The
Reluctant
Metropolis

Also by William Fulton
GUIDE TO CALIFORNIA PLANNING

William Fulton

The
Reluctant
Metropolis

The Politics of
Urban Growth in Los Angeles

Solano Press Books

Library of Congress Cataloging-in-Publication Data

Fulton, William B., 1955–
    The reluctant metropolis : the politics of urban growth
  in Los Angeles / William Fulton.
        p. cm.
    Includes bibliographical references and index.
    ISBN 0-923956-22-0 (hardcover)
    1. Urbanization—California—Los Angeles Metropolitan
  Area—Case studies. 2. Community development, Urban—
  California—Los Angeles Metropolitan Area—Case studies. I. Title.
  HT384.U52C245 1997   97-6374
  307.1'216'0979494—dc21   CIP

Solano Press Books • P.O. Box 773 • Point Arena, CA 95468
Telephone (800) 931-9373 • Facsimile (707) 884-4109

Printed in the United States of America.
10 9 8 7 6 5 4 3 2 1

For Vicki

Contents

LIST OF MAPS

The Collapse of the Growth Machine

If you define the Los Angeles megalopolis broadly enough, which most people are unwilling to do, I live at one end of it.

I live in Ventura, shorthand for San Buenaventura. It's a working-class oil town turned typical Southern California suburb, located where Highway 101 hits the ocean after a sixty-five mile trip north and west from downtown Los Angeles. L.A.'s sprawl has crept toward Ventura along the 101 Corridor across the fertile, flat soil of the Oxnard Plain. It's blocked from moving farther because of the ocean and an imposing set of rugged hills up toward Santa Barbara known as the Rincon. In a very real sense, this is where L.A. ends.

Most of my neighbors, of course, don't want to believe that we are part of Los Angeles. A lot of them moved to Ventura or thereabouts to register a vote with their feet on how they feel about L.A. The irony of this attitude is rich indeed. Geographically we are close. We watch L.A.'s television shows and listen to its radio stations. Economically we are linked, much more than we used to be in the oil boom days, when our strongest economic ties were to Bakersfield and Houston. And when something bad happens in L.A.—a fire, an earthquake, a riot—our friends and relatives call to make sure we are okay. Our response is usually that everything is fine because we don't really live there. We have decided that we live somewhere else.

It should have come as no surprise to me, then, to learn that the people at the other end feel pretty much the same way.

I remember the day I found the other end. It was a moody, rainy morning in the spring of 1990, and I braved the freeways for three-plus

1

hours in my thirteen-year-old Honda Civic to go to Moreno Valley in Riverside County. Skidding across the wet lanes of the freeway—Southern Californians are terrible wet-weather drivers, treating every rainstorm as if it were a blizzard—I traveled through suburb after suburb, past shopping center after shopping center and tract after tract. Camarillo. Calabasas. Woodland Hills. Sherman Oaks. Studio City. Glendale. Pasadena. Duarte. San Dimas. Pomona. Corona. The suburban monotony was so continuous that it was numbing.

Then, after a hundred and thirty miles, I stopped and saw a meadow. Rich and green from the spring rains, hard up against the San Jacinto Mountains, this was obviously the edge of town. Roads trailed off into ruts. Houses had a ramshackle look, with old tools and cars in the yards. Retail establishments were made of cinder blocks. Of course, there are more towns past the mountains: Banning, Beaumont, Palm Springs. But nothing else I had seen that day conveyed quite the same sense of termination.

It had taken almost half a day, and I had covered a distance that would have taken me through three or four Northeastern states, but I had finally found the other end of Los Angeles. And as I traveled around Moreno Valley that day, the people I talked to felt as much alienation from Los Angeles as my neighbors in Ventura.

Moreno Valley had grown in size from ten thousand people to more than one hundred thousand in less than a decade, and it was almost a parody of the typical 1980s suburb: subdivision after subdivision along

Moreno Valley, the prototypical Southern California suburb of the 1980s.

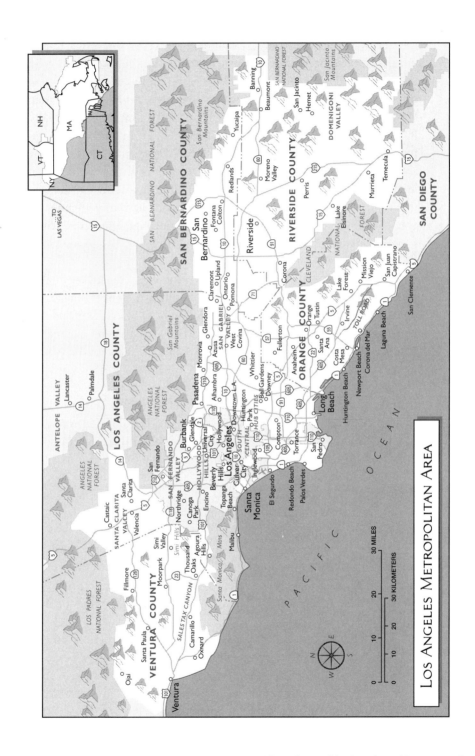

LOS ANGELES METROPOLITAN AREA

the freeway, punctuated only by shopping centers and franchise restaurants, all linked together by overgrown arterials that the traffic engineers had demanded up front. Mini-malls were so ubiquitous that they even housed churches, which had nowhere else to go. And even more than Ventura, Moreno Valley was dependent on the Los Angeles megalopolis. It was largely vacant during working hours, with a third of the breadwinners off in Los Angeles or Orange County or Riverside making the money they would import back to their Moreno Valley tracts. The trick for making the seventy-mile trip bearable, the long-distance commuters said, was to hit the critical interchange of Highway 60 and Highway 91—the main road to Orange County—before five in the morning, when it began to jam up. The interchange of Highway 60 and Highway 91 is located fifty-six miles east of downtown Los Angeles.

And yet it was here, in this unlikely place on the desert's edge, that people said they found a semblance of community no longer available to them in Los Angeles or Lakewood or Fullerton or El Monte. Some combination of "low" prices for housing ($130,000 for a starter home), an illusion of spaciousness, and the old suburban ideal that everybody here was starting fresh had so much appeal that it seemed worth the hassle.

One local resident, who endured the two-hour commute to Orange County for several years, told me that he could have found a house closer to his work, "but I wouldn't have been able to have a pool." A former flight instructor employed by a local developer who wanted to build more than three thousand houses and a business park (on that meadow I found) said he didn't really mind living in a half-built, auto-bound community in the middle of nowhere. In fact, he said, it made him nostalgic. It reminded him of his boyhood in Orange County thirty years earlier.

Given these attitudes, it should have been equally unsurprising that when a large portion of urban Los Angeles erupted in flames and riots almost exactly two years later, people in places like Ventura and Moreno Valley didn't think it had much to do with their lives or their communities.

Triggered by the acquittal of four white Los Angeles police officers accused of beating black motorist Rodney King, the riots raged over an enormous area—a hundred square miles or more, an area bigger than most large American cities. The riot zone encompassed L.A.'s historically black neighborhoods, as well as dozens of other crowded districts that were the entry points for recent immigrants from Asia, Mexico, and Central America. Many of the names were familiar enough to people anywhere in Southern California. Watts. Central Avenue. West Adams. USC and the Coliseum. Koreatown. MacArthur Park. Even Hollywood. But to the suburbanites watching the tragedy on television, most of these places were nothing more than names—poor, neglected places that had been thrown away, decades earlier, by their parents or grandparents. In the mental map of Southern California that most people carry around in their heads, the riot zone was a hole in the metropolitan doughnut.

The riots touched people in the outer suburbs, of course. Most had a friend or relative in danger who had never escaped the urban detritus; many opened their homes to these unfortunate souls during the riots. Older suburbanites remembered living and working in neighborhoods that were going up in flames. One friend, a woman in her fifties, said that watching the riots brought back vivid memories of crouching in her Wilshire District home during the Watts riots of 1965 while chaos reined on the street outside. For her, the whole experience simply confirmed the wisdom of her decision to flee many years before to Camarillo, fifty miles away.

In the months and years that followed, there was considerable evidence that the riots had profoundly affected all of Southern California's suburbs and all of its suburbanites. In Ventura County, where I live, Korean merchants arrived *en masse* from L.A., looking for retail stores to operate without having to fear for their lives. They quickly learned that they needed a gun in a poor neighborhood in Oxnard just as much as in South Central. In Moreno Valley, where working-class black neighborhoods had grown up around a local air force base, South Central kids arrived regularly, sent to live with aunts and uncles located far from the turmoil of urban life. The result, as Moreno Valley quickly discovered, was not a reduction of gang activity but a geographical expansion of it. (The gang member "Monster" Kody Scott, who wrote a well-publicized autobiography, divided his time between South Central and Moreno Valley and was arrested in Moreno Valley for beating up a man who allegedly derided his gang.) And all over Southern California—as the region reeled from a devastating recession and a series of natural disasters—businesses, workers, and families suffered from bad publicity worldwide and a resulting reluctance by tourists, investors, and others to make a commitment to the region.

Yet none of this drew people together. If anything, it pushed them further apart. Nothing has changed in my neighborhood, people said; I have nothing to worry about. Maybe the people in South Central burned down each other's mini-malls, but in our town the chaos seemed about as real as the Gulf War. (The riots didn't come within thirty miles of Simi Valley, the conservative suburban enclave in Ventura County where the Rodney King trial was held.) Those who feared their neighborhoods were changing moved farther away. And those who were still afraid moved behind walls and gates where, they hoped, the rest of society couldn't follow. Even people who really did live in Los Angeles continued to atomize, bombarding the U.S. Postal Service with requests to list their residences as being located in North Hills, West Hills, Sherman Village, or anything but Los Angeles. (In 1996, the San Fernando Valley even pursued one of its periodic attempts to secede from the City of Los Angeles.) Instead of trying to fix Los Angeles, we all simply decided that we live somewhere else.

⤜⤏

By all conventional notions, Los Angeles is a foolish location for a big city. It gets only one-third the rainfall of New York. Its rivers flow sporadically, and its natural water could sustain a city of perhaps a half-million people. It is the largest city in the world located so near a geologically unstable mountain range; the uplifts, mudslides, and debris flows from the San Gabriels are kept at bay only through the efforts of an army of public works employees and equipment that would be the envy of many Third World dictators. Almost every scenic and heavily foliated canyon in the region is a fire trap because of the annual summer drought, which usually lingers until November. Los Angeles has no natural harbors or ports; it is not located near sources of raw material; and even before Europeans settled in the region the air was filled with haze and smoke. Only its remarkably mild climate is a natural advantage, though admittedly a compelling one. The sociologist Harvey Molotch, a perceptive student of urban growth, once wrote that L.A.'s rise to prominence "can only be explained as a remarkable victory of human cunning over the so-called limits of nature."

Conducting academic research on cities in the 1970s, Molotch coined the term "growth machine" to explain the political and economic structure of the typical American city. Places are commodities, he wrote, whose success is driven not by natural advantages but by the efforts of "place entrepreneurs" such as land speculators, bankers, newspaper publishers, politicians, and public utilities with a stake in the economic growth of a particular geographical area. Taken together, these place entrepreneurs make up a cartel of powerful interests—a growth machine—dedicated to fueling a virtually endless and presumably profitable cycle of growth, no matter what the consequences.

For the last hundred years, Los Angeles has been one of the most effective growth machines ever created. It was set into motion, very deliberately, by a small group of visionary (and greedy) business leaders who understood Southern California and set out to exploit its potential allure. The story of this group has been told many times and fictionalized in the film *Chinatown* and elsewhere. Originally it included many of the most famous names in Southern California history, names that are imprinted on streets, buildings, and neighborhoods throughout Los Angeles.

Henry Huntington, heir to a San Francisco railroad fortune, built the Red Car system, subdivided vast amounts of land, and amassed more than $40 million in profits during the first decade of the twentieth century. Water engineer William Mulholland built the great aqueduct from the Owens Valley. Harry Chandler, the publisher of the *Los Angeles Times*, led a cartel of investors who manipulated politics, business, media coverage, and public works investments in an unprecedented manner to build a great city. The son-in-law of *Times* founder Harrison Gray Otis, Chandler was an aggressive real estate speculator who shamelessly used his paper to promote business, bust unions, and lure people out to new real estate developments. The cartel was small. According to one estimate, there were fewer than ninety growth barons in Southern California during the first two decades of the century.

Whatever their number, they succeeded magnificently. Lacking water, the cartel simply imported it from hundreds of miles away, using whatever political clout and legal skullduggery was required. ("If we don't get it," William Mulholland once said, "we won't need it.") Lacking people, they imported bodies, luring trainload after trainload from the frigid winter climes of the Midwest with the promise of an eternal summer, a moral society, and a nice little bungalow. Lacking an economy, they invented one, using a Ponzi scheme of real estate speculation until they could kick-start other industries, such as entertainment, oil, and aerospace. No challenge in this task of city-building was too great.

Once, in the 1920s, a *Saturday Evening Post* reporter commented to his tour guide that a particular mountain had been moved. "Oh yes," said the guide. "Harry Chandler wanted to move it a little farther to the north to improve the view."

These engineers of the growth machine engaged in a wide variety of activities—streetcar companies, electric utilities, water service, publishing. But many of these tasks were loss leaders that didn't see a profit. Their real purpose was to facilitate the growth machine's underlying goal: to consume land profitably. And for everything that Los Angeles lacked, land was one raw material available in abundance. The region's topography was defined by a group of valleys and plains ringed by a series of mountain ranges that helped shape L.A.'s pattern of growth. But the valleys and plains themselves were vast, offering what seemed to be boundless opportunity to lay down subdivision after subdivision for the Sioux Falls immigrants disembarking at local rail stations.

The Los Angeles Basin, the coastal plain stretching almost without interruption from the Hollywood Hills deep into Orange County, provided a vast chessboard on which to play the game of urban development. Hot, dry interior valleys, especially the San Gabriel, which had groundwater, were ideal for the small-scale farming that many Midwesterners brought with them as a counterpoint to urban life. The result was a decentralized settlement pattern quite different from the industrial cities in the East and Midwest. Unlike almost every other city in the world, metropolitan Los Angeles did not grow by radiating from a single center. It appeared when many different centers blurred together.

Early in the century, Huntington's Red Cars connected disparate settlements from San Bernardino to Santa Monica with a vast interurban system. (More ambitious plans to link up Santa Barbara and San Diego were never realized.) The interurbans gave the emerging region a backbone, but also made sprawl permanent by facilitating long-distance commuting. Soon the automobile began to fill in the gaps. But not all of this growth was chaotic. Historian Greg Hise has discovered that much decentralization was, in fact, a planned effort to create a string of small industrial suburbs, each with its own adjoining bedroom community. In any event, this decentralization was fostered by an unusually strong attachment to the automobile. By 1940, a time when most Americans struggled simply to keep a roof over their heads, virtually every family in Southern California had a car.

To process the consumption of all this land, a huge real estate infra-structure emerged. The modern homebuilding industry was practically invented in Los Angeles. So, ironically enough, was modern zoning, originally promoted by local subdividers as a tool to ensure high-quality (and high-profit) development. As early as the 1920s, traffic engineers began working on designs for the freeway system that would be the region's most visible and impressive human achievement. From a few dozen land barons, the growth machine grew to include thousands of middle- and working-class people who were engaged in planning, proc-essing, and building L.A.'s new neighborhoods and towns.

After World War II, Los Angeles—now sprawling, metropolitan Southern California—continued to consume land with extraordinary skill and for extraordinary profit. Fueled by a strong industrial base that emerged during the war, and supported by the aggressive infrastructure investments of Governors Earl Warren and Pat Brown, Los Angeles reached deep into outlying regions. The population of the San Fernando Valley quintupled in sixteen years, from 1944 to 1960. Orange County, an agricultural region, topped one million people by the mid-1960s.

During this period, the Los Angeles growth machine grew even more sophisticated. Mass-produced housing, invented by William Levitt on the East Coast, was perfected by firms like Kaufman and Broad, which even today excels in the purchase of inexpensive remote farmland for building serviceable seven-lots-per-acre subdivisions. The modern savings-and-loan business, which provided stable sources of home mortgages for the middle class, flourished in Southern California as nowhere else, pro-viding vast fortunes for the likes of Mark Taper (Great Western Savings) and Howard Ahmanson (Home Savings). And modern urban planning techniques emerged in order to facilitate development on a vast scale. These were later exported worldwide by local planners and architects such as William Pereira. A flamboyant "black-cape" architect who headed his own firm, Pereira dabbled in large-scale city planning and left his imprint on the landscape with his ambitious, circular, auto-oriented urban designs for UC Irvine and The Irvine Company's Fashion Island shopping center in Newport Beach. By the 1960s, the Los Angeles growth machine had been transformed into a vast industry.

The resulting scale of Los Angeles in the 1960s was so staggering and unprecedented that distinguished urban planners were left speech-less. This was no simple hub-and-spoke industrial city, with boulevards and rail lines radiating outward from a central downtown core. It was, in the words of one scholar of the period, a "fragmented metropolis"— a multi-headed beast with no center, with a system of urban organization that Easterners and Europeans couldn't fathom, and with such a sense of urgent destiny that it clearly preferred movement over history. "Like earlier generations of English intellectuals who taught themselves Italian in order to read Dante in the original," the English architectural historian Reyner Banham wrote in 1971, "I learned to drive in order to read Los Angeles in the original."

During this period the consequences of the growth machine first became evident. As the plains of the Los Angeles Basin were eaten up, the growth machine chewed deep into the desert and the mountains, leading a nascent environmental movement to complain. As the metropolis moved outward, neglect and decay were left in the inner city. Until the 1950s, Los Angeles had seemed a benign alternative to Southern racism for many hopeful blacks from Texas and Louisiana. But the same efficient real estate industry that built a great metropolis worked hard to keep most of the city off-limits to African-Americans. According to Robert Conot's classic account of the Watts riot, *Rivers of Blood, Years of Darkness,* the San Fernando Valley more than doubled in population during the 1950s, from three hundred thousand to seven hundred thousand. But the black population actually declined, from eleven hundred to nine hundred—dropping from four-tenths of one percent to only one-tenth of one percent. By the mid-1960s, Los Angeles was the most segregated city in the country—a fact which, among others, led to the Watts riots of 1965.

Because the growth machine couldn't handle regional problems like smog, planners and politicians struggled to embrace these concerns. In the mid-1960s, local governments banded together to form a kind of regional government, the Southern California Association of Governments, which they hoped would be able to lasso the region. But there would be no lassoing Los Angeles. During the 1970s and especially the go-go years of the 1980s, the growth machine continued to churn.

In part it churned from necessity, because population growth and a vision of economic opportunity had become a self-fulfilling prophecy. During the 1980s, the Southern California region added more than three million people, a population the size of Chicago, and most were not arriving by train from the Midwest. They were stepping off planes from Asia or crossing the border, legally and illegally, at San Diego. Lured by the seductive international image of Los Angeles, they were not deterred by smog or overcrowding or crime or segregation. And the immigrants were joined by thousands of investors from around the world who poured billions of dollars into real estate investment. Hundreds of thousands more people were simply born to the fate of living here, often in the families of recent immigrants. These folks were not going anywhere. To them, and to millions more from the postwar generation, Los Angeles was home and always had been. Having been set into motion a hundred years earlier, the growth machine couldn't stop.

In part, however, the growth machine continued to churn because, for better or worse, churning growth is what the region's economy was designed to do.

By the 1980s, Los Angeles had one of the world's most vibrant and diversified economies. The aerospace industry, Hollywood, the garment business, agriculture, international trade—all were important components of this diversified metropolitan powerhouse. Underlying all of them, however, was the familiar process of consuming land profitably, which had become so intertwined with the region's economy that it was impossible to disentangle.

Orange County developers, having played out their home territory, searched for new land elsewhere as a means of staying in business; they became, in effect, exporters of land development. A vast collection of brokers and lawyers all over Southern California churned deals in order to make their Porsche payments. Labor unions pushed for more growth to keep their members employed; at one point during the 1980s, more than twenty percent of Riverside County's employment base was connected, directly or indirectly, to the construction industry. And most of Southern California's other basic industries turned to the real estate business sooner or later in search of profits. (One ongoing trend throughout the 1980s was the repeated attempts by land-rich movie studios to convert their backlots to more profitable uses such as theme parks, shopping centers, and condominium complexes.) Prosperity depended on growth, and in the 1980s, as in the 1920s, growth meant expanding the metropolis, creating more subdivisions, and converting more land on the fringe to urban use.

By the end of the 1980s, the scale of metropolitan Southern California was so vast that even the speechless urban planners of the 1960s couldn't have foreseen it. The megalopolis was now more than a hundred

New subdivisions in the Antelope Valley just before the real estate bust, 1990.

miles from north to south and a similar distance east to west. Business centers had decentralized so dramatically that Orange County, a generation removed from lima beans, now had a "downtown" larger than San Francisco, and its own suburbs an hour even farther away from central Los Angeles.

The region was so large that it now encompassed several different climates. Bosses sitting in balmy Universal City or Beverly Hills were often dumbfounded by employees calling from their high-desert starter homes in the Antelope Valley to say they were snowed in. Of course, being snowed in might seem preferable to the wrenching sixty- or seventy-mile commute along crowded freeways that no longer seemed an apt symbol for a society based on movement. The area once known simply as Los Angeles was now home to fifteen million people, all living and working in such close proximity that if all Americans were jammed that close together they would fit inside Missouri.

In building a metropolis far beyond the dreams of Chandler, Mulholland, and Huntington, the growth machine also laid the foundation for its own destruction. Because no other metropolis had ever grown so large by promoting an essentially anti-urban way of life.

Other cities, such as industrial-era Chicago and New York, produced growth machines that were L.A.'s equal. But these were based on the gritty realities of urban life: factories and railroads and ports and sweatshops. The people drawn to them, though they dreamed of a better life, recognized that they would be living in a crowded, often dirty, and difficult urban place.

From the beginning, Los Angeles was different. It marketed itself, especially in the Midwest, as the anti-city, and the Midwestern settlers it attracted were profoundly anti-urban in attitude. Many came to Southern California hoping to build a subsistence agricultural lifestyle on five or ten acres of irrigated land. Others sought to use Los Angeles as a transition between a rural past and an urban, industrial present. They worked urban jobs, but reveled in the decentralized small-town life Los Angeles had deliberately produced. Those who thought of themselves as rural folk eagerly bought up the hobby farms being created all over Southern California. (The 100-by-400-foot lot was a popular subdivision in the first half of the century. Ideal for hobby farming, it proved equally useful decades later for "shotgun" apartment buildings.) These dreams were equally true for black and Latino immigrants, many of whom lived, and live, on solid single-family streets that seem the antithesis of urban decay even when they are located in the middle of poor and troubled neighborhoods.

California's Progressive-era political structure, which had decentralized and depoliticized local government, reinforced these anti-urban attitudes. Southern Californians have an almost inborn mistrust of big government, and especially of political machines, which they regard as exactly the sort of corrupt urban ill they moved to Los Angeles to avoid. (At the same time, Los Angeles residents have been traditionally accepting of, or blissfully ignorant about, the business-oriented growth machine that truly ran things.) By around 1920, Los Angeles had become a kind of national suburb for old-line Protestants wanting nothing to do with the immigrant politics of big urban cities elsewhere in the country.

This attitude played nicely into the region's decentralized nature, creating a plethora of small, self-governing cities and establishing local government close to the people as the norm. During the 1950s and 1960s, thanks to the so-called "Lakewood system," the number of small cities grew dramatically. By contracting with Los Angeles County for essential but expensive services such as police protection, dozens of small municipalities were created on the cheap. The Lakewood system helped atomize the Los Angeles Basin into a series of small duchies with little interest in one another or in the region as a whole.

The exception was the City of Los Angeles, which grew large early in the century via forced annexation of areas such as Hollywood that needed a steady water supply. But even Los Angeles had a nonpartisan

The dream: The *faux* rural Southern California landscape early in the twentieth century.

government that vested little power in the mayor, minimizing the possibility of machine politics.

All these components of L.A.'s allure—hobby farms, an anti-urban bias, the small-town atmosphere, localized governments—represent the American suburban ideal. Multiplied by a postwar population of approximately four million, however, these attitudes created a huge metropolis in self-denial about what it was. Most residents benefited from the industrial economy but continued to think of themselves as rural or small-town folk. (In the 1970s, this attitude led to an explosion in the sale of Japanese import pick-up trucks, a boom Japanese manufacturers could not explain because they thought urbanites didn't need trucks.) In contrast to other cities, most residents had no commitment to or even memory of L.A.'s urban core, since people moved straight to their particular neighborhood or suburb without stopping in a crowded immigrant district near downtown. (This was as true for African-Americans as for Midwestern whites; poor transportation stranded the black neighborhoods, making travel to downtown difficult and even more alien.)

After World War II, then, Southern Californians willingly accepted a fraud. To fulfill their anti-urban dream, they relied on the growth machine to continue manufacturing *faux*-rural suburbs. But as new suburbs were created, the metropolis grew bigger and more unmanageable, further and further from the ideal most residents carried in their heads while driving their pick-up trucks to work.

The reality: The emerging suburb of Westchester,
near Los Angeles International Airport, in 1949.

But as long as people could count on a quiet existence in their homes and neighborhoods, and as long as the builders and the bankers continued to stamp out new suburbs to prolong the dream, Southern Californians were able to live with this paradox.

Thus, the members of the postwar Los Angeles growth machine—the bankers and the homebuilders and the building trades unions—lived off the deception for decades, even persuading themselves that they were heroes for perpetuating it. But by perpetuating the illusion, they embedded the anti-urban ideal deeper in the region's psyche. A few years ago, a senior executive of The Irvine Company, the landowning company that developed much of Orange County, lamented the way the growth machine had marketed its postwar suburbs. In the 1960s, he recalled, the company's slogan had been: "Come to Irvine and hear the asparagus grow." In retrospect, he said, perhaps they should have marketed Irvine as "a dynamic and growing community." After all, he said, "When you live between two freeways, it's hard to hear the asparagus grow." But there was a darned good reason why the company didn't market the idea of a bustling future: It wouldn't have sold any houses.

So it is not surprising that when Los Angeles finally grew so vast as to be unfathomable even to those who lived there—when the gap between the illusion of a spacious suburban lifestyle and the daily reality of a massive metropolis could no longer be papered over with dreams—the growth machine began to collapse under its own weight. Happy suburbanites turned angry about traffic jams and high taxes, reducing their tolerance for more suburbs. Struggling inner cities began to rise up against decades of neglect. Farmers and environmentalists protested the loss of open land. In short, the formula that had built Los Angeles so quickly no longer worked.

It took a long time, two decades or more, to reach this crisis. Perhaps the first inkling came in the early 1960s, when dairy farmers in southern Los Angeles County (then still one of the leading agricultural counties in the nation) actually created three new cities in the hope of controlling their own destiny. But Dairy City, Dairyland, and Dairy Valley quickly gave way to the growth machine, becoming Cypress, La Palma, and Cerritos.

During the 1960s, discontent continued to build, especially among the affluent suburban homeowners who lived on pristine hillsides on both sides of the Santa Monica Mountains. A decade earlier, homeowner groups in the area had organized into an umbrella organization, the Federation of Hillside and Canyon Associations. Now, fearing large-scale development of the mountains west of Sepulveda Pass, the Hillside Federation staged a mini-revolution to halt construction of a large four-lane highway along the route of winding and scenic Mulholland Drive. Backed by the Sierra Club and other environmental groups, homeowners began a decades-long effort to block development in the Santa Monicas by creating a regional park. (See chapter 7, The Education of Maria VanderKolk.)

In the late 1960s and early 1970s, homeowner unrest led to a number of electoral victories. In 1967, an iconoclastic homeowner association president, Marvin Braude, was elected to the Los Angeles City Council from a Westside-Santa Monica Mountains district on the strength of the anti-growth issue, which he continued to champion for more than thirty years. And in a startling victory in 1972, environmentalists succeeded in passing Proposition 20, a statewide initiative to restrict development up and down the coast. (The proposal had gone nowhere in the legislature, where it had been introduced by a young Assemblyman named Pete Wilson.) Thus, in a period of only a few years, a homeowner/

environmentalist coalition succeeded in hobbling the growth machine in two key areas of Los Angeles, the mountains and the beach.

But it did not spread. The agitators at the beach and in the mountains were affluent homeowners who lived directly adjacent to these areas. The homeowners and their environmentalist allies were never able to broaden their appeal to include L.A.'s vast working-class neighborhoods in the Los Angeles Basin and along the interior valleys—what Reyner Banham called "The Plains of Id," those vast flat plains of single-family homes where working- and middle-class Angelenos had come to seek their membership in the national suburb. Despite occasional dissatisfaction, most people there thought the system still worked. Living closer to the edge, they weren't willing to take political risks that might affect their jobs. So the growth machine continued to operate pretty much as it always had.

Predictably, the only issue related to the growth machine that could move the voters of the Plains of Id was taxes. And the most dramatic expression of discontent came with the passage of Proposition 13 in 1978.

Proposition 13, which cut property taxes by two-thirds, was widely credited with kicking off a nationwide tax revolt. The initiative was devised by apartment owners (ironically, a pro-growth group) who wanted to cut their own taxes in the face of rising property values. And it was marketed as a means of allowing fixed-income senior citizens to keep their homes. But Proposition 13 had a profound impact on the growth machine, as many of the working-class folks who voted for it well understood.

Even after Los Angeles outgrew its land-speculation phase, growth continued to be fueled by a fiscal Ponzi scheme. Current property owners and residents paid higher taxes to support the debt-financed construction of new facilities (roads, water pipes, parks, etc.) to be used by newcomers who would then help finance the next phase, and so on. (The Metropolitan Water District of Southern California still finances growth this way; everybody in the region pays the same rate for water.) It is amazing that this system worked for so long in a region as individualistic and anti-urban as Southern California.

When property values, and hence property taxes, rose rapidly in the 1970s, it was not difficult for folks on the Plains of Id to understand that they were subsidizing the growth machine with their property taxes. The passage of Proposition 13 put an end to that fiscal system.

With so little property tax revenue available, local governments around Los Angeles could no longer finance growth from their current tax base. Instead, they had to hit up the components of the growth machine—landowners, developers, and home buyers—directly for the funds.

Above all else, the passage of Proposition 13 reasserted the anti-urbanism of most Southern California urbanites. And it marked the beginning of an era of xenophobic hunkering down. Throughout the 1980s, most Southern Californians wrapped themselves up in a self-centered political cocoon. Spread across a vast landscape by eighty years of sprawling development patterns, cut off from one another fiscally and socially, weary of sharing their space with fifteen million other people, and fueled by an enduring anti-urban ideal, Southern Californians simply ceased to be citizens in the larger sense and withdrew into their subdivisions. They would emerge to go to work and an occasional ball game, and perhaps to hit the beach or Disneyland. But then they would retreat quickly into Rancho Vista or Woodbridge or whatever other ready-made pseudo-community the growth machine had manufactured for their consumption.

Once inside, they did not venture out. Many felt disconnected not only from the teeming and volatile metropolis of which they were a part, but also from their own small cities, from which they were often physically separated by gates or large roads. Their sense of community shrunk to include only their tract. After Proposition 13, working-class suburbanites did not emerge from this cocoon to challenge the growth machine, even though they had clearly lost faith. Instead they simply stayed put. Middle-class suburbanites, by contrast, occasionally rose up and vented their anger as citizens—though politically they had been transformed into a peculiar class of citizens best described as "tract-home environmentalists."

Heirs to the middle-class suburban dreams of the hobby-farming "rural folk" two generations before, tract-home environmentalists had already received all the benefits they were going to get from the growth machine: a house, a plot of land, and a middle-class job. They saw no reason to permit the machine to continue operating, at least not in their neighborhood. And so they tried to shut it down. It was not uncommon, for example, to see Phase Two of a subdivision scrapped because residents of Phase One adamantly opposed construction of a neighborhood exactly like theirs filled with people exactly like them. All over the region homeowner groups agitated for gates around their neighborhoods, for separately incorporated cities, and for exclusive access to schools and parks and other supposedly public places which had been paid for by up-front development fees or special neighborhood-based taxes. It is surprising that no neighborhood tried to dig a moat.

And so the political basis for the growth machine collapsed. A vast metropolis, founded on a vision of land profits and sustained for decades by the faith of rank-and-file suburbanites who consumed its products, suddenly seemed to have no consensus among its own residents even to exist. In the absence of an overarching vision, the former components of the growth machine began breaking apart and scrambling for their own survival, rather than working together. Some old-time homebuilders simply griped that they were no longer heroes. Other elements of the growth machine, such as the Metropolitan Water District, tried to buy political support by wrapping their projects in environmentally friendly packages. Still others tried to buy off opposition by coughing up band-aid solutions to the symptoms: fewer houses, more parkland, schools, community infrastructure, often just plain money.

While the growth consensus has collapsed, no new paradigm has emerged to take its place. As I realized the day of my long commute to Moreno Valley in 1990, there is a void at the center of Los Angeles. Not just a void in the physical center, where neglect has created slums. But a void in the political and psychological center, where we decline to take responsibility for a metropolis and an urban landscape that we ought to think is ours.

↩

That lush meadow I saw in Moreno Valley doesn't have three thousand houses and a business park on it today, as the developer of the property anticipated. In part that's because real estate and capital markets collapsed shortly after my visit. But it's also because, predictably, there was no consensus in Moreno Valley about what should be done. Many of the town's political leaders supported the project, because the developer promised that businesses locating there would provide local jobs. But a lot of local homeowners, who felt that jobs would never materialize, did not want to chew up a beautiful meadow to build houses for a few more commuters competing for space on the freeway at four-thirty in the morning.

As for myself, I didn't stick around long enough to form a strong opinion one way or the other. By the end of the day it had stopped raining, so I got back into my Civic and headed west on the freeway. Moreno Valley was interesting, but it was just another suburb of Los Angeles. It wasn't really a part of where I live. It was too distant, too remote, too filled with cars and shopping centers and commuting suburbanites who didn't fit the ambiguously anti-urban image I had of the town where I live. Like everybody else in metropolitan Los Angeles, I just wanted to get home to my own tract.

PART ONE

Power

The collapse of the Southern California growth machine took a long time. Almost thirty years elapsed from the first rumblings of dissent to the wholesale breakdown that accompanied the real estate boom of the late 1980s and the subsequent bust of the 1990s. The path to this restructuring was littered with the carcasses of the once-invincible land developers and their political friends.

Starting in the latter part of the nineteenth century when the growth machine began churning in earnest, the foundation for L.A.'s expansion was laid by the businesses that profited—the real estate developers, the bankers, newspaper publishers, and so on. And over the decades these business interests necessarily became intertwined with Los Angeles's political leadership. Local politics in Southern California may have been weak and nominally non-partisan, but developers still had to obtain approval for their plans and permits from cities and counties in the region. So they did what special interests everywhere do: They groomed candidates, contributed to campaigns, and subtly co-opted the political process to advance their own ends.

Nowhere was this intermingling of politics and business more skillfully accomplished than at the Los Angeles County Hall of Administration where the local Board of Supervisors—or the "Five Little Kings," as they were known in local parlance—presided over the urbanization of a sprawling four-thousand-square-mile area stretching from the desert to the sea. The supervisors met (and still meet) during the daytime in downtown Los Angeles, far from the communities whose futures they were shaping. They accepted campaign contributions (and in the old days perhaps much more) from the powerful land developers who were their friends. They changed and circumvented the zoning and planning ordinances whenever it suited them. And in public they insisted that most of the resulting problems were beyond their control.

In the case of Diamond Bar, an eastern suburb in the San Gabriel Valley, authors Bill and Nancy Boyarsky described in their book *Backyard Politics* how local residents were originally promised a low-density master-planned community, but wound up being forced to live with re-zonings that called for high-rise apartments and commercial development. To make the project even more profitable for the landowner, Transamerica Corporation, the supervisors threw in a golf course at county expense (backed by a pension fund in order to avoid a public vote on a bond issue). Yet in television interviews, the Boyarskys wrote, supervisors blamed "the state for high welfare costs, the federal government for smog, and everyone for bad transportation.... The public believed the myth of powerlessness that the supervisors had cultivated over the years."

In time, the citizenry wised up, a process that began in the late 1960s when an eccentric electronics millionaire named Marvin Braude organized homeowners in the Santa Monica Mountains against new development. It stepped up in the seventies—indeed, Proposition 13 was in its own way a rejection of Los Angeles's long-standing growth alliance. By the 1980s, fighting the growth alliance became good politics throughout the region—from the liberal beachfront towns to the vast sea of single-family homes stretched out across the flats of the Los Angeles plain, and even in the crowded barrios that were emerging in formerly white working-class suburbs east and south of L.A. This *perestroika* profoundly changed Southern California's political rhetoric. But whether it ultimately changed the way things work around town is another question altogether.

CHAPTER 1

The Beachhead

Leaning against the wood-rail fence that runs along the edge of Palisades Park on Ocean Avenue in Santa Monica, you look out over one of the most spectacular urban settings in America. Only a foot or two beyond the fence, the jagged hundred-foot drop of the Pacific Palisades begins. At the bottom of the cliffs is the scenic Pacific Coast Highway, and beyond the highway lie sumptuous beach houses once owned by the likes of Cary Grant, Darryl F. Zanuck, and Mae West. The beach itself is so large and alluring, and so accessible to people all over metropolitan Los Angeles, that it regularly attracts a half-million sun worshippers on summer Sundays when the rest of the Los Angeles Basin is sweltering under heat and smog. Beyond the beach, of course, lies the Pacific Ocean, a glimmering blue reflection of the sky framed by the gentle curve of Santa Monica Bay and the mountains that rise up from its shore.

Reaching America's western shore at Santa Monica, most cross-country travelers are overwhelmed, practically tearful at what lies at their feet. And no wonder. They arrive at the ocean after covering almost three thousand miles of landlocked territory. The last thousand miles of this land is the hottest, driest, and most inhospitable desert in the United States. The last fifty or sixty miles is endless city—nothing but buildings and cars and streets and pavement and sun and heat and, often, smog and haze.

Yet here it is different. Suddenly, where there was land, there is ocean; where there was pavement and blistering stillness and stifling traffic, there is nothing but clear, serene blue water and ocean breeze. Anyone who has seen the ocean knows how liberating a view such as

Downtown Santa Monica, the beach, and the pier. The "wedding cake" building and the skyscraper next to it were built by the bandleader Lawrence Welk.

this can be. Multiply that feeling by a continent, and you begin to understand how Santa Monica appears to the grateful land-bound escapees from the East and Midwest who have been migrating here for decades.

For a century, the engineers of the growth machine understood Santa Monica's appeal and exploited it shamelessly and profitably. In the 1870s the first resorts popped up—tents at the mouth of Santa Monica Canyon, accessible by horse-car from Los Angeles. Subdivision soon followed, and in succeeding decades Santa Monica evolved into a peculiar combination of beachfront resort and bedroom suburb located at the end of the Red Car line. An attempt to create a deep-harbor port there lost out to San Pedro in the 1890s, establishing a basic development pattern followed ever since: recreation on the west side, industry on the south side.

After World War II, frost-bitten soldiers decided to stay in Los Angeles, and the defense industry gave them middle-class jobs. Swarming into Santa Monica and other beachfront suburbs looking for places to live, they sometimes stood three-deep at local newspaper offices waiting for apartment ads to come rolling off the press. And the local growth machine was more than happy to accommodate. Funded by Santa Monica Bank and publicized by the *Santa Monica Evening Outlook*, local developers built tracts of starter homes and small apartment buildings all over the city. Except for the beach, postwar Santa Monica was indistinguishable from the Plains of Id. It was a suburban paradise for working people.

But when the Santa Monica Freeway opened in 1966, everything changed. With a beach town now only twenty minutes from downtown offices and South Bay aerospace factories, the growth machine went into high gear. An entire generation of homes was torn down and replaced with block after block of large apartment buildings that boosted the city's

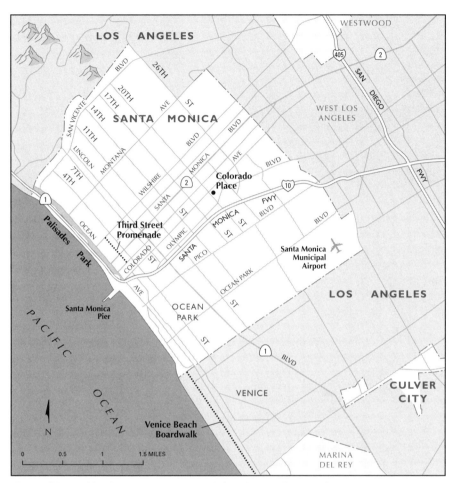

The People's Republic of Santa Monica, surrounded by the City of Los Angeles.

population. Between 1960 and 1972, fourteen thousand apartments were built—forty percent of the city's total housing stock. And most came in the form of large buildings with ten or more apartments. The renter population rose from sixty-five to eighty percent. The resulting boom fueled the local economy, and put money into the pockets of town bankers, builders, and retailers. Perhaps the most famous member of this growth machine, if not the most typical, was Lawrence Welk, who bought up almost all the property along the Palisades after arriving from the bitter cold of North Dakota and eventually developed three large buildings there, including an apartment house called Champagne Towers.

The Santa Monica Pier, as seen from Palisades Park.

For three decades after the war, young families, Frost Belt retirees, and others in search of L.A.'s version of the American Dream lived quietly and more or less peacefully. From the affluent streets north of Montana Avenue to the poor neighborhoods along the freeway, and even in the great apartment belts along Wilshire and Santa Monica Boulevards, the city retained a sleepy small-town atmosphere. Oshkosh-by-the-Sea, some people called it. But the building boom that followed the freeway dramatically changed the city. The very apartment buildings that had proven so profitable to the growth machine contained the people who would engineer the beginning of its demise.

⮌

In 1970, fresh from the Chicago 7 trial and reeling from a variety of personal tragedies, thirty-year-old Tom Hayden arrived in Venice, a seedy, bohemian Los Angeles neighborhood along the beach just south of Santa Monica. An intellectual leader of the movement against the Vietnam war, Hayden had been kicked out of his Berkeley collective for being a power-oriented male chauvinist. He was burned out by the 1960s and wanted to hide out and regroup, so he rented a room in an apartment house on the seediest corner of Venice and registered under the name of his grandfather, Emmett Garity.

In this way Hayden was typical of left-wing protesters in the early 1970s, who had become embittered by the Nixon era and decided to turn inward, focusing their attention on raising children and putting in skylights instead of changing the world. At first glance Los Angeles might seem an odd place for someone like Hayden to hide. Though the Westside contained a thin veneer of liberalism because of Hollywood, most of Los Angeles was profoundly conservative. And yet at the same time it was an open place where almost anyone could reinvent himself—even rock-ribbed Republican immigrants (including Illinois-born Ronald Reagan) who had successfully made themselves over in a sun-baked image.

The area where Hayden chose to settle had a colorful history that appealed to him and others like him. South of Santa Monica's apartment belt, where the hills ended and the city was no longer separated from the beach by the Palisades, the feel of the neighborhoods changed noticeably. Just below the Santa Monica city line lay the remnants of developer Abbott Kinney's gaudy, turn-of-the-century "Venice of America"—a re-creation of his favorite European city, complete with canals. Just north of Venice was the Ocean Park neighborhood, where rundown, small bungalows were all that remained of a once-thriving resort destination that had revolved around the Pacific Ocean Park amusement park.

After World War II, both Ocean Park and Venice had fallen into shabbiness. By the 1960s they were considered dangerous slums, filled with the homeless and drug activity. But Ocean Park and Venice were not without their charm. Both neighborhoods were inexpensive. They were near the ocean, so the air was clean and temperatures were mild; and they were filled with small, old, interesting resort cottages that retained a strong flavor of pre-war Southern California.

In 1973, Hayden married Jane Fonda and bought a house in Ocean Park, but they were far from the only significant new additions to the neighborhood. During this period Venice and Ocean Park became a staging ground for the counterculture. Single mothers, thirtyish activists succumbing to marriage and family, and a slew of other folks arrived, seeking to build an alternative community out of the ashes of the 1960s.

And they did, indeed, build a thriving neighborhood on their own terms. When the local Methodist Church folded, a liberal young minister who lived in the area started the congregation anew, calling it simply The Church in Ocean Park, and it became a focal point for the community. The affiliated Ocean Park Community Center attracted federal anti-poverty grants for such neighborhood projects as crime prevention programs and legal services for the poor. The activists created day care centers, alternative schools, and support groups of all kinds. Though the neighborhood was still considered rundown, the presence of these activists was already changing Santa Monica in subtle ways. A city carried by Barry Goldwater in 1964, for example, went for George McGovern eight years later. To those who lived there, Ocean Park was a beachhead of liberalism on an increasingly conservative continent.

At first, the Ocean Park activists were not overtly political, preferring instead to focus on family and neighborhood. But putting in skylights gives you a lot of time to think, and over time this group dreamed up a new political vision that grew quite logically out of their experience in Ocean Park. They advocated grassroots activism at the neighborhood scale. Their goal, they said, was to give ordinary people more power over their own lives, and especially more power to shape the community and business institutions on which they must rely— much as they themselves had done in Ocean Park. Intellectually, this idea came to be known—in a book by New Left writer Derek Shearer, who lived in the neighborhood, and in the name of a political organization founded by Tom Hayden—as "economic democracy."

Though self-centered, the little community of activists in Ocean Park was not insulated from the outside world, nor from the Santa Monica growth machine. Even before the activists arrived, the city government had been engaged in a bulldozer-style effort at urban renewal. Seeking to arrest the growing seediness of the neighborhood after the closure of Pacific Ocean Park, the city moved out ten percent of the neighborhood's population and more than two hundred businesses in the name of slum clearance. They were replaced by two seventeen-story apartment towers on the beach, known as Santa Monica Shores.

To residents of Ocean Park, Santa Monica Shores stood as a daily reminder that the city had shoved them aside. A recession left the rest of the land vacant for a while, but in 1972 the city approved a plan to build an additional fourteen hundred luxury apartments near the Shores. Before groundbreaking, however, California voters passed the coastal initiative, a law designed to discourage coastal development, increase public access, and make affordable housing a high priority.

The hated Santa Monica Shores apartment buildings in Ocean Park.

Led by, among others, a young urban planner named Ruth Galanter, Ocean Park activists quickly mastered the complexities of the coastal initiative and used them to the neighborhood's advantage. They persuaded the new Coastal Commission to veto the city's plan. Subsequently they filed several lawsuits, forcing the city to negotiate an agreement to include one hundred units of low-cost housing for the elderly, a maximum height of five stories, adequate parking, and six acres of public parks on the site. With this they set the standard for coastal development up and down the state of California.

Later in the decade, Ocean Park activists worked with middle-class reformers to oppose other large development proposals, such as a plan to tear down Santa Monica Pier and replace it with an offshore island with condominiums and a hotel. They also fought against one of Lawrence Welk's high-rise buildings and a downtown shopping mall developed jointly by the city and the Rouse Corporation.

The Ocean Park urban renewal fight was crucial in organizing the activists into a cohesive group confident of their political clout. Many of them felt they had saved their neighborhood from a forest of expensive high-rises. In this way they were not so different from homeowner activists in the Hillside Federation, who lived just a few miles away.

But Ocean Park activists had two things the Hillside Federation never had. First, they had a broad political agenda, which grew not out of their own self-interest but out of a sense of social justice strongly rooted in the 1960s. If such an agenda was not really within Southern California's political tradition—and it wasn't—that fact made it all the more powerful. Second, they had a keen understanding of how to mobilize a constituency politically and how to organize and run campaigns.

Though the Hillside Federation had achieved campaign successes, notably the Braude council victory in 1967, the homeowners had always hit an electoral wall. The very nature of their agenda—protecting a single-family lifestyle that itself had evolved out of an anti-political, anti-urban mentality—prevented them from broadening their constituency and attacking the growth machine on a larger scale. Middle-class Angelenos often reacted violently to the bulldozer on their block; but once it was successfully pushed onto the next block, they retreated once again to their sealed-off backyards.

In Santa Monica, however, there would be no electoral walls.

↬

In 1976, six years after his penniless arrival in Venice, Tom Hayden decided to enter the political mainstream as a candidate for the Democratic nomination for U.S. Senate. Running against incumbent John Tunney (who would subsequently emerge as a member of the Los Angeles growth machine), Hayden did not win, but he attracted more than a million votes. With Ocean Park serving as the campaign's epicenter, many local activists returned to electoral politics for the first time in years.

A year later, the same group worked in support of Ruth Yannatta in a race for state Assembly. Yannatta, who had been married to the writer Derek Shearer in a wedding ceremony at The Church in Ocean Park, was a consumer activist who dropped out of graduate school to organize a nationwide meat boycott. Like Hayden, she did not win the Democratic nomination. But even more than the Hayden campaign, the Yannatta campaign proved to be a turning point for the Ocean Park activists, and for two reasons. First, it gave them momentum independent of Tom Hayden. (Hayden used his political organization to win a seat in the state legislature in 1982 and has remained there ever since, serving as a lightning rod of attention in Santa Monica but never really a central figure in municipal politics.) Second, the campaign, managed by Derek Shearer, helped Ocean Park activists develop the skill and experience to run state-of-the-art political campaigns with sophisticated direct-mail operations and computerized precinct walking. By 1978, the Ocean Park activists amounted to a group in search of a cause. All they needed was a galvanizing political issue at which all this political passion and organizing skill could be aimed.

⌒

While Tom Hayden and Ruth Yannatta were campaigning, a real estate boom of unprecedented proportions overran the Westside of Los Angeles. Faced with inflation, cold weather on the East Coast, volatile political situations abroad, and smog in other parts of Southern California, people flocked to Beverly Hills, West Los Angeles, and Santa Monica in search of a comfortable place to live and a safe way to invest their money. The result was price inflation on real estate everywhere on the West Side and all over Santa Monica in particular. As the financial writer Adam Smith put it, for the first time in history people were "hoarding houses."

Heavy speculation in the apartment building market soon followed. Rents doubled and tripled, and in many cases tenants were simply pushed out the door to make way for new buildings or condominiums. Five percent of the city's apartments were demolished.

Yuppies flocked to the area, paying high rents and purchasing expensive condos. Ocean Park's once-derelict Main Street was revived as an area of chic bars, restaurants, and boutiques. Seeing Santa Monica as a fertile market, office developers began buying up properties near the poor neighborhoods along the freeway because of their easy access.

To many in Santa Monica, the issues of land speculation and rent increases were intertwined, adding up to a gigantic attack on people of modest means. The elderly who lived in Santa Monica apartments were not in classic pursuit of the Southern California dream—they did not own a single-family home—but they understood that as working-class people their deal with the growth machine was going sour.

Some of the elderly renters were New York liberals, but many were not. Still, it was not long before they were leading a zealous campaign against the landlords. Well organized, the senior citizens placed a rent control measure on the ballot in 1978. Faced with a $200,000 landlord-led counterattack, they lost. But their efforts gained the attention of Ocean Park activists. Their cause was further aided by the passage of Proposition 13, which apartment owners had promised would lead to lower rents. A year later, rents were still going up, fomenting more unrest among renters. So the activists and the elderly renters—now organized into a nonpartisan group called Santa Monicans for Renters' Rights— went to a young Legal Aid lawyer named Robert Myers and asked him to write a new, tougher rent control initiative. The new measure called for an elected Rent Control Board and strict limits on rent increases. If passed, it would be the strictest rent control law in the country.*

The zeal of the elderly renters was now combined with the Army-like political efficiency of the Ocean Park activists to make a formidable campaign organization. To turn out the vote, the Renters' Rights group ran a highly disciplined campaign. Though operating before the age of personal computers, they developed a programmatic system of walking precincts. Knocking on doors, they determined whether a voter was pro-rent control, anti-, or on the fence. This information was fed into a computer, which was then used to develop the strategy for future

* Santa Monica was not alone in pursuing rent control in the late 1970s. Property inflation made rising rents an issue all over California, and coincidentally in the late 1970s the state Supreme Court issued a ruling clarifying that rent control was legal. Tenants' rights became a statewide issue, and dozens of rent control ordinances were passed, including ordinances in the City of Los Angeles and L.A. County. But no ordinance was as tough as the one that Santa Monica passed in 1979.

precinct-walking and phone-bank efforts. The antis were left alone. But the pros and the fence-sitters were visited again and again; precinct walkers even carried printouts with them as they walked.

And ironically, it was the nature of the city as created by the growth machine that made a successful rent control campaign possible. Packed cheek by jowl with apartment buildings, Santa Monica's precincts were eminently walkable, with more than eleven thousand residents per square mile. And the precinct walkers had a compelling message for these people to listen to. Traditionally tenants had been difficult to mobilize. They were transient, poorly educated and informed, or complacent. But the real estate boom had created a new group of "permanent" tenants who could not afford to buy a house. Historically disinterested in local elections which didn't affect them, the city's renters—eighty percent of the population—now had a pocketbook issue on the municipal ballot. And as renters, a lot of these folks were feeling cheated out of the Southern California dream as it had been sold to them by the growth machine. As the president of Santa Monica Bank declared a few years later, "We dug our own grave."

In an off-year, nonpartisan local election in April 1979, voters overwhelmed the polls and passed the rent control ordinance. In the same election, Ruth Goldway (formerly Ruth Yannatta, now using her maiden name rather than the name of her first husband) was elected to the city council. Two months later, the Renters' Rights group called out its army of precinct walkers to engineer a victory in the first elections for the new city Rent Control Board. And in November the troops came through yet again by electing another Ocean Park activist to an unexpired term on the city council. By the end of the year Goldway had a working majority on some issues, reallocating federal funds to grassroots neighborhood efforts and making a major commitment to defending the rent control law (the strictest in the country) in court.

For those unfamiliar with local politics in Los Angeles, it is hard to explain what a remarkable achievement these three campaigns in 1979 represented. This was not New York or Chicago or Boston, where local politics is religion, pastime, and in many ways the lifeblood of the community. This was local politics in a Southern California suburb, where elections are held in April of odd-numbered years, a twenty percent turnout is considered exceptional, and political parties aren't allowed to participate. Prior to the rent control campaign, many people didn't even know what city they lived in. There were no local career politicians, nor any patronage jobs, and the council positions themselves paid almost nothing.

For decades the council seats had been held by bankers, lawyers, landlords, and other members of the growth machine who represented only those few homeowners who actually voted, and who didn't differentiate between their business jobs promoting growth and their political jobs on the council. In the 1970s, Santa Monica had begun to elect reformers opposed to rampant growth, but these too had been homeowner candidates with a homeowner constituency. Now, virtually overnight, a century of political custom in Santa Monica was obliterated by dedicated and poorly financed left-wingers, who figured out how to systematically extract thousands of votes from apartment dwellers who'd never before cast municipal ballots. This was electoral skill and dominance that had never been seen in Southern California—that the Hillside Federation in Los Angeles, with a narrower agenda and a more spread-out constituency, had never come close to matching.

When four city council seats became available in the April 1981 election, the Renters' Rights forces swept to power with a solid victory for their entire slate, including James Conn, the easygoing young minister who had founded The Church in Ocean Park, and Dennis Zane, an intense rent control organizer long involved in liberal causes. Typical of its organizational skill, the Renters' Rights group put together a list of fifteen thousand supporters, and then used computers to transfer each person's name and address onto individual door hangers displaying each voter's polling place. At four a.m. on election day, a hundred volunteers began placing hangers on doorknobs and wound up in an early-morning chase with kids hired by the other side removing them.

"We're not going to be taking trips to Havana or renaming Main Street 'Ho Chi Minh Boulevard'," Derek Shearer quipped shortly after the Renters' Rights group assumed power in 1981. Nevertheless, with their victory coming only a few months after Ronald Reagan's election as president, Santa Monica became a symbol to both left and right across the nation. "Revolt in Reagan's Backyard!" the *Village Voice* proclaimed, taking the victory as evidence that there was no tilt to the right in the United States after all. (Reagan had lived for years in Pacific Palisades, a

Los Angeles neighborhood just north of Santa Monica.) Right-wingers quickly dubbed the town "The People's Republic of Santa Monica" (landlords even printed bumper stickers with the nickname in Russian-looking letters), and *The Wall Street Journal* accused the group of being "suburban radicals" who were hiding middle-class values underneath all their rhetoric.

Though Tom Hayden and Jane Fonda remained special favorites of the conservative press, Santa Monica's new First Couple, Ruth Goldway and Derek Shearer, made an easy target for right-wing attacks. A serious woman, Goldway plunged full-time into her $150-a-month job as the new mayor, usually saying whatever was on her mind, no matter how harsh or strident.* When the new council appointed Shearer to the city planning commission, she responded to charges of nepotism by saying: "I think it's really just a coincidence that he happens to be my husband." Shearer himself was the main target of the suburban radical charge; a solid son of Culver City, he was a self-described jock who looked more than a little like the Dodgers star Steve Garvey. And while he had a sense of humor, Shearer too was given to the arrogance that power sometimes bestows on liberal activists.[†]

Although it was the hot-button issue, in truth rent control was just part of the larger Renters' Rights agenda of taming the growth machine—an agenda that stretched beyond apartment rents to questions of land prices and, especially, demand for office space. At the same time that the residential real estate market was heating up on the Westside, the demand for office space near the beach was growing. Land prices soared so much that the dirt underneath the city's only ice-skating rink fetched $80 per square foot as potential office space. From 1976 to 1979, new office space approved by the city grew from fifty thousand square

---

* Like most Southern California towns, Santa Monica retains the Progressive-era tradition of not electing a mayor independently of the council. Instead, the mayor is selected by the other council members, and the mayor's job—a mostly ceremonial one—is usually rotated among the council's ruling faction. Designed to prevent the creation of political machines by eliminating the role of an elected executive, this tradition has not stopped ambitious politicians like Goldway from using the job as a bully pulpit.

[†] Having spent time at Oxford in the late 1960s, Shearer emerged years later as a certified "FOB"—Friend of Bill Clinton, with whom he had remained in contact for more than two decades. Shearer served briefly as Deputy Assistant Secretary of Commerce in the Clinton Administration and later became ambassador to Finland. But with conservative organs such as the *Wall Street Journal* gunning for him, he was dogged by his leftist past—and especially his political activities in Santa Monica—as if he were Tom Hayden himself.

feet to four hundred thousand to seven hundred thousand and finally to one million—a figure almost as large as the entire amount of office space in the city at the beginning of the decade.

Though not as politically divisive, the pressure for more large-scale office development in the city was as important as rent control in the minds of Ocean Park activists—intertwined with it, in fact. In the same three-year period, more than three hundred apartments had been demolished to make way for office development. At its very first meeting the highest priority of the new council was not to control rents, which were covered by the rent control law, but to control growth.

In April 1981, Santa Monica, a city of eight square miles, had sixty-one development projects in the pipeline at City Hall, including thirty-one that already had some sort of city permit. The first thing the new council did, before appointing Bob Myers as city attorney or selecting Ruth Goldway as mayor, was to impose a six-month building moratorium that stopped all sixty-one projects. The new council wanted to revamp the city's entire General Plan before allowing any major construction. One developer sued the city for permission to proceed, and a couple of others who could have sued began to negotiate.

To reform the city's planning process, the council appointed three citizen task forces to modify the planning policies. But Goldway and the other council members knew what they wanted: new ordinances requiring developers of all kinds to cough up money for parks and day care centers, and other "exactions" that would help offset the squeeze on land that Santa Monica's speculators had created.

More than anything else, council members wanted—needed—the office developers to build or pay for low-cost housing. Housing was at the cornerstone of their political agenda. Affordable housing, they believed, was the key to winning over working-class voters from the defenders of the growth machine; it was the price of housing, after all, that was making the growth machine a bad deal for the working class. To these folks, local politics was, indeed, a class struggle.

Furthermore, the Ocean Park activists had some experience in exacting low-cost housing from developers by means of the Coastal Commission; and, at a time of waning federal support and dramatic property tax cuts, the council had no place else to turn. Other left-leaning cities—San Francisco, Boston—were also moving in this direction, but Santa Monica was the first city in Southern California, and probably the first small city in the nation, to start hitting developers hard for housing and other social "goodies."

Of the three task forces, the one addressing commercial and industrial development issues received the most publicity, simply because so many office buildings were on the drawing board. And although it was supposed to be setting up guidelines for all developers to follow, the committee ended up spending most of its time dealing with one project: a proposal by Welton Becket Associates to turn a fifteen-acre former garbage dump into a multi-million-square-foot office complex near the Santa Monica Freeway.

The Renters' Rights group could not have asked for a more perfect foil in its fight against the growth machine than Welton Becket. Though the Colorado Place project was the company's first venture into real estate development, Becket was an old-line Los Angeles architectural firm, the seventh-largest in the country, specializing in large corporate clients. During the Depression, the firm designed Santa Monica's beloved Civic Auditorium, where the Oscars have often been held. After World War II, Becket designed many of the large, vaguely modernist structures that have given so much of postwar Los Angeles a feeling of impersonality, including the skyscrapers rising from the former movie backlot at Century City, the Dorothy Chandler Pavilion at Los Angeles Music Center, and the hated Santa Monica Shores apartment buildings. The firm's president, N. David O'Malley, was a pin-stripe architect who typified the thinking-big mentality of the postwar growth machine. "At a time when so many architects seem unsure of their present role," he said in 1982, "our staffers dream of building the cities of the future." In addition to the Santa Monica project, Becket was a partner with the Chinese government on the one-thousand-room Great Wall Hotel.

In 1980, before the Renters' Rights group assumed full control, Becket had won preliminary approval to build what would be the largest real estate development in the city. On a fifteen-acre site in the industrial corridor, amid clusters of old factories and not far from the apartment belt, Becket envisioned a half-million square feet of office space and a three-hundred-fifty-room hotel, all in a group of three-story buildings. In the first phase, Becket would build the office buildings. Phase Two would include the hotel. As a tightly packed business park almost independent from the outside world, Colorado Place prefigured many large-scale real estate development projects of 1980s Los Angeles.

Becket was planning to move its own offices into the building and had also lined up one other key tenant: Systems Development Corporation, a spinoff of the RAND Corporation and Santa Monica's largest employer. Having spent $7 million on the project, Becket was excavating the site at the time of the council election. But because it did not yet have a final building permit, the firm had to apply for an exemption from the moratorium.

Reluctantly concluding that he would have to pay a price to get the go-ahead, O'Malley came to the council in June with a package that any other city would have welcomed. He agreed to subject the Becket plans to many public hearings, proposed that Becket build fifty units of low-income housing, and offered the firm's professional services to the city without charge for use on public development projects.

Buoyed by electoral victory and a real estate market that was going through the roof, Ruth Goldway responded by saying: "I'm not impressed at all." In spite of a threat by Systems Development to move fifty miles away to Camarillo if the project weren't built, the new council majority voted against allowing Becket to move ahead. The project seemed dead.

But the threat that many of SDC's fourteen hundred employees might lose their jobs weighed heavily on a council supposedly elected to protect working people from the ravages of larger economic forces. When they held a hearing in July, the commercial and industrial task force members were deluged with pleas from SDC employees to let the project go forward. In early August, the task force released its recommendations on Becket, and the price was stiff indeed. On the fifteen-acre site, Becket would be asked to reduce the size of the office project by twenty percent and build forty units of low-cost housing, a park, a day care center, and a community room. In addition, the task force said, Becket should pay a fee of one-and-a-half percent of the project's cost to assist arts and social services. "If the private market and federal and state government will not build rental housing," fumed the chairman of the task force, "then, by God, the developer will." The task force suggested that the office buildings and the hotel could be made taller to make room for the park.

O'Malley was livid at the prospect of these concessions. The delays, he claimed, were nearly bankrupting his company. The controversy gained state and national attention as the first big test of the People's Republic against the forces of capitalism, and after the task force recommendations were announced it seemed like a stalemate.

Into this breach stepped Dennis Zane, one of the new council members elected with the support of the renters' coalition. At the age of thirty-four, Zane was not the most popular renter activist—he had finished last among the council winners—but he may have been the smartest. Intense and passionate, Zane often appeared to be the most openly radical member of the council—an ex-philosophy major who once organized a self-management system among inner-city transients who worked with him on the night shift of a Boston restaurant. He had worked as a precinct walker on the Hayden and Yannatta campaigns and had been one of the few young activists to work with elderly tenants on the rent control issue from the beginning. He did not seem like the kind of guy to make a deal with David O'Malley.

But Zane was more pragmatic than he first appeared. A private-school math teacher, he seemed like the smartest kid in the high school chess club, the guy who has played out all the scenarios in his head and knows just how far he has to go to beat you. Characteristically, he had been a chief architect of the computerized precinct-walking system. Furthermore, he was particularly sensitive to the possible plight of SDC employees. Born into a working-class family in San Bernardino County, Zane had seen his father thrown out of work during economic downturns.

In August 1981, to the astonishment of his fellow council members and his own constituents, Zane sat down with O'Malley and worked out a framework for a deal. The size of the office space was reduced slightly. Becket would build one hundred units of low-income housing on the site, half in Phase One and half in Phase Two. Becket would commit three acres, twenty percent of the total site, to a park, which would be included in Phase Two. But in return, the hotel would be made larger—ninety-five-feet high, so large that it would tower over the rest of what was essentially a two-story neighborhood. (Because it would generate an enormous amount of sales and bed taxes, the hotel was far more profitable for the city than the office buildings. To a council with a lengthy social agenda, this was no small consideration.)

Hard-line rent control organizers were dismayed at Zane's conciliatory attitude toward Becket. The task force members felt sold down the river, and Goldway refused to vote in favor of the deal. But the rest of the Santa Monica Renters' Rights council supported it. The final development agreement, which ran to some forty pages, was approved as an ordinance by the Santa Monica City Council on October 27, 1981—almost exactly six months after the election.

Despite Goldway's resistance, it was a remarkable achievement. The Renters' Rights group had stared down the growth machine and gotten what it wanted: a smaller project, low-cost housing, and lots of social goodies that fit in with the new council's agenda. Though not unlike the legal settlement over the Santa Monica Shores project, the Colorado Place deal had two important differences. The Shores project was a city redevelopment project, not a private development. And the legal settlement had been forced through the regulatory clout of the Coastal Commission, a state agency with sweeping authority. By contrast, the Colorado Place deal represented the first time a local government in Los Angeles had translated sheer electoral power into direct leverage over a private developer. Welton Becket had to back down because the Renters' Rights group could deliver working-class votes on election day.

                             ↭

Colorado Place does not stand today as originally negotiated. Becket completed Phase One more or less as planned—a low-slung, boxy-looking set of buildings along Colorado Boulevard housing some corporate and professional offices and a Yuppie restaurant or two. But Becket ran into financing problems, and the project went belly-up before the firm could build Phase Two, which was to include more housing, the park, community space, and most of the other exactions the Renters' Rights group had demanded. After Welton Becket turned the project over to Southmark Pacific in 1985, the new developer and the city entered into an extended legal fight over proposed changes that would have cut into the social agenda called for in the 1981 development agreement. Phase Two was eventually completed in a somewhat different form, but the recession held up plans to complete the project.

As the 1980s wore on, the Renters' Rights coalition lost its majority twice, most significantly in 1983 when Ruth Goldway lost her bid for re-election. (She has never sought public office again, though she did portray the Secretary of Education in the movie *Dave*.) After each defeat, the suburban radicals recaptured power by being a little less radical and a little more suburban as—rent control or not—the working class gave way to the Yuppies. Perhaps the most telling change came over the issue of homelessness.

Beginning in 1990, the Renters' Rights coalition began backing away from its sympathetic view toward the homeless when most Santa Monica residents, even renters of modest means, began complaining about their proliferation in the city's parks and public spaces. Then, during an election season in 1992, City Attorney Robert Myers, the revered author of the city's rent control law and an outspoken advocate for the homeless, became a political liability. Sensing a shift in public opinion, the Renters' Rights group retreated from its position of tolerance. When Myers refused to cooperate on anti-homeless ordinances, Dennis Zane, once again engaging in a sophisticated game of political calculus, engineered the ouster of his longtime political ally. By this time, it was clear that the Renters' Rights group had become an entrenched political machine, exactly the sort of political operation Southern Californians traditionally disdained.

Along the way, the concept of "economic democracy" died a slow, unnoticed death. When apartment construction soared and rents declined during the Reagan years, rent control disappeared as a galvanizing political issue almost everywhere but Santa Monica. As a liberal political movement countering the conservatism of the 1980s, Santa Monica has always remained a beachhead and nothing more.

Phase 1 of the Colorado Place project as it was eventually built by Welton Becket.

Yet the Ocean Park activists did start a revolution. In a very real sense, their rise to power was the first true challenge to the Los Angeles growth machine. This was partly a result of their policies, which slowed growth considerably and shaped it to meet their political agenda. The Renters' Rights group helped to pass two rounds of zone changes that significantly cut the amount of development permitted in the city. The group engineered the approval of a wide range of large office and retail projects and, as in Colorado Place, the group extracted a long list of social benefits as part of the price. All these policies became models for other cities around Southern California.

More important, however, the Renters' Rights group broke through the electoral wall that Los Angeles slow-growthers had always run up against. Certainly the Hillside Federation had scored some of the first political victories against the growth machine, and many suburban cities, Thousand Oaks and Riverside among them, passed slow-growth initiatives during the late 1970s. But Santa Monica was the first city to prove that an attack on growth could be the basis for a mass political movement in municipal government.

Bluntly stated, the Ocean Park activists made local politics in a small Los Angeles city truly political for the first time in decades. They walked precincts and used computerized lists to keep track of likely voters and likely supporters. They organized their campaign like a military operation and rounded up votes—working-class votes—that other slow-growth groups before them had never been able to obtain. After seizing control of City Hall, they worked very much like a traditional political machine, rewarding friends, punishing enemies, and whipping political sentiment into a frenzy to retain power.

In other words, they did all the things that local politicians do as a means of involving voters and making them care. Their enemy was the landlord, the banker, the developer, the speculator—all the cogs in the growth machine. Their success did not go unnoticed in Los Angeles, in Pasadena, in Redlands, or even in Orange County. Soon, demonizing the growth machine became good politics in Southern California. And, once the electorate had been stirred against them, the landlords and bankers and developers soon discovered that it was not easy to put them back to sleep.

CHAPTER 2

Perestroika Co-opted

In 1987, Tom Bradley stood on the east lawn of the Los Angeles Central Library and proclaimed that growth was good.

Bradley was helping to commemorate the groundbreaking for the Library Tower, the tallest office building on the West Coast, just across Fifth Street from the library. Library Tower was part of a deal—typical in Los Angeles in the 1980s—to pay for a civic renovation by skimming cream from the profits of growth. Bradley and other city officials had permitted a prominent developer, Maguire Thomas Partners, to exceed zoning requirements for two buildings across the street (one more than seventy stories high, the other over fifty). In return, Maguire Thomas had agreed to foot the bill to renovate the magnificent sixty-year-old library.

At a time when there were few other ways to pay for anything, the library was one deal Bradley could firmly support. It fit in well with his decade-long effort to recreate Los Angeles as a "world-class" city—a center of commerce and culture equal to Tokyo, New York, Paris, or London. In one deal, Los Angeles would get a renovated historic building and a glitzy corporate center in the downtown area.

Three years after the stunning success of the 1984 Olympics, and only two years after his greatest electoral victory, Bradley took the occasion of the groundbreaking to declare his unequivocal faith in growth as the driving principle of the city's urban development. "All cities must grow to survive and prosper," Bradley said with a rare tone of stridency. "Every city that has ever tried to do otherwise has died."

The following January, the *Atlantic Monthly*, that paragon of Eastern establishment media, portrayed "The Big Orange" on its cover wearing a business suit and carrying a briefcase—a serious and prosperous image of Los Angeles never before seen in the national press. It seemed the ultimate victory during what political scientist Raphael J. Sonenshein has called Bradley's "pro-growth" period.

But the Library Tower groundbreaking was probably the last time any Los Angeles politician, including Tom Bradley, dared to say anything good about growth in public.

⌒

The City of Los Angeles is about as different from Santa Monica as one can imagine—some four-hundred-sixty-odd square miles of squiggling, squirming property created by the changing political and economic necessities of an entire century. Los Angeles reaches over this mountain to grab a choice ranch, runs down that corridor to capture a harbor, slices inward here and there to avoid a dump site or some other noxious use, and runs completely around at least four small cities including Santa Monica. These boundaries are largely the product of the growth machine. Eighty years ago, Los Angeles gobbled up cities fearful of a future without water, such as Hollywood, in exchange for water service. At the same time, the city annexed the entire San Fernando Valley as part of the famous water scheme on which the film *Chinatown* was based. Old cities that survived, like Beverly Hills, generally had their own sources of water. New cities avoided geographically natural annexation via the Lakewood system, which made the boundaries of Los Angeles all the more nonsensical.

If L.A.'s boundaries are vast and illogical, so are its politics. Ruled by a set of Progressive-era reforms designed to prevent the creation of political machines, the diffuse and complicated governmental structure of Los Angeles has left more than one newcomer wondering exactly where the power lies. Unlike his counterparts in Chicago or Boston, a Los Angeles mayor has very little authority. Independent boards and commissions wield much of L.A.'s power. Even department heads who are political appointees elsewhere are covered by civil service protection.

To the extent that it is focused anywhere, power resides with the city council. And while they are elected by district, council members are hardly neighborhood ward-heelers. Like the mayor, they are elected on a nonpartisan basis in odd-numbered years, meaning that they cannot rely on formal support from organized political parties. Perhaps

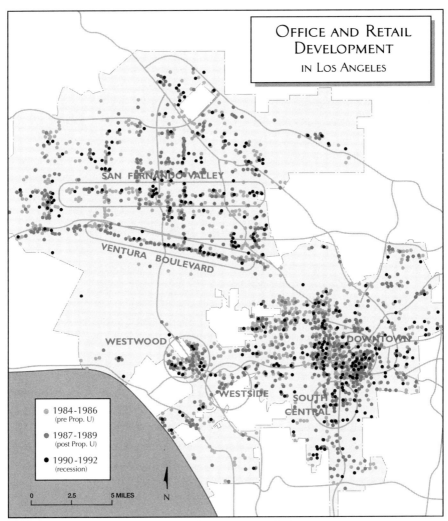

1984-1986
(pre Prop. U)

1987-1989
(post Prop. U)

1990-1992
(recession)

SAN FERNANDO VALLEY

VENTURA BOULEVARD

WESTWOOD

DOWNTOWN

WESTSIDE

SOUTH CENTRAL

0   2.5   5 MILES   N

The City of Los Angeles before, during, and after Proposition U. Each
dot represents a separate retail or commercial development project.

most important, only fifteen council members govern this vast, sprawling city. Every council member represents around thirty square miles
and a couple of hundred thousand people. In effect, each is the mayor
of a city the size of Syracuse or Toledo or Riverside.

In such a large city, operating on such a large scale with no formal
party structure, retail politics is impossible. The precinct-walking system
that Santa Monica's rent control coalition used so effectively to mobilize

voters would succeed in turning out only a handful of voters in a typical L.A. council election. Occasionally an angry grassroots candidate can sweep to victory on public emotion, as the slow-growther Marvin Braude did in 1967 and the young Jewish activist Zev Yaroslavsky did in 1975. In general, however, running a campaign for mayor or council in Los Angeles requires big money for big media buys and big direct-mail campaigns. And only one group has historically fronted that kind of money: the real estate developers who form the core of the Los Angeles growth machine.

Obviously, there was a lot of tit-for-tat between developers and politicians over campaign contributions and new real estate projects, just as there is everywhere. But the flow of power and money and people around City Hall was a good deal more complicated than that.

In a city without strong parties, political insiders usually look for a substitute that can serve as an effective organizing principle and vote-getting technique. This is why the Westside political operation known as the "Berman-Waxman machine" achieved almost mythical power in Los Angeles; using highly sophisticated direct-mail techniques, the group was able to slice through a weak institutional structure and consistently deliver votes.* But the Berman-Waxman operation largely stayed out of city politics, and in that arena the real estate development business played an important role.

The offices of development companies, their law firms, and their consultants filled the role of the nonexistent Democratic clubhouses. In a city where almost no one seemed interested in local politics, real estate was a base from which to operate—a business intertwined with local politics, where people could gossip about City Hall and plot political comebacks and coups while at the same time making money. It could serve as a launching pad, a staging ground, or a back-end gold mine to finance future activism.

John Tunney, for example, went into the development business after being defeated for re-election to the U.S. Senate (and put his name on the door of a prominent Democratic law firm at the same time). While serving as state Democratic chairman, Peter Kelley was a partner

* The Berman-Waxman "machine" was not really a machine at all because, typical of Los Angeles, it did not have party loyalists on the ground or political patronage to dispense. Instead, it depended on an affluent, largely Jewish Westside fundraising base and state-of-the-art mailing techniques. The machine's principals were Henry Waxman and Howard Berman, both veteran Democratic members of Congress from Los Angeles, and Berman's brother Michael, a political operative.

in a bitterly fought development proposal in Santa Monica. Nelson Rising, who managed Tunney's and Bradley's campaigns in the 1970s, subsequently became a partner with Maguire Thomas and shepherded two politically explosive development projects through City Hall (including the Library Tower). Bradley confidante Dan Garcia, who for ten years was president of the planning commission, became a developer's lawyer and later vice president for real estate at Warner Brothers, making him a rare and powerful combination of development, entertainment, and politics. The list goes on and on.

In short, power in Los Angeles city politics revolved largely around an iron triangle of nominally nonpartisan politicians, developer/contributors, and the Democratic party—an iron triangle which, though theoretically liberal in political philosophy, was really part of the business-oriented growth machine. Labor unions, even though they were institutionally weak in Los Angeles, also played an important role in this triangle because they wanted sympathetic Democrats in office and a booming development business to provide jobs for their members.

Republicans, who had stronger political support in Orange County and elsewhere outside the city, played essentially the same game in the suburban counties, with developers contributing to supervisorial campaigns and often rewarding politicians with land or jobs after they left office. The occasional conservative Democrat with staying power at Los Angeles City Hall, such as longtime City Council President John Ferraro, also had little choice but to operate within the power structure created by the liberal Democratic developers.

The result was that sooner or later virtually all of L.A.'s politicians found themselves closely tied to the growth machine and its dizzying web of relationships. Tom Bradley had been elected as a reform mayor and had spent the 1970s pursuing a liberal social agenda. In the 1980s, however, he promoted Los Angeles as a world-class city and downtown as a corporate center, creating strong relationships with developers in the process. The same web ensnared any number of politicians, such as Bradley ally Pat Russell, who represented an area around Los Angeles International Airport containing several choice pieces of undeveloped land. Even the sanctimonious slow-growther Marvin Braude got about forty percent of his campaign contributions from developers.

To the extent that it existed, structured opposition to the Democratic developer iron triangle came from the Hillside Federation and its fifty-odd member homeowner associations scattered throughout the Westside and the Valley. For decades the Hillside Federation had been the city's only grassroots political organization, defending what social historian Mike Davis once described as middle-class L.A.'s obsession with "homestead exclusivism." The Federation's coming of age had been the Braude-led campaign against a large highway atop the Santa Monica Mountains in the 1960s. Beginning in the 1970s, however, the Federation took on the broader task of breaking the growth machine's power in City Hall as a means of protecting single-family neighborhoods. Though often allied with environmentalists concerned about sensitive land in the mountains, the homeowners were classic NIMBYs, people to whom "Not In My Backyard" was not just a phrase but a mantra.

The first attempt came in the early 1970s, when the visionary Calvin Hamilton, then planning director, drew up a new General Plan. At the time Los Angeles was viewed as the nation's most unsolvable urban planning problem, a vast sea of undifferentiated low-density neighborhoods experiencing seemingly random growth. Hamilton's creative breakthrough, known as "the centers concept," called for concentrating high-density commercial and apartment development in thirty-five centers around the city, which would be linked together by mass transit. Channeling development into these locations would allow the city to dramatically down-zone single-family neighborhoods and undeveloped areas in order to keep out further urbanization.

A consummate piece of urban planning theory, Hamilton's proposal was a threat to the merchants of growth. While accommodating development and giving the city a more orderly geographical framework, the plan actually challenged the basic precept of the growth machine: that raw land must be continually consumed for the local economy to prosper. Hamilton was the first city planning director to actively solicit citizen participation, and he once claimed that twenty thousand Los Angeles residents (mostly homeowner activists) had participated in the plan's creation.

The Hillside Federation loved the plan and the process. But the Democratic developer power structure hated both. The plan reduced the opportunity for profits in areas of low density where land was relatively cheap. Developers didn't want to be channeled into "centers." They wanted to make big money creating new ones. So Cal Hamilton's General Plan sat on the shelf, and the city continued to operate under the very liberal provisions of the 1946 zoning ordinance, which anticipated a city of ten million people. Despite Hamilton's efforts, it was possible well into the 1980s to build a twenty-story office building without any environmental review—just an "over-the-counter" permit from the Los Angeles Planning Department. The Democratic developer iron triangle justified this system by saying it was good for business and good for jobs. Just because a bunch of "rich" homeowners like the Hillside Federation wanted to shut down the city's economy didn't mean that working-class homeowners all over the city agreed.

This wide-open system of zoning was still in place when the city emerged from the 1982–83 recession with a roaring economy and a series of successes, such as the 1984 Olympics, that established Los Angeles as a world-class city. With the prosperity had come a real estate boom—the second in a decade—that drove land and home prices through the roof. But as the Santa Monica experience foreshadowed, this boom was different. This one was driven not only by rising home prices in "nice" parts of town, such as beachfront areas, but also by a dramatic decentralization of employment and retailing. Los Angeles, of course, had never been as centralized as other cities. But during the 1980s, as telecommunications improved and traffic worsened, more and more people, especially corporate honchos, wanted to work and shop near where they lived.

The result was tremendous pressure to build large office buildings and retail centers in middle- and upper-class neighborhoods all over the city, especially in the Hillside Federation's strongholds, the Westside and the San Fernando Valley. As land prices shot up, dry cleaners and drug-stores were uprooted and replaced with multilevel urban shopping malls and multistory office buildings. Near West Hollywood, the eight-story Beverly Center mall emerged on a piece of land formerly devoted to pony rides. In West Los Angeles, a nondescript low-rise industrial district on West Olympic Boulevard erupted with large, bulky office buildings.

Making matters worse was the fact that, unlike most other American cities, Los Angeles was almost exclusively a "strip" city. Except for down-town, Hollywood, Westwood, and a few other areas, there were no con-centrated shopping or employment districts. Commercial areas were usually just one parcel deep along a boulevard such as Wilshire or Santa

The forest of skyscrapers, adjacent to single-family neighborhoods, on Westwood Boulevard in Westwood, part of Zev Yaroslavsky's former city council district.

Monica or Ventura, which is what prompted Cal Hamilton to pursue the centers concept. So it was almost impossible to build a large structure anywhere in the city without casting shadows or otherwise interfering with the life of a quiet residential neighborhood. In the 1980s the most notorious example was the Fujita building on Ventura Boulevard in Encino, an affluent district in the San Fernando Valley, where a sheer six-story wall butted against swimming pools in the backyards of a single-family neighborhood.

All these problems were not unique to Los Angeles. They were being replicated all around the state and the nation, especially in suburban areas where pressure for large shopping and office developments were squeezing previously bucolic suburbs. Homeowner unrest was strong all over California, especially in evolving suburbs like Walnut Creek (east of San Francisco), Riverside, San Diego, Newport Beach and Costa Mesa in Orange County, and Thousand Oaks (just west of the San Fernando Valley). A decade or two earlier, the only political option for these homeowners would have been to recall their local council members. By the 1980s, however, they had two exceptionally sturdy tools at their disposal: the ballot and the courtroom.

In the 1970s, the California Supreme Court, traditionally protective of the initiative and referendum process, had liberalized the rules affecting the placement of land use issues on local ballots. The result was an explosion of initiatives restricting growth, mostly in the San Francisco area at first, but gradually moving into Southern California. Also during the 1970s, the state legislature passed tougher environmental and planning laws, giving citizen groups much greater power to challenge local planning decisions in court. One law specifically required that a city's zoning ordinance conform to its General Plan. Another ordered Los Angeles to rezone the city according to Hamilton's General Plan.

The Los Angeles growth machine's response to the state law had been to ignore it. The rezoning was supposed to be complete by 1982; by 1984, it was only one-fourth done. Hamilton pleaded with the city council for funds to finish the job. For obvious reasons, the council refused to furnish the money. "Many of the homeowner groups were surprised and amazed and dismayed when they found out all the work they had done on community plans made no difference whatever," recalled Carlyle Hall, a veteran public interest lawyer in Los Angeles.

In 1984, the Hillside Federation hired Carlyle Hall to sue the city. And in January 1985, a local judge ordered the city to complete the rezoning. The city council dickered for months and finally, in September of that year, allocated $5 million to get the job done. The result, if anyone had been up to the task, was a rare opportunity to reshape urban planning in one of the largest cities in America. Hamilton's proposal could have been updated and implemented through a rezoning. At last, the city's future growth patterns could have been rooted in solid planning principles, rather than the real estate industry's land-consuming appetite.

But it was clear that the growth-oriented power structure hoped the entire issue would disappear. (In fact, Bradley forced Planning Director Hamilton out of office in late 1985.) And the Hillside Federation, though supportive of Hamilton's plan, was equally unwilling to address the actual nuts and bolts of reshaping the city, because it was institutionally bound to protect the status quo in all single-family neighborhoods, even those near a designated center. So a rare opportunity was lost. Instead of serving as the vehicle for constructive debate, growth became a political football between two ambitious politicians.

In February 1986, sensing a political opportunity, Marvin Braude and his council colleague Zev Yaroslavsky called a press conference to announce an initiative for the November ballot that would reduce growth dramatically. Proposition U, as it would eventually come to be known, was nothing if not a blunt instrument. The measure would cut commercial zoning in half almost everywhere in the city. The only exceptions were downtown and Hollywood (which had true commercial districts) and the mid-Wilshire area (which, though a strip, was heavily developed with skyscrapers). An initiative was needed, the two council members declared, because a regular ordinance funneled through the city council would be watered down by developer interests. Proposition U, Yaroslavsky promised, would ensure "no lobbyists, no compromises, no backroom deals." Having watched the passage of California's Proposition 13, the two council members also understood the way a well-timed initiative could tap into voter resentment in a politically powerful way.

That the iconoclastic Braude would back such a measure was no surprise; he had been tilting at windmills such as these for more than two decades. But Yaroslavsky was another matter. Then thirty-seven, Yaroslavsky was already an eleven-year veteran of the council—a powerful, highly quotable, and brazenly ambitious politician who made no secret of the fact that he wanted to be the next mayor of Los Angeles.

A student protester at UCLA in the 1960s, Yaroslavsky later became an activist operating on behalf of Soviet Jewry in the Fairfax area, a Jewish working-class neighborhood. In 1975, at the age of twenty-six, he scored a stunning upset victory over Bradley insider Fran Savitch for a council seat from a heavily Jewish Westside district. Early in his council career, Yaroslavsky had been a firebrand, supporting school busing and tangling with the Los Angeles Police Department, and he generally backed the Bradley line. But his ambition was untempered. During the 1980s, he forged a political alliance with the Berman-Waxman machine. Both, for example, endorsed Gary Hart in 1984, while Bradley endorsed Walter Mondale.

By the mid-1980s, it was clear Yaroslavsky was eyeing Bradley's seat. And there was no question that a Yaroslavsky challenge with Berman-Waxman support posed a problem for Tom Bradley. Then in his fourth term, Bradley was probably the most extraordinary politician in the city's history. One of the first black police lieutenants on the LAPD force, he had retired in the early 1960s to pursue a career in law and politics. In 1963, at a time when the black community was agitating for reapportionment to assure a black district on the city council, the calm and moderate Bradley won election to a district that was racially mixed. During the 1960s, he emerged as a responsible reformer who won widespread support among southside blacks and Westside Jews, who have always played an important role in city politics.

With the support of the black-Jewish coalition, Bradley was elected mayor in 1973, the first African-American ever elected mayor of a predominantly white American city. He had not been challenged seriously since then, scaring off potentially strong opponents and winning three re-election campaigns by at least thirty percentage points. In 1982, he missed being elected the nation's first black governor by the slimmest of margins, losing to George Deukmejian on absentee ballots. In Los Angeles, Bradley was a Reaganesque figure, a "Teflon mayor" whose durable personal popularity seemed undiminished by actual events.

Zev Yaroslavsky in his West Los Angeles field office, 1988.

Yet during the 1980s, Bradley had changed. He had become more business-oriented, leaving behind what political scientist Sonenshein called his "progressive period." Focusing on developing L.A.'s global reputation, Bradley traveled abroad frequently and grew more remote from his constituency. In 1986, he geared up for a second challenge to Deukmejian—a race few people thought he could win, but one that would require big campaign contributions from L.A.'s business community and its developers.

In short, after thirteen years as mayor, Bradley was vulnerable. A challenge from Yaroslavsky, whose Westside district formed the core of Bradley's vital Jewish support, threatened to sever Bradley's biracial coalition and cut into his fundraising ability on the Westside. For Yaroslavsky, the growth issue was a way to differentiate himself from Bradley, and a ballot initiative would test the issue's electoral strength.

Tom Bradley, the most extraordinary politician in Los Angeles history, speaking in 1985.

Yet, on the issue of growth, Yaroslavsky himself was vulnerable. It was no coincidence that the initiative came at a time when he was being pounded by some homeowners in his district, especially the Westwood area near UCLA. Like every council member who represented affluent Westside and Valley neighborhoods, Yaroslavsky had little choice but to play both sides of the fence. It was true, as he once insisted to the *L.A. Times,* that "from the day I walked into office...we have done nothing but roll back and impose limitations on development rights on every single commercial street district in my district." (Given the liberal 1946 zoning, it would have been difficult to do otherwise.) But it was also true that his district had the hottest real estate market in the city, and to an ambitious Los Angeles politician this situation was too tempting not to exploit.

Between 1980 and 1986, Yaroslavsky raised about $1 million in campaign contributions, and almost $400,000 of that money came from developers. He had also selectively supported large projects crucial to the development community. He backed several skyscrapers, including the controversial twenty-two-story Center West project in Westwood (on the site of a landmark coffee shop), and the Beverly Center and Westside Pavilion, two enormous shopping centers that were squeezed into existing urban neighborhoods. Most recently, Yaroslavsky had expressed support for a major expansion of the Westside Pavilion, one that would have been prohibited under Proposition U.

All this was reported in the press during 1986, but none of it mattered. Slow-growth fever was rising throughout California; and the slow-growthers were learning how to use ballot initiatives to blast away the longstanding web of developer-politician relationships. In San Francisco, slow-growthers placed a measure on the ballot to restrict downtown office development. In Moorpark and Simi Valley, working-to-middle-class suburbs of Los Angeles in Ventura County, restrictions on residential growth won decisively. According to one survey, there had been ten ballot measures related to land use planning on California ballots in 1985. In 1986, there were forty-five.

In Los Angeles, Braude and Yaroslavsky used their own campaign war chests, including a lot of money raised from the real estate business, to mount an aggressive Proposition U campaign attacking "greedy developers." But the rest of the power structure tried to muscle slow-growth sentiment aside. With Bradley off running for governor, his longtime ally, council president Pat Russell, took the lead in ramming through more than thirty exceptions to Proposition U prior to the election, including areas west of downtown and near Los Angeles International Airport controlled by key developers. (Some portions of South Central were also on the list.) Under a storm of protest from Braude and Yaroslavsky that it had not provided proper notice for the exemptions, the council backed off. But in a move that would be fatal to her political career, Russell made sure that one favored project in her district—

the three-million-square-foot Howard Hughes Center along the San Diego Freeway—was approved prior to the election.

Election Day 1986 brought a sea change to the politics of growth in Los Angeles and throughout California. San Francisco's office development restrictions passed; so did dozens of other measures around the state that trimmed, tucked, and otherwise pruned local development policies. And in Los Angeles, Proposition U received sixty-nine percent of the vote. The measure passed overwhelmingly on the traffic-choked Westside and in the homeowner-dominated San Fernando Valley. But it also passed by healthy margins in neglected and underdeveloped black and Latino neighborhoods on the south and east sides. Meanwhile, Bradley was soundly trounced by incumbent governor Deukmejian. The California slow-growth revolution had begun. And the most astounding development, or so it seemed to pundits at the time, was the depth of its victory in the heart of the growth machine's own territories in Southern California. This was not just Encino or Brentwood; this was Simi Valley and South Central talking.

&

Yaroslavsky and Braude lost no time exploiting the moment. Less than a month later, they proposed a sweeping ten-point program to change growth policies in the city, including planning commission review of all buildings over fifty thousand square feet, citywide urban design criteria, and height limits on apartment buildings near single-family homes. Meanwhile, a citizen committee appointed by planning commission president Garcia called for thirty-five neighborhood planning boards throughout the city to review projects on a local level.

In early 1987, events swung even more toward Yaroslavsky. At the end of March, an appellate court in Los Angeles overturned the city's approval of the Center West office building in Westwood, ruling that the city's pro forma approval of the project violated state environmental laws. In the anti-growth mood of the moment, it was easy to forget that Yaroslavsky had actually supported the Center West project; facts aside, the court ruling played into his slow-growth political agenda.

The April municipal elections brought more evidence of the voters' changing mood. Council president Pat Russell was getting hit hard by community activists for her support of many large development projects, including two controlled by the interests of the late Howard Hughes: the

Hughes Center and, nearby, the massive proposal at Playa Vista, an undeveloped nine-hundred-acre lowland along Ballona Creek. In the April primary, facing opposition from a half-dozen anti-growth advocates, Russell was forced into a runoff. The challenger was Ruth Galanter.

Fifteen years after she first fought Santa Monica's plan to build high-rise apartment buildings along the beach in Ocean Park, Galanter was making her first run for public office. Well known among planning insiders as a savvy activist—she had served on the regional Coastal Commission in the late 1970s—Galanter was unknown as a politician. But she emerged from the pack of Russell critics thanks to her connections to Santa Monica and to Westside liberal causes. Though raising only $32,000 for the primary, compared with $260,000 for Russell, Galanter had the support of Tom Hayden (with whom she had gone to college), the League of Conservation Voters, and liberal stalwarts such as television producer Norman Lear. Despite the fundraising gap, she trailed Russell in the primary by only eight percentage points.

A week after Galanter forced Russell into a runoff, Zev Yaroslavsky filed papers at City Hall indicating that he would begin raising funds for a mayoral campaign in 1989.

In early May, just a month before the runoff, Galanter was stabbed in the neck by an intruder in her Venice home. Seriously wounded, she underwent two rounds of surgery at UCLA Medical Center, and there were many questions about whether she would be well enough to serve if elected. Ironically, the tragedy seemed to help. It focused media attention on Galanter when her campaign might otherwise have struggled. (Russell had been seeking to paint her as a radical with close ties to Hayden.)

In mid-May, Galanter was endorsed by Braude, and later in the month, only two weeks before the runoff, the growth issue surfaced yet again when the city's Hyperion sewage treatment plant failed, dumping millions of gallons of raw sewage into Santa Monica Bay. The failure of Hyperion, coincidentally located in Russell's district, played into Galanter's hands, allowing her to highlight her Coastal Commission experience and her longstanding work to improve the Bay. On June 2, while still in the hospital, Galanter overwhelmed Russell in the runoff, fifty-eight to forty-two percent.

It was clear that Galanter's victory held the potential to serve as a turning point in L.A.'s growth politics. Galanter was not a Hillside Federation NIMBY interested only in protecting single-family neighborhoods. She was a Santa Monica/ Venice activist with a long history of fighting for environmental and social causes. Her Coastal Commission work had been characterized not only by environmental advocacy, but also by aggressive support for low-income housing and eco-

Expansion work on the mammoth Hyperion sewage treatment plant near Los Angeles International Airport. Note beachfront bike path in forefront.

nomic development in poor neighborhoods. She showed no inclination to change her approach now that she had been elected to the council.

In the race against Russell, she had done well in the liberal Venice neighborhoods because of her record on social issues. She had done well in the homeowner neighborhoods around the airport because of her opposition to growth. And she had done well in the working-to-middle-class black area around Crenshaw because she had promised to stimulate economic development there. Indeed, Galanter's council race was in many ways a rerun of Santa Monica's early days, because the Playa Vista project was being designed by David O'Malley of Welton Becket Associates—whose skill at mollifying community concerns had not noticeably improved in the intervening six years since the Colorado Place controversy in Santa Monica.

In short, Galanter's victory proved it was possible to win elections in the City of Los Angeles by wedding Hillside Federation-style anti-growth sentiment to Santa Monica-style social activism. This was a potentially powerful breakthrough, because Bradley and other growth advocates had always offset Hillside votes by playing to the inner city's desire for more development.

In the wake of her victory, Galanter and other like-minded West-siders predicted an emerging alliance between inner-city social activists and suburban slow-growthers. Galanter's victory had come just as a festering battle over a city proposal to build a trash incinerator in South Central—the so-called LANCER project—was coming to a head. Galanter and other Westside slow-growthers, especially the vocal Westwood group in Yaroslavsky's district, made a big deal about teaming up with inner-city activists to oppose LANCER. (A surprised Bradley had little choice but to kill the project despite intense lobbying at City Hall from its proponents.) In a *Los Angeles Times* opinion piece, Derek Shearer, now long retired from the Santa Monica Planning Commission, announced that in Los Angeles "the post-Bradley era" had begun, fueled by "the growing neighborhood-based revolt against the city's policies and priorities." Clearly, he believed the Santa Monica revolution had at last been vindicated.

Galanter's victory was indicative of the emerging strength of what was now being called "the slow-growth movement." Three weeks after her election, the San Diego City Council acted to cut residential construction in the city by sixty percent. In October 1987, developers attending a nationwide conference in Los Angeles identified growth control as their number-one concern. Later that fall, an odd coalition of liberals and conservatives began circulating petitions for a slow-growth initiative in that symbol of California suburban development, Orange County, and an initial *L.A. Times* poll showed that more than seventy percent of the voters favored the measure. With a white-hot real estate market still churning, it was clear that 1988 would be a critical year for slow-growth politics, and an important prelude to the Los Angeles mayoral election in April 1989.

Bradley had been slow to respond to the slow-growth trend. In March he had proposed a mild set of restrictions which would permit "vigorous and fair enforcement" of Proposition U; at the same time, he had declared, "We will continue to grow. That is the American destiny." Later that month he called for more restrictions on "mini-malls," the small, cheap shopping centers that had popped up on busy corners all over town. But the loyal Bradley was steadfast in his support of his protégé Russell, and even part of his agenda, the idea of jacking up fees on office developers rather than reducing the size of their buildings, was borrowed from her.

After the June election, Bradley realized he was in trouble and began positioning himself to outmaneuver Yaroslavsky on the growth issue. His first step—and, as it turned out, his most important—was to hire Mike Gage as his chief deputy.

Bradley was Reaganesque in more ways than one. Besides his Teflon popularity, he also had Ronald Reagan's gift for leaving the details of governance to others. The polite term used in City Hall was that Bradley was "staff-driven." In four terms as mayor, he had brought in a new cadre of aides every few years and, essentially, allowed them to re-invent his approach based on what he thought he needed to survive. His last deputy mayor had been Tom Houston, a veteran political operative who tried to help Bradley catapult himself into the governor's chair. In the process Houston had misread the local political mood and allowed the mayor to fall behind on the growth issue. Gage's job was to turn this problem around in time for Bradley's re-election in 1989.

At forty-two, Gage was one of the most interesting figures in California politics. A big, beefy man with a backslapping manner and a quick temper, he was equal parts environmentalist, political sharpie, and bully. Growing up in Northern California, Gage had gone to work as a legislative aide in Sacramento and then won an Assembly seat for himself in 1976 at the age of thirty-one. After four years of service as a liberal environmentalist, Gage abruptly quit and earned his living leading river-rafting tours—a decision that mystified Sacramento's inside-the-beltway types. He then drifted into campaign consulting and eventually moved to Southern California, managing Bradley's hugely successful 1985 re-election race.

Talkative, blustery, and combative, Gage had a confrontational style quite the opposite of Bradley's. He alienated many people at City Hall and once got into a fistfight with another mayoral aide in a budget meeting. But Gage was a shrewd political operative who understood how to outmaneuver the opposition and slipstream between seemingly conflicting constituencies. (His own Assembly district had included both blue-collar neighborhoods and white-collar "environmental" suburbs.)

It did not take long for Gage to take the offensive on the growth issue. In late July, just a few weeks after Galanter defeated Russell, Bradley announced that the city would comply with the Westwood court ruling by subjecting all large projects to formal environmental review, including office buildings, shopping centers, and even large mini-malls. The days of over-the-counter office buildings in Los Angeles were over. The move had Gage's fingerprints all over it: It was a bald co-option of the Braude-Yaroslavsky political agenda, cloaked in the political cover of merely implementing a court ruling.

In the months that followed, Bradley moved further into the slow-growth camp. During early 1988, with Gage's assistance, he proposed restrictions on growth to buy time for the city's sewage system until its treatment capacity could be expanded. The sewer moratorium was significant because the City of Los Angeles served, essentially, as a regional wholesaler of sewage treatment facilities, contracting with thirty other cities and special districts in the L.A. basin. None of the cities, including Los Angeles, had ever thought about whether the sewer system could accommodate the new developments they were approving. When Bradley proposed that all these cities be subject to a moratorium, most of the other municipalities—including, ironically, Santa Monica—complained that Los Angeles would be violating their sovereignty.

In early May 1988, the city council approved Bradley's recommendation for sweeping restrictions on growth, including a thirty percent cut in city building permits, because of the sewer crisis. Cleverly, Bradley insisted that he had not pushed the sewer restrictions to mollify any particular constituencies. He insisted that he was acting "on information from engineering experts—not the alleged pressure from the slow-growth movement."* And, though this did not make headlines, the Bradley plan had several large loopholes for pet projects, including Library Square.

In short, Gage helped Bradley master the game of playing both ends of the growth issue with middle-of-the-road rhetoric—a clear attempt to outmaneuver Yaroslavsky, who was, according to one insider, intent on "riding the issue all the way." And Bradley needed the boost, because Zev's fortunes were soaring. In early 1988, the *L.A. Times* reported that Yaroslavsky had amassed $800,000 for the mayoral race a year hence. Bradley, by comparison, had only $550,000, because he had been forced to pay off debts left over from his failed governor's race.

~

* Bradley made this statement in a letter to the editor rebutting an opinion piece I had written for the *Los Angeles Times*, in which I argued that he had buckled under to slow-growthers. In the same letter he also disputed my contention that he had often made "ringing declarations against growth control," saying that he favored "managed growth." *L.A. Times*, April 16, 1988. In retrospect, it is clear that the sewer restrictions, while necessary for health and safety, were part of a strategy to co-opt as much of the slow-growth agenda as was necessary to secure re-election the following year.

At the time the Los Angeles City Council passed the sewer restrictions, the power of the slow-growth movement was at its peak. The Orange County initiative had qualified for the June 1988 ballot and apparently tapped into longstanding voter resentment about traffic congestion and lengthy response times for police and fire calls; polls showed support for the initiative dropping but still strong. Meanwhile, an attempt by builders to remove the measure from the June ballot had failed. Another initiative measure was proposed in Riverside County, the fastest-growing large county in the country and the emerging capital of the Plains of Id. (Working-class people of all colors were fleeing there from Los Angeles and Orange Counties.) In response, the Riverside Board of Supervisors bumped the measure from the June election to November and rammed through approval of more than one hundred thousand new homes. The move was a little too clever, and seemed to alienate even the residents of a county where virtually the entire economy was tied to the construction industry.

In April, slow-growthers from across California convened in Riverside to "put the Legislature on notice" that they would oppose end-runs by the building community in Sacramento. (The groups included Not Yet New York from Los Angeles, Prevent Los Angelization Now from San Diego, and slow-growthers from smaller cities that did not want to become either of the above). A few weeks later, they pressured one member of the Assembly to withdraw a bill that would have subjected slow-growth initiatives to environmental review, a clear attempt by builders to turn environmental laws on their head in order to block the movement.

Slowly, however, the cogs of the growth machine were beginning to turn. The key battleground was Orange County. The initiative there had been put forward by a relatively small group of environmental activists from Laguna Beach, which had always been more liberal and anti-growth than the rest of the county. They were joined by a variety of liberal politicians and conservative old-timers, including the odd couple of Irvine Mayor Larry Agran, an ex-Naderite and fringe presidential candidate, and former Republican party chairman Tom Rogers, a rancher. (When asked about attending a reception Agran had put together for the Nicaraguan basketball team, Rogers responded, "I just hope they were whoever the good guys are, the Contras or whoever. I didn't ask.")

The Orange County slow-growthers knew that support for their initiative was broad but not deep. They also knew that, unlike political activists in a compact municipality like Santa Monica, they could not hope to shore up their support by walking precincts in a sprawling county of two million people. Beyond that, they had little organization and even less money. They simply hoped that the building industry would mount a mass-media campaign so slick and expensive that it would backfire, something that had happened in other places. Given the incendiary atmosphere of the time, it was not an unreasonable strategy.

As expected, the building industry raised $2 million, compared to $50,000 for the initiative's supporters. But the builders' campaign consultants spent the money far more shrewdly than anyone could have expected. Deliberately rejecting a glitzy media campaign because it might backfire, the builders hired five hundred people at $7 per hour to walk precincts and work phone banks. At front doors and on the phones, campaign workers pushed the notion that the initiative would destroy the local economy, dependent for so long on construction and development. In short, the builders spent a fortune to make their campaign look like a Santa Monica-style grassroots effort.

And it worked. On election day, the initiative won only forty-four percent of the vote—and only thirty-nine percent in the northern part of the county, where working-class neighborhoods cared far more about protecting their jobs than protecting undeveloped land around far away (and far-out) Laguna Beach.

The Orange County election was a turning point. Adopting a similar strategy, builders trounced the Riverside County initiative even more decisively in November and brought down two initiatives in San Diego. In suburban counties, the lesson was clear: The dynamics driving growth were regional, but opposition to growth was local. People might vote against development in their neighborhood or in their small municipality, but they probably wouldn't vote against sweeping restrictions all across the region—in part because they didn't want to risk their jobs (especially if they are working class), and in part because they just didn't care.

&

In April 1988—the same week, coincidentally, that slow-growthers from around the region met in Riverside—Tom Bradley went to the Gilbert Lindsay Community Center at 43rd and Avalon to meet with local black homeowners about the court-ordered rezoning brought about by the

Hillside Federation's lawsuit. The black homeowners, as always, were skeptical about the white middle-class agenda for Los Angeles. Many of them thought that rezoning would cause the closure of neighborhood churches and maybe even force them from their homes. In short, inner-city residents were convinced that the political power of Westside and Valley homeowners would do them in once again.

"It just isn't going to happen," Bradley assured them, and then, after forty-five minutes, "left briskly, out a side door, with the more vocal activists giving chase to get in a few last words," according to an account in the *Times*. After he left, one prominent black activist said simply, "He's lying."

After her election in 1987, Ruth Galanter and other Westside slow-growth activists talked at length about the emerging alliance between inner-city residents and homeowner activists, neither of whom wanted to suffer at the hands of City Hall. This alliance was always implicit in the Santa Monica agenda, and Galanter and others had hoped it could be used as a lever against the growth machine in Los Angeles.

But just as the coalitions in Orange and Riverside Counties could not win over the working class, neither could slow-growthers in L.A. succeed with their inner-city counterparts. The slow-growth movement had peaked without creating real reform. Bradley could not wade into the movement too far without risking discontent from his black base in South Central, where he had grown up.

Bradley had neither the luxury nor the inclination to build an entire campaign around opposition to growth. As the incumbent, he didn't have to. (In the intervening months he had worked hard at fund-raising, and had pulled even with Yaroslavsky at $1 million apiece.) And he knew that Yaroslavsky, though he had come from modest immigrant roots, could not hope to capture inner-city black support. All that remained was for Gage to devise a plan to undermine Yaroslavsky's position on the growth issue in a way that would discredit Zev with the slow-growthers. This proved surprisingly easy to do.

Through the fall, Bradley took small steps to remind slow-growthers of his modest shift in their direction. In September, he asked that city ordinances be tightened to require hotel developers to obtain conditional use permits before serving liquor. The move played nicely with angry homeowners in Yaroslavsky's district, who were miffed over construction of the large Ma Maison hotel near the Beverly Center. At about the same time, Bradley reopened public comment on one hundred fifty projects that had been approved in the last year; this won praise from a Westwood activist who wanted to run for Zev's council seat. And in mid-November, he endorsed the recommendations of a blue-ribbon commission (which he had appointed) calling for two regional agencies to deal with growth and environmental issues.

Just before Christmas, Bradley fired his last shot. While crafting his slow-growth campaign, Yaroslavsky had also been working on a large expansion of the Westside Pavilion shopping center at Pico and Westwood Boulevards, a project that backed up to an angry residential neighborhood. Supportive of the expansion, Yaroslavsky had brokered a compromise making the project smaller, although it retained a sky-bridge, with shops along it, over Westwood Boulevard. Ever wary of treading in each other's districts, council members unanimously approved the expansion.

On the morning of December 22, Bradley held a press conference on the sidewalk in front of the shopping center to veto the expansion. The city's lawyers, he said, had concluded that the retail shops along the skywalk violated Proposition U.

Yaroslavsky was livid, calling the move "hypocritical, disingenu-ous, and insincere," and adding, "He never once raised a concern about this until eleven o'clock this morning." But the challenger soon had to admit the genius of his opponent's political move. Twelve days later, on January 3, Yaroslavsky agreed to Bradley's demand that retail shops be removed from the sky-bridge in order to comply with Proposition U.

And two days after that—on Thursday, January 5, 1989—Yaroslavsky announced that he would not run for mayor in the April election. There were other reasons for his decision, including a damaging cam-paign memo deriding Bradley's intelligence and campaign polling showing that the mayor was still remarkably popular. But the death blow had come from the Westside Pavilion, the culmination of a careful eighteen-month campaign by Tom Bradley and Mike Gage to eliminate the one campaign weapon Zev had at his disposal.

↜

As it turned out, Bradley was vulnerable in the April 1989 election after all. Serious questions were raised during the campaign about his rela-tionship with two financial institutions that did business with the city, leaving him open to conflict-of-interest charges for the first time. He was challenged by black city councilman Nate Holden and former county supervisor Baxter Ward, who was from the San Fernando Valley. Though underfunded, Ward and Holden between them received more than forty percent of the vote, while Bradley narrowly missed a runoff by drawing only fifty-two percent. It was his closest re-election campaign by far, and led to Bradley's diminishing political stature as the 1992 riots approached. Deputy Mayor Michael Gage left the mayor's staff in November 1989 to work for Ted Stein, a homebuilder and Bradley supporter. He later emerged as a reform leader in water politics.

The court-ordered rezoning was eventually completed. But by and large the effort was complicated and difficult for average citizens to decipher. Predictably, the Hamilton plan was not followed. In some cases, the zoning was reduced to match Hamilton's General Plan. In other cases, the General Plan was changed to accommodate the liberal zoning that had been in effect for almost fifty years. And the much-ballyhooed attempt to create elected neighborhood planning commissions vanished as well, usurped by an alternative proposal to create citizen advisory committees appointed by members of the city council. In the end, the council members—Ruth Galanter included—were not about to give up control over their fiefdoms to the Hillside Federation and other homeowner activists voluntarily.

Meanwhile Proposition U proved to be more useful as political rhetoric than as a tool for urban planning. Two urban planning professors later concluded that because Proposition U exempted most commercial centers in the city, commercial development had proceeded more or less as it would have otherwise. (The only exception, Ventura Boulevard, attracted less office development and more retail development—which, ironically, created more traffic problems.) Meanwhile, the bridge over Westwood Boulevard was built as part of the Westside Pavilion expansion.

So, homeowners went back to fighting development projects one at a time, because that seemed like a better way to protect single-family neighborhoods than trying to dismantle the Democratic developer iron triangle. They gave up trying to forge broad alliances with working-class and inner-city residents elsewhere in the city and the region. Politicians and developers continued to play tit-for-tat on projects around town, even during the recession that hit in 1990. Tom Bradley did not run again for mayor in 1993, his credibility having been badly damaged by the riots. And Zev Yaroslavsky, who eventually moved on to the Los Angeles County Board of Supervisors, played both ends against the middle until his very last week on the council, eight years after Proposition U, when he opposed changes to the city's affordable housing ordinance in order to appease the Hillside Federation.

In other words, all the politics, all the homeowner activism, all the campaigns, and all the failed development projects had not changed or reformed planning in Los Angeles. The system was as chaotic and riddled with political favoritism as ever. The growth machine adapted and resisted just enough to stay more or less in control, buying off the homeowners and scaring off the working-class folk who might have turned the slow-growth movement into a real revolution. The net result of all this breathless political activity was to make everyone lose faith in the system, so that nobody trusted the politicians or the developers or the homeowner activists to look after any interests but their own—and especially not the interests of the broad range of Southern California's Plains of Id, whether in Watts or Westminster or Moreno Valley. The consensus for growth had been demolished, and nothing had been built in its place.

CHAPTER 3

Suburbs of Extraction

From the rustic mountain homes and spectacular hillside views of the slow-growthers on the Westside and in the San Fernando Valley, it is hard to imagine anywhere that seems farther away than Alameda Street.

Alameda is perhaps L.A.'s grittiest industrial street—an endless strip of factories and warehouses running south from the rail yards downtown thirty or so miles to the ports in Long Beach. Especially for the first five miles, from downtown to the Randolph Street rail corridor, Alameda is unrelentingly bumpy and unrelentingly ugly. It's the kind of place from which the Westside cocktail-party set might extract some profit, but it's not a place one would discuss in polite conversation at those cocktail parties. At first glance, it's a relic that seems more suited to Akron or Pittsburgh than to Los Angeles.

But Alameda is, in many ways, a more important part of today's Los Angeles than Beverly Hills. In particular, it's the gateway to a critical group of working-class post-industrial suburbs that have come to symbolize the way the city is changing. During the same time that Los Angeles and Santa Monica were undergoing their slow-growth *perestroika*, the suburbs springing east and south from Alameda Street were undergoing an even more profound change—one that didn't fit in neatly with the pro-growth/slow-growth paradigm that dominated politics in the rest of the metropolis.

In the disaster-ridden, racially charged atmosphere of Los Angeles in the 1990s, perhaps nothing symbolized this different kind of *perestroika*—and the tension that came with the change—more than the mountain of concrete rubble rising some thirty feet in the air just off Alameda Street south of Randolph.

The mountain was actually a heavy-duty recycling location run by a man named Sam Chew, a onetime corporate pilot and former business finance specialist who had never worked in industrial recycling before. Chew's operation ground the rubble into aggregate that could be re-used in other construction projects. When he proposed the project in 1993, it seemed like a good idea to city council members in Huntington Park, the three-square-mile city that adjoins South Central Los Angeles along Alameda Street. Who could be against jobs, recycling, and productive use of vacant industrial land?

Then the Northridge earthquake hit in January 1994, and suddenly six hundred thousand tons of the Santa Monica Freeway arrived at Sam Chew's door. At one point it rose some eighty feet into the air, and though it subsequently dropped in height, its girth spread to encompass an entire city block.

Viewed from the west, the mountain hardly seemed out of place amid the railroad tracks, the scrap metal shops, and the truck-chewed roadbeds of the Alameda corridor. But from the other side—the east side—things looked a little different. The mountain ran a full block's length along Cottage Street in Huntington Park, a small residential area filled with bungalows and small apartment buildings indistinguishable from a hundred other typical neighborhoods throughout Los Angeles.

Cottage Street had always been located on the edge of an industrial area. Next door to Chew's operation, for example, was a large lumberyard. But with the arrival of the mountain the feel of the neighborhood changed. All through 1994 and 1995, while the mountain was growing, the grind of machinery was constant. Even after the mountain shrank, dust was everywhere—on people's porches, in their houses, and in their lungs as well. "It used to be quiet here," one Cottage Street resident told a reporter in 1995. "Now I feel as though being in my house is like being in prison."

In most cities, the rubble mountain might have seemed like the usual neighborhood dispute, important to local residents but little more than a minor diversion for everyone else. In Los Angeles, however, the mountain came to assume a somewhat larger significance. Because the pile of concrete along Cottage Street was not usually called "the mountain," but, rather, *La Montaña*. The residents who complained about it were part of the area's emerging Latino population—and so were

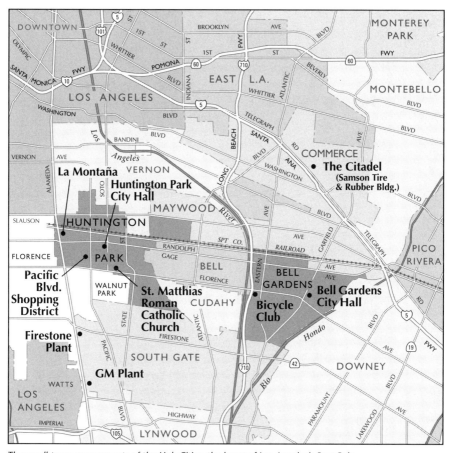

The small-town governments of the Hub Cities, the heart of Los Angeles's Rust Belt.

the members of the city council who approved the recycling project in the first place. *La Montaña* had become an important test for a generation of politicians in what some commentators have dubbed "The Latino Metropolis."

Over the past twenty years, the suburbs around Huntington Park have been transformed from blue-collar Anglo towns tied to an industrial economy to blue-collar Latino towns tied to a post-industrial economy. Indeed, they have come to symbolize what Rodolfo Torres and Victor Valle have called the emerging Latino landscape of L.A.'s "Greater Eastside." As such, they are something more than traditional working-class suburbs. They have become laboratories of democracy—test cases to see how smoothly suburban political power can be transferred from one race to another in a metropolis that has suffered more than its share of racial tension in recent years.

For decades, these eight suburbs—the "Hub Cities," as they are called—had remained in the iron grip of an entrenched Anglo power structure. At least from the 1970s onward, this group had served as a kind of extractive successor to the original growth machine, strip-mining the area for the benefit of those few exploitative business enterprises—junk recycling, gambling, apartment rentals—that saw shards of opportunity in the Los Angeles Rust Belt.

Finally, in the volatile political atmosphere of the early 1990s, the Latinos took political control. As L.A.'s slow-growth sentiment began to give way to anti-immigration rhetoric and rising racial tension, every local political tug-of-war came to be viewed as a test of the new Latino power structure. In the days when the Anglos were still in power, the Latino dissidents could always blame them for what went wrong. Now that Latinos were in power, things were supposed to be different. But it was not clear *how* they were supposed to be different. "We thought when we finally elected Latinos that they would help us," said one resident of Huntington Park. "But look what has happened with *La Montaña*."

It was an understandable complaint. In a metropolis where race had become the major fault line, many people looked at politics on the basis of race alone, and believed that if the right race were in charge, things would be okay. But in the Hub Cities it became clear that race alone was not what mattered. A century of parochialism had sliced the political landscape into odd little pieces. Those pieces, in turn, had served as the foundation of a tight-knit world in which the extractive businesses and small-town politics were closely intertwined. And a mere change of race at City Hall was not enough to disentangle them.

⌐

The ring of suburbs known as the Hub Cities includes some three hundred thousand people living in an area approximately eight miles across and five miles deep, stretching roughly from Alameda Street on the west to the Santa Ana Freeway (Interstate 5) on the east. The residents here are a mixture of long-established Latino families and new immigrants from Mexico, along with Cuban families and refugees from all over the world. Increasingly, these Latinos, and especially the recent immigrants, provide the labor force for the low-end, post-industrial economy that is springing up on the old industrial landscape. Among other things, their presence has revived previously struggling shopping districts such as Pacific Boulevard, an old Midwestern-style downtown just eight blocks east of *La Montaña* that's been reborn as a thriving center of Latino retailing.

Though the area can be clearly defined geographically and demographically, it's sliced politically into eight small subdivisions. On the north side are two industrial cities (Commerce and Vernon) with wealthy tax bases, strong business leaders, and few residents. (Commerce has only eleven thousand people, and Vernon has almost none.) To the south are six other towns—towns with some industry and some middle-class prosperity, but also great stretches of immigrant poverty.

Five of these towns are strung across a swath of land—once a rancho owned by the Lugo family—that straddles the Randolph Street rail corridor and crosses the Los Angeles River. The westernmost town, the one with perhaps the proudest history of upscale aspirations, is Huntington Park. The easternmost town, the one with the most volatile and downscale history, is known as Bell Gardens. For geographical as well other reasons, these two cities have always served as the polar opposites that define the Hub Cities. In between are three tiny, extremely poor small cities: Bell, Maywood, and Cudahy. (Just to the south is South Gate, more industrial and middle class but still very much within the Hub Cities' orbit.)

Some of these towns measure barely a square mile, and even the biggest is not as large as the City of Santa Monica. Some have an industrial base, or at least the remnants of one. But increasingly the six residential Hub Cities represent places where upwardly mobile Latinos buy a house and put down roots, and where new immigrants are warehoused in the remaining space, occupying overcrowded houses, apartment buildings, and even garages. All six cities had an official population in the 1990 census that was at least eighty-three percent Latino. And all six rank among the twenty most crowded cities anywhere in California. More than three hundred thousand people live within the seventeen square miles that define these six towns, giving the area a higher population density than San Francisco, Chicago, or Boston.

This peculiar political geography exists today because of the way the Southeast area evolved into, and out of, a district that can best be described as L.A.'s "Little Akron."

Up until the 1920s, the commercial life of Los Angeles revolved around downtown. But the city was poised on the edge of a massive industrial expansion fueled by two related developments: L.A.'s love affair with cars and the recent local discovery of oil. Seeking to break free from the monopolistic grip of streetcar companies, Angelenos embraced the car with an enthusiasm that rivaled Detroit's. (See chapter 5, The Money Train.) Because it was located so far from Detroit, Los Angeles had to develop an outsized industrial infrastructure that revolved around oil, cars, aircraft, and tires.

Anticipating this massive expansion, L.A.'s growth brokers set out to create a deliberately suburban industrial base. Different industries were focused in different suburban areas, and surrounding residential neighborhoods emerged to support them. The movies went to Hollywood and Burbank. The aircraft industry went along the ocean, in a swath stretching from Santa Monica to what is now Los Angeles International Airport. Cars and tires went to the lowlands, creating an industrial belt south and east of downtown, along the Los Angeles River and the major rail lines that followed the river from the rail yards south to the ports near Long Beach. This created what some sociologists have called "suburbs of production," rather than the more stereotypical "suburbs of consumption." Far from escaping the gritty reality of daily life in their suburb, residents of Little Akron, like their counterparts in the Midwest, were surrounded by it.

As early as the turn of the century, residential districts grew up alongside industrial areas. In 1905, the rough-and-tumble town of Vernon incorporated as the nation's first purely industrial city. A year later, civic boosters in a developing area just to the south won incorporation for their town as well. Soon Huntington Park—named for the streetcar magnate who had placed the area within a nickel car ride of downtown— had a broad main street, a stately Spanish-style city hall, cozy bungalow neighborhoods, and upscale pretensions. It had become the residential moon to Vernon's industrial sun.

During the oil-and-rubber boom of the 1920s, this sun-and-moon pattern was repeated again and again. East of Vernon, for example, Adolph Schleicher, president of Samson Tire and Rubber Company, constructed an $8 million tire plant modeled after a royal palace once built by the king of Assyria. As before, working-class residential neighborhoods formed around such industrial behemoths.

In those days, the urban geography of the Southeast area resembled a series of self-contained Midwestern factory towns. Factories, residential neighborhoods, and retailing centers like Pacific Boulevard were bunched together, and the whole arrangement was separated from surrounding towns by farms and fields. One local newspaper trumpeted "the suburban ideal of moderate decentralization."

The Citadel shopping center in Commerce, originally a tire manufacturing plant designed with an Assyrian theme.

Appropriately enough, given the aspirations of the residents, this decentralization also encouraged the creation of cities so small that they were almost neighborhood governments. During the real estate boom of the 1920s, three more residential suburbs in the area were incorporated as separate cities—Maywood, Bell, and South Gate, which covered a new stretch of subdivisions just west of the Los Angeles River. None encompassed more than a few square miles.

When the boom of the 1920s ended, there remained a good deal of flood-prone land in the lowlands along the Los Angeles River that hadn't been developed. In the 1930s and 1940s, these areas began to fill in—but haphazardly, further dividing the Southeast's urban landscape and laying the foundation for the peculiar politics of the future.

Whereas communities such as Huntington Park and South Gate included formal townsites, the lowlands were marketed to low-end buyers who wanted to combine a rural lifestyle with an approach that today might be called "self-help." On the west bank of the river, the area known as Cudahy was divided and subdivided into ranchettes with few formal roads. On the east bank was the even more isolated Bell Gardens, which during the Depression developed in much the same manner.

Cut off on the east and west by rivers (the Los Angeles and the Rio Hondo), and on the north and south by railroad tracks, Bell Gardens had been cultivated by Japanese sharecroppers who grew vegetables. Beginning in the 1930s, however, a local developer started selling off homestead sites to new immigrants from Texas, Arkansas, Kansas, and

The concrete channels of the Los Angeles River, the border between Bell and Bell Gardens.

Oklahoma—California's infamous "Okies." For $15 down and $10 restricted third of an acre, pitched tents, and began building houses and growing crops.

To the new residents, the community seemed ideal, a friendly place where everyone looked out for everyone else. "We had to live on goat's milk," recalled Claude Booker, who would play an important role in the city's later history, "but we all loved it." To the surrounding communities with upscale pretensions—especially Huntington Park, the opposing pole of Hub Cities' life—the Okies were a disturbing presence who degraded the Southeast area's image. Before long, Bell Gardens had acquired the nickname "Billy Goat Acres."

When the Los Angeles County Flood Control District turned the Los Angeles River into a huge concrete culvert in order to facilitate runoff and prevent flooding, the area seemed more isolated. And to aspiring cities all around, Bell Gardens never quite shed its Dogpatch image, dragging down, in their view, whatever prestige the surrounding towns could muster.

But during and after World War II, the whole area rose with the tide of industrialization. With booming industrial factories (including a major General Motors plant opened in South Gate in 1936) and the growing incomes of unionized workers, the Southeast area became a Los Angeles version of the humming working-class neighborhoods of Detroit or Pittsburgh. "For children of the Dustbowl," wrote social critic Mike Davis, "the smokestacks of Bethlehem Steel and GM South Gate represented a happy ending to *The Grapes of Wrath*." This working-class ideal even extended to typically virulent working-class racism. Pacific Boulevard was only a few blocks from the historically black neighborhoods in South Central, but Alameda Street became a line blacks simply did not cross.

During this period the Hub Cities in general—and Huntington Park in particular—remained strong and influential working-to-middle-class suburbs. In the 1950s, Huntington Park had more than thirty auto dealerships, and city leaders deftly retained Pacific Boulevard's retailing lead by adding a series of parking lots behind the strip's stores. Several local politicians used the Huntington Park City Council as a steppingstone to higher political office. One typical example was Lawrence Walsh, the son of a union organizer at Bethlehem Steel, who eventually became the majority leader in the State Senate. Like so many other politicians from the Hub Cities, Walsh was what would be known today as a "Reagan Democrat"—a white working-class stalwart who supported industrial unions but opposed civil rights and open housing laws.

East of the Los Angeles River, most of the lowland areas remained under the iron grip of Los Angeles County well into the 1950s, as local residents resisted cityhood. While L.A.'s postwar suburbs grew in power and influence, however, so did their dreams of grandeur. With the creation of the Lakewood system in 1954, which permitted cities to operate on the cheap by contracting with the county for services, a rash of incorporations and annexations began.

In the Southeast area, municipal raids upon surrounding county territory became common. In particular, voracious cities coveted the tax-rich industrial area east of Vernon—a triangle around the Samson tire plant, created by the Long Beach and Santa Ana Freeways and the major rail line along Randolph Street. In 1960, local residents and industrial leaders created the "City of Commerce," a mostly industrial 6.5-square-mile city with eighty-three hundred residents and fifty thousand workers.

With all the good industrial property gone, Bell Gardens and Cudahy had little choice but to create patchwork cities out of the remaining working-class neighborhoods, apartment belts, and a few commercial strips. The effect of this landscape was to make residential Bell Gardens a southern moon to Commerce's northern industrial sun, just as Huntington Park was to Vernon. For better or worse, the political landscape was complete.

By the early 1960s, no less than eight different city halls were located within a four-mile radius of Florence and Atlantic in the City of Bell. Though some cities were richer than others, the whole area appeared to be an almost perfect manifestation of the Los Angeles dream. It was a decentralized area with a small-town feeling, sliced up politically into small pieces that permitted the area's power brokers to deliver what their constituents needed: an unfettered, low-tax environment for the industries in Vernon and Commerce to the north, and a series of small, self-governed communities for the workers to the south. But it wouldn't stay that way for long.

⌐

In 1965, the Watts riots accelerated Anglo flight from all over central Los Angeles and reshaped the urban geography of the entire metropolis. Before the Watts riots, Los Angeles was being pulled outward by the lure of cheap suburban homes and a planned decentralization of industrial jobs. After the riots, it was pushed outward by working- and middle-class Anglos who were suddenly afraid to live in or near what they now referred to as "the inner city."

Larry Walsh, who was mayor of Huntington Park at the time, tried to keep the riot from spilling over into the Hub Cities by calling Southern Pacific and getting the railroad to line Alameda with rail cars. "We put boxcars at intersections all the way down to Compton," he recalled years later. The boxcar blockage minimized the damage, but it didn't change the public perception of the Hub Cities after the riots. Suddenly, the Southeast's cozy neighborhoods and close proximity to industrial plants didn't seem so attractive, especially at a time when freeways made it easy to escape to newer, more distant suburbs.

So, the neighborhoods of the Southeast cities began to empty out. Many people escaped east across the Rio Hondo to Downey, which seemed to refugees of the Hub Cities to be a suburban paradise of large lots and postwar homes. But Downey was simply a gateway to more distant suburban paradises. From Bell Gardens, it was only a nine-mile drive down the Golden State Freeway to the Orange County line.

After growing steadily for decades, the Southeast cities' population dropped for the first time during the early 1970s and leveled off at about one hundred eighty thousand in 1975—not much more than it had been in the glory days of the 1950s. Before long the plants that had brought people there in the first place began to leave as well. The Assyrian-style tire plant in Commerce, by then controlled by Uniroyal, shut down in 1978.

In a world of freeways and suburban subdivisions, the Hub Cities were left behind. Cities with an industrial base, like Commerce and South Gate, struggled with figuring out how to replace the shuttered plants. Pacific Boulevard in Huntington Park was located three long miles from any freeway, and like many Main Streets it fell into decline; by 1968, more than sixty storefronts were vacant. Huntington Park also lost almost all of its thirty-odd auto dealerships to more freeway-friendly locations. And the four tiny residential suburbs—Maywood, Bell, Bell Gardens, and Cudahy—were left with little hope for prosperity.

Not surprisingly, local politicians desperately searched for a formula that would save their towns. But as they searched, they discovered that their options were limited. No longer was a wide range of businesses interested in locating in these towns. Instead, as so often happens with declining cities, most of the businesses with an interest were engaged in the process of what might be called "urban extraction."

These included apartment builders seeking to extract rent from tenants with few other choices; gambling enterprises coveting the few leisure dollars that were left; and junk and recycling companies wanting a cheap place to set up where no one would give them much trouble. All these companies were in the business of urban extraction—that is, they were mostly designed to suck from a community whatever economic vitality might remain. But they all needed a friendly local government to help them out with zone changes, pro-business ordinances, police protection, urban renewal subsidies, and the like. In return, they held out the promise of providing tax revenue the cities desperately needed.

Gradually then, the Hub Cities ceased to be suburbs of production. Instead, they were transformed into what might be called "suburbs of extraction," catering to businesses that mined the remaining wealth from their towns. In essence, the small islands of self-government in the Southeast area became little Nevadas, seeking to exploit the powers of sovereignty in whatever way they could for the closely entangled economic benefit of both the city treasuries and local businesses of urban extraction. As more residents left and the voter base dwindled, the politicians became entrenched, some serving twenty or thirty years without much opposition. (In some of these cities it was possible to win election to the city council with only a few hundred votes.) With not many voters to worry about, the politicians focused on the narrow range of businesses that still showed an interest in their communities.

Suburbs of extraction.

All of the Hub Cities, east and west of the river, started using urban renewal subsidies to assist the extractive businesses in trying to revive their towns. Between 1972 and 1980, the eight Hub Cities created eleven different redevelopment areas under state law. These redevelopment projects gave the city governments direct control, including the power of eminent domain, over some seven square miles of territory, or about twenty-five percent of the entire Hub Cities area.

Some of the cities were able to exploit their now valuable freeway frontage—as did South Gate, which kept some auto dealers along the freeway, and Commerce, which used the Assyrian theme of the Uniroyal plant to attract developers willing to recast it as a retailing mecca now known as "The Citadel." Others were not so lucky, and circumstance, aided by a political hardening of the arteries, led to more desperate measures.

Huntington Park was the proudest of all the Hub Cities, but after the Watts riots it also found itself farther from any freeway. (It was often left off maps and freeway signs for this reason.) Huntington Park used redevelopment aggressively in a desperate attempt to bring back Pacific Boulevard and shore up its declining industrial and residential areas. The city put half of its territory inside redevelopment boundaries during the 1970s, demolishing fifteen hundred housing units in pursuit of some one hundred different real estate development projects. This hard-charging effort was led by an all-Anglo city council, made up mostly of homegrown small business owners. Kept in power by a dwindling base of longtime residents who remembered the city's glory years, the council's membership did not change for fifteen years, from 1973 to 1988.

The most durable member of this group was Tom Jackson, a sandy-haired and moustachioed local florist with a North Carolina drawl who had moved to Huntington Park as a young man and married a local girl. Like Larry Walsh and countless local politicians before him, Jackson had entered politics through the Huntington Park Jaycees, and more often than not during this period his colleagues selected him for the ceremonial post of mayor.

Though parochial in outlook, Jackson was shrewd, and like his colleagues he viewed city government simply as a business operation. "We liked each other," he recalled years later, when he was the lone remaining Anglo on the city council. "We were like a board of directors. We never dealt with personalities. We had fun." Jackson and his colleagues had to withstand a good deal of political heat over the redevelopment projects, which displaced local residents and disrupted local businesses in their attempts to revive the economy. Typical of extractive politics, these projects made money for developers and landowners—and sometimes for the city as well—but they did not alter the town's basic trajectory.

Inevitably, in their desperation, Huntington Park and the Hub Cities began to subsidize the most tantalizing extractive industry of all: gambling. Most forms of gambling were illegal in California, but card clubs were not. Featuring highly regulated versions of poker and other card games, a successful club could be a gold mine for a city, which could tax the gambling revenue. Huntington Park set up a card club in a tiny redevelopment pocket west of Alameda Street, away from the rest of the city and adjacent to historically black South Central Los Angeles. Bell and Commerce also went into the card club business. But no city worked the card club angle better than Bell Gardens.

No less than in the 1930s, Bell Gardens in the 1970s and 1980s was still the Dogpatch of the Hub Cities—a low-end community with lots of apartments, declining commercial strips, and little respect from neighboring cities. Like the other Hub Cities, Bell Gardens created two big redevelopment areas in the 1970s. But despite good frontage along the Long Beach Freeway, the city met with only middling success in retail development.

The key figure shaping Bell Gardens' redevelopment efforts was Claude Booker, whose Kansas family had moved onto a $10-a-month lot during the Depression. In the 1960s and 1970s, Booker served as a planning commissioner and member of the city council. Twice during the late 1970s and early 1980s, he also served as city manager. City managers in Southern California typically serve as a "professional class," and it is very unusual for a politician to cross the line and become a manager. But all anyone needs to be appointed city manager is three out of five votes on the city council. Booker was able to meet this criterion whenever his supporters regained council control.

In 1982, Booker returned from the working-class resort community of Clear Lake, in Northern California, where he had been managing a mobile home park, to take over as city manager a third time. Once in office, he quickly negotiated a redevelopment deal with gambling promoter George Hardie to bring the Bicycle Club to a prime parcel next to the Long Beach Freeway on Florence Avenue.

Business grew slowly at first, but in 1986 the Bicycle Club added two Asian poker games, allowing it to tap into the lucrative Asian gambling market. Soon it became the most successful card club in Southern California, grossing upwards of $80 million a year, and it gave the government of Dogpatch a gold-plated feel. By 1990, the city was reaping some $9 million a year in tax revenue. Thanks to the Bicycle Club, the Bell Gardens budget was larger than the budgets of Bell, Cudahy, and Maywood combined.

Success at the Bicycle Club carried a price tag, of course. In 1990, four original investors were convicted of putting laundered drug profits into the Bicycle Club. The federal government seized thirty-six percent of the club's ownership, but according to state prosecutors, money-laundering and loan-sharking continued. Despite these shady undertones, the club's presence and its money helped to solidify Claude Booker's base of power. Indeed, the whole Bell Gardens' story appeared to send a clear message: With a dwindling voter base and a group of eager businesses like card clubs, you could make the politics of extraction "work" in the Hub Cities—"work," at least, for the politicians and the city governments that played the game.

The assumption underlying this municipal mining operation was that the business-government cartel would thrive as the population of the cities emptied out, leaving the area with few residents and even fewer votes. In the decade after the Watts riots, this is exactly what happened. Beginning in the late 1970s, however, a dramatic reversal occurred. Instead of dropping, the Hub Cities' population went up—and not just by a little, but by a lot. Between 1975 and 1980, Bell grew by twenty-five percent, Bell Gardens by thirty percent, Huntington Park by thirty-six percent. Overall, the eight Hub Cities—which were, by this time, almost completely built-out, with little new residential construction—grew from one hundred eighty thousand to two hundred twenty-two thousand in only five years, a growth rate of almost five percent per year.

The new faces were no longer Anglo. And they weren't black, as the Hub City political structure had always feared. Instead they were brown, coming mostly from the historically Mexican-American communities in East Los Angeles (immediately to the north), from other Latino homelands such as Cuba, and from Mexico itself. By 1980, Latino residents in the Hub Cities outnumbered Anglo residents by more than two to one. In Huntington Park, Latinos accounted for about eighty-one percent of the population in the 1980 census, compared to seventeen percent for Anglos. This new wave of Latino residents into the Hub Cities was part of a much larger pattern of immigration and family creation that was, during the 1970s and 1980s, driving a dramatic Latinization of the entire Los Angeles area.

During the 1980s California was receiving an estimated four hundred thousand immigrants a year, half of them illegal. As a team of sociologists led by Douglas Massey has written, "To many observers, mass migration seemed to develop out of nowhere. Americans wondered where the millions of Spanish-speaking migrants had suddenly come from, and Mexicans fretted over the rapidly increasing influence of Anglo-American culture and the English language. Both became uneasy about the mutually dependent relationship into which they had fallen."

Of course, this migration had not developed out of nowhere. In fact, it was the latest chapter in the long and complicated history of Mexican immigration to the United States.* As Massey and his col-

---

* This chapter deals primarily with the phenomenon of Mexican immigrants and Mexican-Americans in the Southeast cities of Los Angeles. Of course, the Latino population in the United States and even in Los Angeles is far from homogenous, and to describe them all as Latino is about as useful as describing all white Americans as European. Many Latinos in Los Angeles—sometimes known as Chicanos—have family roots that predate the U.S. takeover of Southern California in 1846. Immigration has been strong from the Caribbean and Central America as well as from Mexico. In the 1980s, Central Americans emigrated to Los Angeles in large numbers, settling principally in the Wilshire/MacArthur Park area. However, the politics of the Eastside communities in Los Angeles are dominated by Mexican immigrants and Americans of Mexican descent.

leagues have shown in their book *Return to Aztlán*, Mexicans of different economic classes have migrated to the U.S., and California in particular, throughout the twentieth century, depending on economic conditions.

The population of Mexican immigrants and Mexican-Americans in Los Angeles has ebbed and flowed throughout the twentieth century, depending on this country's labor needs, economic situation, and racial attitudes. After being segregated into an Eastside *barrio* in the early years of the century, the Mexican population grew dramatically in the 1920s, when Mexican immigrants benefitted from anti-Asian immigration laws. During the Depression, when a quarter of all Americans were out of work, a half-million Mexicans (including many Mexican-Americans born in the United States) were shipped to Mexico—many at the expense of the relief-plagued Los Angeles County government—only to be accepted back during World War II, when labor shortages again surfaced.

But the guest worker program that began during the war only strengthened the ties between Los Angeles and Mexico and laid the groundwork for a permanent flow of immigrants northward. According to Massey and other researchers, as farm jobs have been lost to mechanization, rural folk have moved to major cities in Mexico and, often, on to Los Angeles. Once in Los Angeles, the Mexican immigrants often find menial day-laborer jobs or work for low wages in the garment industry or in the city's post-industrial service economy. In this way, the *El Norte* aspirations of today's immigrants are not so different from the *Grapes of Wrath* aspirations of the Okies sixty years ago.

With L.A.'s Latino population exploding, the Hub Cities became a logical spillover area. The Hub Cities have always had a significant Latino population, and, because of the geographical connections, they have often been linked to the Latino Eastside. With the Anglo population in flight and landowners playing extractive politics in order to build apartment buildings, a large stock of urban housing was available—not only as shelter for immigrants, but also as investments for the upwardly mobile Latino working class.

Thus, between the mid-1970s and the late 1980s, the Hub Cities were Latinized. By the time the 1990 census was taken, the official population had grown to almost three hundred thousand, a sixty percent increase from fifteen years earlier. (The real population, of course, was likely even higher.) Latinos made up eighty-eight percent of the residents and Anglos less than ten percent, a swing of about twenty percent since 1980.*

Household size, which was below two persons per household and declining in the slow-growth hotbeds on the Westside and in the San Fernando Valley, approached four persons per household throughout the Hub Cities. Schools were

Pacific Boulevard in Huntington Park.

bulging with students. Many apartment neighborhoods were overcrowded, and gangs had become a problem. At the same time, many of the Hub Cities' tidy bungalow neighborhoods had been revived, usually with Mexican touches like a fence around the front yard, which created sociability with neighbors. Pacific Boulevard was transformed from a declining downtown into a center of Latino commerce. Though it wasn't near a freeway, Pacific Boulevard was easily accessible by car from most parts of the Hub Cities and by foot from the crowded neighborhoods in Huntington Park, and good bus service put it within reach of even the working poor.

These changes did not sit well with the remaining Anglo population. Members of one Huntington Park Anglo family interviewed in 1990 revealed that they didn't know their Latino neighbors nextdoor, even though the neighbors had lived there for thirteen years. Others complained that they couldn't buy any Anglo items on Pacific Boulevard despite its prosperity. "It is heartbreaking to see this happen in this city," an elderly woman told a reporter.

The extractive machinery, of course, profited from the change, as unsophisticated tenants paid more and more rent for overcrowded apartments. The politicians weren't threatened, at least not at first.

---

* Though it was pronounced in the Hub Cities, this change was hardly an isolated phenomenon in Southern California. According to planner/demographer Dowell Myers, Los Angeles County in 1990 had twenty-three cities with a Latino majority. By contrast, forty-four cities had an Anglo majority, two an African-American majority, one an Asian majority, and sixteen had no majority at all.

Transient apartment dwellers tend not to vote regularly, especially in poorly publicized local elections held in April. And many of the new Latino residents were not eligible to vote because they weren't citizens. So many politicians ignored the Latino residents. For a long while, even the traditional Latino political organizations didn't pay much attention to the Hub Cities, preferring instead to focus on traditional centers of power such as the Los Angeles City Council and the Los Angeles County Board of Supervisors. Eventually, however, demography and chronology combined to erode the entrenched power of the Anglo politicians.

﹏

In Huntington Park, aspiring Latino politicians emerged as early as the 1970s, when the demographic shift first became evident. Perhaps the most persistent Latino politician in Huntington Park was Raul Perez, who had emigrated to the city in the 1960s after graduating from the University of Guadalajara in western Mexico. Friendly and open, Perez was first a salesman and later a mortgage broker; he liked Huntington Park's small-town atmosphere and often cruised around the city on a bicycle. Like other upwardly mobile Latinos, Perez saved his money and began to invest in apartments. And like Larry Walsh, Tom Jackson, and a previous generation of Huntington Park leaders, he gained entry into politics by joining the local Jaycees. Though he retained a thick Spanish accent, Perez was the personification of small-town American boosterism, supporting anything he thought would help local business.

Perez and Ric Loya, a native-born Mexican-American teacher and liberal activist, began running for city council as a team during the 1970s. Perez persisted and continued to lose. "But every time," he recalled years later, "I lost by fewer votes." The trend was clear. If it did not take very many Anglo voters to keep Anglos in office in a mostly Latino city—and in Huntington Park it took fewer than fourteen hundred votes to win an election—then it did not take very many Latino votes to turn them out.

In 1988, Perez mounted a serious challenge, and focused his attacks on Tom Jackson, who was then running for his sixth term. Perez claimed that Jackson, who doesn't speak Spanish, couldn't represent Latinos effectively because he was Anglo. Jackson responded, as always, that people turned to him because he knew how to get things done. In a technique that would be duplicated elsewhere in the Southeast cities, Perez also made aggressive use of absentee ballots, which brought reluctant Latinos more readily into the electoral arena.

When local voters went to the polls in April 1988, Perez had almost enough support to win. After a recount, it was determined that Jackson and his Anglo colleagues had won re-election by only a few votes. But it was clear that, politically speaking, the Latinos' time was almost at hand. Jackson's narrow victory had occurred in a city populated by, as the 1990 census would soon show, more than fifty thousand Latinos and about three thousand Anglos.

But *perestroika* in the Hub Cities wasn't achieved by a quiet and gradual political transition in Huntington Park. Instead, it came amid the harsh glare of publicity in the boisterous atmosphere of Bell Gardens—and more than ever linked all the Hub Cities to this volatile Dogpatch scene.

In 1990, as Perez prepared to mount another challenge in Huntington Park, Bell Gardens was still under Claude Booker's political control, with an all-Anglo council in charge of an overwhelmingly Latino city where almost no one voted. In April of that year, two Anglo incumbents in Bell Gardens won re-election with, respectively, 473 and 472 votes, about fifty-five percent of the 800 or so votes cast. The 1990 census, taken within two weeks of the election, showed that the city's population included 37,000 Latinos and 4,200 Anglos. Significantly, however, two Latina challengers each won about thirty percent of the vote.

In spite of these political changes, or maybe because of them, Claude Booker soon proposed a dramatic rezoning. In the Billy Goat Acres days, Bell Gardens had developed haphazardly. Now Booker suggested a revision that called for many residential areas to be rezoned for commercial use. Many apartment districts would be rezoned for single-family or other low-density homes. The phase-in would be slow—no changes would be required for twenty years—but eventually the plan would affect a third of Bell Gardens' nine thousand parcels of land.

Booker always claimed that he'd had such a vision in mind for many years. He had accumulated various studies showing that the city's infrastructure was strained to the breaking point by a population that had grown, officially, by sixty-one percent in fifteen years. And his proposal was certainly consistent with the slow-growth attitudes then prevailing in more affluent white areas. But the timing suggested that he hoped to punish or undercut his political opposition by removing both landlords and tenants from the city. Payback time was not long in coming.

At an explosive city council meeting in December 1990, six hundred people—almost as many as had voted in the election eight months before—showed up at the city council to protest the rezoning plan. The residents had been whipped up in advance by flyers accusing the city council of seeking to "get rid of all Bell Gardens residents," "lower the price of all land to zero," and then buy the land for redevelopment, making them "the richest public officials in the history of Southern California." And when he claimed that "not one house, not one apartment, not one tenant will be disturbed for the next twenty years," Booker was greeted with calls of "*mentiras, mentiras.*" Lies, lies. Despite the spectacle, Booker's city council voted 5–0 for the rezoning plan.

Over the next few months, Booker tried to engage in damage control, but it didn't work. In April 1991, one of his longtime council members resigned to move to Utah. Booker replaced him with Rosa Hernandez, the top Latina vote-getter in the previous year's election. It wasn't long, however, before Hernandez was being accused of betrayal, setting the tone for a seemingly endless parade of factional charges and counter-charges in Bell Gardens.

In June 1991, Booker's opponents—now calling themselves the No Rezoning Committee—filed petitions to recall all four Anglo members of the council. Meanwhile, Latino activist groups held citizenship classes and voter registration drives in order to line up new voters. As in Huntington Park, the Bell Gardens activists also made heavy use of absentee ballots. In December 1991, all four Anglo incumbents were removed from office in a recall election.

The recall set up a dramatic special election for March 1992 which pitted the No Rezoning slate against one allied with Booker. The No Rezoning group ran a slate of three Latinos, including Josefina Macias, who had run well in the 1990 election, and Rodolfo Garcia, head of the local office of the League of United Latin American Citizens. They also ran George Deitch, an Anglo landlord allied with them against Booker, and conducted an aggressive campaign poking fun at "King Claude." The pro-Booker forces also ran a mostly Latino slate and, in turn, lampooned "Boss Deitch." But history, at this point, was running against Claude Booker. The March election saw voter turnout more than double from the 1990 election. More than half the votes, one thousand fifty in all, came from absentee ballots distributed by the No Rezoning group, and some eighty percent of the absentees voted for the No Rezoning slate.

The No Rezoning team easily swept into office, and the Booker era came to an unceremonious end. New council members entered their first city council meeting to the sounds of "Diana" and "La Negra," played by a mariachi band that sprung spontaneously from the crowd. They were sworn in by State Senator Art Torres, with the Mexican consul looking on. Josefina Macias, who was selected mayor by the council, promised that other city employees would keep their jobs, saying, "If we cut off the head of the snake, Booker, then the other employees will do their job." Booker responded by telling the new council, "It is a great honor to be fired by you." All these exchanges were recorded by the national media, which dutifully depicted the dramatic events in Bell Gardens as a story of self-liberation by the Latino masses. "This is the first time Latinos in a community have taken charge of their community, of their neighborhood, and made people listen to their voices," said Torres, one of the leading politicians on the Eastside. "We are no longer a sleeping giant."

The Bell Gardens story completely overpowered news of the more peaceful transition in Huntington Park. In the 1990 election, a veteran member of the Tom Jackson council retired, and Raul Perez won an overwhelming victory. Another Latino activist scored a more modest victory over one of the incumbents, and suddenly Huntington Park was only one vote shy of a Latino majority on the five-member city council.

In 1991, while the recall campaign was going on in Bell Gardens, another longtime Jackson crony died in office, and Ric Loya, the high school health teacher, was appointed to replace him. With Loya's vote, the Huntington Park council selected Perez as the first Latino mayor in the Hub Cities area. The following year, on the same day the Latino slate was elected to office in Bell Gardens, Loya won election to a full term in Huntington Park. Henceforth the question in Huntington Park, as in Bell Gardens, would not be whether there would be a Latino majority but what it would do.

⤺

At this point, the story of Latino power in the Hub Cities, at least as it was depicted in the national media, became almost entirely the story of Bell Gardens. One by one, the other cities also elected Latino councils, which in turn selected Latino mayors. And Huntington Park slowly began wrestling with its own transition as well. But in Bell Gardens, the politics of race and the politics of urban extraction hurtled toward a spectacular collision that would set the tone for the politics of the entire area.

For the media, the flashpoint came during a closed session of the council in January 1993, ten months after the Latinos won. Josie Macias, the diminutive mayor, picked up a chair and threw it at Councilman Frank Duran in the middle of a dispute over who the city attorney should be. Afterward she told the press, "He has always wanted me to step back and let him run the show." Duran simply said, "You know how women are." A day later, the council dumped Macias as mayor and replaced her with Duran.

The chair-throwing incident made national news, pushing Bell Gardens, for better or worse, into the limelight as the nation's leading illustration of what can go wrong when an inexperienced group of politicians is running a town. Because since the election, *everything* had gone wrong. Having rid itself of Booker, the council had trouble agreeing on a new city manager. The council also had to field a lot of questions about the No Rezoning Committee's absentee-ballot campaign tactics, which opponents claimed had been coercive, and about Claude Booker's contract, which had more than two years to run. (Refusing a severance, Booker sued for, and eventually won, the complete sum of about $266,000.)

It was true that the No Rezoning group in Bell Gardens had little experience in politics. But inexperience was only part of the story. In large part, Bell Gardens' problems arose from the way the politics of extraction has wrapped itself around the city. The media and other Latino politicians sought to portray Bell Gardens as a tale of Latino self-liberation. To some extent this was true. To a considerable degree, however, the whole No Rezoning effort was not a mass movement but, rather, an attempt by local landlords to protect their own interests. The No Rezoning group had raised and spent $50,000 on the election—far more than had ever been spent on a local council campaign—and most of it came from landlords. Many of the movement's leaders owned rental units in Bell Gardens.

After the chair-throwing incident, Bell Gardens politics became, if this was possible, even more volatile. In 1994, a flamboyant woman named Maria Chacon, who had managed the 1992 campaign, ran for the council herself, challenging the very people whose campaign she had managed two years earlier. The voter turnout increased significantly—more than three thousand votes were cast, as compared with eight hundred in 1990—and Chacon won easily. But Macias quickly accused Chacon and the No Rezoning Committee of coercing voters, just as Booker had done.

Soon, Bell Gardens fractured into so many pieces that it is difficult to say with certainty who was allied with whom. The main instrument of political intimidation among these factions was the recall. A populist idea originally designed to permit voters to oust unresponsive officials, the recall now became the hackneyed plot twist in Bell Gardens' comic political opera. Whenever one faction wanted to gain leverage over another, recall petitions were circulated around town, and soon it was an unusual week if a recall *wasn't* being threatened.

The reason for all the volatility, of course, was that so much in Bell Gardens was riding on the Bicycle Club and the city's $9-million-a-year cut from the club's gross revenue. While permitting Bell Gardens to finance some social programs to assist low-income Latino residents, this pot of money also led the council into an endless series of spats over who should occupy the high-paying top jobs in city government. The council went through three city attorneys and four city managers. For long stretches of time, the council did without any city manager because of political turmoil over how much power should rest with the mayor, ordinarily a ceremonial post.

To make matters worse, as time went on, the Bicycle Club's finances deteriorated, and this strained the extractive relationship between the club and the city. Even with the federal government claiming one-third ownership, state prosecutors still alleged that illegal activity went on. One of the managers, suspected of skimming millions from club revenue, was forced out by government officials. Another key employee, who had been lured away from the Huntington Park Casino to run the Bicycle Club's Asian games, was arrested on loan-sharking charges. Soon the city's revenue from the club began to fall. The bickering and recall threats increased.

And the council meetings themselves became spectacular examples of political theater. At one meeting, where the council fought openly about background checks on Bicycle Club employees and routine appointments to minor city commissions, one angry citizen was ejected after calling Chacon *pinche vieja*, a "fucking old woman." After the meeting one city official remarked that the evening had not been as boisterous as usual.

⬿

With no golden goose to fight over, the new Latino majority in Huntington Park did not engage in the same kind of comic antics that were found in Bell Gardens. Just as they had done for decades, Huntington Park politicians distanced themselves from Bell Gardens, making it clear that Beverly Hills had little in common with Dogpatch. But even though extractive businesses had not wound themselves so tightly around the city government in Huntington Park, it was not long before the new Latino council was faced with the problem of *La Montaña*—and it became clear just how difficult it was even in Huntington Park to disentangle community interest, political ambition, and the politics of extraction.

While the Latino politics of Bell Gardens was fracturing in a way that made national headlines, the Latino politics of Huntington Park was fracturing in a less dramatic fashion. In 1994, two Latinas were elected to the council. One was Jessica Maes, a local real estate broker and public relations specialist who had long been active in local business circles. Like Ric Loya, Maes was a native-born Mexican-American who had a track record of activism in Democratic party politics. The second was Rosario Marin, an energetic advocate for the disabled whose political star was rising because of a high-level appointment in the administration of Governor Pete Wilson. Marin, like Raul Perez, was a Mexican immigrant, having moved to Huntington Park from Mexico City with her parents when she was a teenager. Her career was heavily promoted by Republican Party activists, who were always looking for a demographically correct fresh face. Among other things, Marin was featured at the 1996 Republican National Convention.

At first, the new Latino council was unabashedly pro-business. This was a no-lose situation, at least in the abstract, since it allowed local politicians to demand more local jobs for the Latino working class while at the same time cozying up to businesses that might contribute to their campaigns. So it was not too surprising that Sam Chew's Aggregate Recycling Systems Inc. got a warm reception.

Chew was a slim, balding, middle-aged man who had worked as a business loan advisor in South Central Los Angeles for many years. A native of Los Angeles, Chew himself was sensitive to racial slights and gave up a career as a cargo pilot because he felt he was targeted for trips to Asia and Hawaii. After helping to obtain financing for a gravel business, he decided to try the aggregate recycling business himself. Wanting an industrial site near downtown and rail lines, he chose a vacant property between Alameda and Cottage Streets and approached the city for a permit in 1993. Everyone on the new council liked his business; it would fill up an empty industrial lot with a going concern and generate some tax revenue for the city at minor inconvenience to the neighbors, who already lived next to an industrial neighborhood.

Originally, the city anticipated only a small hill about eight feet high, surrounded by an eight-foot fence. But wanting to appear pro-business, the council never imposed tough conditions on Chew's business that might restrict his ability to operate. As a result, once the Northridge earthquake hit and the rubble came rolling in, the city could do nothing to stop the creation of *La Montaña*.

Soon, Chew's grinder was in operation all day long, and trucks hauling the concrete rubble into his shop were lined up even at night. The residents of Cottage Street—mostly working-class, Spanish-speaking families—endured the business for eight long months without complaint. Then, at two-thirty in the morning on a hot night in August 1994, one woman who had been awakened by the noise called the police.

It was not long before *La Montaña*, then reaching some eighty feet into the air, became the most controversial public issue in Huntington Park. Chew's conditional use permit was up for renewal in November 1994, but the public debate had become so vociferous that the city council never acted on it.

La Montaña polarized the community, split the Latino majority, and confused many residents who expected politics in the town to change. Communities for a Better Environment, a San Francisco-based environmental justice group that

La Montaña, Cottage Street, Huntington Park.

had recently set up an office in Los Angeles and was looking for causes to support, began to organize Cottage Street residents. A more established Eastside community group, United Neighborhoods Organization, also began working to resolve the problem of *La Montaña*, using the leadership of Father Rody Gorman of St. Matthias Church. St. Matthias was Huntington Park's largest Roman Catholic church, running fourteen masses every weekend—one in English, one bilingual, and twelve in Spanish. The white-haired, ruddy-faced Gorman, who often called himself "the last Irishman in Huntington Park," was one of the most influential figures in town.

All through 1995, the citizens and the city fought over *La Montaña*, by conducting air quality tests, debating each other in public, holding press conferences. As the year went on, the citizens became more and more militant. They demanded immediate action and denounced the pro-business Latinos. But the pro-business majority remained firmly at Chew's side—especially Rosario Marin, who was a longtime acquaintance of Chew's from causes for the disabled. (Both had children with Down's syndrome, and they had met lobbying in Sacramento to advance the rights of the disabled.) Marin had a charismatic, jovial personality, and she often claimed she was firmly in favor of the underdog. But some Cottage Street residents disliked her, saying she often made fun of them.

The Cottage Street residents' biggest booster on the council was Ric Loya, the high school health teacher, who suffered from respiratory problems himself. Though of Mexican descent, Loya—first name Richard, not Ricardo—was an assimilated Latino who had grown up around the surf spots of Long Beach and didn't even speak Spanish. But he was a Democrat of the old school and could always be relied upon to fight for liberal causes like unions and the environment. He viewed his split with his old ally Raul Perez as progress of a sort. "Just because we're all Latino," he said, "doesn't mean there'll be harmony."

In February 1996, after more than a year of divisiveness, Father Gorman brokered a deal between Chew and the city that would have permitted Chew to receive concrete rubble for three months, until May 1, and completely shut down his operation within a year. Gorman fully expected that Loya and Maes, the more liberal Mexican-Americans, would support the deal, while Marin and Perez, the more business-oriented Mexican immigrants, would oppose it. Much to his surprise,

Communities for a Better Environment felt cut out of the deal Gorman had put together, and therefore pressured Loya and Maes to oppose the deal. So Gorman went to Perez and Marin—both of whom were his parishioners—and leaned on them to support it. "When Father Gorman asks you to do something, it is very difficult not to do it," Marin recalled later. With Jackson's vote, the Gorman deal was approved by the city council.

No sooner had the council acted, however, than the city was sued by both sides, thus continuing the local media barrage. Chew sued for $1 million in damages, claiming that local air pollution authorities had determined that his operation was not a hazard and therefore he should not be shut down. CBE and the Cottage Street residents also sued, insisting that the council had violated the Brown Act, the state's open-meetings law, in taking the February action without advance notice.

In March, Loya conducted his own analysis of data from the pulmonary tests of fifty residents of the Cottage Street area. Half, he claimed, had abnormal pulmonary readings—and, on the whole, they had a ten percent higher reading than the typical resident of an industrial area. Jackson and Perez insisted that the area's health problems were due to sawdust coming from the lumberyard next door.

With CBE backing him up and litigation pending on both sides, Loya demanded throughout the spring of 1996 that the city declare *La Montaña* a public nuisance. At the same time, the Latino majority couldn't decide which of the council's two new Latinas, Marin or Maes, should assume the largely ceremonial post of mayor, and neither could muster the necessary three votes. As a result, when the problem of *La Montaña* came to a head, the mayor's chair in Huntington Park was occupied—as it had been most of the time for thirty years—by Tom Jackson.

Tom Jackson might have seemed like an archaeological relic in modern-day Huntington Park, but he had won re-election to a seventh term in 1992. Jackson frequently expressed frustration with all the political infighting among the ambitious Latinos and longed for the good old days when a businesslike council had moved forward with the business of doing redevelopment deals. And he continued to believe that if he applied his own brand of common sense to problems in Huntington Park he could solve them.

At the time of the controversy over *La Montaña*, Jackson had already announced that he would not run for an eighth term. He expected to give up his flower shop and move to his vacation home in Riverside County. At the same time, he was considering a bit of extractive politics himself, toying with the idea of taking a $70,000-a-year job as a top City Hall staff deputy. Such a move would have been unthinkable in other parts of Los Angeles, but, at least as far back as Claude Booker, it had been a viable possibility in the suburbs of extraction. (He later dropped the idea.)

On a Monday night in early May 1996, Jackson convened yet another meeting of the city council to deal with *La Montaña*. The council meets in an elegant eighty-year-old council chambers on Miles Avenue, just five blocks from Pacific Boulevard, and business is conducted under an inspiring, chiseled slogan: WHERE THERE IS NO VISION THE PEOPLE PERISH.

Loya and the Cottage Street residents were lobbying the city to declare the Chew site a public nuisance and require an environmental impact report. Jackson, for his part, thought the whole exercise was ridiculous. "Why make the guy do an EIR for $45,000?" he asked later. "We've already revoked his permit."

But Jackson was not the only politician being attacked from the audience that night. So were the other members of the pro-business faction, Latino or not—including Marin, for whom the Cottage Street residents always held special contempt.

"Los hijos han estado echando sangre por sus narices!" yelled a resident of the Cottage Street neighborhood at one point during the meeting. "The children have been bleeding through their noses!" Through a translator she had brought with her,* the woman zeroed in on Rosario Marin, accusing her of making fun of their situation and advising them to lock their children up so they won't have to breathe the air.

Only a few moments before, Marin had joked with Mayor Jackson when he had accidentally referred to the Latino boxing star Oscar de la Hoya as de la *Loya*. Now she dropped her usual jovial pose. And even

---

* Unlike Bell Gardens, which had installed a United Nations-style electronic translation system, Huntington Park did not provide translations of city council meetings, so Spanish-speaking residents had to bring friends or relatives to translate for the official council sessions.

though there was no official translator, she did not speak in English. *"Nunca, nunca dije que sus hijos deben ser encerrado. Estos son mentiras,"* she said. "I never, never said that your children should be locked up. Those are lies."

A little while later, an Anglo resident named Thomas Lunde complained that the concrete dust was so pervasive that he spit up dirt every morning. "It's like having grits for breakfast. Grits is really good for a Southerner, but it's not good for us." Lunde called Sam Chew "a poor Chinese coolie immigrant," and the mostly Latino crowd erupted in applause.

Around midnight, with only eight people left in the audience, Mayor Jackson called for a closed session—permissible because the council was dealing with an issue in litigation. Behind closed doors, the council majority voted to rescind the February order calling for Sam Chew to shut down. This move dissolved the basis for both lawsuits. It also gave Sam Chew the unfettered ability to keep operating.

In the months that followed, the pro-business council members continued to seek a solution to *La Montaña* in a way that would make them look both pro-business and pro-Latino. Finally they agreed to bring in a hearing officer to decide whether *La Montaña* should be declared a public nuisance. The hearing officer, Colin Lennard, was an experienced and respected lawyer in both municipal and environmental law. But he was also a gray-haired white male from a downtown firm. And when the hearing began in the council chambers in September, it was clear that neither the lawyer nor the city's staff had thought about whether or how to translate the testimony of the Cottage Street residents.

Though he did his best to sort out the legal issues associated with *La Montaña*, there was no question that Lennard's job was to provide the city council with political cover and allow the city to buy some time. (He eventually did declare *La Montaña* a public nuisance.) In Huntington Park, as in Bell Gardens, politicians who had been elected mostly because of their race could not disengage themselves from the economic forces that had taken root in the Hub Cities long before their election.

⌐

On the day before Halloween of 1996, a thousand people crowded into St. Matthias Roman Catholic Church on Florence Avenue in Huntington

Park—one of the largest churches in the Archdiocese of Los Angeles—to pay their last respects to Raul Perez.

Only fifty-four years old, Perez had been suffering for several months from gall bladder cancer, though he had not revealed his suffering to the general public. The day of the funeral was moody, the first rainy day of the fall in Southern California. The wet weather seemed to accentuate the surrounding street noise and the distant hum of jets beginning their descent into LAX. To an Easterner, the scene would have resembled nothing so much as an Italian funeral in Queens.

Built in 1950, St. Matthias is a classic older church. It's the largest structure for blocks around, tucked snugly and elegantly onto a corner lot along a busy street. For Perez's funeral, St. Matthias proved big enough to accommodate both political bigwigs and ordinary working people. As Perez himself often mused, it is impossible to hide in a small town like Huntington Park. Though the church conducts almost all Masses in Spanish every weekend, Perez's service was conducted in English, meaning many congregants had a hard time following along.

Afterward, Perez's casket was carried through the rain to a waiting hearse, accompanied by Huntington Park police officers in dress uniform complete with Mountie-style hats and white dickeys. As dozens of people stood in front of the church with their umbrellas open, County Supervisor Gloria Molina, the first Latina elected to such a prominent position, emerged to console Perez's family. Later, Mayor Tom Jackson came down the church steps without even a raincoat. Having recently announced plans to run for an eighth four-year term, Jackson darted from one umbrella to another, consoling some constituents and waving to others.

Given the divided nature of the the City Council. Perez's death cast doubt on the political future of *La Montaña* and many other issues in Huntington Park. (Among other things, a dispute quickly arose over whether to name a new community center for Perez or for Jackson's longteam council colleague Jack Parks, whose death in 1991 led to the appointment of Ric Loya.) Yet in a broader sense, his departure represented something more important. Born and raised in Mexico, Raul Perez was laid to rest in Resurrection Cemetery in Montebello as an important political figure in suburban Los Angeles—a symbol of the Hub Cities' political change and their ongoing struggle to free themselves from extractive politics. His trip from St. Matthias to the cemetery required a motorcade including one Los Angeles County fire truck, nine Huntington Park Police Department motorcycles, four patrol cars, one limousine, and one hearse bearing the name, appropriately enough, of the Cunningham-Guerra Funeral Home.

In the midst of all the turmoil, the Hub Cities continue to receive national attention—not just because politicians throw chairs, but because of the peculiar phenomenon of Latino political power in suburban cities. In the spring of 1995, for example, Secretary Henry Cisneros of the U.S. Department of Housing and Urban Development toured the Hub Cities and came away with a typically optimistic attitude. "I can't imagine anywhere in the U.S.," Cisneros said afterward, "that is more ripe for moving people into the middle class than here."

Cisneros may well be right. Few recent groups have embraced the traditional working-class aspirations of the American dream as firmly as the Latinos who have settled in the Hub Cities. Yet just as surely, few are so poorly served by the growth machine—or, more accurately, by the peculiar tattered remnants of the growth machine that remain.

Huntington Park and Bell Gardens are very different places and in some ways, their stories are very different. But surely both stories reveal how difficult it has been for Latino politicians to disentangle themselves from the extractive politics that followed the original growth machine's departure.

The politics of extraction is a dirty business in any declining urban area, creating an alliance between municipal fiefdoms, in search of power and money, and nefarious or noxious businesses looking for a safe haven in which to operate. Once a community becomes a suburb of extraction, only a political revolution can change things. And in a critical sense, the sequence of events in the Hub Cities has been far from revolutionary, however dramatic that sequence may have seemed. So the bonfire of political vanities goes on, deeply intertwined with the narrow economic interests that have traditionally ruled. In the Hub City lowlands no less than the mountains of Malibu, the *perestroika* is something less than complete.

PART TWO

Structure

L os Angeles may be a reluctant metropolis, but it is not an inadvertent one. The Los Angeles area is a large metropolis today mostly because the fathers of the growth machine built the economic infrastructure required to sustain it—water and power, ports and airports, freeways and railways, and so on. Far superior to that in most other American metropolitan areas, this infrastructure has shaped the growth of the Los Angeles region for decades.

It has also shaped the construction of large bureaucratic structures. Along with the infrastructure, Los Angeles has created a set of large regional organizations dedicated to feeding and guiding the sprawling regional growth machine. But the structure and infrastructure have not operated smoothly, especially in the last twenty years or so. The reason is simple: Once they were created, L.A.'s structure and infrastructure, like the region's growth dynamic itself, took on a life of their own.

Virtually all of the regional organizations were formed in Los Angeles by Los Angeles interests, and most of them are still headquartered there. Most of them—including, to varying degrees, the three organizations highlighted in these chapters—were essentially created in the modest offices of the Greater Los Angeles Chamber of Commerce on Bixel Street just west of the Harbor Freeway in downtown L.A. With its close ties to Los Angeles City Hall and to the business executives who ran the growth machine—developers, bankers, publishers, and the like—the Chamber of Commerce has set the regional agenda for eight decades or more.

Ironically, the regional infrastructure these organizations built has created far-flung rival centers of power and money in Orange County to the South and the so-called "Inland Empire" to the East. As they grew, the outlying areas chafed under L.A.'s colonial rule and demanded a larger voice in regional affairs. Yet the traditional power structures have been reluctant to yield control to the burgeoning metropolises they created. "Power," complains one Orange County official, "remains embedded at Bixel Street."

Not surprisingly, both structure and infrastructure have nearly buckled under the resulting pressure. In the case of water, L.A.'s most famously scarce resource, intra-regional jealousies have traditionally been papered over by the ongoing common quest to import more water from elsewhere in the West. In the case of transportation, the struggle to build an urban rail system became, in part, a struggle over money between business leaders in downtown Los Angeles and politicians in the outlying areas. And in the case of regional planning, local potentates have proven unwilling to yield parochial power, while at the same time Bixel Street has sought to maintain a strong hold on even the most far-flung outposts in the empire.

In short, while the infrastructure of the Los Angeles region has largely been equal to the task of dealing with growth, the bureaucratic structure has not. Absent a common purpose, Southern California and its hundreds of power centers have simply muddled through, hoping against hope that ad hoc political deals can take the place of strong-minded political leadership. It should be no surprise, then, that the regional structures were caught off-guard by the collapse of the growth machine and now appear ill-prepared to guide the future of the reluctant metropolis.

CHAPTER 4

Redefining Chinatown

There aren't very many places left in Southern California where you can stand on top of a mountain and feel like you're in a scene from the movie *Chinatown*—where you can look across a vast, barren landscape and imagine the power brokers of the growth machine conspiring to transform it into money. In fact, maybe the only place left for that kind of fantasy is the Domenigoni Valley.

The Domenigoni lies on the edge of Riverside County's San Jacinto Mountains. It's only a few miles from the farming community of Hemet, and less than a half-hour's drive from Moreno Valley, the prototypical Southern California suburb. It's the classic Western irrigated landscape—flat, usually hot, often windy, with green farm fields punctuated on two sides by a dramatic set of mountains rising from the valley floor. For more than a century, the valley has been cultivated by a hundred agricultural families who were confident that their out-of-the-way spot would never be of much interest to the power elite in Los Angeles.

From atop one of the nearby mountains, however, the signs of change are obvious. Some farms appear abandoned, their fields withering. In a few spots, huge trenches have been dug in the ground. And halfway up the side of the opposite mountain, perhaps five or six hundred feet above the valley floor, stands a large orange marker.

The marker is significant, because it represents what will eventually become the surface of Eastside Reservoir. Here, in a dusty agricultural valley eighty miles from Los Angeles, the Metropolitan Water District of Southern California is spending $2 billion to build one of the largest bathtubs in human history.

And bathtub is, indeed, the word. Eastside will not be a reservoir in a natural drainage basin, but a six-square-mile vat, blocked off on all sides by dams and pumped full of water diverted from its natural flow hundreds of miles away. If it were a movie, an observer once said, it would be called *No River Runs Through It*.

Eastside Reservoir is the kind of exercise in bigness Southern California rarely sees anymore. It will be as big as all the other reservoirs in Southern California put together. It will take five years just to fill. The Met is spending almost another $1 billion to construct a forty-mile canal to bring in water from the California aqueduct. Eastside will be so big, a Met press release once chortled enthusiastically, that it could hold seventeen hundred Rose Bowls. Its purpose is to help eliminate the question of water supply as an obstacle to growth in Southern California for decades.

Given all that, you'd think that the Eastside project would be so big that environmentalists would hate it. And, in fact, some do criticize the reservoir as costly and needless. But most environmentalists now love the Met, a massive wholesaler of water to all of Southern California traditionally at the center of the web of relationships making up the Los Angeles growth machine. And if they are not exactly enthusiastic about a six-square-mile artificial lake near Hemet, at least they haven't sued to stop its construction.

That so many environmentalists have bought into the Eastside project largely reflects the reinvention of the Met in the 1980s by Carl Boronkay, an avuncular lawyer who emerged from the wreckage of a divisive campaign over the Peripheral Canal as the agency's general manager. Reversing decades of rigid stonewalling, Boronkay—a soft-spoken, wry, and popular figure at the Met—understood that in order to build big water projects like Eastside, the Met had to be willing to do environmental penance.

Even before the Met decided where the reservoir would be built, Boronkay and the Met's directors authorized $15 million to help buy a critical piece of land environmentalists wanted to save. Boronkay also engineered the donation of nine thousand acres of Met land to solve a variety of thorny endangered species problems facing Riverside County. After these deals, it became fashionable for the press to applaud Boronkay as a far-sighted public servant who forced a hidebound agency to change with the times and become more envi-

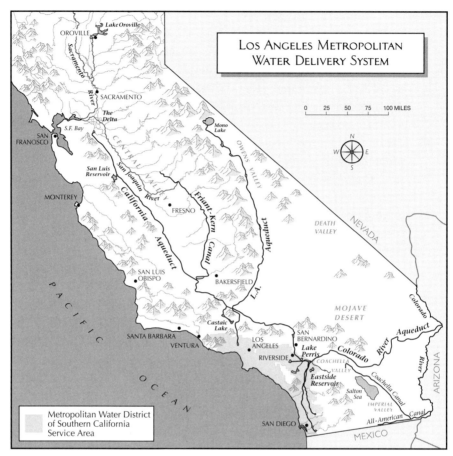

The Los Angeles water system, stretching hundreds of miles to the east and north.

ronmentally sensitive. And this reputation washed over onto other issues Boronkay was confronting, especially environmental concerns in the Sacramento-San Joaquin Delta, the state's massive switching yard for water.

In many respects, Boronkay's sterling reputation is well deserved. Less often noted is the fact that the Eastside business was simply a new version of the same old Met approach. The collapse of Southern California's growth consensus had forced Boronkay to rethink the Met's treatment of environmental issues and environmental groups. But it had not forced him to rethink the Met's ideology, its goals, or its way of getting things done.

On Eastside, the Met gave the environmentalists certain things they wanted, with the understanding that the larger issue of water as an inducer of growth regionwide would be taken off the table. Extolling the natural wonders of the Met's Riverside County preserves, most environmentalists never doubted that the deal was worth it. But environmental penance obscured the fact that the Met had not really changed. Wielding so much power and money, trading one thing off against another, determining what's worth eliminating in the name of progress—all this has been the Met's business for nearly seventy years.

From this point of view, the Domenigoni Valley script contained nothing new. Thanks to Boronkay's considerable skill, the old script with a few variations worked for a remarkably long time. But given the collapse of the Southern California growth coalition, it couldn't work forever.

⌐

Like every great metropolis, Los Angeles is a drain. A vast supply of goods flows toward it—food, commodities, electricity, water—to be consumed by the millions who live there, with the remnants disposed of beyond the consumers' view. Cars come to Los Angeles from all over the world and end up in the region's junkyards. Food comes from the Central Valley to the north and the Imperial Valley to the east, and the resulting waste is flushed to the ocean. Electricity generated as far as a thousand miles away, in the hydroelectric plants of the Northwest and the coal plants of the Rockies, is used to power L.A.'s air conditioners, traffic signals, and home computers (including the one being used to write this book).

Of all of these commodities, none is so precious and valuable as water. Like most of the American West, Southern California is a desert. Not a true desert, climatologically speaking, but a semi-arid region that suffers from an annual six-month summer drought and volatile winter rainfall. In a wet year, the region might see twenty to twenty-five inches of rain; in a dry year only six or seven. On average, Los Angeles gets about fifteen inches of rain per year. That's a quarter of Miami's rainfall, a third of New York's, and less than half of Chicago's. Despite an extensive system of natural underground water basins, it cannot support a fast-growing metropolitan area of fifteen million people or more.

It should not be surprising, then, that the Los Angeles growth machine has been obsessed with water from the beginning. Starting in the 1880s, the land speculators, newspaper publishers, and other members of the growth machine understood that, while they could try to sell Southern California's climate and image, the number of buyers would always be limited by the region's natural water supply. So for a century, one of the leading missions has been to find and import water. And not just a little water, but so much water that the issue of water would become irrelevant to Southern California's growth. Pursuing this goal has required Los Angeles to create an impressive pool of political and organizational talent—in effect, a whole water industry, half-hidden from the public, to ensure that when people in Westwood or Watts or West Covina turn on the shower in the middle of a drought, they actually get wet.

The first and most famous effort to import water came in the first decade of the twentieth century, when the City of Los Angeles moved successfully to bring a huge supply of water from the Owens Valley, more than two hundred miles to the north. In order to secure the rights to the Owens River, then the main source of water for a growing agricultural valley, the city used subterfuge, secret agents, and the intervention of President Theodore Roosevelt. To build an aqueduct unprecedented in human history, the growth machine whipped up a frenzy of public concern about an impending drought (always a useful technique in Los Angeles bond elections) and relied on the self-taught skills of Irish water engineer William Mulholland. When the first rush of Owens Valley water moved swiftly down a spillway into the San Fernando Valley in 1913, Mulholland uttered a now-famous phrase that aptly sums up L.A.'s approach to water: "There it is. Take it."

With those words, the future of Los Angeles as a center of growth was assured, and so was the method by which this growth would be achieved. As the fictionalized retelling of this story in the 1970s film *Chinatown* suggests, L.A.'s growth brokers had learned the most basic lesson about surviving in the West: Water is power, plain and simple. Whoever controls the water controls the future, and Los Angeles boosters proved willing to be as muscular, imperial, and ruthless as necessary to secure enough water to ensure unlimited future growth. They also understood, in a way that *Chinatown*'s oversimplifications could not possibly convey, that acquiring so much water required political clout and sophisticated coalition-building in Washington and Sacramento.

As soon as Mulholland finished the Owens Valley aqueduct, he began looking eastward to the next most obvious source of water. The Colorado River sat some two hundred miles away, draining the entire western slope of the Rocky Mountains to the Gulf of Mexico in Baja California. Not a large river by most standards—it was only one-tenth the size of the Columbia—the Colorado was subject to brackishness, wild drops in elevation, and even wilder episodes of flooding. And it didn't really belong to California. Although sharing its banks with Arizona, California contributed no water to the river. (Most came from Colorado, Wyoming, and Utah.) But, as Mulholland might have said, it was there. So Los Angeles decided to take it.

Beginning in the 1910s, California's congressional delegation proposed damming the wild Colorado and diverting the water—most for agriculture in the adjacent Imperial Valley in southeastern California and some for urban Los Angeles. It took more than ten years to make a deal with the other six states in the Colorado basin and get it through Congress, but by the early 1930s the U.S. Bureau of Reclamation was building the massive Hoover Dam near Las Vegas, one of the most remarkable engineering feats ever undertaken, and Parker Dam farther downstream, where California would divert the water. Soon, California would have legal rights to 4.4 million acre-feet of Colorado River water per year—the equivalent of 1.4 trillion gallons, or enough to serve perhaps ten million new residents of Southern California.* While much of the water was destined for the Imperial Valley, most of the money and political clout to get the job done had come from Los Angeles.

⤶

To bring Colorado River water to Los Angeles, the growth machine created what may have been its most brilliant organizational achievement. Stimulated by a special report from the Los Angeles Chamber of Commerce, eleven cities in Los Angeles and Orange Counties joined together in 1928 to form the Metropolitan Water District of Southern

---

* The most common measurement of water supply, an acre-foot, is equivalent to 325,000 gallons of water, or the amount required to fill one acre to the depth of one foot. By traditional judgments this is approximately the amount of water required by a family of four for one year.

California.* Los Angeles dominated the board, but the Colorado project was too big even for Los Angeles. For the first time a truly regional vehicle for development had emerged, and it laid the foundation for the region's decentralized, growth-oriented municipal system. As UCLA water historian Norris Hundley Jr. explained: "[T]he presence of scores of cities throughout the region (smaller but no less ambitious versions of Los Angeles) meant that there could never be quite enough water to provide complete peace of mind or make possible a metropolis that could not somehow be grander with just a little more water."

Building the aqueduct took eight long Depression-filled years and cost more than $200 million in taxpayer bond money. Yet in contrast to Mulholland's dramatic ceremony in the Owens Valley twenty-eight years earlier, when water from the Colorado River arrived in Los Angeles in 1941, hardly anyone cared. The event received little publicity, and in the first year, a wet year, the Met sold only thirty thousand acre-feet.

From this inauspicious beginning, the Met grew to become the leading instrument for rapid and expansive urban development in metropolitan L.A. The agency has always insisted that its job was not to stimulate growth but merely to provide water wherever growth occurred. But in fact, the Met's goal was, and continues to be, to acquire such vast amounts that water would not be an issue in planning Southern California's future. In this task, the Met succeeded.

Because lack of demand from the original members threatened its financial stability, the Met aggressively expanded to incorporate newly suburbanizing areas outside Los Angeles, including San Diego, which even today is almost entirely dependent on the Met's water. When agricultural areas threatened to import water independently, the Met changed its charter to permit water to be used for agricultural as well as urban purposes.

The Met annexed the agricultural areas and, with ample water available, they soon turned into postwar suburbs. Between 1942 and 1954 the Met's service area grew from seven hundred seventy square miles to more than forty-five hundred, and the growth patterns of the megalopolis pretty much followed its boundaries. In the decade of the

* The original eleven cities were Los Angeles, Pasadena, Burbank, Glendale, Beverly Hills, San Marino, Santa Monica, Anaheim, Colton, Santa Ana, and San Bernardino. In 1931, Colton and San Bernardino withdrew, while Fullerton, Long Beach, Torrance, and Compton joined. These were the thirteen cities that completed the aqueduct.

California Aqueduct, San Joaquin Valley.

1950s, the period of Southern California's most explosive postwar growth, the Met's Colorado River water sales quadrupled to more than one million acre-feet per year. With a few additional annexations in the early 1960s, the Met's empire expanded to cover the entire reach of the Southern California megalopolis, from present-day Moreno Valley in the east to Oxnard in the west and from Simi Valley in the north to the Mexican border in the south.

The role of the Met in shaping the region's growth patterns was not lost on members of the growth machine. From the beginning, the Met's board was dominated by men—and they almost exclusively were men—who profited from urban development or, at least, shared the growth coalition's vision of a limitless future. During its aggressive postwar expansion, the Met was led by a steely and powerful board chairman, Joseph Jensen, an executive with Getty Oil Company who had written the original Chamber of Commerce report in the 1920s. "Land is just land," Jensen once said, "until it gets water on it."

In China-like fashion, men like Jensen held positions of power well into their dotage. The board elected Jensen to ten consecutive two-year terms as chairman. Many others served as board members for two decades or more. "The term of office," water historian Erwin Cooper wrote in the 1960s, "is construed to be for life." According to one estimate, in 1982—the year of the Peripheral Canal defeat, the Met's greatest public humiliation—the average age of a board member was sixty-seven.

Given these circumstances, the Met's unpaid directors-for-life branded the agency with a distinctive type of "corporate culture." Though some were suited, corporate types, others had the leathery skin and bolo ties that marked them as old-time California outdoorsmen. "Mostly," recalled one woman who served on the board, "they were white, gray-haired, polite, and patronizing gentlemen." The water industry was not only the center of their professional lives, but of their social lives. And they believed passionately in "developing" water—that is, harnessing the rivers of the West with dams and diverting its water through aqueducts and canals for human use. In time they came to be called "The Water Buffaloes."

The Water Buffaloes' clubby insularity was reinforced by the fact that they were, for the most part, shielded from public scrutiny. Though they made critical decisions affecting the growth of the entire region, and the agency had sweeping power to impose property taxes region-wide, most of the Met's fifty-one members were unknown to the general public. Board members were not directly elected; instead, they were selected for membership by one of the twenty-seven cities and water districts belonging to the Met. (The local water districts, in particular, operated almost out of public view even though they were public agencies.) The Met's staff consisted largely of highly skilled engineers and technicians who shared the board members' passion for building dams, aqueducts, and other water facilities. And in the best Los Angeles tradition, the Met also had enough wealth and influence to create a great public relations machine, which produced slick and expensive publications and helped control the flow of information to the press and the citizenry.

If this arrangement helped the Water Buffaloes acquire and hold power, it also insulated the Met from change. When the growth machine began to collapse in the late 1960s and early 1970s, the Water Buffaloes didn't seem to notice. And when they were threatened with demise, it was not because the desert had parched their thirst, as they had always feared. It was because they almost drowned in the roiling politics of a delta more than three hundred miles away.

About half of the imported water the Met sells today to member cities and water districts in Southern California is diverted from its natural flow almost four hundred fifty miles north of Los Angeles at a place in Butte County called Oroville. Here, on the edge of the far northern Sierra Nevada mountains, the largest earthen dam in the world—a mile wide and seven hundred feet high—holds some three-and-a-half-million acre-feet of water from the northern Sierras, awaiting shipment south. Released from behind Oroville Dam according to need and supply, the water is sent down the Feather and Sacramento Rivers. It is then sucked south across the fragile Sacramento-San Joaquin Delta—natural flow

The Sacramento-San Joaquin Delta.

would move it west, toward San Francisco Bay—and shipped hundreds of miles down an open-cover aqueduct across some of America's hottest and driest terrain. In a final engineering miracle, the water is electrically lifted two thousand feet over the Tehachapi mountains before being distributed to the state's reservoirs in Castaic and Moreno Valley.

Completed in 1972, California's State Water Project is the third, and probably last, leg of the stool on which the Los Angeles megalopolis relies day after day for its continued existence. At capacity, it is designed to carry four million acre-feet of water per year south. The Met has paid billions of dollars for Feather River water over the last thirty years, about seventy percent of the full cost of the State Water Project, and with good reason. Much of Southern California's growth during that period was predicated on the assumption that Feather River water would be available. Unfortunately for the Met, however, not all of this water actually arrives. The reasons lie in the Delta itself.

After more than a century of human fiddling, the Delta is now a bewildering collection of streams, creeks, channels, levees, and islands—stretching more than forty miles all the way from Sacramento south to Tracy, and then west for another forty miles until the water pours into a series of bays heading toward the San Francisco Bay and the Pacific Ocean. Receiving the runoff from four important rivers, draining most of Central and Northern California, the Sacramento-San Joaquin Delta carries more water seaward than the Colorado River.

On top of this, the Delta is a crossroads for all of California. Its flush of fresh water contains almost half the runoff in the state, and helps forestall saltwater intrusion that would harm people and wildlife. The Delta contains vital shipping channels that serve long-established industrial ports in Martinez, Pittsburg, and Stockton east of San Francisco. It is a heavily used recreation area prized by fishing interests, boaters, and others. It is home to several towns, including at least two below sea level. Thanks to a system of levees constructed over a century, the Delta has hundreds of thousands of acres in farmland, including some one hundred fifty thousand acres that lie below sea level. And finally, the Delta is a switching station for California's water. Most of the water used in the state—from municipal and federal dams to the east and state dams to the north—is stored, flushed, and pumped across the Delta to reach farm and urban customers to the west and south. Sixty percent of the state's drinking water travels through the Delta, along with water to irrigate almost half the fruits and vegetables in the United States. If there is one reason for a divided and contentious California to stay together as a single state, it is simply that everyone from San Francisco to San Diego uses water flowing through the Delta.

The Delta is not supposed to be a bottleneck, of course. The State Water Project was to have included a large aqueduct that would skirt the Delta, bringing water from the Sacramento River south to what is now known as the Edmund G. Brown Aqueduct. Constructing this "peripheral canal" has been the principal objective of a longstanding, if stormy, alliance between the Met and the state's other powerful growth machine—the agricultural barons of the San Joaquin Valley, whose otherwise dry, barren land lies on the banks of the concrete river now named for Pat Brown. The demise of the Peripheral Canal plan was one of the major episodes contributing to the collapse of the Southern California growth machine. And it also served as a wake-up call for the Met.

The State Water Project is largely a product of Pat Brown's political leadership and the creation of the Met-grower alliance. When he became governor in 1959, Brown began to promote the Feather River project enthusiastically. Though Brown himself seemed motivated by a desire to provide water for urban Southern California, most of the behind-the-scenes political muscle came from the San Joaquin Valley growers.

In only a century, the San Joaquin Valley has been transformed from a vast, dry plain into one of the world's leading breadbaskets, delivering an astonishing array of agricultural products to the entire country at a low price. Like Southern California, the San Joaquin Valley is built on the use of large amounts of water in an unlikely place. Southern California uses four million acre-feet of water a year, but Central

Valley farmers use fourteen million acre-feet on their crops. That's about five trillion gallons of water annually.

The Valley's agricultural empires were fueled initially by water from underground aquifers. Later the water came from the Central Valley Project, a huge network of dams and canals planned by the state but built by the federal government because of the expense. Even after the Central Valley Project was completed in the 1950s, however, groundwater levels continued to drop, and large farm interests in the area feared that the federal government would enforce its seldom-used requirement that federal water users be limited to ownership of one hundred sixty acres of land. So Valley farmers began lobbying Sacramento for more water development.

But agricultural interests could not afford the full cost of another water project. They needed urban water customers, who would pay far more per acre-foot than the richest farmer. Only one customer would be able to foot a bill that large, and that was the Met.

The Water Buffaloes wanted water from the North, because, like the growers, they knew of no other place to get it. Indeed, during the 1950s the Met had frequently threatened to dam the Eel River. But the agency balked at the idea of a State Water Project, fearing the financial burden it would be forced to carry for Valley growers.*

When Pat Brown bullied a $1.75 billion bond issue onto the 1960 ballot, the Met folded. In a rare public split, Jensen held out, but a majority of the board agreed to sign state contracts for the delivery of one-and-a-half-million acre-feet of Feather River water a year. Four days later, the State Water Project was approved by 174,000 votes out of 5.8 million cast, with the Met's service area in Southern California delivering the margin of victory.

Oroville Dam and the Pat Brown aqueduct were built, along with the two-million-acre-foot San Luis Reservoir in Merced County. The dry, desolate stretches of land in the southern part of the San Joaquin Valley bloomed with all kinds of high-profit specialty crops, enriching many farmers, including some large corporations that owned land in the area. The Met and the Valley landowners were now partners. The

---

* It seems likely that Met directors were also concerned that the State Water Project would damage its longstanding legal dispute with Arizona over Colorado River water, which rested largely on the argument that Southern California had no other sources of imported water.

growers needed the Met's subsidies, and the Met, though powerful in its own right, needed the remarkable political strength of the state's farming industry in Sacramento. And in the 1970s, each needed the other to pursue construction of the final piece of the State Water Project, the Peripheral Canal.

By the time Pat Brown's unpredictable son Jerry was elected governor in 1974, Northern California environmentalists had made the ecological health of the Delta a major issue, and they also feared that construction of the Peripheral Canal would open the way for the damming of even more rivers in Northern California for diversion southward. Laboring under the legacy of his father, Jerry Brown decided to support the canal's construction. Closely tied to the environmental movement, however, he attached an enormous laundry list of environmental conditions, and demanded a public vote on the canal, which was scheduled for the June 1982 ballot.

Led by a forceful chairman, former Burbank mayor Earl Blaise, the Met firmed up its alliances with the growers. According to former Met director and author Robert Gottlieb, Blaise used the canal referendum as a way to instill a new sense of intensity and mission in the Met that had been missing since Joe Jensen stepped down in the early 1970s. Blaise and other directors went on the offensive in a highly public campaign that turned the canal vote into a referendum on the Southern California growth machine. But 1982 turned out to be exactly the wrong time for a referendum on growth. Unrest with growth was rampant in Northern California and spreading to Southern California. Environmentalists were publicly linking the water establishment to unbridled growth for the first time. Worst of all, it was a wet year.

The Met-grower alliance was further weakened when two key San Joaquin Valley growers, J.G. Boswell Company and Salyer Land Company, bolted from the ranks, saying they opposed the canal deal because the environmental protections were too severe. Then, unbelievably, Boswell and Salyer joined forces with environmentalists and bankrolled the anti-canal campaign.

Suddenly, environmentalists had enough money to compete in the high-cost, media-oriented world of California state politics. On election day, the canal carried Southern California, but not by an overwhelming margin (about sixty percent in the Los Angeles megalopolis). And most of the populous San Francisco Bay counties voted against the canal by ninety percent or more.* Statewide, sixty-three percent of all voters rejected the referendum. Later attempts to push through a series of Delta improvements also failed in the wake of the canal defeat. Finally, it appeared, the Water Buffaloes were dead.

⌣

In the inevitable shakeup that followed the canal debacle, the board selected Carl Boronkay, the Met's top lawyer, as the organization's new general manager. Tall, affable, and erudite, Boronkay represented a clean break from the past.

Boronkay was not the first lawyer to serve as the Met's general manager, but he was the first person who had enough of an outsider's perspective to see what was really going on. Then fifty-five years old, Boronkay had come to the Met only eight years before, following a distinguished career in the California attorney general's office. Unlike virtually all of his predecessors, who had been lifers either at the Met or the U.S. Bureau of Reclamation, Boronkay had not devoted his career to building dams and delivering water. Instead, he had spent twenty years defending California's environmental and natural resources agencies in court. Boronkay was no environmentalist, and he was not about to challenge the Met's basic assumptions, as a few renegade Met board members from older, liberal cities (including Santa Monica) had begun to do. But he understood that things were changing. "The Met had a one-track mind—how to go forward with the State Water Project," Boronkay recalled years later. "But after the canal vote, it became clear that the State Water Project wasn't going to be completed in any reasonably foreseeable period."

And the canal defeat was only part of the story, as Boronkay well knew. Environmentalists were engaged in a fierce legal battle against the City of Los Angeles, a battle which would eventually lead to a reduction of the city's water supply from the Owens Valley in order to improve the ecology of Mono Lake. As general counsel, Boronkay had watched the Met's claim on Colorado River water drop as Arizona asserted its legal right to large amounts. Boronkay could see that Southern California's long-established sources of water were shrinking, and

---

* Even in Santa Clara County, which would have received some of the canal's benefits, eighty-nine percent of the voters rejected the canal.

no new rivers were going to be dammed. At the same time, the region continued to grow. Southern California added more than three million new residents in the 1980s, and the Met tripled its State Water Project deliveries between 1983 and 1989.

For growth to continue, the Met would have to find another way to achieve its goals. So Boronkay gradually nudged the board—its composition slowly changing, as the Water Buffaloes began to depart—in a new direction. He brought in a new cadre of middle managers and shook up the bureaucracy, which began to refer to life "B.C." (Before Carl) and "A.C." (After Carl). And while he didn't challenge its basic mission, he did change the way the Met did business.

Carl Boronkay, general manager of the Metropolitan Water District until 1993.

The Domenigoni project was classic Boronkay. It was a large, even audacious, public works project in the classic Met style. Yet his approach to building it was unlike anything that had come before.

For the Met, the next best thing to more water flowing southward through the Peripheral Canal was a huge new reservoir, where Colorado and Feather River water could be banked in wet years for use in dry years. So shortly after Boronkay took over, the Met began planning a reservoir of breathtaking proportions. The reservoir would probably cover about six square miles, approximately the size of Beverly Hills, and hold close to one million acre-feet of water, doubling Southern California's storage capacity. The severe drought that began in 1987 bolstered the argument that wet years had to be banked. But just as important was the way Boronkay used his understanding of environmental law and the political landscape of Southern California to win support.

In late 1988, as the Met was analyzing prospective sites, the U.S. Fish and Wildlife Service declared a small rodent, the Stephens' kangaroo rat, an endangered species. The K-rat, as it came to be called, burrowed in the grasslands of western Riverside County, where homebuilders were scrambling to construct one hundred thousand houses while the real estate market was hot and, not incidentally, where the Met wanted to build its reservoir. Because of the strength of the Endangered Species Act, which prohibits disruption of an endangered species habitat even on private property, the K-rat's listing brought all construction in the area to a halt.

Experienced in environmental law, Boronkay understood that, instead of suing or bullying, he had to "mitigate" his way through the project. Under the Endangered Species Act and other environmental laws, many construction projects are allowed to go forward if environmental regulators approve a "mitigation plan"—in essence, a plan to solve or improve other environmental problems in order to compensate for those created by the project. In 1989, the U.S. Fish and Wildlife Service informed county officials that they could not move ahead with development projects unless some twenty-five thousand acres or more—that's forty square miles, almost the size of San Francisco—were preserved just for the K-rat.

Heavily dependent on the construction industry and politically conservative besides, Riverside County was thrown into turmoil by these demands. Adding to the problem was the fact that the K-rat's listing mobilized a coalition of environmentalists from all over Southern California who now targeted western Riverside County as the focus of their preservation efforts. In particular, environmentalists, calling themselves the Endangered Habitats League, had made a *cause celebre* out of saving the Santa Rosa Plateau, a beautiful hilly area on the back side of the Santa Ana Mountains near Temecula.

Determined to mitigate, Boronkay hired an old friend from the attorney general's office, a lawyer named Greg Taylor, as a special assistant and sent him to Riverside County with instructions to offer a gold-plated mitigation deal.

The Santa Rosa Plateau had been bought for $15 million in 1988 by Won Yoo, an influential local developer. Yoo then proposed building twenty-four hundred houses and a golf course. By 1990, he was offering to scrap the plan and sell the property for conservation purposes for $35 million. The state and the county came up with $20 million, but no more. As instructed, Taylor used the Met's deep pockets to solve everyone's problems. In early 1991, even before choosing a site for the reservoir, the Met committed $15 million for the Santa Rosa Plateau, along with a couple of million more as an endowment for site maintenance. The environmentalists got their land and, thanks to the Met's deep pockets, Won Yoo turned a substantial profit.

Having saved Santa Rosa Plateau, the next step was for the Met to do everything possible to solve the overall K-rat problem. The county had established its own mitigation plan, which might produce a few thousand acres, but by itself the plan would never make federal biologists happy. So, once the Met decided on the Domenigoni site near Hemet, Taylor again went to work. First the Met agreed to set aside most of the land around the Domenigoni Reservoir as a kangaroo rat preserve. Then the agency agreed to do the same with its land around Lake Skinner, an existing reservoir a few miles to the south.

The Domenigoni Valley near Hemet in 1993, shortly before reservoir construction commenced. An abandoned chicken ranch can be seen in the foreground.

Finally, the Met spent more than $10 million to buy the four-square-mile ranch in between the two reservoirs, creating a continuous fourteen-square-mile preserve stretching from Hemet south toward Temecula.

With more goodwill in the bank, in 1992 the Met began to acquire the Domenigoni Valley property from families that had farmed there for a century—most by purchase, some by hostile eminent domain. (In 1995, a Riverside County court ruled that the Domenigoni family should receive more than $40 million for the property, six times what the Met had offered. This led the Met to change the name to the Eastside Reservoir.) The reservoir will be created not by damming a river canyon, as most reservoirs are created, but simply by constructing two huge walls along the sides of the valley, both around two miles long, and then filling it with Feather and Colorado River water. Construction on Domenigoni began in 1995, and is scheduled to be finished by 1999, after which it will take five years to fill.

Some water-oriented environmentalists criticized the reservoir, calling it unnecessary and too expensive. But "water" environmentalists in Southern California don't get nearly as much publicity as "land" environmentalists. It's hard to get on television by complaining about the cost of regional water resources, but it's easy to get on TV by protesting construction of new subdivisions on pretty pieces of property such as the Santa Rosa Plateau. Whatever the implications of Eastside Reservoir on the future growth of Southern California—and on the pressure for urban growth in environmentally sensitive areas in the region—the "land" environmentalists now loved the Met. "To me," said one, "the most important question is, were conservation goals advanced. And Greg Taylor has turned these projects into conservation opportunities."

While characteristic of the Boronkay approach, Domenigoni was not the whole story. The Boronkay agenda had one other component that could hardly have been a surprise to anyone who knew the Met's history. Having brought Domenigoni to the verge of construction, he had to find a new source of water to fill it, the equivalent of another Feather or Colorado River. He had an idea where the water might be found. But in order to succeed, Boronkay had to go back to the Delta and turn history upside-down.

⤺

Because he was not an engineer, Carl Boronkay did not automatically think in terms of building dams as a way to bring more water to Southern California. As a lawyer with thirty years' experience, he knew that changing a law could be just as effective. It is this insight, as much as anything else, that set him apart as a member of the Los Angeles growth machine.

From Boronkay's point of view, the best potential source of water, as big or bigger than some new river in Northern California, was the fourteen million acre-feet of water that Central Valley farmers were sitting on through their groundwater wells and their state and federal water contracts. The farmers were already under intense pressure from environmentalists to cut down on profligate use of water. And given the low cost of Central Valley water, many farmers could flip the liquid to the Met at an enormous profit.

The idea of "water transfers"—creating a statewide market for water somebody already held title to—was not new. Since the 1970s, some environmentalists had argued that water markets would encourage more efficient use, thereby reducing the need for new dams. In particular, water transfers were promoted by the Environmental Defense Fund, a creative organization that often dreamed up market-oriented solutions to environmental problems.

Shortly after becoming general manager, Boronkay became mesmerized by water transfers. "We got nervous about the future," he said. "We didn't see any major projects coming on line." And, he added: "The logic of these things was really compelling." In particular, he was impressed by economic analyses showing that the same amount of water that produces nine farm jobs produces three thousand urban jobs. Before long, Boronkay came to believe that water transfers were the best way to ensure Southern California's continued expansion.

He began working with EDF on a water trading plan with the Imperial Irrigation District, the agency that takes some of California's Colorado River water and sells it to farmers in the Imperial Valley. State water regulators had been pushing Imperial to line its earthen canals, and EDF proposed simply that the Met pay for the lining and use the conserved water in return. Water Buffaloes at both the Met and Imperial had blown the idea off. But Boronkay negotiated a deal, which brought the Met one hundred six thousand acre-feet of water a year, and, as in the Domenigoni Reservoir situation, lots of ink as an environmental good guy.

The Imperial Valley was small potatoes, however. Boronkay really had his eye on the Central Valley, where many farmers got water dirt-cheap from the federal government as part of the Central Valley Project. But he faced huge obstacles. Under CVP law, reselling federally subsidized water for profit was illegal. And even though individual farmers might profit from it, water marketing was a heresy to most California farming communities because it conjured up images of the Owens Valley being raped by Los Angeles.

Beginning in 1991, an opportunity emerged. Senator Bill Bradley of New Jersey became interested in Western water and began to promote a bill to reform the Central Valley Project. That same year, the chairmanship of the House Interior Committee, traditionally one of the chief protectors of Central Valley farming interests, passed to George Miller, a liberal Democrat from the Delta who had made environmental protection one of the cornerstones of his career.

Working together, Bradley and Miller had a huge agenda, but two of the items were an anathema to California's water establishment. One was a crackdown on large farmers who violated the federal government's acreage limit. The other was a plan to set aside a large amount of CVP water to improve the Delta's ecology.

Central Valley farmers immediately attacked the proposal, lining up Governor Pete Wilson and John Seymour, Wilson's hand-picked successor in the U.S. Senate. Seymour introduced an alternative to the Miller-Bradley bill with weaker environmental protections and fewer controls on CVP farmers.

Going into it, there was no question that the Met should have sided with the farmers and supported the Seymour bill. The board passed a resolution of support, and Boronkay says he tried to work with Seymour. But over time he became convinced that Seymour's bill wouldn't pass, and he began talking to Miller and Bradley. As one director recalled: "Carl totally ignored the board's action."

All through 1991, Boronkay edged the Met away from the farmers and closer to the Miller-Bradley bill. He moved gingerly, first committing the Met to the principle of water transfers, then using that principle to pull away from the farmers.

In the spring of 1991, Boronkay testified before Bradley's senate subcommittee on water and power, publicly advocating water transfers as a part of the CVP reform legislation. "Substantial increases in water transfers," he said, "will be essential as urban water agencies work to meet water needs during the 1990s and later."

It was an historic moment, because it indicated that, with the right deal, the Met might be willing to break with the growers. At the hearing, Boronkay recalled later, Bradley created a stir simply by greeting him warmly. "I'm sitting in the second row," he said. "The first row is all environmentalists. He stands up and turns around, and he leans over—remember, he's six-foot-seven or something—and shakes my hand. And there's this audible 'huh' in the crowd."

By fall, Boronkay had persuaded his board to adopt a policy stating that the agency would "vigorously pursue" the development of water transfers, primarily from agricultural users. A few months later, the Met board backed away from the Seymour bill altogether and agreed to support any CVP reform package that included water transfers, environmental protection, and CVP economic reforms.

The message between the lines was clear: Boronkay believed that his Feather River, his Colorado River, lay not in any stream or creek or aqueduct but in the wording of Central Valley Project water contracts.* The Met would not automatically side with the farmers. It would hold out for the best deal on water transfers, no matter the source.

---

* It is also worth noting that if the increased flow of water into the Delta for environmental reasons came from the Central Valley Project, which the Met was not part of, then that increased flow would likely not come from the State Water Project, on which the Met depended heavily.

Working with the Met's Washington lobbyists, Boronkay traveled to the Capitol frequently to lobby for the water transfer provisions. House staffers remember that the agency's understated influence was awesome. "It's an odd organization," one recalled. "Not like the AARP, flooding the place with letters and phone calls. It was only one or two people who wandered around. But they're like an eight-hundred-pound gorilla." Boronkay would come alone, or with a lobbyist; but everybody on Capitol Hill knew he represented fifteen million urban dwellers.

The longer the Met held out for water transfer provisions, the more important the Met became in the final outcome. By the fall of 1992, the Met was supporting a Miller-Bradley bill that set aside eight hundred thousand acre-feet of Central Valley Project water for environmental and wildlife purposes, established a $50 million environmental enhancement fund, cut CVP subsidies to farmers, and reduced the length of their contracts. In return, Miller, Bradley, and environmental groups supported provisions to allow CVP farmers to sell CVP water voluntarily to any urban water agency anywhere in California.

Congress approved the legislation in October 1992 and, despite Pete Wilson's pleas for a veto, President George Bush signed the bill just before the election. The alliance of thirty years had been shattered. The Met and the environmentalists had ganged up on the farmers and divvied up the spoils. As with Domenigoni, the Met got two seemingly contradictory things: the chance to bring more water to Southern California and an enhanced reputation as an environmental good guy. "There's not a representative from the Met that's welcome at any water district board meeting in the Central Valley," the CVP farmers' chief lobbyist said a few months later. "They've made themselves our enemy."

"I told the farmers, you haven't offended us," Carl Boronkay said in response. "We've just figured out where our interest is." That interest, as always, lay in the direction of finding water wherever it resided and moving it to Los Angeles by whatever technological, financial, or political means necessary. More than ever, however, there was now a price for pursuing that interest.

⁋

When Carl Boronkay retired as general manager of the Metropolitan Water District in the spring of 1993, William L. Kahrl of the *Sacramento Bee* called him "one of the most important big-time water developers in

California—the equal of William Mulholland and Pat Brown." Kahrl, who knows California water politics better than anyone, did not mean this as a compliment. Speaking with characteristic Northern Californian anger, Kahrl argued that Boronkay's actions on the Central Valley Project reform bill had turned all of California's agricultural areas into a water colony for Los Angeles.

In a way, Kahrl's angry editorial was proof that Boronkay had done his job. He had found his Feather River and, using his own particular skills, he had secured it for the future use of urban Southern California.* But, as Kahrl pointed out, Boronkay was really no different than Mulholland or Pat Brown or any of his predecessors. He had viewed his job as importing more water into Southern California. What Boronkay could not see, even with his skills as a lawyer and an understanding of environmental issues, was that this was no longer good enough because the growth machine was collapsing. Yet the consequences of the collapse were taking its toll on the Met and its board members.

During the drought, the Met's eternal spiral of more customers paying more money for more water ended. While this reversal helped the region through the drought, it was a financial disaster for the Met. Suddenly the Met was selling less water to its twenty-seven member agencies; but it still had to shoulder the fixed costs for its huge water-delivery infrastructure. With few revenue sources other than water sales, the Met began to raise rates.

The result was a deep division among the Met members, one that Boronkay readily acknowledges he ignored during his tenure. The agencies that had access to groundwater (and more than one million acre-feet of groundwater was available in Southern California) began threatening to abandon the Met altogether if the price increases didn't stop. But agencies completely dependent on the Met's imported water—especially San Diego, located "at the end of the pipe"—felt more vulnerable than ever.

* In the years following the 1992 Central Valley Project deal, the story of the Met and the Delta took many twists and turns. Few farmers proved willing to sell out to the Met, at least at first. The Republican Congress elected in 1994 appeared likely to reverse some of the law's water transfer provisions, but no action was taken. Most important, state and federal regulators reached a breakthrough agreement in 1994 on how to approach restoration of the Delta. As part of Carl Boronkay's legacy of gold-plated mitigation, the Met provided crucial funding at key points to help this process along.

At the same time, older cities such as Pasadena and Santa Monica began clamoring for a different rate structure. Under the Met's longstanding policy, everyone was charged a blended rate, meaning that all water customers paid equally for new facilities. But now the older cities were no longer willing to subsidize high-growth areas, such as Riverside County. They wanted high-growth areas to pay more, perhaps in the form of a connection fee for new hookups.

So in Boronkay's wake the agency belatedly undertook a wrenching re-examination of what it is and what it's supposed to do. Mike Gage, Mayor Bradley's voluble former chief of staff, briefly served as board chairman and began agitating for change. (See chapter 2, Perestroika Co-opted.) A new general manager, John Wodraska, was recruited from Florida, the first from outside California. Board membership turned over seventy percent in only three years, and bore little resemblance to the fossilized group of the past. And the Met began to examine how to deal with a future of shrinking water supplies, a growing population, and no reliable set of political allies.

It was not long, however, before the Met began to fly apart. Ironically, the crisis was precipitated by a water-marketing idea that emerged from Boronkay's work.

Shortly after his arrival, Wodraska began playing a complicated, long-term game of water acquisition as ambitious as any of his predecessors'. Among other things, he sought to persuade the Interior Department to give the Met priority on some of the water in the Colorado Reservoir, and he made a deal to ship some water to Las Vegas as the price of Nevada's support. (This move eventually fell apart. See chapter 12, Cloning Los Angeles.)

During this same period, however, the Imperial Valley acquired a new pair of landowning "farmers" who understood the potential of selling water: Sid and Lee Bass, the Fort Worth-based speculators who had made a fortune in greenmail. The Bass brothers bought up forty thousand acres of land in the Imperial Valley and began peddling the Colorado River water rights for $400 an acre-foot, or about thirty-five times the amount they paid the federal government.

The Met turned down the Bass brothers, and so did Las Vegas. Then the Basses tried ever-vulnerable San Diego and hit the jackpot. With the Met splitting into "haves" and "have-nots," San Diego moved quickly to accept the offer as a way, albeit expensive, to win more independence from the Los Angeles water barons. San Diego then demanded that the Met use the Colorado Aqueduct to ship the water to San Diego, instead of shipping the Met's own water.

Suddenly, the very idea that Carl Boronkay had promoted in order to save the Met—transferring water from farms to cities—was pulling it apart. San Diego accounts for twenty-five percent of the Met's water sales, providing the agency with a critical source of revenue. Without San Diego as a customer, the Met faced the possibility of winding up without enough water on hand to fill the Eastside Reservoir, or enough money to pay back the $2 billion in bonds floated to build it.

Back to Joe Jensen and before, the Met's Water Buffaloes had acted with unwavering confidence in an ever-expanding future for Southern California fueled by an ever-expanding water supply. While recognizing that the 1980s were not the 1950s or the 1920s, Carl Boronkay had not really changed the equation. He set his sights on Domenigoni, garnishing it with environmental mitigation to make it more palatable, because his engineers said the project was needed. He pursued water transfers with the tenacity and singularity of purpose that William Mulholland had once exhibited in pursuing the Owens River.

Now, in the 1990s, the Met is paying the price for its inability to see the collapse of the growth machine—or its own vulnerability as a critical component of it. Too often in Los Angeles the quest for water itself, like the quest for growth, has overshadowed the consequences of its pursuit. As the San Diego episode reveals, the L.A. growth machine's most elegant creations can be used against the machine itself when the consensus for growth breaks down. Even surrounded by kangaroo rat preserves and the loving reviews of local environmentalists, Eastside Reservoir—full or empty, solvent or bankrupt—may stand as silent testimony to the folly of this pursuit.

CHAPTER 5

The Money Train

There is probably no more peculiar feeling in all of Southern California than riding on a train. Traveling along the backsides of industrial buildings in Northridge, or slipping underneath downtown's Wilshire Boulevard, or passing the county courthouse in troubled Compton, the feeling a rail rider gets is not fear or frustration, relief or relaxation, but sheer irrelevance. Somewhere, a great city is pulsating toward the beginning or ending of another day. In that world, everyone is hooked in with everyone else, constantly monitoring the metropolis around them. The middle-class masses are pushing along the freeways in their cars, listening to reports from traffic helicopters, or scanning lanes in the rear-view mirror, or yelling at their kids on a cellular phone. Even in the middle of a freeway-stopping traffic jam, there's a sense of urgency, a feeling that things are happening, that people must keep moving forward for the metropolis to survive.

Freeway travel is often viewed as a precondition for understanding the Los Angeles experience. Unless you are on a freeway, most observers have concluded, you are not really participating in the city's daily life, nor can you understand its magical allure. "As you acquire the special skills involved," Reyner Banham wrote in 1971, at the height of the city's love affair with them, "the Los Angeles freeways become a special way of being alive." Freeways have come to define Los Angeles in the popular mind so completely that even the O.J. Simpson saga could not be viewed as a true Los Angeles story until it included a surreal road trip worthy of Nathaniel West or Joan Didion.

The trains, on the other hand, seem quieter even when they're crowded, and slower even when they're moving fast. For most people, trains are inconvenient; among millions of possible destinations in the vast Southern California urban landscape, roads provide transportation to virtually all of them, while trains stop at only a few. There's something futile about riding a train in Los Angeles, something unsettling and out of step, and most of all there's a feeling that one is engaged in an activity that is profoundly un-Angeleno.

So it's something of a surprise to roll past the quasi-industrial and mostly poor neighborhoods north and east of downtown and see a brand-new skyscraper going up just to the east of the tracks. Trains in Los Angeles generally run through industrial neighborhoods or along concrete riverbeds, while glitzy skyscrapers are off in the distance, alongside wide automobile boulevards and massive parking garages. But this particular skyscraper isn't near the others. It's separated by a mile or so from the grove of tall buildings in the downtown financial district further west. In fact, it is being built hard alongside the tracks at Union Station, the last, and most pointless, magnificent train station ever built in the United States.

The skyscraper provides a symbol for those who would redefine Los Angeles so that it does not revolve around the freeways. The building is the headquarters of the Los Angeles Metropolitan Transportation Authority. Folly or not, it stands as a reminder that, as the Southern California growth machine has collapsed, the region has bet tens of billions of dollars—more, probably, than has ever been spent on the imported water that made the megalopolis possible—on the proposition that somehow or other riding on trains can save Los Angeles.

～

Los Angeles's status as the world's pre-eminent car-oriented city was by no means pre-ordained. It's true that the region's topography creates a natural set of transportation arteries radiating from downtown. But these roadways, as Reyner Banham pointed out, constitute a "transportation palimpsest"—a natural tablet written upon, over and over again, to provide routes for wagons, railroads, interurbans, surface streets, and freeways. Nothing about it is inherently auto-oriented. Los Angeles emerged as the prototypical automobile city for other reasons, including the peculiar aspirations of its settlers, the time in history that

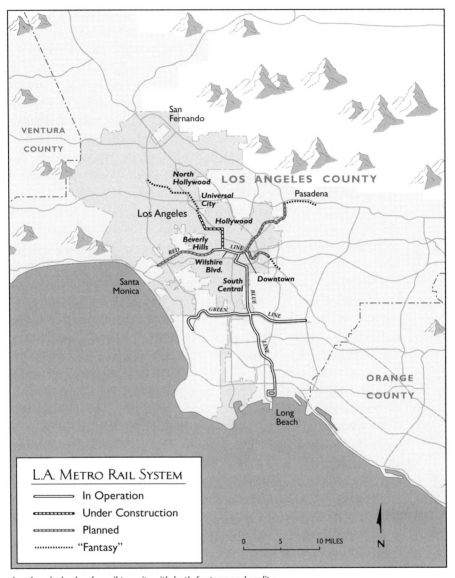

Los Angeles's plan for rail transit, with both fantasy and reality.

L.A. grew to significance, and, not least, the way members of the growth machine used the region as a vehicle for real estate speculation.

The first big real estate boom came in the 1880s, when competing rail connections from St. Louis drove the price of a one-way ticket down to a dollar. Faced with a massive influx of immigrants from the

Midwest, the city's fledgling growth merchants had to choose between growing up or growing out. Eager to market land in outlying areas, they chose to grow outward, using the then-new technology of street railways to achieve their goal.

Thus, the Los Angeles growth machine was born, along with its most enduring unspoken principle: that it is possible to perpetuate profit forever by expanding the city endlessly outward, consuming land along the way. And to satisfy the goals of the growth machine, the primary purpose of transportation would not be to move people to and fro on a daily basis, but to lure them to otherwise inaccessible areas where they could buy property in new subdivisions.*

The city did not have much of a settled urban form prior to the arrival of the street railway and the real estate speculators who thrived on it. Though downtown Los Angeles was the region's crucial hub up through the 1920s, it had nothing like the cachet of Manhattan or close-in areas of Boston and Philadelphia, which had been centers of commerce and culture for hundreds of years. (A downtown height limit, imposed in part to encourage the city to spread out, also contributed to this phenomenon.) Unlike other American cities, Los Angeles began decentralizing before it had been able to centralize.

Decentralization succeeded not only because of the emergence of the street railway, but because the growth machine knew how to use it and immigrants were receptive to the idea. From the 1880s onward, real estate speculators created highly sophisticated techniques for marketing outlying land. The rail lines were usually paid for by the landowners, and wiggled oddly on the landscape in order to reach the property of everyone who'd paid. (The arcing balloon shape of modern Santa Monica Boulevard, which follows an interurban route, is a relic of this practice.) And the landowners themselves were really part of a cartel—the original members of the growth machine—which worked in harmony to market their property.

As conceived by Harry Chandler, real estate magnate and publisher of the *Los Angeles Times*, every member of the growth machine had a role to play in promoting development: bankers, newspaper pub-

---

* This idea was not unique. All through the nineteenth century, American railroads were used in a speculative manner to move people westward. And in the East and Midwest, the street railway was used as a tool for suburban real estate speculation as well.

lishers, title insurers, politicians, and especially streetcar builders. Without an orchestrated effort (and, especially, without the streetcar builder), the profitable expansion of the metropolis could not be achieved. "It would never do for an electric line to wait until the demand for it came," streetcar tycoon Henry E. Huntington, who made most of his money in real estate, said in 1904. "It must anticipate the growth of communities and be there when the homebuilders arrive—or they are very likely not to arrive at all, but to go to some section already provided with arteries of traffic." It was Huntington's way of restating William Mulholland's philosophy: "If we don't get it, we won't need it."

And to the arriving hordes of Midwesterners, many of whom had cashed handsomely out of the family farm, the new subdivisions offered exactly what they wanted: a reminder of a rural past without the harsh realities of the hardscrabble life they'd left behind. The popularity of the car was the *result* of L.A.'s suburban ethos, not its cause.

The net effect was a decentralized city unlike any other in America. As Robert Fogelson pointed out in his seminal book *The Fragmented Metropolis,* by 1930 the ratio of population density between the central city and the outlying suburbs was less than 3 to 1 in Los Angeles, compared with 30 to 1 in San Francisco, 26 to 1 in New York, 23 to 1 in St. Louis, and 15 to 1 in Philadelphia, which was then considered a sprawling city of single-family homes. Yet while the population was radically dispersed, most people continued to work and shop (at least until the 1920s) in the downtown area, much like residents of more conventional cities. A city with so much commuting was obviously far more dependent on streetcars than a typical city, and for this reason the operation of L.A.'s two major streetcar companies was a public obsession, especially in the first two decades of the twentieth century.

The streetcar era in Los Angeles was dominated by Henry Huntington, who built a $60 million real estate fortune around the Pacific Electric in a little more than a decade. A nephew of Collis Huntington, the head of the Southern Pacific Railroad, Henry Huntington incorporated the Pacific Electric in 1901 and eventually built the PE's "Red Cars" into the largest interurban rail system in the country—more than eleven hundred miles stretching from Santa Monica to San Bernardino and from the San Gabriel Mountains to Newport Beach. In 1911, Huntington consolidated his operations with the Los Angeles Railway Company, the streetcar system that served urban Los Angeles. After this merger, the daily functioning of America's fastest-growing city was almost entirely dependent on the business decisions of Henry Huntington and his managers. And while he ran his operations more efficiently than most of his counterparts elsewhere in the country, Huntington was always more interested in the streetcar as a real estate device than as a transportation service.

Not surprisingly given the city's urban form, streetcar travel in and out of downtown became intolerable. Virtually every streetcar line ran through the downtown, and the mixing of large PE interurbans with smaller Los Angeles Railway streetcars on busy streets caused extensive delays. It would often take a PE Red Car longer to leave the downtown area than to make the entire run to Pasadena or Santa Monica.

Despite complaints about the system and the service, the PE and LARY operated throughout much of the streetcar era with very little public oversight. When the Progressive political movement took over City Hall in 1906, one of its most important actions was to create a Board of Public Utility Commissioners to regulate the city's gas, electric, telephone, and streetcar utilities. But the board did not deal aggressively with street railway issues, so middle-class commuters lost faith in the Progressives' ability to solve the city's transportation problems. By the 1910s, however, middle-class commuters had already obtained the means of their liberation: the car.

⌣

The Los Angeles middle class embraced the car earlier and more quickly than residents of any other city in the country except Detroit, where the cars were made. As early as 1915, Angelenos were five times more likely than Americans in general to own a car, and almost eight times more likely than residents of Chicago. And then the real boom occurred. According to one estimate, there were nine streetcar commuters for every driving commuter in 1920; four years later, the ratio was almost one to one. By 1925, Los Angeles already boasted more than one car for every two residents, essentially a car in every garage.

The traffic volume and traffic jams created by this rapid rise in automobile use were staggering. As historian Kevin Starr has pointed out, by the end of 1924 more cars traveled in and out of downtown Los Angeles each day (310,000) than were registered in the entire state of New York. And these cars were not traveling unimpeded on modern highways. They competed with hundreds of streetcars and PE interurbans which had stretched the street system to its breaking point even before the cars came.

In spite of the congestion, middle-class commuters embraced the automobile for the simple reason that it freed them from the clutches of the growth machine. Frustrated by crowded streetcars and bad service, angry that the city's growth brokers would rather

Streetcar days: A congested street corner in downtown Los Angeles.

expand the system outward than improve service on existing lines, the middle class turned to the car as an act of rebellion. "The individual citizen began using his car because the reform movement could not assert its control over the traction companies," wrote Los Angeles transportation historian Scott Bottles. "By jumping in their cars, urban denizens thumbed their noses at their long-standing antagonist—the railway executive."

In short, the switch represented a rejection of the growth machine every bit as intense and emotional as the slow-growth movement of the 1980s. The irony was that, in this very act of rebellion, the growth machine found the basis for its own perpetuation.

By freeing commuters from the street railway, the car freed real estate speculators as well. No longer did employment or shopping districts have to be conveniently located along streetcar lines. Now they could be literally anywhere, as long as they were within easy commuting distance by car. Over the next several decades, this revelation would have a profound impact on the urban form of Los Angeles and, indeed, of all American cities. In the 1920s, however, this trend was foreshadowed by creating decentralization of shopping districts to an unprecedented degree.

The area west of downtown along Wilshire Boulevard became the first serious competitor to downtown entirely because of the car. In 1921, drawing a line around several affluent residential areas, developer A.W. Ross realized that they were all within easy driving distance of the bean fields at Wilshire Boulevard and Fairfax Avenue. So he developed a new shopping district there which eventually came to be known as Miracle Mile. Parking lots were placed behind the stores, and on-street parking was banned along Wilshire to ease traffic. The landmark Ambassador Hotel opened on Wilshire Boulevard that same year. And in 1929, the Bullocks department store also broke with tradition, building the magnificent Art Deco department store on Wilshire Boulevard, complete with porte-cochere and parking lot behind.* "For the first time in urban history," wrote Kevin Starr, "a city was building itself around the automobile."

In succeeding decades, decentralization became a self-accelerating cycle, as residential subdivisions moved farther and farther away from the center of the city, followed by shopping centers and office buildings chasing them across the landscape. This outward push-and-pull, facilitated by the automobile and by a system of land economics that seeks cheap land for new houses, lay at the heart of the growth machine's quest for profit.

City planners and politicians, paralyzed by the political infighting involved in improving transportation in downtown Los Angeles, welcomed decentralization. They had successfully updated and improved the street system in the 1920s, but their attempts to create a comprehensive solution to improve mobility stalled.

In 1925, transportation experts R.F. Kelker and Charles DeLeuw proposed a comprehensive transportation plan for Los Angeles that called for constructing an extensive rail system, which would probably be elevated through the downtown area to separate it from traffic, as well as rail extensions to Hollywood and the San Fernando Valley.

The Kelker-DeLeuw plan met stiff opposition, because it proposed elevated railways. Then it evaporated into a political conflagration over rerouting trains from L.A.'s three transcontinental railroads, which at the time used city streets to enter downtown. In 1926, a plebiscite overwhelmingly supported the construction of Union Station on the edge of downtown, ending plans to build an elevated system above downtown streets. But by the time it opened in 1939, Union Station was practically

* Wilshire Boulevard retains its flavor today as the first car-oriented commercial corridor. In addition to Bullocks' Wilshire building (which closed in 1992) and many outstanding commercial buildings in the Miracle Mile area, Wilshire Boulevard contains many of the best examples of early small shopping centers with parking courts, such as the Chapman Market on Sixth Street, recently restored by developer Wayne Ratkovich.

obsolete and in the wrong place. Meanwhile, LARY and PE traffic dropped precipitously, from one million passengers a day in the peak year of 1924 to half that a decade later.*

Unlike the debacle over rail transit, the city and the region proved remarkably savvy at forging a consensus for accommodating the car. In large part, this consensus was a tribute to the organizing skill of the Automobile Club of Southern California, which quickly became the region's most influential transportation organization. In 1937, when traffic congestion was again reaching intolerable levels all over the city, the Auto Club proposed a breakthrough of breathtaking proportions— "a network of traffic routes for the exclusive use of motor vehicles over which there shall be no crossing at grade and along which there shall be no interference from land use activities." The Auto Club's accompanying "Map Showing General Location of Proposed Motorways in the Los Angeles Metropolitan Area" outlined, almost exactly, the Los Angeles freeway system as it was eventually realized.

Limited-access highways had already been built in many locations. But nothing of this scope had ever been proposed before. After conducting a traffic survey that revealed dismal conditions (motorists spent thirty percent of their time waiting at intersections, for example), both city and county embraced the idea.

Making the freeways a reality took some time. Financially, building the system was beyond the capacity of local government, to say nothing of the real estate speculators who comprised the heart of the growth machine. And while the state Division of Highways expanded the state highway system during the Depression, it balked for many years at taking responsibility for urban highways. But in 1947, the state legislature approved the Collier-Burns Act, which increased the state tax on gasoline sales and placed the revenue in a special trust fund for highway construction. Aided by the federal Interstate Highway Act of 1956, which provided up to ninety percent of the funding for certain routes, the Collier-Burns Act touched off the golden age of freeway con-

---

* The problem of at-grade rail crossings also contributed to the decline of urban rail in Los Angeles. A city so dependent on automobiles was, unsurprisingly, little tolerant of commuting delays caused by passing interurbans. And to avoid accidents with cars, interurbans slowed down at crossings, thus making trips longer—and making car trips faster by comparison. Ironically, most at-grade crossing problems resulted from the arrival of roads for automobiles, which were built after the rail lines.

Construction on the Hollywood Freeway plows through an urban neighborhood near downtown Los Angeles.

struction. Virtually the entire Southern California freeway system was built in twenty years, between 1950 and 1970.

By bringing new areas within commuting distance of existing job centers, the freeways created a new generation of opportunity for the growth machine, which, in turn, exploded in size and sophistication in the 1950s and 1960s. Best of all for the growth machine, this new era of transportation construction was self-financing. People wanted to drive cars so much that they willingly paid enough gas tax to build and maintain new roads. No subsidy from developers was needed. "In the mid-1960s, when I was on the California Highway Commission," Joseph C. Houghteling once wrote, "it was believed with some justification that there was a perpetual-motion money machine in the back room. This marvelous mechanism cranked out gas tax revenues that constructed freeways that promoted higher consumption of gasoline that generated more gas tax revenues to construct more freeways *ad infinitum*. Platoons of surveyors were dotting California's landscape with straight-lined markers, presaging the construction to follow."

Freeways became the perfect metaphor for a sprawling, indecipherable city built on the idea of constant movement. Some writers viewed the freeway system as a critical organizing element, giving the region a shape and structure it simply did not have in the days of willy-nilly subdivision in the 1920s and 1930s. "As the end result of the automotive revolution, the freeway system has tended to stabilize a particular order of social change," wrote essayist David Brodsly. Others simply celebrated the rapture of driving on the freeway. "Actual participation requires a total surrender," Joan Didion wrote in 1976, "a concentration so intense as to seem a kind of narcosis, a rapture-of-the-freeway. The mind goes clean. The rhythm takes over."

Still others saw freeways as the defining aspect of Southern California life, a thesis that met with astonishing validation. In 1966, the magazine *Cry California* published an interview with Frank and Marilee Ferrier, a middle-class couple who lived in a camper and traveled the freeways constantly. In extreme detail, Frank and Marilee described how they shuttled between Frank's job at Lockheed in Burbank, Marilee's mother's house in West Covina (where they did the laundry), and a downtown parking lot where they spent each night near Frank's second job. After an explosion of publicity, *Cry California* had to admit that the story was a hoax. "What was designed as a satire," the writer said, "was too close to the truth."

Finally, in the mid-1970s, the well ran dry, when the California Department of Transportation—Caltrans, as it is universally known—stopped building new freeways. Even worse, under the administration of Governor Jerry Brown, Caltrans began taking them *away*. The most famous example was the case of the so-called "Diamond Lane," a special lane on the Santa Monica Freeway which was closed to regular traffic and reserved only for buses and three-person carpools. The resulting public outcry was so intense that it undermined the authority of Brown's Caltrans director, Adriana Gianturco, and gave carpool lanes a taint that still exists in Southern California today.

But Jerry Brown's ideology was only part of the story. The reason Caltrans wasn't building more freeways was that the perpetual-motion money machine in the back room stopped pumping. The equilibrium between gas tax revenues and the cost of planning and constructing freeways was overturned by a series of events in the early 1970s: the Arab oil embargo, the recessions of 1969–70 and 1974–75, environmental regulations, and Caltrans labor contracts. Caltrans simply couldn't afford to build more freeways, and the ones that were built took a lot longer to complete. (Halted by litigation from poverty lawyers who wanted the agency to replace demolished housing units, the Century Freeway took more than twenty years to finish.) When population and driving began to rise again in the late 1970s, the freeway system could not keep up with demand, and traffic congestion grew measurably worse all over the region.

It was during this period, too, that the car in general and freeways in particular began to take the blame for a panoply of urban ills. Contrary to the original expectations of L.A.'s urban planners, freeways accelerated urban decay by cutting up city neighborhoods, making it easier to flee to the suburbs. And tailpipe emissions from cars were identified as one of the leading sources of Southern California's now-characteristic "smog," the worst urban air pollution problem in the country.

At the same time, the politics of transportation nostalgia began to gather force. Because the Red Cars had been gone for a long time, few people remembered how slow or cumbersome they had been, or the problems they created at grade crossings. Now the Red Cars became the focal point of a time-weathered view that somehow things were better in the old days, when Los Angeles wasn't big and bustling. All of a sudden trains didn't look so bad.

When this political opportunity presented itself, one wealthy and powerful group in Los Angeles was ready to pounce. This was a coalition of business leaders from downtown and the Wilshire Boulevard corridor. Once the beneficiaries of the growth machine's efforts, they were now the victims of its endless outward path, losing business and traffic to suburbanization every day. Downtown, for example, lost twenty percent of its traffic between 1941 and 1955. And Wilshire Boulevard, ironically, quickly ceased to be competitive with newer and more modern auto-oriented areas in the suburbs farther out.

Ever since the Kelker-DeLeuw report in 1925, the downtown business community had continued to push hard for a rail system. Beginning in the 1960s, when it became clear that a rail system could not be privately financed, downtown-Wilshire business leaders began to lobby for government help. The vehicle that they wanted to use to build the system was the Southern California Rapid Transit District. Created in 1964 after a lengthy fight in the legislature, the RTD was charged with running the existing transit system, now made up entirely of buses. (The last Red Car line, to Long Beach, shut down in 1961; the final trolley rolled into the Vernon car barn in 1963.) But its real task was to make sure that the downtown-Wilshire subway was built. The RTD was controlled by city and county offi-

The interchange of the Interstate 10 and Interstate 110 near downtown Los Angeles.

cials in Los Angeles County, who appointed board members. And the new RTD was given the power to submit tax proposals to the voters. Shortly after its formation, the RTD set for itself the task of winning voter approval for a rail plan.

From the beginning, however, the RTD had to contend with opposition from politicians in outlying areas. It was no surprise that these politicians opposed a rail system, for they were literally the children of decentralization. Their towns had grown rapidly, thanks to the car. And they had been empowered politically under the Lakewood system, which allowed them independence from downtown. They simply didn't see how their cities would benefit from rail construction.

Suburban politicians were not the only obstacle to downtown rail. Because it ran a large bus system, the RTD also became a vehicle for the political activism of two other groups—groups that did not necessarily share the business leaders' rail agenda, but whose power and influence grew as a result of the RTD's creation. These were the bus riders and the transit unions.

Using state and federal subsidies, the RTD had bought up local bus companies throughout Southern California and integrated them into its regional system. This ended the isolation of transit-dependent minority residents of the south and east sides—isolation which had contributed to the civil unrest of the 1960s.* Between 1966 and 1978, ridership doubled to more than three-quarters of a million passengers per day, and the RTD became a lifeline to poor and working-class people who didn't have cars.

Just as important as the riders, however, were the unions. As the RTD grew larger and better financed, it became a key source of high-paying union jobs for blacks, furthering another social goal that had grown in significance because of the civil rights movement and the Watts riots. By the 1970s, some ninety percent of the RTD's employees were unionized—strikes were frequent—and a third were black.

Thus, from the very beginning, the downtown-Wilshire agenda of using the RTD to construct a rail system always had to be balanced against a whole series of competing agendas: bus drivers and other unionized transit workers who wanted higher wages; poor and working-

* Later, the RTD spun off several transit agencies in outlying areas such as Orange County, Riverside, San Bernardino, and the San Gabriel Valley.

class bus patrons who wanted better day-to-day service; and suburban politicians who had no desire to increase the power of the central city.

Throughout the 1960s and 1970s, a political consensus for a rail system was never reached. A campaign to enact a half-cent sales tax to finance construction failed in 1968, and a similar campaign, this time calling for a one-cent sales tax, was defeated in 1974, despite vigorous support from the newly elected Tom Bradley, who committed himself to reviving the downtown. One final gasp came in 1976, when County Supervisor Baxter Ward, a San Fernando Valley suburbanite but a rail buff, placed yet another tax measure on the ballot that would have financed a suburb-oriented system. The measure lost easily.

After the defeat of the Baxter Ward plan, two new developments helped lay the foundation for a political deal that seemed to work. First, the RTD devised a new and somewhat different subway proposal. And second, the state legislature, frustrated by RTD's inability to get the job done, created an entirely new entity devoted to transportation planning, the Los Angeles County Transportation Commission.

The RTD's Red Line proposal, unveiled in 1978, was shaped partly by the need to win the backing of several important politicians, especially the powerful State Senator David Roberti of Hollywood. Serving downtown and part of the Wilshire corridor, the Red Line also veered north to include Hollywood and the San Fernando Valley, home to an important suburban-style constituency in the City of Los Angeles. At the same time, the RTD was able to interest federal transportation officials in financing part of the Red Line. Every dollar that Washington provided was a dollar that didn't have to come from taxpayers in the suburbs.

Meanwhile, the L.A. County Transportation Commission emerged as a rival power center to the RTD, especially for some politicians from outlying areas who wanted rail transit funding sprinkled more broadly around the county.

In early 1980, the Transportation Commission staff proposed yet another sales tax election, this time suggesting a half-cent sales tax, which would produce several hundred million dollars a year. Some of the revenue would underwrite the Red Line, but a lot would go for a wide-ranging light rail system in the suburbs.

Ward, who supported the plan, short-circuited the predictable opposition from other suburban politicians in a very clever way: He proposed that some portion of the remaining funds be turned over to local cities for whatever transit projects they chose. And to satisfy bus riders, Ward made a deal with with Kenny Hahn, the popular county supervisor from South Central. A public works builder of the old school, Hahn liked the light rail plan—indeed, at his insistence a map of the rail system was included in the tax proposal. But he wanted to make sure his bus-riding constituents got something as well. So, in exchange for Hahn's support for the tax proposal, Ward agreed that some of the money, in addition to building a light rail system and financing local transit operations, would be used to lower RTD bus fares from 85 to 50 cents for three years.

In November 1980, while the anti-government Angeleno Ronald Reagan was being elected president, Proposition A passed easily. The political deal had been consummated. A huge light rail system would be built in the suburbs. Suburban cities would receive money for their own transit programs. Bus riders would have cheap fares, at least for a while. And all of these other things would create enough political equilibrium for the downtown-Wilshire business interests to build a subway. But such a complicated deal was not deep enough or strong enough to withstand the pressures that lay ahead.

⌐⌐

"I've written dozens of stories on the subject," wrote *L.A. Times* political columnist Bill Boyarsky ten years later, "but I've never been able to understand why the dispute goes on."

The dispute Boyarsky was referring to was the decade-long feud between the RTD and the Transportation Commission. The feud was touched off by the passage of Proposition A, which gave the Transportation Commission tremendous financial control over transit investments in Los Angeles. It was eventually won, more or less, by the Transportation Commission. But along the way, it just about destroyed the credibility of public transportation in Los Angeles, and especially the idea of a rail system. And it proved how fragile the political deal made in 1980 really was.

On the surface, the feud seemed foolish. Though they had somewhat different functions, both agencies were devoted to countywide transportation. Furthermore, their boards were selected by exactly the same political power centers: the L.A. County supervisors, the Los Angeles mayor, and the smaller cities in Los Angeles County. Yet the feud's depth and durability was astonishing.

One reason was that the passage of Proposition A had changed the debate about public transit into a high-stakes game. For more than a half century, transit had been a political loser, little more than a social services backwater assisting those too poor to have a car. Now, however, the Transportation Commission was a powerful agency with a half-billion dollars a year or more sloshing through it—much of it earmarked for contractors, bond houses, consultants, and others who could provide important campaign contributions for local politicians. For the RTD these changes posed a serious threat. Proposition A diverted attention from the Wilshire subway, established the light rail system as a competitor for public attention and public money, and placed the RTD under the Transportation Commission's thumb because the commission had to approve RTD's bus subsidies.

And the rivalry was made worse by the huge cultural schism between the two agencies at the staff level. Working out of a windowless building on Main Street near Skid Row, the RTD thought of itself as decidedly blue-collar. As the unionized successor to generations of trolley and bus companies, the agency was large and labor-intensive, almost New Yorkish in style. Having lived through a series of strikes, RTD managers saw everything through the prism of managing union labor.

Furthermore, both RTD's managers and board members—many of whom were part of the downtown-Wilshire power structure—were firmly committed to building the Wilshire subway, believing it to be a logical extension of the overburdened bus system. They viewed the countywide light rail system as folly and their Transportation Commission counterparts as pointy-headed planners.

The staff of the Transportation Commission, by contrast, saw the RTD as bloated and inefficient. Operating out of a series of white-collar office buildings in more fashionable areas of downtown, they saw their organization, at least at first, as "lean and mean." They were few in number, highly educated, and non-unionized. And, of course, they were not responsible for the daily operation of a huge bus system running at a loss. Freer to dream, they were determined to build a countywide light rail system quickly and cheaply and use it to change the course of the whole region's development.

From the time of Proposition A's passage, then, the RTD played a defensive game—seeking to fend off Transportation Commission planners, keep the bus system running with a minimum of labor problems, and, most of all, build the Wilshire subway at all costs. Four months after Proposition A passed, the RTD hired as its executive director John Dyer, a smooth-talking Tennesseean who had succeeded in constructing a rail system in Miami. Dyer immediately stated that better bus service was his highest priority, but there was no question he had been hired to make sure that the Wilshire subway was built.

When the Proposition A bus subsidies went into effect in 1982,* RTD ridership rose dramatically, to more than one-and-a-half-million boardings a day. Yet during this period, Dyer typically spent part of every week in Washington, lobbying Congress and the Reagan Administration for money for the Wilshire subway. It was an uphill battle, because President Reagan was cutting back on federal funding for rail projects. All through Reagan's first term, Dyer was unable to secure a long-term deal with Washington, and construction was delayed.

But it was still easier for Dyer to squeeze money for the Wilshire subway from the Reagan Administration than from his crosstown rivals at the Transportation Commission, who were pursuing their own agenda. While he was lobbying Washington to build the Red Line, the Transportation Commission was determined to use Proposition A money to show that it was possible to build a rail system in Los Angeles— any rail system.

The completion of the San Diego Trolley in 1981 put tremendous pressure on Los Angeles to duplicate the feat. The San Diego system didn't solve any particular transportation needs, but it had been built cheaply and quickly, and it soon became a source of civic pride. San Diego's achievement bred envy among Los Angeles politicians. Waxing nostalgic about the Red Line era, Assemblyman Bruce Young of Norwalk, chairman of the Assembly Transportation Committee, questioned the wisdom of expensive subways, and insisted that "San Diego has pointed the way." Supervisor Kenny Hahn, the godfather of Proposition A, was more insistent. "We've been dilly-dallying in this county for the last thirty-five to forty years with studies," Hahn fumed shortly after Proposition A passed. "Let's take the bull by the horns and get going." It was no coincidence, of course, that the most probable quick-and-

---

* The bus subsidies had been held up by a court challenge, brought by the Transportation Commission itself to determine whether the sales tax measure was exempt from Proposition 13, the 1978 initiative that subjected many new taxes to a two-thirds vote requirement. In 1982, the California Supreme Court ruled that simple majority passage was sufficient.

dirty solution was the old Red Car route to Long Beach, which went through the heart of both Hahn's and Young's districts.

In early 1985, using money freed up from the end of its three-year bus subsidy, the Transportation Commission approved the downtown-to-Long Beach light rail line. Expected to cost $700 million (it eventually came to almost $900 million), the twenty-two-mile line would serve approximately thirty-five thousand passengers per day, about half the number carried by buses along Wilshire Boulevard. At the same time, the Transportation Commission continued to plan for a vast web of light rail lines all over metropolitan Los Angeles.

Dyer, meanwhile, did not obtain a funding commitment from Washington for the Red Line until the summer of 1986. Ground was broken in September 1986, almost a year after the groundbreaking for the Blue Line. Now the two agencies were engaged in separate rail construction activities. But by then it was too late for the RTD. The problems of the nation's largest bus system, and the political opportunities those problems provided, spelled the end.

All through 1986 and into 1987, while Dyer was wrapping up the Metro Rail deal, the RTD was plagued with highly publicized personnel and operational problems. One bus guided by an inexperienced driver flipped over on the Hollywood Freeway; in another incident two RTD buses collided, injuring more than two dozen people. Several other bus drivers were found to be operating buses without valid licenses. Absenteeism and drug use were also problems. It wasn't long before RTD had become a convenient scapegoat for all of L.A.'s transit problems, especially among conservative politicians who wanted to break it up. RTD defenders say the problems were blown out of proportion. Nevertheless, they fed the Transportation Commission's view of the RTD as bungling and inept.

A year after the Red Line groundbreaking, Dyer took the fall for all the problems and quit. It would be five more years before the Transportation Commission and the RTD were fully merged into the Los Angeles Metropolitan Transportation Authority. But for all practical purposes, the war was over the day Dyer left.

⌐

The Transportation Commission's victory over the RTD ushered in an era best described as a bonfire of political vanities. In succeeding years, politicians from both the left and right seized on the Transportation

Commission's revenue stream and high profile to promote their own causes, usually to the detriment of the political deal that had initially created the agency.

The first person to move into the Transportation Commission with his own agenda was L.A. County Supervisor Pete Schabarum, a conservative ex-football player who had made anti-government rhetoric the centerpiece of a long career as an elected official. Schabarum disliked unions, and on the Board of Supervisors he championed the idea of "privatization," contracting out government services to private firms. He didn't have much success with the unmanageable Los Angeles County bureaucracy (see chapter 9, The Taking of Parcel K). But the Transportation Commission, which Schabarum chaired the year Dyer quit the RTD, was a different story. During his term as chairman, Schabarum ruthlessly used the Transportation Commission's newly won power to pursue his own political agenda.

First, he persuaded the commissioners to cancel a $20 million order for driver-operated rail cars on Green Line between L.A. International Airport and Norwalk, then in the planning stages, and switch to an untested automated technology that required no drivers. "Automated is an idea whose time has come," Schabarum said—meaning, quite simply, that he liked driverless cars because they would never go on strike.

Schabarum's second move was even more bold, because it struck directly at the heart of the RTD's union-labor culture. He established a set of pro-management labor rules that recipients of the Transportation Commission's money, principally RTD, had to follow. As part of the same initiative, he proposed privatizing the RTD's San Gabriel Valley service, spinning it off to a non-union organization.

All through the fall of 1988, while the RTD refused to adjust its labor contracts to meet new Transportation Commission policies, Schabarum held the agency's $9-million-a-month Proposition A subsidy hostage. The RTD threatened a fifty-percent cut in service and sued the Transportation Commission. Desperately, Mayor Tom Bradley, then under attack from Zev Yaroslavsky (see chapter 2), intervened and made a deal. The RTD labor contracts would stand as written. But the price was spinning off the San Gabriel Valley lines into a non-union Foothill Transit District, a stunning victory for Schabarum.

In transportation terms, Schabarum's initiatives were a mixed success. Foothill Transit became an outstanding example of the benefits of contracting out, providing excellent service at a lower cost. Driverless trains, on the other hand, never made much sense. Because of the two different technologies, airport travelers would have to change in Norwalk from driver-operated cars on the Blue Line to driverless cars on the Green Line.*

But transportation was beginning to matter less and less at the Transportation Commission. Schabarum had found an effective vehicle to move his anti-union agenda. And other politicians were recognizing that, with the RTD out of the way, the L.A. County Transportation Commission—soon to become the L.A. County Metropolitan Transportation Authority—had become the best political game in town.

When the Green Line's driverless cars were ordered from Sumitomo Corporation of Japan, Yaroslavsky and several other board members held up the sale, screaming about the need to "buy American." In 1991, when the recession hit Los Angeles County and the aerospace industry collapsed, Yaroslavsky and others pressured the Transportation Commission to finance economic research so that the aerospace companies could be re-tooled to manufacture parts for buses and rail cars. Indeed, all during the recession, the Transportation Commission and its rail construction projects were viewed, WPA-style, as one of the few glimmering hopes for re-energizing the economy.

During this period, the Transportation Commission and the RTD took their first steps toward a merger when many board members began to serve jointly on the boards of both organizations. This situation gave many rail advocates a broader forum to call for the construction of a rail system. Perhaps the strongest advocate was Nicholas Patsouras, a well-to-do Greek immigrant who served on both boards. Believing rail transit to be the solution to most of Los Angeles's urban ills, Patsouras tirelessly paraded a dog-and-pony show about the rail system at any public forum anywhere in the city for many years.

Patsouras's persistence, along with the RTD's decline, placed great political pressure on the Transportation Commission to mollify many political constituencies by promising many rail lines. The job of meeting these heightened political ambitions fell to Neal Peterson, who was hired as the Transportation Commission's executive director in 1989. Peterson had been credited with turning around transit systems in

---

* When it finally opened in 1995, the Green Line used human-driver technology.

Seattle and Oakland, and he proved to be a master salesman of rail transit in Los Angeles. Deftly playing a game of political chess, Peterson exploited the ambitions of his own board members in order to expand the scope and wealth of the agency. But in so doing, he left behind a financial time bomb that would almost wipe out the rail transit effort.

In 1990, the same year the Blue Line to Long Beach opened, the Transportation Commission persuaded voters to pass Proposition C, a second countywide half-cent sales tax. Proposition C increased the amount of local money available for transit programs, at least on paper, to nearly a billion dollars a year.

Peterson had engaged in lots of machinations even to get Proposition C on the ballot. Among other things, he had to fend off a competing wish by Sheriff Sherman Block to place a sales tax measure on the ballot to pay for jails. Once passed, however, Proposition C created another problem for Peterson: It attracted an ever-expanding political wish list from the politicians on the Transportation Commission's board. Peterson's solution was to promise the fulfillment of every politician's dream, no matter which part of the region the politician was from. In 1992, the Transportation Commission approved a broad-ranging thirty-year construction plan that encompassed some four hundred miles of track. By 2001, the new plan promised, the Transportation Commission would build lines to the Westside and Pasadena, a subway extension into East Los Angeles, a rail system across the San Fernando Valley, and a line running from Los Angeles International Airport some seventy-five miles north to Palmdale. Buoyed by Proposition C, the Transportation Commission worked with surrounding counties to establish a commuter rail system funneling downtown commuters from throughout the region into Union Station. While promising everything to everyone, the plan contained no demographic and economic forecasts on which to base these transportation decisions.

In the fall of 1992, the commuter rail system began operating. And in early 1993, after more than five years of construction, the first four-mile leg of the Red Line opened. At the same time, the Transportation Commission swallowed the enormous RTD bureaucracy, and the agency was rechristened the Metropolitan Transportation Authority. The new organization was not without problems: Peterson, for example, was bogged down by highly publicized criticism of costly trips and retreats for the executive staff. This mini-scandal knocked him out of the run-

Union Station, the last, and most pointless, magnificent train station ever built in the United States.

ning for the top job at the new MTA. Nevertheless, few politicians in town appeared to doubt the MTA's ability to deliver on whatever political agenda happened to be hot at the moment.

A month after the agency was formed, Franklin E. White, New York State's transportation commissioner, arrived at the MTA's executive offices at 818 West Seventh Street to take over as its first chief executive officer. In a way, White symbolized the MTA's goal of solving all political problems for all politicians. He was experienced, having run large transportation programs in both New York and Virginia. He had a lawyerly reputation as a problem-solver and consensus-builder. And he was black, no insignificant matter in a city divided less than a year before by race riots.

But it did not take White long to figure out that even though it had just been born, the MTA was in deep trouble. The Peterson scandal was hanging over his head, and another damaging story was brewing over the MTA's apparent inability to manage its subway contractors to assure high-quality tunneling work. The cultural schism between the two former staffs remained palpable, so much so that each was proceeding with plans to build separate headquarters. Worst of all, the MTA was broke.

Money was supposed to be the means by which the complicated political deal on transit in L.A. would stick together. Money was needed because, even after almost seventy years, there was still no consensus in Los Angeles that an expensive rail system should be built. Despite commitment to many component parts, nobody trusted the overall package. The old RTD folks didn't believe in the light rail system. The old Transportation Commission folks didn't believe in spending an endless amount of money on the Red Line. And a lot of people in town, including ideologically opposed urban planning professors at UCLA and USC, didn't believe the rail system should be built at all.

Four months after he arrived, Franklin White announced that, because the recession had cut into sales tax revenues, the MTA would never see the $180 billion required to build the rail system. In fact,

White said, the agency was faced with a yearly deficit of perhaps as much as a half-billion dollars. Over the next year, he and his financial advisors worked on a scaled-back rail construction plan. They didn't cut bus service, but in the spring of 1994 they proposed a twenty-percent increase in the bus fare, from $1.10 to $1.35. Soon, however, their proposal became the crowbar by which the rail system's opponents would pry L.A.'s political deal on transit apart.

Back in the RTD's heyday, Dyer had often threatened fare increases during hard times, just as White was doing in 1994. But few people paid any attention. Dyer's fare increases were usually little more than ploys to extract a bigger Proposition A subsidy from the Transportation Commission, and even the reporters who covered transit had long ago lost interest in this obscure bureaucratic tug of war.

The new headquarters of the Metropolitan Transportation Authority rises from amid the railyards at Union Station.

The MTA, however, was a different kind of forum. Now the rail construction money and the bus subsidies were in the same budget—a budget controlled by the MTA's board, which included the city's most visible politicians. And the politicians had learned how to use the MTA's high profile for publicity. Instead of sending alternates, they often attended MTA board meetings personally, followed by a gaggle of newspaper reporters and TV cameras.

So when Franklin White proposed a fare increase in 1994, the poverty advocates and the labor unions who complained began to get big headlines and lots of TV time. And complain they did. Relentlessly, they attacked the idea that people of modest means would have to pay higher bus fares because the MTA was wasting money building rail systems no one would use—mostly for the benefit of contractors who contributed heavily to MTA board members' campaigns. Even the new mayor, Richard Riordan, was embarrassed when it was revealed that he owned a major stake in an environmental consulting company doing work on MTA rail projects.

The critics focused their attack on the long-planned Pasadena light rail line, on which construction was about to begin. Poverty advocates argued that the MTA's financial woes could be solved without a fare increase if only the agency would postpone the Pasadena line. "This is politics as usual," one poverty advocate charged, in a typical bit of class warfare. "We're subsidizing wealth flight from Los Angeles on the backs of poor people in the inner city." (In 1996, poverty advocates won a legal settlement from the MTA forcing, among other things, a rollback in the fares and a reduction in the cost of monthly bus passes.)

In the middle of the siege, the MTA passed a $2.9 billion budget that contained enough dynamite to blow up almost any deal. The budget included the twenty-percent fare hike, but also allocated $123 million to construct the Pasadena line. Seeking more cost-cutting measures, the MTA held out in its labor contracts for more flexibility in parceling out work to non-union employees. The agency's reward for this hard line was a lawsuit against the fare increase by poverty activists and an eight-day strike by the unions. After the fare went up, bus ridership continued to decline, until it reached a level of one million boardings per day—a forty-percent drop from the peak in 1986, and about the same as the city's transit ridership when the Kelker-DeLeuw plan was issued in 1925.

Throughout the budget debacle, White held firm on the Red Line construction to Hollywood and the Valley, saying, "There can be no deviation from the Red Line timetable." Because it was the core of the political deal leading to the passage of Proposition A, he believed the Red Line had to be finished. But in the fall of 1994, the Red Line was almost finished prematurely, when it was discovered that tunnel contractors had used plywood or odd-sized blocks of wood, rather than concrete or grout, in the joints of the tunnel. The next day, the federal government cut off funding for the Red Line.

Though the federal spigot was later turned back on, the embarrassments did not end. One of every three Red Line tunnels, it turned out, was misaligned and in need of re-excavation. Later, a huge sinkhole appeared at an MTA construction site on Hollywood Boulevard, creating the perfect visual metaphor for the agency and its roiling, expansive agenda. After some fifteen years, the deal that led to the construction of a rail system in Los Angeles was on the verge of disappearing into a political sinkhole. Nobody seemed to want the darn thing.

In February 1995, Zev Yaroslavsky, perhaps the city's most accurate political weathervane, began to back away from the deal. "There's going to come a point where some people at the MTA will say, We're out of the capital business," he said, "and we're going to focus on the people who already depend on the transit system." In two years, the MTA had gone from being L.A.'s savior to its scapegoat.

～

In the spring of 1995, Franklin White arrived at the MTA board meeting at the county Hall of Administration bearing a scaled-down rail construction plan that he said Los Angeles could afford. The plan was still big, calling for some $70 billion over a twenty-year period. And, unlike its predecessor, the new proposal contained technical analysis on which the transportation decisions had been based. But nobody claimed it would be the largest public works project in the country, and nobody was promoting the plan as a way to rescue Los Angeles from a seemingly interminable recession.

White still proposed building the Pasadena light rail line and finishing the Red Line, along with a couple of other projects. But a half-dozen rail lines or more were scrapped. "The original long-range plan," he said, "incorporated some far-reaching ideas that just aren't attainable." The new plan focused heavily on improved bus service and labor productivity. Soberly, with repeated assertions that Los Angeles could no longer afford to spend freely, Mayor Richard Riordan, all the county supervisors, and representatives from smaller cities voted for the plan.

The idea that the rail system would somehow turn the growth machine inside out was forgotten. The notion that the Red Line was needed to revive downtown and the Wilshire corridor was scarcely mentioned. The remnants of the political deal of fifteen years before lay scattered, a testimony to the region's inability to find a deeply felt political consensus and stick to it. Nothing was left—except, of course, a bonfire of political vanities.

In fact, the new plan had hardly been constructed from the ground up, with the best interests of the region's transportation needs at heart. Most of MTA's funds were committed to rail projects designed to mollify various political constituencies, including the cross-Valley rail line, which few agency staffers thought should be a high priority. The plan also contained a major funding commitment for the Alameda freight corridor from Long Beach to downtown—the city's latest political fad, and one that had little to do with MTA's mission as a passenger transportation operation.

Literally from the moment the plan passed, the political vanities reasserted themselves, and White lacked the strength to bat them down. As soon as the board voted its approval, individual members stood up one by one, demanding that their pet rail project be included. Joining in the spirit of this spectacle, one director jokingly scrawled out a handwritten motion to insert an entirely new rail project, one that no one at the MTA had ever considered or analyzed.

In the months that followed, scandal after scandal unfolded, especially regarding the MTA's inability to supervise the Red Line tunnel contractors. The Green Line opened along the Century Freeway, but few experts believed anyone would ride it. The state legislature considered reorganizing the agency again, and some people proposed that the board be elected directly. Mayor Richard Riordan took the opportunity of MTA's trouble to call for a new board structure—one that, incidentally, would give him more power.

Perhaps the crowning blow came in August 1995, five months after the scaled-down plan was passed. Faced with a massive budget deficit that threatened to close all county hospitals, Los Angeles County supervisors went to Sacramento and convinced the legislature to change state law so that the MTA could transfer $150 million to the county general fund. The agency's credibility had fallen so low that five of its own board members had lobbied to take some of its money away. It wasn't long before Mayor Riordan, who had a strong influence over the board, began looking for a fall guy, and it was no surprise when he found one. Five days before Christmas 1995, Franklin White was fired, on Riordan's initiative, by a nine-to-four vote. "This is a money train," White said. "And if you get between the people who want the money and the people who spend the money, you've got problems." (White's successor, Joseph Drew, faced similar pressures and quit after nine months on the job.)

In short, fifteen years after Proposition A passed, the participants still didn't believe in the original political deal. The supervisors and Mayor Riordan—like the unions and the bus riders, the rail contractors, and the other city politicians—attacked and undermined it at every opportunity, hoping that political trouble for one part of the transit package would mean that more money would come their way. In the end, after seventy years of political haggling, the city had a rail system. But Los Angeles still had no consensus about whether that system should have been built.

CHAPTER **6**

The Reluctant Metropolis

At three o'clock in the morning on December 6, 1994, five stunned and sleepy members of the Orange County Board of Supervisors were roused from their beds and headed to the Hall of Administration in downtown Santa Ana to figure out why they didn't have any money.

The supervisors had gone to bed the night before secure in the belief that Robert Citron, the veteran county treasurer, was earning high returns on the county's investments, just as he had for many years. They were awakened to learn that Citron had made a mess of the county's investment portfolio. Simply put, Citron had laid most of the county's $7 billion investment fund on a bet that interest rates would go up, and they'd gone down. Suddenly, the county was short by about $1.7 billion, and the bond houses were demanding their money. After meeting all day, the supervisors had little choice but to declare bankruptcy immediately.

The bankruptcy sent shock waves to Sacramento, where politicians fought over whether to bail the county out, and to Wall Street, where investor confidence in Orange County bonds was shaken. More important in the long run, however, was the impact the bankruptcy had in Orange County itself.

In an area with no dominant city, the Orange County government had long been the dominant institution guiding the county's startling rise from a lima bean backwater to one of America's greatest economic powerhouses. The county's credibility had been eroding gradually, as slow-growth sentiment grew and as various politicians were embarrassed by minor corruption scandals, usually involving their connections to

Orange County's landowners and developers. The bankruptcy, however, deep-sixed the county's credibility once and for all. And that set the stage for a carnivorous expedition by almost every other center of bureaucratic power in the county outside the Hall of Administration.

The investment fund included not only the county's own money, but other people's money as well, including cities in Orange County and elsewhere, local school districts, two transportation agencies, the Orange County Sanitation District, and assorted other units of local government. Many of these agencies were required by law to invest with the county; others were lured to place their funds there voluntarily by the prospect of high returns. At first, the bankruptcy triggered a round of intergovernmental jealousies over who would bear the cost. The county wanted everyone to share the pain, whereas all the other agencies wanted the county to absorb the entire cost. But it wasn't long before all the cities and agencies began to realize that they could make a play not just for the county's money but for the county's power as well.

A poll taken a few months after the bankruptcy found that public support for the county had dropped dramatically, and residents now had more confidence in the ability of the county's thirty-one cities to deal with public problems. Soon the cities proposed that the county government be partially dismantled, leaving all the fun and profitable government work to them (transportation, landfills, land use policy), while leaving the weakened county with the work no one else would want (welfare, health care). The Orange County Transportation Authority, which ran the county's bus system, agreed to take a small financial hit, but at the same time beat its breast about the need to accumulate more power. Even Curt Pringle, who became Speaker of the State Assembly in 1996, suggested consolidating a lot of the county's special districts for the sake of greater efficiency, putting him in the odd position of being a conservative Orange County Republican advocating more centralized government. Soon, a county charter was proposed in the hope of restoring credibility, but voters turned it down.

Bankruptcy gloom: Orange County Supervisors Tom Riley (left) and Harriett Wieder consult with County Counsel Terry Andrus at the December 6, 1994, meeting, where bankruptcy was declared.

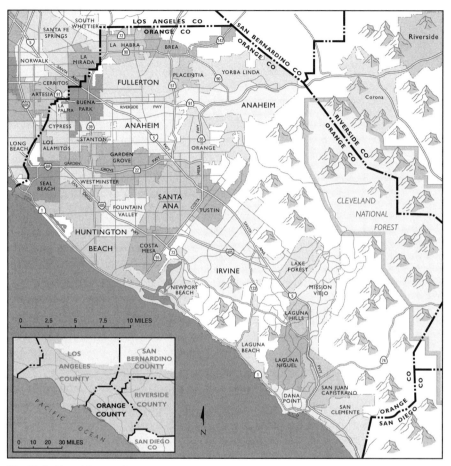

The 31 duchies of Orange County.

Even as its people and businesses sought to rebound from the bankruptcy, Orange County's assortment of local government agencies remained a motley and contentious bunch, bickering over power and money and turf at every turn. Though this may have been unfortunate, it was not exactly unplanned. In fact, Orange County's fiefdoms had spent most of the last decade—especially during the boom years of the late 1980s—resisting attempts to organize themselves in a more rational way. And they had long refused to participate constructively in governing the reluctant metropolis of which their county is undeniably a part.

⌐⌐

After a century or so of rapid and expansive growth, metropolitan Los Angeles sometimes looks as though it was deliberately designed to be ungovernable. Some fifteen million people are slathered across a landscape larger than many states. This urban blob covers an area so large that if it were laid down on the East Coast, it would stretch from New York well into Delaware, and from the Atlantic Ocean into the mountains of Pennsylvania. It can take all afternoon, and sometimes all day, to snake along the freeways from one end of this empire to the other.

The expanse alone makes it hard for the fifteen million to have any sense of belonging to a region larger than the one encompassed by their daily commute. But there are other obstacles as well. Southern California's geography—with its mountains and valleys, its extreme microclimates, and its lack of any unifying feature such as a large bay—tends to divide people rather than unify them. So does the anti-urban sentiment that has characterized the region from the start. Perhaps most important, however, is the fact that because of these other obstacles the fifteen million and their territory have been sliced and diced into literally thousands of local governmental units. Southern California today includes five counties, more than a hundred cities, and so many police and fire districts, school districts, water and sewer entities, regional pollution authorities, and other agencies that just listing them all would fill a book.

As confusing and disjointed as this system is, one of the basic facts of life in the region is that most people seem to think it's just fine. In a metropolis suspicious of government to begin with, people tend to trust government only if it's close to them. They also tend to support government that's limited in scope, like school districts, water agencies, or libraries—agencies that can stay focused on specific objectives with an obvious benefit to the community. If, as a result, there is chaos in the region, a lack of broader vision, and frequent confrontation and litigation among neighboring governments—well, that seems just fine as well. Because the only thing Southern Californians dislike more than an inefficient government at war with itself is an efficient government that knows what it's doing.

All this is not so fine, however, with some people outside Southern California, especially the politicians and bureaucrats in Sacramento and Washington, who see things in a different light. Whenever runaway growth begins to consume the Los Angeles area, the out-of-towners start moving in with their own solutions. When the region began to boom with growth again in the late 1980s, it was once again besieged by attempts to lasso it.

When two deadlines to meet federal air quality standards came and went, environmentalists and federal regulators began an aggressive attempt to force significant lifestyle changes on the fifteen million. When traffic got so bad that even the plodding Governor George Deukmejian noticed, the state stripped some authority from Southern California's local governments, forcing them to produce elaborate "congestion management" plans in order to qualify for the gasoline tax revenue they believed was rightfully theirs. Indeed, things took such a turn for the worse that in 1988 a task force of Southern California's own business leaders and good-government types concluded that the Los Angeles area required two large and powerful regional agencies to manage growth.

But the biggest threat began shortly after that, when the "growth management" issue got so much publicity that the flamboyant Willie Brown became interested. One day in 1988, the powerful Assembly Speaker offhandedly remarked that maybe the state's thousands of local governments should be abolished, replaced by streamlined regional governments that could get things done much more quickly and efficiently. Soon Brown introduced a bill in the legislature to create powerful regional governments and weaken the control of the locals—the most direct threat in decades to L.A.'s crazy-quilt of local jurisdictions.

At the time of this onslaught, the Los Angeles area actually had a regional planning agency in place—a rickety, somewhat arcane structure called the Southern California Association of Governments, known universally by the unfortunate acronym "SCAG." SCAG, however, was ridiculed even by the local officials who participated in it. Throughout its entire history, SCAG's real purpose has been to protect the local governments in Southern California from the creation of something worse.

When state and federal money began rolling into Los Angeles and other large cities in a big way in the 1960s, Sacramento and Washington struggled to find a way to make sure their funds were spent properly. Fearing that the alternative would be more onerous, Los Angeles, like most other metropolitan areas, decided that the funnel for all this revenue should be a "council of governments," a kind of United Nations of cities and counties in the region. Mayors, county supervisors, and city council members doubled as regional leaders by serving on SCAG's board and its various committees. They helped prepare regional plans required mostly by the federal government, and sought to assure that federal money was being spent in ways that were consistent with those plans. Yet the same local officials who served on SCAG's committees often torpedoed its power and effectiveness.

These cities held an almost theological conviction that they should be masters of their own fate, free to pursue whatever future they envisioned for themselves without the interference of outside forces—and, especially, without the interference of state or federal government. They may have wanted to grow quickly or slowly; they may have wanted to build housing or prevent its construction; they may have wanted to be known for equestrian trails or card clubs. But one characteristic they shared was that, Greta Garbo-like, they just wanted to be left alone. (For a fuller discussion of the resulting competition among local cities, see chapter 10, Sales Tax Canyon.)

Given this kind of bureaucratic environment, it was no surprise that the locals were not very hard on one another when doling out the money. To the cities of Southern California, SCAG was a kind of diluted castor oil. A voluntary organization, it was the weak medicine they administered to themselves in order to show the doctors from out of town that they were doing something about their health. "SCAG's biggest accomplishment," a local politician once said, "is just to continue to exist."

In spite of this record of ineffectiveness—or because of it—SCAG assumed great value to the cities and counties of the Los Angeles region when the experts from Washington and Sacramento began knocking on their doors in 1988. Mayors, county supervisors, and city managers grimaced as they prepared to accept yet another dose of SCAG's medicine in order to send the out-of-town experts away. Surely a little SCAG was better than a lot of whatever Sacramento or Washington might prescribe.

⌐

There was, however, one minor glitch in this plan, and his name was Mark Pisano.

Then in his mid-forties, Pisano was the executive director of SCAG—an eternally boyish man who had spent his entire life toiling in the bureaucratic vineyards. By the time Willie Brown started tossing around the idea of a regional government for Southern California, Mark Pisano had spent more than a decade watching the reluctant metropolis at work. And, oddly, he believed more passionately than anyone else in Southern California that it could be made to work better.

Born into an Italian-American fruit-ranching family near San Jose, Pisano had moved effortlessly as a young man into the rarified intellectual atmosphere of Washington, D.C. He earned a Ph.D. from Georgetown University and then went to work at the Environmental Protection Agency during the Nixon years. In the mid-1970s, he returned to California to run SCAG—a job that was perfect for his wonkish skills.

Mark Pisano, executive director of the Southern California Association of Governments and the Gorbachev of the region.

From the beginning, Pisano relished the opportunity SCAG gave him to look at regional problems. When it came to regional planning, Pisano was so intense, earnest, and relentless that he could render a listener numb. On any given day, he might discuss the many ways that Southern California has proposed restructuring its government agencies over the past few decades, or hold forth on how "the region" and "the neighborhood" might interact most effectively for the well-being of both, or lament the loss of "intermediary institutions" and the decline of the "civil society." He frequently expressed concern about the future of democracy, and pointed to Los Angeles, the Bosnia of American metropolises, as the ultimate laboratory for working out America's political future.

In spite of this airy, academic tone, Pisano was an adept bureaucratic survivor, and he never accepted the idea that SCAG was just regional eyewash. Throughout the 1980s, he fought an apparently losing battle for power against other arcane agencies, especially the South Coast Air Quality Management District, which regulated sources of air pollution in a four-county area around Los Angeles. Outdistancing SCAG in power and reach, the AQMD became the most influential of L.A.'s regional agencies for many reasons. One was that the issue of air pollution had a certain sexiness; another was tougher legislation from Sacramento and Washington as well as tough-minded litigation from environmentalists to enforce these laws. Not the least, however, was the public relations skill of Pisano's counterpart at AQMD, a steely-eyed chemist from Tennessee named James Lents, who always said he moved to Los Angeles to play in the "Super Bowl of Smog." By the late 1980s, the AQMD had a staff several times the size of SCAG's and had imposed onerous regulations on the region ranging from carpooling requirements to a ban on the sale of charcoal lighter fluid.

Despite an erosion of power, Pisano did not give up hope. Ever the social engineer, he was always tinkering with SCAG's conceptual framework, or with its mission statement, or even with the titles of the staff members, hoping to find the magic formula that would make SCAG powerful. And when the movement for stronger regional planning began in Sacramento in 1988, Pisano realized he had an opening. The local officials in Southern California would, quite naturally, turn to SCAG as the lesser evil. And that, in turn, would give Pisano the leverage to make SCAG stronger.

At SCAG, however, Pisano had his own political problems to overcome. Because as it began losing what little bureaucratic power it once held, the agency also began to lose its fragile grip on member cities and counties.

As they began to reap the spoils of growth in the 1980s, the cities of Southern California became restless and independent, and they were less willing to tolerate association with a remote and academic entity like SCAG. For the cities, SCAG was a double-edged sword. On the one hand, the agency's existence made it difficult for the state and federal governments to exert more control over the Los Angeles area. On the other, SCAG's bureaucratic paper-pushing posed a threat to the independence of the locals even in its current weakened state.

Under both state and federal law, SCAG was responsible for preparing growth forecasts for the region and then drawing up a series of plans—transportation, solid waste, the allocation of low-income housing—designed to deal with the consequences. Often as not, SCAG's plans represented paper solutions, intellectual tricks designed to comply with the law even though they had little to do with the real world. Nevertheless, the locals were afraid of SCAG's paper. Once some SCAG bureaucrat put into a plan that there would be an airport in Palmdale, or a hazardous waste facility in West Covina, or lots of low-income housing in Artesia, the ideas earned a kind of legitimacy. Politicians and high-level bureaucrats from Sacramento and Washington would begin to refer to them, and sooner or later one of these ideas might turn up in a state or federal program, fully funded and ready for construction. This fear was especially strong from outlying areas, such as Orange

County and the Riverside-San Bernardino area. They believed SCAG was a creation of the Bixel Street crowd (indeed, Pisano's predecessor had gone on to become president of the Chamber of Commerce), and that Los Angeles was determined to use SCAG to dump what Los Angeles didn't want into the outlying counties.

So the locals would battle endlessly with SCAG over the methodology used in the growth projections, forcing those projections downward through a highly political negotiation process. SCAG could try to resist, of course, but resistance carried a price. Though SCAG was bound to carry out state and federal policy, the political reality was that because it was a voluntary union, SCAG's primary mission always had to be retention of membership. If Pisano pushed too hard, the cities might quit, further eroding SCAG's credibility and, possibly, causing the state and federal governments to withdraw financial support.

As the battles became more petty and SCAG came to seem less important, attendance at meetings dwindled down to only the die-hard "Pisanistes"—a few loyal local officials from around the region who, for personal or political reasons, had come under Pisano's sway and committed themselves firmly to SCAG's future. Increasingly, Mark Pisano looked like the Mikhail Gorbachev of regional planning, working desperately to hold together an empire that no one else thought had any reason to exist.

⤹

If Mark Pisano was Southern California's Gorbachev, then Orange County was its Estonia, the proud and independent stepchild always plotting a coup for independence. Pisano sometimes had trouble with the "eastern provinces" of San Bernardino and Riverside, but they usually followed Orange County's lead. So from his weakened position, Pisano's ability to leverage the external threat from Sacramento into more power for SCAG depended almost entirely on his ability to win over Orange County.

Having broken away from Los Angeles County a hundred years ago in the first of many assertions of independence, Orange County is the geographically smallest and wealthiest county in the Southern California megalopolis. Beginning with the postwar suburban boom, the county underwent an almost unbelievable transformation from an agricultural center to a prototypical suburb to an economic powerhouse rivaling San Francisco in money and power. In 1950, it had two hundred thousand people and a lot of lima bean fields. By 1990, Orange County had almost two and a half million people. Alone, it was the fifteenth largest metropolis in America, bigger than Baltimore, Phoenix, Pittsburgh, Denver, or Kansas City. Furthermore, it had grown increasingly independent of Los Angeles over time. It had a local economy totalling more than $60 billion, home prices that were among the highest in the nation, a "downtown" around John Wayne Airport bigger than downtown San Francisco, and even its own bedroom suburbs (principally in western Riverside County, just to the east).

During this period, Orange County's politicians and business leaders came to see the county as a separate entity, an independent region that needed to be recognized and respected as such. As the prototypical "edge city" suburban metropolis, these "Orange Firsters" hated Los Angeles and hated to be associated with it. They viewed SCAG as the creation of Bixel Street, an operation designed to prevent outlying counties from receiving federal money, while dumping on them facilities, like landfills, that caused political problems downtown.

Many of the elected officials and bureaucrats in Orange County saw Pisano as the figurehead emperor in Los Angeles who refused to release them from bondage. And they believed SCAG's control over regional plans would hold back Orange County's own manifest destiny. One good example was the San Joaquin Hills toll road, one of three major highway initiatives undertaken by the county and the cities with mostly local funding. The Orange-Firsters wanted the San Joaquin to be a regular highway without any restrictions on the use of lanes. But SCAG wanted to force the county to provide toll-free carpool lanes, because regional policy discouraged construction of "mixed-flow" highways with no transit or carpool lanes. On this point SCAG's opinion mattered, because it was the designated federal transportation planning agency (the "metropolitan planning organization," in federal bureaucratic language) for six counties in Southern California, including Orange.

For years, then, the county and SCAG fought over whether the San Joaquin would receive SCAG's blessing, making it eligible for federal transportation funds. At one point, a SCAG committee even voted to remove the San Joaquin Hills toll road from the regional transportation plan. Orange County immediately complained, insisting once again that its transportation policies shouldn't be subject to bureaucratic scrutiny in Los Angeles. "A major new freeway for Orange County, financed mostly by Orange County, is being deleted from the (transportation plan) by a group far removed from the concerns and interests of the majority of affected Orange County elected officials," fumed Supervisor Harriett Wieder, normally a supporter of regional planning. (For a more detailed discussion of the toll road, see chapter 8, The Politics of Extinction.)

Of course, many of Orange County's leading politicians had been trying to pull out of SCAG for years. As early as 1973, the county and its cities had created the Intergovernmental Coordinating Council of Orange County. In 1980, they created the Orange County Sub-Regional Planning Council. In 1987, they created the City-County Coordination Committee. None of these efforts succeeded in freeing the county from SCAG. The reason was that local politics in Orange County was wrapped up in its own tangled web of petty jealousies that made SCAG's internal politics seem simple by comparison.

Given the staggering dimensions of its growth, it is not surprising that Orange County has been controlled for decades by a powerful combine of politicians and real estate developers. The most important unit of governance in Orange County is not the city or the county but the ranch. Almost a century and a half after large Mexican land grants were honored by statehood, the county remains dominated by a few companies that still own huge tracts of land—especially The Irvine Company (with almost one hundred square miles), the Mission Viejo Company, and the Rancho Santa Margarita Company. Since the early 1980s, both Irvine and Mission Viejo had been controlled by billionaire Donald Bren, who was perhaps the single most important supporter of Republican politicians anywhere in California.

For decades, the Orange County version of the growth machine worked quite simply. The land developers—along with hundreds of smaller developers—bankrolled supervisors' campaigns, awarded them small indulgences while in office (mini-scandals involving supervisors and developers have been common), and sometimes gave them jobs after they left office. In return, the supervisors facilitated the construction of Orange County's huge master-planned communities and built up a businesslike planning department that prided itself on getting things done.

Houses and office buildings rise from Irvine's bean fields, 1987.

As support for growth eroded in the 1970s and 1980s, cracks appeared in this system. Established cities disliked the way big developers used the county to push through projects they didn't want. And in many new neighborhoods, unhappy residents formed new cities in hopes of keeping at bay the very same county and developers that had created their communities in the first place.

As the county grew, a labyrinth of special government agencies was set up to deal with water supplies, transportation, and trash—each of them forming a separate power center for aspiring politicians and turf-grabbing bureaucrats. And as the county became more diverse, a strong north-south split appeared among the cities. With a racially mixed population, the mature northern cities (Los Alamitos, Westminster, Brea) identified more with Los Angeles. But the new cities in southern Orange County—affluent, mostly white subdivisions carved out of the hills by Irvine, Mission Viejo, and Santa Margarita—were classic suburbs that wanted nothing to do with the rest of the area, whether that meant being connected to Los Angeles or to Los Alamitos.

In 1989, Orange County sought to negotiate the terms of its liberation from SCAG by proposing the Orange County Regional Association. When this joust failed, the county simply stopped paying its dues, and several cities followed suit. At the same time, several key Orange County legislators introduced a series of bills in Sacramento that would eliminate SCAG, or gut it, or create an independent regional planning agency just for Orange County. In 1992, Orange County congressmen tried to add language to federal transportation law making it easier for Orange County to set up its own transportation planning agency. The idea was killed in Washington only through the personal intervention of Los Angeles Mayor Tom Bradley—which may have kept Orange County in SCAG for the time being, but didn't do anything to diminish the agency's reputation as a Los Angeles-dominated institution.

In short, throughout this period, Orange County desperately wanted to be free of SCAG. But Pisano desperately needed to keep Orange County in the fold in order to strengthen his political hand as the spectre of regional growth management emerged in Sacramento.

〜

Once Willie Brown proposed the idea of replacing local governments with powerful regional agencies, the concept of regional growth management began to gain momentum. In 1988, the year Brown first made his proposal, several other legislators introduced bills in Sacramento that would take power away from local governments. Then, in November 1988, a blue-ribbon task force of regional leaders in Los Angeles came to the same conclusion.

The "L.A. 2000 Committee" was classic Bixel Street. Its membership included a long list of local luminaries, such as future Secretary of State Warren Christopher, the wife of former Attorney General William French Smith, real estate superbroker John Cushman, and Roger Mahony, the powerful archbishop of the Roman Catholic diocese. Staff work was directed by Pisano's wife, Jane, an acknowledged public policy expert in her own right.

The L.A. 2000 Committee began its sweeping set of recommendations by singling out Lents's South Coast air district for heavy criticism. "This single-purpose agency has become our regional government," the final report said. To remedy the problem of fragmented growth policy, and to cut the air district down to size, the committee called for the creation of a powerful regional growth management agency that "would have the authority to set overall policy and guidelines for development with area-wide impacts," and even have veto power over big development projects approved by local governments. The L.A. 2000 Committee also proposed a second powerful regional agency to deal with environmental problems. In short, the committee was calling for a far more powerful regional planning agency than Mark Pisano had ever dared to demand.

Armed with the committee report, Pisano suddenly had the perfect opportunity to strengthen his hand—not just with Lents and the other regional agencies, but also with the rebellious local governments he was trying to keep under control. Not only was Willie Brown trying to undermine the locals in Southern California, but so was Tom Bradley and the Los Angeles Chamber of Commerce! Recognizing the power of these external threats, Pisano moved quickly.

On December 1, 1988, only days after the L.A. 2000 Committee report came out, Pisano circulated a memo announcing that it was "time to reassess SCAG's mandate." Attached to the memo was the first draft of a proposal for SCAG to assume stronger control of regional planning, giving the agency better funding sources and more power over development and implementation of regional growth policies.

In the months that followed, the barrage against SCAG was stepped up, especially from Orange County's leading local-government expert in the legislature, Marian Bergeson. One bill would have stripped SCAG of its charter. Another would have transferred responsibility for state transit funds to the county transportation commission. A third would have declared that Orange County could administer its own federal transportation funds free of SCAG interference.

In response, Pisano set up a special task force to examine "intra-regional relations." The task force was chaired by veteran Supervisor John Flynn of Ventura County. A onetime SCAG opponent, Flynn had recently become a Pisaniste, apparently because, like some local politicians before him, he saw in SCAG the potential to step into a position of broader power. Throughout 1989 and into 1990, as the legislature grappled with the regional planning proposals from Willie Brown and others, the Flynn committee drew up a plan to reinvent SCAG.

The Flynn proposal was shaped by volatile political dynamics that seemed to change almost every day. Though Flynn was the chairman, and other local politicians served on the committee, the entire effort inevitably reflected Pisano's own political posturing. At the time, Pisano was determined to make SCAG a stronger force for shaping the region, and his own staff was pressuring him to be pro-active and visionary. But he couldn't afford to get out in front of the political will of his member local governments. When the state legislature recessed in late 1989, the growth management bills had not moved, and they did not seem to local officials to be much of a threat.

By the spring and summer of 1990, however, the situation had changed. In May and June, the Willie Brown bill gathered steam, and passage appeared likely. Thus, when the Flynn committee came out with its final proposal in the spring of 1990, it seemed politically possible to cast the reinvention of SCAG in sweeping terms. Regional planning would be done by a revamped SCAG (renamed the Southern California Assembly of Governance) that would include the powers of the air district and other regional planning agencies. The agency would be run by a legislative-style regional council, with half of its members elected directly by the public. And the new agency would be responsible for putting together an "Overall Regional Plan" that all local governments would have to follow.

Throughout the debate, Pisano had continually insisted that in its new form, SCAG would be more "bottom-up" in nature—the inevitable result, he argued, of a regional council that included directly elected officials. It was true that SCAG had a reputation for being clubby and remote, and any such change might have opened up the process. Astutely, however, Pisano had used this political cover to propose something quite different from bottom-up planning. With the threat of a much tougher Willie Brown bill looming, he had actually engineered a demand from some of SCAG's own members to create what amounted to a more centralized regional government with far greater political power.

In the months that followed, Pisano transformed the Flynn committee's recommendations into a concrete legislative proposal to take to Sacramento, and he convinced the L.A. 2000 Committee to sign off on a similar set of recommendations calling for a regional plan and an elected regional legislature.

Meanwhile, in the State Capitol, the pressure continued to mount. In the fall of 1990, a Republican governor and a Democratic legislature, which had agreed on almost nothing for eight years, agreed to reduce local planning power as part of a gas tax increase.* Then, in the gubernatorial campaign, Dianne Feinstein unhesitatingly adopted Willie Brown's proposal for centralized control of growth, and hammered on the growth theme in her campaign. (She even cribbed the word "growth" on her hand during a gubernatorial debate in which notes were prohibited, as a reminder to pound the issue.) Her Republican opponent, Pete Wilson, insisted that he would "not do land use planning from Sacramento," but nobody believed him. Wilson had been an advocate of

---

* SCAG did not gain power as a result of this legislation, but the Los Angeles County Transportation Commission did. The legislation required local governments to submit traffic congestion "management plans" to their county transportation commissions, such as LACTC, for approval.

growth management as mayor of San Diego, and everybody knew he would have to come up with a growth management proposal if he won. As the election approached, Pisano lay in wait. And Southern California's local potentates held their breath, pondering just exactly how their power would be taken away from them.

⤺

The first thing Willie Brown did when the California legislature reconvened in December 1990 was to re-introduce his growth management bill. In fact, he moved so quickly that the bill, which had been known in the last session as AB 4242, was assigned the legislative number AB 3, meaning that it was only the third bill of the year to cross the Assembly clerk's desk.

Like its predecessor, the bill called for the creation of powerful "Regional Development and Infrastructure Agencies" in metropolitan areas throughout the state. These agencies would determine when and where key pieces of infrastructure would be built. They would pass judgment on large development projects which were previously the exclusive province of local cities and counties. And they would be governed by a board directly elected by district. In essence, Brown was proposing the creation of a regional growth "legislature" for Los Angeles, the San Francisco Bay Area, San Diego, and other metropolitan areas in California.

One of the first things Pete Wilson did after becoming governor in January 1991 was to send out the message that he wanted to drag his feet on the growth issue. He established a task force to study the question and asked Brown to hold off for a year until the task force made recommendations. Wilson, as usual, had read the political climate flawlessly. After an eight-year boom, the California economy was faltering badly. The joke around Wilson's office was that the governor would gladly come up with a growth management strategy if only he had a little growth to manage. Manfully, Willie Brown insisted he was not going to back off. But it quickly became clear that he was not twisting anybody's arm very hard in order to get AB 3 onto the governor's desk.

At SCAG's annual meeting in February 1991, the local governments of Southern California approved the concept of restructuring the organization. But, as if sensing that the threat from Sacramento was no longer serious, the individual members of SCAG began to hammer Pisano and Flynn (who was now SCAG's president) about the restructuring proposal. "This proposal," wrote Roy Paul, the mayor of Downey, "reads like an attempt by SCAG to expand its powers and acquire authority over local government that it does not now enjoy. If SCAG's primary focus would be the region, how could we as local governments trust it to create a 'bottom-up' process that truly ensures effective local government and public participation?" Simi Valley, the conservative city just west of the San Fernando Valley in Ventura County, threatened to pull out if membership in SCAG was made mandatory. Such complaints were typical.

Most significantly, Orange County began flexing its muscles again. In early 1991, the county government and the cities set up yet another joint entity, the Orange County Regional Advisory and Planning Council. Its purpose was clearly to figure out how to pull Orange County out of SCAG so that it could set up its own federally designated transportation planning agency. In response to SCAG's proposal, the board president of the Orange County Transportation Authority (which believed it should replace SCAG as Orange County's regional planning agency) told Flynn in a letter: "There is an undeniable feeling in Orange County that opportunity for input before the fact has often not been adequate and that plans and proposals are many times only perfunctorily circulated for comment by local agencies." With growth management's prospects on the wane in Sacramento, Orange County was on the attack against SCAG.

Not surprisingly, Pisano and Flynn quickly retreated. By the fall of 1991—with Pete Wilson's own task force dragging its feet and Willie Brown's bill going nowhere—the SCAG proposal had changed dramatically. Pisano would not give up his longstanding dream of creating an overall plan for the whole region, now to be called the "Regional Comprehensive Plan." But he surrendered on almost everything else. The new SCAG would not be mandatory, at least not for the first two years. The SCAG board would be expanded, but the directors would not be directly elected, meaning they would be no threat to the power of local officials. And SCAG would begin to surrender some decision-making and number-crunching power to "subregional" organizations—a sop to Orange County and other outlying areas that were chafing under the perceived control of downtown.

The political payoff for this watered-down approach was immediate. Within four weeks after the new proposal was floated to the SCAG executive committee, the Orange County Board of Supervisors began to talk about rejoining SCAG. The Orange-Firsters, of course, were still talking tough about secession. "I look at San Diego, which is about the same size as us and has its own planning board, and I am envious," said Don Roth, a county supervisor with close ties to many developers. But the power brokers of Orange County realized that all they had accomplished in withdrawing from SCAG was to eliminate their right to vote on regional issues that still affected them. And they were much more interested in rejoining a toothless and voluntary SCAG than a mandatory regional planning agency with independent political power.

By early 1992, then, the idea of regional planning imposed from Sacramento appeared dead. Orange County was back in the fold. The SCAG membership had accepted the watered-down reorganization plan, which expanded the executive committee from twenty to seventy members but didn't include any independently elected directors. Even the much-maligned name was retained, although at Pisano's direction the receptionist started answering the phone "Association of Governments" instead of "SCAG." All that remained of Pisano's dream was the Regional Comprehensive Plan.

⏤

Toward the end of 1991, desperate to show that he had a serious domestic policy agenda, George Bush signed the Intermodal Surface Transportation Efficiency Act—a five-year extension of the federal transportation program that increased its funding (to around $30 billion a year nationwide) and broadened its scope (to encourage more mass transit). The political impetus for the bill, known universally as ISTEA (pronounced "ice-tea"), was to allow Bush to claim credit for signing "a jobs bill." Buried deep in its language, however, ISTEA contained a bureaucratic revolution.

Transportation planning agencies such as SCAG would no longer be mere rubber stamps of federal money to local governments. Instead, they would have real power. All agencies that wanted federal funding, including the once-omnipotent Caltrans, would have to grovel in front of SCAG for approval. Since the reviews required for SCAG to make its decisions were highly technical readings of laws and plans, ISTEA tended to vest more power in SCAG's bureaucrats, rather than the local officials who served on its board.

Although the new federal law gave the agency more power and money, on the surface it appeared to narrow SCAG's purpose. It was still a coalition of local governments, all of whom paid dues, but SCAG received more than eighty percent of its money from the federal and state governments to undertake broad-based regional transportation planning. As SCAG's chief source of money and power, ISTEA seemed to seal the agency's fate as a pusher of transportation paper.

Dreaming of a Regional Comprehensive Plan, however, Pisano managed to stand ISTEA on its head. Instead of narrowing SCAG's focus, he used ISTEA's power and money to broaden the organization's scope and reach. Cleverly, he obtained a political consensus, at least from his expanded seventy-member Regional Council, to use a lot of the ISTEA money not for transportation but to create the regional plan. To gain enough political clout to undertake this bold move, Pisano hit on the idea of using the economy as the common thread of a regional plan.

Between the defense cutbacks and the 1992 riots, everyone in the region was hurting economically. Furthermore, the worse the economy became, the more business leaders and politicians blamed Jim Lents and the South Coast Air Quality Management District for imposing burdensome regulations—such as mandatory carpooling requirements—that supposedly harmed the region's ability to compete for business. Pisano positioned his regional plan so that he was on the right side of the economic issue while Lents was on the wrong side. As Lents was clinging to burdensome regulations, SCAG was forming regional task forces on NAFTA and streamlined permits for film companies. At a time when local voters throughout Southern California were electing more conservative leaders, this was not an insignificant point.

From the beginning, the Orange-Firsters were reluctant to go along with the Pisanistes in backing the idea of a regional plan. In their resistance, they had growing support from their counterparts in inland areas—and from the homebuilding industry, which feared that the SCAG effort would result in regional government that would rein in their far-flung construction efforts on the edge of the metropolis.

In 1991, just as SCAG was reorganizing, the Orange-Firsters engineered an important merger of transportation bureaucracies in Orange County. The local bus company, the county transportation commission (which distributed some state transportation funds), and scattered other organizations were combined into a new agency known as the Orange County Transportation Agency, or OCTA. Led by an ambitious former journalist named Stan Oftelie, OCTA quickly established itself as a rival power center to SCAG, intent on wresting bureaucratic strength southward. Wisecracking and informal, Oftelie's staffers were poles apart from the cerebral and earnest regional planners on Pisano's staff, and they seemed to view their rivalry with Pisano in personal terms. They jokingly referred to Pisano as their devil, and more seriously accused him of personally lobbying Congress on ISTEA to give SCAG more power over Orange County.* "Why should the mayor of Brawley have anything to say about transportation projects in Orange County," one Oftelie aide once asked. (At the time, the president of the SCAG board was Stella Mendoza, a loyal Pisaniste who was the mayor of Brawley, a city of eighteen thousand people located in Imperial County about one hundred forty miles southeast of OCTA's headquarters in Santa Ana.)

In Oftelie and OCTA, the Orange-Firsters had a vehicle that could serve as their own, one-county transportation planning agency. They also hired a UC Irvine planning professor, Scott Bollens, to conduct a study. Bollens concluded that Southern California was, in fact, a "super-region," and nowhere else in the country—not even in New York—was a centralized regional planning agency exerting so much control over transportation. At last, momentum seemed to be building for liberation from SCAG. In the meantime, however, the Orange-Firsters had to deal with Pisano's Regional Comprehensive Plan, which was sucking up most of Southern California's ISTEA planning dollars.

At the first RCP meeting, the Orange-Firsters sat, spoke, and voted as a bloc, requiring a resolution from the Pisanistes that regional representatives distribute themselves randomly around the table in the future. They frequently complained that Pisano was misusing millions of dollars of ISTEA money by pursuing a regional plan no one had authorized. Later, Pisano established planning efforts on the subregional level (using more ISTEA money)—presumably for more input, but probably also to mollify the plan's opponents. The response of the Orange-Firsters was to demand, and receive, special treatment along the

* Whatever Pisano's personal role in lobbying on ISTEA might have been, the provisions that strengthened organizations like SCAG primarily resulted from an insurrection in the San Francisco Bay Area, where local governments had chafed under the authoritarian dictates of Caltrans over which transportation projects would be funded and built.

lines of Quebec's Meach Lake Accord. SCAG agreed to a memorandum of understanding spelling out exactly what Orange County's role would be in preparing the technical data used in the plan.

In fact, Orange County resistance might have killed the Regional Comprehensive Plan had not cracks appeared in the Orange-Firster armor. After the initial unified resistance, some representatives from cities in north Orange County began to support the plan. Ron Bates, an ambitious city council member in Los Alamitos, just over the county line, became an active Pisaniste and played an important role in lining up Orange County support. Other north county politicians, such as Bev Perry, the mayor of Brea, openly admitted that their cities had a strong connection to Los Angeles that couldn't be ignored. In 1993, SCAG's Regional Council gave the go-ahead to the Regional Comprehensive Plan, partly because of north Orange County support, and partly because of Pisano's skill at turning out votes in SCAG meetings. "Whenever they needed the votes," one Orange-Firster complained, "they'd go dig up John Flynn, Stella Mendoza, and those folks."

Once the plan moved forward, the next question was whether it would have any teeth that would hold Orange County and other out-lying areas legally accountable to the broad regional goals the plan would contain. Soon this boiled down to a fight over the power of the plan's "non-mandated" chapters.

Everyone agreed that SCAG had statutory authority to create regional plans, in areas such as transportation and solid waste, where state or federal laws mandated that such plans be prepared. But as Pisano envisioned it, the Regional Comprehensive Plan also included several other sections that clearly were not mandated under law. These sections dealt with a wide range of issues—water, open space, housing, growth management, human resources—that had long been considered the purview of local government or other agencies. Not only did the Pisan-istes insist that these chapters be prepared (mostly with ISTEA money), but they also demanded that the policies among all the chapters be linked together to ensure that the Regional Comprehensive Plan had a consistent set of regional strategies.

The last thing the Orange-Firsters wanted was for SCAG, up in Los Angeles, to broaden its power so that the Pisanistes could tell some city in Orange County it had to set aside land for a wildlife preserve or an air-port because that's what was called for in the Regional Comprehensive

Plan. So vehement was their opposition that they refused even to comment on the non-mandated chapters, believing them to be, in essence, illegal chapters that SCAG had undertaken without authority. When released in draft form in late 1993, the regional plan stood a very good chance of defeat at the hands of Orange-Firsters and their friends.

At the beginning of 1994, then, a group of Pisanistes on the SCAG staff drove down to Santa Ana to meet with representatives from the Orange First crowd. Over a long lunch, the Pisanistes threw in the towel. They agreed to split the regional plan into two parts: "core" chapters and "ancillary" chapters.

The core chapters would consist of the regional plans SCAG had the authority to prepare, and everyone agreed that localities around Southern California would be required to use them as the basis for their own plans. The ancillary chapters would consist of the additional non-mandated plans—such as open space—that Pisano had made part of the RCP. During the Santa Ana lunch, SCAG's staffers sacrificed them in order to obtain political acceptance for the plan as a whole. As SCAG stated in its own newsletter, the ancillary chapters, "do not contain actions or policies required of local governments" as the result of the regional plan. In other words, SCAG would adopt the ancillary chapters as part of the plan, but nobody had to pay any attention to them.

After six years of maneuvering, Pisano had completed the reassessment and reorganization of Southern California's only true regional planning agency. There was no question that he had made some important strides. The seventy-member regional council broadened the agency's political base, even if it did not give the council's members any political incentive to look at issues from a regional perspective. SCAG had successfully fostered the creation of several subregional planning efforts, in which neighboring local governments (usually stimulated by a SCAG subsidy) worked together to solve common problems. And Pisano had, for the first time, persuaded his local potentates to buy into the idea of a regional plan, at least on paper.

Yet he had not succeeded in truly reorganizing the way the region functions. There were no elected officials who were accountable to the region as a whole, rather than simply to the local neighborhoods that elected them. Membership in SCAG was still voluntary, not mandatory.

Furthermore, the division of the regional plan into core and ancillary chapters had destroyed the idea that local governments would be truly accountable to one another. With a single, Bobbitt-like stroke, SCAG had been reduced once again to a loose confederation of local fiefdoms unwilling to ask each other to make any sacrifices. And the whole effort had not quelled the Orange-Firsters' desire to secede. In November 1994, just as the final sections of the Regional Comprehensive Plan were being approved, Orange County's Regional Advisory Planning Council went on record that the county's transportation planning agency should not be Pisano's SCAG but, rather, Stan Oftelie's Orange County Transportation Authority.

↜

Three weeks after the Regional Advisory Planning Council's vote, Orange County's dramatic plunge into bankruptcy began. Oddly, despite early predictions to the contrary, the bankruptcy did not have a long-term impact on Sacramento or Wall Street. It was an isolated incident, and the municipal bond market was soon humming along as if nothing had happened. The bankruptcy did turn the political dynamics of local-regional power in Orange County upside down, however, for the simple reason that it gave the cities and the special government agencies one more reason to hate the county government.

Investors in the county's doomed $7-billion fund included OCTA, the county's retirement system, the Sanitation District, more than forty school districts, thirty-seven cities, thirteen water districts, and a variety of other agencies. Some of these outfits had a huge amount of money in the fund—over a half-billion dollars for OCTA, for example, and some $200 million for Irvine, one of Orange County's most important cities. (The agency least at risk was the Dana Point Sanitary District, with $31.17 in the fund.)

Eventually, the cities and school districts got almost all their money back, though the transportation and sanitation agencies had to help with the bail-out. But in the weeks and months after the bankruptcy, animosity among local officials toward the county was high. The county, along with the big developers, had always dominated Orange County politics, while the bickering small cities had little clout. Now, however, the situation was reversed. And instead of working together to improve the county's governance, the county, the cities, and the special agencies revived the old game of turf-poaching and turf-protection.

Shortly after the bankruptcy, Orange County's cities came out with a plan to strip the county government of most of its powers and replace it with a "council of governments"—an Orange County SCAG —to manage land use policies, transportation, landfills, and other regional matters previously handled by the county or by SCAG. The plan was also supported by Marian Bergeson, a former state legislator who had taken office as a county supervisor just as the bankruptcy hit. In seeking to give the cities more power, Bergeson declared that the county's "days as a land baron... [are] long gone." OCTA also jumped into the act, seeking to consolidate power around its own organization. Meanwhile, the old-line power structure sought to revive the county's credibility with a "county charter" proposal that would have restructured and strengthened the role of top county officials. The charter plan was clobbered at the polls.

In this volatile situation, longstanding petty jealousies broke out into the open more than ever before. When some north county legislators proposed selling off the El Toro air base for an airport in order to pay the bills, the southern cities surrounding the airport threw up roadblocks. And when these same southern cities—representing some of the most affluent and fast-growing areas of the county—sought to annex new property, the county blocked them, fearing a loss of needed revenue in a time of crisis.

In mid-1996, Orange County's cities—with SCAG's assistance—simply created their own "council of governments." Only later did the cities begin negotiating with the county government, OCTA, and other agencies about expanding the organization so that everyone was included. In the wake of the bankruptcy, it was clear that part of the trouble in Orange County was simply the same old problem in a new context. Government agencies with neighboring—or even overlapping—responsibilities shared little sense of identity with the region they served, even when that region was defined narrowly as being Orange County.

Six years of struggle to reinvent itself had not made SCAG a useful forum for warring local governments to resolve their differences. Now the entire region was paying the price—and the Orange-Firsters most of all—as the credibility of all the county's local governments bled away in the constant internal warfare among them. Having evaded Mark Pisano's lasso, the reluctant metropolis had also failed to find within itself a sense of regional purpose strong enough to hold it together.

PART THREE

Land

The growth game gets played on many levels in Southern California, but whenever and wherever it is played, it involves a lot of political juice. In the boom years after World War II, most of this juice came from landowners and real estate developers, who met little resistance in their attempt to mold a great series of suburbs from the stark and fragile landscape around Los Angeles. Beginning in the 1960s and 1970s, however, the political equation changed.

No longer were land developers and their political friends the only people playing the game. Soon enough, the sheer magnitude of the growth itself called into existence a whole series of other players. As home values grew and traffic became increasingly clogged, homeowners organized to protect the serenity of their neighborhoods, to say nothing of their own real estate investments. As environmental degradation became more apparent, environmental activists—"eco-activists," in the words of environmental writer Robert Gottlieb—emerged to fight development and help pass a series of laws that gave them more power over the whole. Lastly, the environmental laws themselves created a whole new kind of government bureaucrat—"enviro-crats," as Gottlieb calls them—who had to administer the new laws and protect the environment, yet still operate within the prevailing political atmosphere in order to save their own skins. And these enviro-crats worked not only in local and state government, but also for the federal land agencies in the U.S. Department of the Interior, which has played a pivotal role in Los Angeles as it has throughout the West.

To all these players, the landscape of Southern California became an enormous chessboard, and the urban development of the region became a kind of floating game played out on that chessboard. Especially in the go-go years of the 1980s, the growth patterns of the region were determined by an endless series of local battles over pretty plateaus and dramatic vistas, in which developers sought to gain enough political power to bulldoze the landscape and environmentalists used every means at their disposal to try to stop them.

Inevitably, most such disputes were settled by giving half a loaf to each side. The developer would scale down the project and dedicate, or sell, the rest of it to some public agency for parkland. Which property was preserved and which was developed depended on the political dynamics of any given situation. In general, however, the resulting patterns of land development did not represent anybody's idea of "good planning." Instead, it was ad-hockery at its finest—a metropolis growing by political deal, driven and informed by some economic imperatives, some environmental preservation, and a lot of give-and-take behind the scenes.

Occasionally, however, an urban development project would contain so much political juice that the half-a-loaf rule would cease to apply. In those cases, the outcome depended on simple political maneuvering all the way up to the Governor of California, the Secretary of the Interior, and the President of the United States. Whether or not the results in these situations constituted "good planning" was equally hard to say. But there was no question that political hardball at all levels was determining the future of the land, and the landscape, all around metropolitan Los Angeles.

CHAPTER 7

The Education of Maria VanderKolk

Of all the freeway escapes from Los Angeles—and there are dozens, or so it sometimes seems—the most beautiful is unquestionably the trip west on Highway 101 toward Thousand Oaks.

The drive begins in the San Fernando Valley, that overgrown suburb-turned-Edge City, whose broad flats now provide homes to more than a million people and jobs to hundreds of thousands more. After Woodland Hills, the freeway suddenly channels into a narrow gap in the surrounding hillsides. The Valley's cluttered commercial strips and prosaic apartment complexes are left behind. Lush hillsides filled with oak trees and fine native grasslands grace both sides of the freeway down the Calabasas Grade and beyond. In the distance lies the majesty of the Santa Monica Mountains—maybe the most important urban mountain range anywhere in America, and certainly the most expensive. It is a landscape familiar to millions of Americans who have never been to Los Angeles, because in hundreds of movies and TV shows it has served as a stand-in for mountain towns in Colorado, Utah, Oregon, and even—though the grass is brown most of the year—the bittersweet Wales of *How Green Was My Valley.*

Over the years, the Santa Monicas have drawn to them a unique collection of self-styled mountain people, mystics, misanthropes, environmentalists, ardent slow-growth suburbanites, and wealthy executives posing as simple rural folk. In the fifteen or so miles before the flats open up again in Thousand Oaks, these people have dotted the landscape with an eclectic collection of hillside hideaways, ostentatious gated subdivisions, ersatz horse farms, and ordinary tract homes that

brush up against nature—all of which they protect from flatland interlopers like West Virginia moonshiners trying to fend off federal agents with a few rusty shotguns.

On a warm spring day in early April 1994, most of these local characters were gathered at one of their favorite mountain spots—the Jordan Ranch just north of the freeway past the rural chic community of Old Agoura—to celebrate their most recent success in chasing the flatlanders off yet again. They came at the invitation of the National Park Service, which had just spent almost $17 million of taxpayer money to rescue the Ranch's twenty-three hundred acres from one of the area's largest and most unpopular landowners, Bob Hope.

There were riders on horseback and riders on mountain bikes, Birkenstocked eco-activists and buttoned-down envirocrats, a veteran Democratic congressman and his ambitious Republican opponent, a Chumash Indian chief who warded off evil spirits, and even an African-American park ranger whose evangelical style moved the all-white crowd to chant in response. In the middle of the group, looking like she would rather be someplace else, sat Maria VanderKolk.

The Calabasas Grade heading west out of the San Fernando Valley along Highway 101.

At twenty-eight years old, VanderKolk was at once a political veteran and a political novice. She was an accidental office-holder who had achieved her most cherished goal. But success had come at a price so high she openly admitted that she could barely stomach it.

Four years before, VanderKolk had been elected to the Ventura County Board of Supervisors by fewer than a hundred votes after running a shoestring campaign based on one issue: saving Jordan Ranch. But now that Jordan Ranch was saved, Maria VanderKolk had learned that it wasn't enough, at least not for the tract-home environmentalists who had originally propelled her into office.

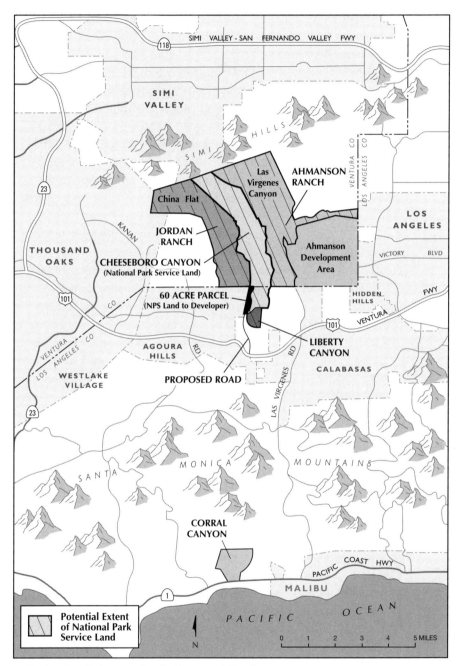

Jordan Ranch and Ahmanson Ranch, almost straddling the
county line between Los Angeles and Ventura Counties.

Today VanderKolk sat on a makeshift podium, in the middle of a grove of oak trees, alongside Mary Weisbrock, president of Save Open Space—Santa Monica Mountains, the woman who had originally persuaded her to run for the Board of Supervisors in the first place. Though they had not spoken for more than two years, they posed quietly next to one another as the congressional candidates traded barbs and the envirocrats made lofty speeches about how much good they had done, and the Chumash chief cleansed everyone with burning sage. When it was her turn to speak, VanderKolk unfolded gracefully to her full six-foot height and gave a short and modest talk. "All the complicated reasons that we are here today," she said, "are not as important as the fact that we are here."

A short time later, Weisbrock stood up—a middle-aged, bespectacled woman in a dress who looked not at all like the typical environmental activist. As she walked to the podium, several other members of SOS unfurled a huge sign at the back of the crowd that read: BOB HOPE'S GREATEST GAG, a reference to the high price the National Park Service paid to acquire the land. As park rangers pushed the sign-holders back, Weisbrock lectured the crowd on the need to mobilize in order to save a different piece of land—Ahmanson Ranch, two canyons to the east, which VanderKolk had agreed to deal away to developers as the price for saving Jordan. Her voice characteristically quavering with emotion, Weisbrock declared, "This is all a big hoax."

So much for reconciliation. Maria VanderKolk may have saved Jordan Ranch. But it was clear that nothing she could ever do would make Mary Weisbrock and the other tract-home environmentalists in the Santa Monica Mountains happy.

⌐

What Maria VanderKolk did not know when she was elected four years earlier—what she could not have been expected to know, given her background—was just how deep emotions ran in the Santa Monicas.

She might have known that the political struggle to preserve the Santa Monicas stretched back thirty years. She certainly knew the fervor with which many eco-activists approached saving the mountains; after all, they had chosen her to run for office in the first place. But she did not really understand how long the local environmentalists held their grudges, or how deeply they felt their wounds. The activists were usually longtime residents who lived in or near the mountains. Whatever their day job might be, they regarded the task of preserving the Santa Monicas as their life's work. Some were rich; others were middle-class. Some lived in tract homes, some in fancy Malibu spreads, and some in rustic quarters deep in the mountains themselves. But they had one thing in common: They constantly agitated against all development in the mountains and cared little about the financial resources or regulatory tools required to achieve that goal.

Many of them were still scarred by the 1970s, when the first battles in the environmental war were fought. After a long struggle, the Santa Monica Mountains Comprehensive Planning Commission was established, and had actually produced an ambitious plan to save the mountains by downzoning some private property and acquiring the rest for public use. One by one, however, the compromises had come. The creation of a powerful regulatory agency, similar to the Coastal Commission, proved to be politically impossible. Some of the plan's recommendations were adopted, but many local officials, especially those in Los Angeles County, often ignored them. The local eco-activists were thrilled when Congress formed the Santa Monica Mountains National Recreation Area. But, as they soon learned to their disappointment, Santa Monica was one of the most peculiar national parks ever created.

For one thing, it encompassed a vast expanse, stretching forty-seven miles end to end, in the middle of a densely built urban area. But maybe more important, when the park was created in 1978, the National Park Service didn't actually own any of the land. Its daunting task in the Santa Monicas was to acquire, after the fact, about forty thousand acres—sixty square miles, the size of Cape Cod National Seashore. And after the Los Angeles real estate boom of the 1970s, that land was among the most expensive in America. Even before the National Recreation Area was established, real estate speculators were scouring the Santa Monicas looking for property that could be developed or resold at a profit.

At first, the Park Service did what any government agency would be expected to do: It obtained land by purchasing it at a very high price. By 1984, the Park Service had purchased seventy-five hundred acres in the Santa Monicas at a cost of $45 million, an average of $6,000 per acre. (Congress had originally estimated that the entire forty thousand acres could be acquired for $125 million, or about $3,000 per acre.) Thanks to L.A.'s influential congressional delegation, in those early years the Santa Monicas received an ample supply of land acquisition money, up to fifteen percent of the Park Service's national acquisition budget in some years.

In the early 1980s, however, the environmental politics of the Santa Monica Mountains changed. Under Interior Secretary James Watt, the Reagan Administration stopped the flow of federal acquisition money for the Santa Monicas. And Los Angeles began to experience one of its periodic real estate booms. Land prices skyrocketed, and a developer-friendly majority on the L.A. County Board of Supervisors permitted construction of expensive subdivisions all over the mountains.

Some state and local funds were available for land acquisition, but it was impossible for the Park Service to match the developers dollar-for-dollar in the private real estate market. For conservationists, the cruelest blow came in the early 1980s, when Bob Hope chose to sell Sampo Farms, a scenic ranch just south of the 101 Freeway in Calabasas, to private developers rather than the Park Service.

Out of necessity, then, the envirocrats working on the park developed a deal-making approach. They could not buy the land or zone development away. So they made deals. They did not oppose major development, and, indeed, sometimes they spoke out in favor of a project. In return, they persuaded private developers to donate critical parcels of land to the public, or at least sell the property at a discount.

The key figure in this deal-making environment was Joseph T. Edmiston. A burly, bearded man in his forties, Edmiston had spent most of his career as an environmental bureaucrat in the Santa Monicas. In the 1970s, he had served as executive director of the Santa Monica Mountains Comprehensive Planning Commission. Since 1980 he had been executive director of the Santa Monica Mountains Conservancy, a state agency created to help the Park Service acquire land after the planning commission shut down.

But Edmiston was more than a bureaucrat. He was, in fact, a larger-than-life figure, a dominating personality who set the agenda and the tone for land acquisition in the Santa Monicas with a Machiavellian taste for political intrigue and financial intricacy. Around the Conservancy he created a confusing maze of interlocking agencies and organizations, permitting him much more leeway than the Park Service in dealing for land. He also aggressively expanded the reach of the Conservancy beyond the Santa Monicas to virtually all the mountain ranges ringing Los Angeles. (A map on the wall of his Malibu office jokingly charted the history of the Conservancy's annexation of all land in California.)

And Edmiston was a grandmaster of the chess game over land in the Santa Monicas. When a trash district sought an environmentally sensitive property for a new landfill, Edmiston—who couldn't afford to buy the land out from under the trash czars—simply optioned an adjoining parcel that was needed for access, thus blocking the project. When he wanted to condemn a key parcel of land, he simply turned to a special subsidiary, the Mountains Conservation and Recreation Authority, that he had established jointly with Ventura County—even though the property in question was across the line in Los Angeles County. And whenever a celebrity wanted to bail out of a mountain property investment with a tax-deductible donation, Edmiston would grab the land as well as the resulting headlines.

In short, Edmiston was aggressive, smart, annoying, and sometimes too clever. Politicians tolerated him for the results he provided; hard-line environmentalists were sharply critical of his willingness to compromise and his blustery manner. Nevertheless, after the National Park Service ran out of money for the Santa Monicas in the early 1980s, Edmiston emerged as the most powerful figure in the mountains, interposing himself into almost every land deal. In Edmiston, developers knew, they had someone with whom they might be able to cut a deal on almost any piece of land.

⌐

The Jordan Ranch, however, was not just any piece of land. Strictly speaking, Jordan was not a part of the Santa Monica Mountains. It lay in the Simi Hills, north of the Highway 101 freeway. But it was a spectacular property. And because it was immediately adjacent to the Santa Monicas, environmental planners viewed it as absolutely critical to the long-term ecological health of the area.

The Jordan Ranch consisted of some twenty-three hundred acres of property stretching in a long, thin configuration from the freeway north toward Simi Valley. The southern portion was a canyon—Palo Camado Canyon—a combination of oak savannahs and grassy plains, long used for cattle farming, and it provided the pathway to the only possible wildlife corridor along the freeway. The northern portion, sometimes called China Flat, was much more rugged, and stretched westward to include Simi Peak, a mountaintop more than two thousand feet above sea level that afforded a 360-degree view of everything from Malibu halfway to Santa Barbara.

In an entertainment industry deal typical of landholding patterns in the vicinity, Bob Hope had bought the property decades ago from Will and Marion Jordan, "Fibber McGee and Molly" of radio fame. Well past his eightieth birthday, Hope wanted to cash Jordan out by developing the land, and as a longtime golf enthusiast he found the perfect partner in Potomac Investment Associates.

A group of investors headquartered near the nation's capital, Potomac appeared to be the ideal development firm for the country club set. Politically well-connected to Washington's Republican establishment, Potomac had already developed one golf course project in suburban Washington for the Professional Golfers Association. On Jordan, Potomac wanted to replicate the lucrative formula: a championship golf links surrounded by almost two thousand tony homes for the rich.

To build the project, Potomac and Hope had to overcome two obstacles. First, the county line skirted the southern edge of the Jordan property. That meant that even though all of Jordan's neighbors were residents of Los Angeles County, final approval for the project rested with the Ventura County Board of Supervisors—historically a much more environmentally oriented group that had discouraged intense development in the Jordan area. In 1986, Ventura County had zoned Jordan for one-hundred-sixty-acre parcels, meaning that Potomac would be limited to only about fifteen houses under current zoning, rather than the eighteen hundred it wanted to build.

More significant, however, was the problem of access. The only entrance to Jordan was a private road across a wealthy, semi-rural section of Old Agoura, whose residents were not about to allow through traffic. There was only one other potential access point: cutting a road farther east, along the edge of Cheeseboro Canyon.

Potomac had optioned part of the required property, just to the south, between Cheeseboro and the freeway. But Potomac still needed to acquire a sixty-acre slice of the Cheeseboro property from its current owner, the National Park Service. So beginning in 1987, Potomac started throwing around its political influence in Washington, hoping to make a deal to obtain sixty acres of national parkland to provide access to a private development.

In most times and in most places, the Park Service wouldn't have considered trading away parkland the federal government already owned. Even if the Park Service had considered it, mainline environmental groups would have flattened it with bad publicity. But the peculiar political history of the Santa Monicas meant two things for Potomac Investment Associates. First, the firm actually did have a chance at making a deal for the sixty acres of parkland in Cheeseboro Canyon. And second, for the deal to fly, sooner or later Joe Edmiston would have to support it.

At first Potomac did not try to make the deal with Edmiston. Instead, beginning in 1987, the firm decided to strongarm the National Park Service in Washington, hiring a slew of lobbyists and lawyers to twist the arms of the Secretary of the Interior on down. (One of Potomac's lawyers was the former law partner of William Clark, who had been Reagan's previous Interior Secretary.) The idea was to obtain Interior's approval for a land "swap," a deal that would give the Park Service a sizeable piece of Jordan in exchange for the sixty acres of parkland at Cheeseboro.

Potomac met with bureaucratic resistance in the field. All through 1987, Daniel Keuhn, then the Park Service's superintendent at Santa Monica, rejected any kind of a deal, and Keuhn's regional superior in San Francisco also balked. But by pummeling the politicos in Washington, Potomac was able to get a second hearing toward the end of the year. After negotiating all winter, Peter Kyros, Potomac's general partner, placed a formal offer on the table in the spring of 1988. Saying that any land swap must be "in the long-term best interests of the Park and in the public interest as well," Kyros proposed giving the Park Service eight hundred of Jordan's twenty-three hundred acres, including five hundred fifty-five acres of China Flat. (The developer wanted to reserve the right to build twenty homes on the other two hundred twenty-five acres of China Flat.) Potomac would also give the Park Service the parking concession at its annual PGA golf tournament and $1 million to build a Visitor Center. (The long-delayed Visitor Center was a delicate subject, especially since the Park Service had originally hoped to build it on Bob Hope's Sampo Farms property.) In return for these riches, the Park

Service would have to sell Potomac sixty acres of national parkland for an access road to the Jordan development.

Under intense lobbying pressure, the Park Service folded. On July 11, 1988, Stanley Albright, the western regional director, reversed his position and issued a press release blessing the deal. The following day, Kuehn testified in favor of the Potomac project before the Ventura County Board of Supervisors, and the board voted to allow Potomac's development application to move forward.

Joe Edmiston, however, did not fold. Like Park Service officials, Edmiston had been strident in his opposition all through 1987. Writing a letter to a Ventura County supervisor in December of that year, Edmiston noted that the Potomac proposal violated the Santa Monica Mountains Comprehensive Plan—a document he had helped draw up that federal, state, and local officials had all agreed to. Indeed, the policies in the mountains plan had been incorporated into the Ventura County General Plan. In typical lofty rhetoric, he wrote that the Potomac proposal "presents a serious danger to the integrity of planning for the Ventura County portion of the Santa Monica Mountains zone" and "rends the fabric of the general plan and shreds its usefulness as a document."

Later in 1988, as an agreement with the Park Service grew near, Potomac threw Edmiston another bone. As part of the deal, Potomac Investment Associates offered to sell the rest of China Flat—where they had planned to build twenty homes—along with critical trailheads and access routes near Cheeseboro Canyon to the Conservancy for $2 million. Edmiston had the money, because only a month before the state's voters had passed Proposition 70, a $770 million parkland acquisition bond issue. Still, Edmiston refused to take the bait.

But he didn't hold firm because he thought the Jordan project was irretrievably bad, or because he opposed the idea of making a deal with Potomac. Rather, Edmiston held firm because he believed he could cut a better deal.

↜

Most of the environmental hard-liners in the mountains thought Joe Edmiston was a sellout. They despised his power-mongering, his political posturing, and most of all his deal-making, which they believed revealed an impure environmental soul. They bickered with him constantly, exchanging petty letters and holding grudges for decades about things he had said and deals he had cut.

For his part, Edmiston engaged them in letters and conversations with great relish, reliving past battles and defending his decisions. Whatever his personal feelings for the eco-activists, Edmiston had a clear-eyed view of their value. Even while criticizing him, they were his constituency, his source of power. For twenty years, as the threat of development spread farther west, neighborhoods throughout the mountains had become radicalized by the threat of development—indeed, often by Edmiston's own actions—and the net result was that Edmiston's bargaining power grew. The more the eco-activists complained, the higher the price Edmiston could extract from some landowner or developer.

Edmiston knew full well that the Jordan situation was no different. The Park Service's acceptance of the Jordan deal in July 1988 was not the end of the story for the environmentalists, and hence did not represent the pinnacle of his bargaining power.

Like dozens of controversies before it, the Jordan deal mobilized a new anti-development constituency along the foothills of the mountains. This time, a small group of opponents emerged from the two communities next to Jordan Ranch: Agoura Hills (in Los Angeles County) and Oak Park (an adjacent neighborhood in Ventura County). Led by Agoura Hills housewife Mary Weisbrock, this group quickly organized into SOS—Save Open Space.

A woman of remarkable energy, and a favorite of newspaper reporters for her ability to provide great sound bites, Weisbrock emerged during 1989 as a pivotal figure in the Jordan debate. Through sheer will, she managed to keep the pressure on the Park Service all that year, as the proposed land swap worked its way through the federal approval process. Though a relative newcomer to eco-activism, Weisbrock also managed to connect her SOS group with older activists in the Santa Monicas—people from Los Angeles and Malibu—who had been fighting battles south of the freeway for many years.

Joining forces with other eco-activists, SOS managed to bring the Jordan Ranch deal to the attention of the environmental establishment in Washington. Once this connection was made, opposition began to mount quickly from sources far from Agoura Hills. In early 1990, the National Wildlife Federation called the land swap "a raid on the federal treasury." Representative Mike Synar of Oklahoma toured the property and announced plans to investigate all federal land exchanges. Hope himself expressed frustration with the opposition, telling one reporter, "It bugs the hell out of me." And he continued to say that Jordan would make a beautiful golf course.

Through all this uproar, Edmiston waited, knowing what Potomac would have to do in response. And in April 1990, Potomac came to the table with two more pieces of Bob Hope's property that Edmiston wanted. The first was the forty-three-hundred-acre Runkle Ranch property in Simi Valley, north of Jordan, which the L.A County Sanitation District had earmarked for a landfill.* The second was a one-hundred-seventy-seven-acre parcel of coastal land in Corral Canyon in Malibu, near Edmiston's office, which already had development approval from L.A. County.

Conveniently forgetting his earlier complaints that the Jordan project violated his own comprehensive plan for the mountains, Edmiston accepted the deal. On April 19, he signed an agreement with Bob Hope calling for Hope to give the Corral Canyon property to the Conservancy and sell the Runkle Ranch property to the Conservancy for $10 million, supposedly far less than the $35 million the sanitation district had offered. The deal was much better than any on the table before, and was in fact one of the most lopsided land deals ever proposed. Some fifty-seven hundred acres of private land would be protected in exchange for sixty acres of National Park land deeded over to Potomac. The Santa Monicas' master dealmaker had made what he thought was the best deal he could make.

The 1990 deal might have made Edmiston happy, but it did not silence Mary Weisbrock. She and her colleagues at SOS were not at all pleased by the deal. Both Runkle Ranch and Corral Canyon were far away from the organization's Agoura Hills base, so the benefits were not immediately apparent to many of the members. Meanwhile, Potomac had not budged from its original plans to develop most of Jordan with a golf course and more than eighteen hundred homes.

Frustrated by their inability to sway either Edmiston or the Park Service, SOS members decided to focus on local politics instead. Potomac

* The Runkle offer had the added benefit of appealing to Ventura County Supervisor Vicki Howard, whose constituents would rather have a park on Runkle Ranch than L.A. County's trash.

still needed Ventura County's approval. Weisbrock and the organization's other leaders wanted to find an anti-Jordan candidate to run against the pro-development incumbent, Madge Schaefer, whose district included Jordan Ranch. But they had a problem: Almost all of the SOS members lived across the county line in Agoura Hills.

Then, one day, Mary Weisbrock read a letter to the editor in the *Los Angeles Daily News,* calling for preservation of the Jordan Ranch. It was signed: "Maria VanderKolk, Thousand Oaks." Characteristically assertive, Weisbrock called VanderKolk and invited her to an SOS meeting at the home of Barry Van Dyke, son of actor Dick Van Dyke, who lived on the private road in Old Agoura adjacent to the Jordan Ranch.

When she walked in the door of Barry Van Dyke's house, Maria Vander-Kolk did not look much like the next Ventura County supervisor from Thousand Oaks. Six feet tall and twenty-five years old, VanderKolk was attractive and well spoken; she worked as a marketing specialist for a local toy company. But unlike almost everyone else in the room, she was not a veteran of the political wars in the Santa Monicas. In fact, she was not a veteran of much of anything in California. Born and raised on a farm in Colorado, VanderKolk had moved to the Los Angeles area only a little over two years before, when her husband accepted a position as an aerospace engineer. She had lived in Ventura County for only fifteen months. And partly because of her age, she was a bit shy and occasionally uncertain.

Oak Park, hotbed of SOS's tract-home environmentalism, with the peaks of Jordan Ranch in the background.

If she was not a typical SOS activist, VanderKolk had several things to recommend her as a potential candidate for supervisor. Her environmental beliefs seemed sincere. Despite her shyness, she projected herself well in public. She was a registered Republican, a distinct advantage for an environmentalist in a conservative suburban area. And most important, she was almost the only person in the room who lived in Madge Schaefer's district in Ventura County.

Less than two weeks after she wrote the letter, Maria VanderKolk called in sick to her employer. She went to the County Government Center in Ventura, paid a $478 filing fee, and began a one-issue campaign for supervisor with SOS's backing. She was horrified, she later recalled, when her photograph appeared in the newspaper the next day. She was afraid her boss would discover that she hadn't really been sick.

The incumbent Schaefer didn't take her seriously, and VanderKolk took maximum advantage of her opponent's complacency. She crisscrossed the district, speaking about saving Jordan Ranch and her environmentalist values at every opportunity. She also received help from Patagonia Inc., the environmentally oriented clothing manufacturer based in Ventura County, whose subtle ads in local newspapers called on voters to save Jordan. SOS quickly incorporated, conducted mail campaigns, and walked precincts.

On election night in June 1990, Maria VanderKolk got tired of the suspense and went to bed. At two-thirty in the morning, she was awakened by a phone call informing her that she had been elected Ventura County supervisor from Thousand Oaks by fewer than one hundred votes. And suddenly, the environmental politics of the Santa Monica Mountains had changed again. Suddenly, the fifty-seven-hundred-acre deal Joe Edmiston had cut just a few weeks before no longer looked like the best deal possible.

⌐

The education of Maria VanderKolk began when she showed up for work at the toy company six hours after being elected. Although she wouldn't take office for six months—not until January 1991—she and her husband had a mortgage to meet, and she wanted to keep her job. But the television cameras arrived at her office that morning before she did. Her bosses didn't appreciate the publicity and she quit, leaving her six unpaid months to figure out how to be a county supervisor representing one hundred forty thousand people.

The learning curve was steep. She knew nothing about county government; she didn't even know the difference between a prosecutor and a public defender. But she did know that if she did nothing else in the following four years, she had to figure out a way to save Jordan Ranch.

Edmiston and the developers had already begun to lay traps for her along the way. In July, for example, Hope's lawyer wrote a letter to the City of Simi Valley, asking that it consider annexing Jordan Ranch.

Simi Valley, not yet the notorious home of the Rodney King trial, was a working-class community with upwardly mobile ambitions and something of an inferiority complex. Simi's leaders could be expected to favor an upscale development like Jordan in their city. And because Runkle Ranch was adjacent to Simi, Hope and Edmiston could hammer away at the benefits of the land swap to local residents. Hope placed a color insert in the local newspaper, emphasizing that the land swap would prevent a landfill from being built in Simi Valley. Meanwhile, the Conservancy hosted tours of Runkle Ranch, which, because it was owned by Hope, had never before been open to the public.

At the end of August, however, Ventura County released its environmental impact report for the Jordan project. The environmental consequences of the Potomac proposal—on air quality, on wildlife, on natural resources—were undeniable. It wasn't long before the Simi Valley annexation idea died on the vine. That meant the Jordan proponents had to step up the pressure on VanderKolk directly. In January 1991, just after VanderKolk was sworn in, Potomac offered a new development plan. Instead of eighteen hundred homes, the Jordan plan now called for only seven hundred fifty, with more property set aside for preservation. That was the carrot. But VanderKolk soon felt the stick as well.

Toward the beginning of March 1991, just two months after she took office, VanderKolk was summoned to a meeting in Sacramento with Pete Wilson, the new governor, to talk about Jordan Ranch. When she arrived, she was not alone; she was joined by Edmiston, several county officials, and leaders of three surrounding cities. They were greeted by Wilson, his planning aide Richard Sybert, and representatives for both Potomac and Bob Hope.

The fact that the meeting took place at all was a testament to Potomac's extraordinary clout. Not only did Wilson attend briefly, but he handed out a letter from Interior Secretary Manuel Lujan—apparently solicited by Potomac just for the meeting—calling the land swap "an innovative partnership I personally find attractive." The young supervisor was overwhelmed that so much highly placed political attention was being focused on her. But she could hardly miss the point of the meeting: she was supposed to stop fighting and make a deal.

In later years, when they tried to explain why Maria VanderKolk had betrayed them, Weisbrock and other SOS leaders often pointed to the meeting with Wilson and Sybert as a turning point. Though sincere, they would argue, VanderKolk was not strong. She did not have the courage of her convictions. Pressured by politically powerful older men, Maria buckled.

There is some truth to this version. The meeting with Wilson was, in fact, a turning point in VanderKolk's thinking. She was indeed intimidated by the governor and his aides. But the change was more subtle than the SOS people suggest. The obvious deal to make, and the one Wilson's staff and Potomac clearly expected to force upon her, was a scaled-down project on Jordan Ranch that would permit the golf course and some houses while still preserving most of the land. That, after all, was the standard deal in Southern California.

Yet VanderKolk held firm in her opposition to such a deal. To find a way around the problem, she began to take a broader view of environmental politics in the Santa Monicas. She later recalled that she came to realize she did not want to spend four years simply saying no to Potomac. She wanted a permanent solution.

In assessing her options, VanderKolk came to understand, as Joe Edmiston did, that environmental politics in the Santa Monicas was a chess game, and you had to look at the whole board to understand how to deal with each piece of property. So she stepped back and looked at the whole board. And that's when she noticed Ahmanson Ranch.

The Ahmanson Ranch was a huge piece of property, some fifty-four hundred acres, located just two canyons to the east of Jordan. It was bordered on the east and south by intensely developed subdivisions in Los Angeles and Calabasas, but like Jordan it was located in Ventura County. For more than twenty years, it had been owned by Los Angeles-based Home Savings of America, the largest savings-and-loan in the country and in the high-rolling 1980s one of the most solvent.

Though VanderKolk did not pay much attention to it prior to her election, Ahmanson's fate had been intertwined with Jordan's for several years. Beginning in 1986, Home Savings proposed an enormous development on Laskey Mesa, a flat portion of the property immediately adjacent to Los Angeles and Calabasas. As part of the deal,

Las Virgenes Canyon at Ahmanson Ranch, which Home Savings agreed to donate to the National Park Service as part of the deal to develop the property.

Home Savings agreed to donate Las Virgenes Canyon, a beautiful thirty-five hundred acre section farther west, near Cheeseboro Canyon, to the Park Service. The Park Service accepted the offer in the same public statement, in July 1988, in which it announced its support of the Jordan land swap.

Ventura County processed the two proposals more or less simultaneously, and the respective environmental impact reports were released on the same day. In the public's mind, Ahmanson and Jordan were virtually indistinguishable. SOS was opposed to Ahmanson but had focused more attention on Jordan, which was closer to Agoura Hills.

Yet the projects were very different. Potomac's front men were slick political types. Ahmanson Development Company was headed by the courtly urban planner Donald Brackenbush, once the partner of legendary environmental planner Ian McHarg, author of the classic book *Design with Nature*. Potomac wanted to build a lavish golf course community with million-dollar houses surrounding the fairways. Home Savings envisioned a fully rounded community on Laskey Mesa, with office and shopping districts, apartments, and single-family homes for various income groups. And, of course, Ahmanson was adjacent to established communities, while Jordan was not.

That is not to say that Ahmanson was not free of public controversy. It was, in many ways, more controversial than Jordan. For one thing, Ahmanson's overall development proposal was much larger: three million square feet of office space (the equivalent of three large downtown office towers), three thousand houses, a large hotel, and a golf course. Environmental degradation was considerable. And because it was located adjacent to existing communities, Ahmanson was an easy political target. In the fall of 1990, local politicians from both Calabasas and Los Angeles stood at the end of dead-end streets, vowing never to permit the roads to be built across the county line to accommodate Ahmanson.

Attempting to read the political climate, Ahmanson had slip-streamed behind Potomac in the development process. And after Vander-Kolk's election, Ahmanson, like Jordan, proposed a much smaller project. The new proposal called for only four hundred thousand square feet of office space and eighteen hundred homes. Both developers appeared to be playing the classic game of downsizing. Each hoped to scale its project back so much that local politicians could, in standard fashion, vote for the projects and still declare a victory for the environment.

Instead, VanderKolk, looking at the chessboard, decided to try a different approach. Since she couldn't seem to kill the Potomac project, she concluded, maybe she could move it—off Jordan Ranch and onto Ahmanson.

Beginning in the spring of 1991, her environmental aides Lenora Kirby and Russ Baggerly began meeting secretly with Brackenbush to discuss the possibility of combining the two projects on the Ahmanson Ranch, thereby freeing the Jordan Ranch to be purchased by the Conservancy or the Park Service. The discussions were tentative at first. The two developers had discussed the idea the year before but, because of their different styles, rejected it. And VanderKolk felt she could not risk alienating her SOS constituency by revealing that she was negotiating with developers. All during the summer of 1991, a summer in which VanderKolk was pregnant, she maintained her public opposition to the Potomac project. Meanwhile, her aides continued to negotiate with Ahmanson and Potomac, pushing for more environmental goodies in the package.

Maria VanderKolk at Jordan Ranch, December 16, 1992, the day after the Ventura County Board of Supervisors approved the combined Jordan-Ahmanson project.

By fall, discussions were almost complete, but word of a deal had leaked to the press. So at a hastily arranged press conference in mid-October 1991, VanderKolk stunned the county with the

announcement that a complex exchange, while not completely negotiated, was in the works. Literally nine months pregnant, she stood in
front of a gigantic map of the entire chessboard and explained how the
pieces would fall into place. The Ahmanson and Potomac projects—
twenty-six hundred homes, two golf courses, and four hundred thousand square feet of commercial space—would be combined on Laskey
Mesa. Jordan Ranch would be sold to the Conservancy or the Park Service as part of a $29.5 million package of Bob Hope properties that also
included Runkle Ranch and Corral Canyon. Ahmanson would still
donate Las Virgenes Canyon to the Park Service.

In all, park agencies would acquire more than ten thousand acres
of land, and would now own three critical adjacent canyons—Jordan
Ranch, Cheeseboro, and Las Virgenes—north of the 101 Freeway. Wilson
aide Richard Sybert, while taking partial credit in a press release, called
it "the park deal of the century."* A spokesman for the National Parks
and Conservation Association, a mainline environmental group, called
the deal "like, wow, a miracle." One SOS leader said he was "thrilled"
with the deal, though he had some concerns. And Mary Weisbrock
said, "I am going to do whatever I can to preserve Ahmanson Ranch as
open space."

⤳

Over the following year, having achieved her main goal, Maria Vander-
Kolk made a serious strategic mistake: she went beyond dealmaker and
became a cheerleader for the combined Ahmanson-Jordan project. She
and her aides worked closely with Ahmanson in shaping several aspects
of the new project, including special parks and a new environmental
institute Ahmanson had agreed to create. She praised the virtues of the
project's supposed "neo-traditional" layout, which was designed to minimize automobile use by making virtually all residences in the project a
short walk from the town's shopping district. And she backed up Brackenbush when he said the project's size had to be increased to accommodate the county's affordable housing requirements.

---

* Claiming credit for the Jordan-Ahmanson deal, Sybert ran for Congress from Thousand Oaks in 1994, losing narrowly to veteran Democrat Anthony Beilenson, who was the
congressional architect of the Santa Monica Mountains National Recreation Area. In 1996,
Beilenson retired, but Sybert lost again, this time to Brad Sherman.

Most important, VanderKolk agreed to push the Ahmanson project through quickly in order to accommodate deadlines established by Bob Hope. Nearing his ninetieth birthday, the entertainer was apparently anxious to see profits from the combined Ahmanson-Jordan deal.

This new combined project was dramatically different than the previous proposal for the Ahmanson site, a situation that would ordinarily require the county to start from square one on environmental documents. At Hope's request, VanderKolk agreed to an expedited schedule calling for approval by July 1992, only nine months after she announced the deal. When that proved impossible, she agreed to push approval back to December 1992. But the county still moved quickly by adding new information to old environmental documents, rather than starting over. All through 1992, the Ahmanson-Jordan project was moving ahead full-throttle, with VanderKolk at the controls.

But her constituency did not move with her. First, opposition in neighboring communities began to mount, especially in Calabasas, just to the south of the Ahmanson Ranch. A newly incorporated city located across the county line, Calabasas would bear the brunt of the traffic from the Ahmanson project. Bashing Ahmanson became good politics in Calabasas in 1992.

Second, Weisbrock and the other SOS leaders felt betrayed and did not hesitate to say so in public. They had helped elect VanderKolk so she could oppose development, they believed, and she had turned around and made a deal, just as Edmiston would have done. The issue was not just Jordan, they insisted; it was keeping development out of the area altogether. It wasn't long before SOS was firing heavy anti-Ahmanson salvos toward VanderKolk in the press.

With Jordan saved, the group now refocused its attention on saving Ahmanson. Though Las Virgenes Canyon was to be deeded to the Park Service and Laskey Mesa was adjacent to existing neighborhoods, SOS sharply criticized the project. Laskey Mesa turned out to have an important stand of California native grasses, a fact that SOS exploited. And while the environmental documents were being rewritten, SOS argued forcefully that the Ahmanson project would harm regional traffic and air quality.

The case against Ahmanson did change some minds. Ventura County's staff planners recommended denial, claiming that the project would set a bad precedent because it would erode the county's open space policies. The county's planning commission, meeting hastily in December 1992, at VanderKolk's request, formally voted against the project.

Ten days before Christmas, the Board of Supervisors met to vote on the Ahmanson project as well. In a lengthy and emotional statement, VanderKolk defended her position but expressed sadness. "I never meant to hurt you," she told Weisbrock and the other environmentalists who had helped elect her. "I'm sorry for the lost friendships. But I'm proud of this proposal." With those words, she extracted approval of the project from the board on a four-to-one vote.

In less than three years, VanderKolk had risen from an unknown to a position of power through a political fluke. Her election changed the rules of the game in the Santa Monicas. She withstood the overtures of both the Governor of California and the Secretary of the Interior, who wanted her to make a deal that would allow development on Jordan Ranch. In her naiveté, she had been perhaps a little too zealous in embracing the eventual Ahmanson project and ramming it through. Even so, she held out for, and achieved, what she wanted and what she thought her constituency wanted: total preservation of Jordan Ranch. And in the end, it cost her the support of almost every political friend she had. "She's a traitor," Mary Weisbrock told a newspaper reporter the day after the Ahmanson vote. "She ran on our principles and that got her elected, and now she's betrayed us. It's that simple."

Even with all that, however, the education of Maria VanderKolk was not quite complete.

⤸

VanderKolk had rushed the Ahmanson approval to accommodate Bob Hope's desire, for whatever reason, to sell Jordan Ranch to the National Park Service by January 15, 1993. But the board's vote in December did not settle the issue. And as it turned out, VanderKolk's much-sought-after Ahmanson approval was not the lever that placed Jordan Ranch in the hands of the Park Service, at least not directly.

The Park Service did not buy the Hope property in January because by that time Ventura County had been peppered with nine different lawsuits challenging the Ahmanson project. Until the lawsuits were settled, Ahmanson Land Company could not start building and, under the terms of the deal with the county, Hope could not sell the property. It was clear that the lawsuits would take months, if not years, to resolve. In the meantime, Bob Hope was eighty-nine years old and counting.

In March, two months after Bob Hope's original deadline, Vander-Kolk awoke one morning to read a startling headline in the *Los Angeles Times:* TALKS IN AHMANSON LAND SWAP SNARLED. Not only was Bob Hope ornery about the delays, but now the National Park Service was threatening to pull the plug on the entire deal if Hope didn't sell the property by the end of the month.

David Gackenbach, who had taken over as the Santa Monica park superintendent in 1989, had $19.5 million in acquisition funds sitting in the bank. But he said that if he failed to spend the money, Congress might not appropriate more funds for acquisition in the Santa Monicas the following year. So Gackenbach made Hope an offer to buy Jordan and Corral Canyon, separate and apart from the Ahmanson deal.*

But Hope nixed this idea, fearing that without Jordan as leverage, the Ahmanson deal would fall apart and he would never realize his expected profits as Ahmanson's partner. During March and April, every-thing was up in the air. Playing a game of chicken with Hope, Gacken-bach withdrew his offer in April. Trying to keep the land from slipping away, Edmiston offered Hope a side deal for Runkle Ranch in Simi Valley.

And Maria VanderKolk sat on the sidelines, dumbfounded that the deal she had worked so hard for refused to stay zipped up.

In May, Hope finally folded, agreeing to accept $16.7 million from the Park Service for Jordan. But Hope and Potomac continued to nego-tiate privately for a settlement with Ahmanson Land Company, which was suddenly in the awkward situation of relying on Bob Hope's good faith in delivering Runkle and Corral Canyon to the Conservancy as a condition of moving its project forward.

By the time she sat on the podium under the oak trees on Jordan Ranch in April 1994, Maria VanderKolk had already made up her mind not to run for re-election. "I don't have much courage," she said later. "And I used it all up on Jordan Ranch." A week after her last board meeting, her education as a politician at last complete, she and her family moved back to Colorado.

---

* Gackenbach was actually an important player in the Jordan story. A former head of concessions for the Park Service, he was more entrepreneurial than most park superin-tendents and worked closely with Edmiston on several land deals during his five-year tenure.

Not surprisingly, the chess game in the Santa Monicas went on much as it had before she arrived. Joe Edmiston moved on quickly to other deals. He accepted Barbra Streisand's lavish Malibu ranch and established an environmental institute there. He settled a development dispute in Topanga Canyon, just east of Calabasas, by offering to buy out the developer with money he didn't have. He tried to work a deal to buy a ranch in Santa Barbara County, a hundred miles from the Santa Monicas, but got his wings clipped by the state legislature.

Potomac Investment Associates went away, but Donald Brackenbush and the Ahmanson Land Company stuck around, grinding it out for years in courtrooms in Los Angeles and Ventura trying to get the Ahmanson Ranch project built. When asked what he did for a living, Brackenbush often replied, "I'm a developer. People sue me and I sue them and then they sue me again."

And Mary Weisbrock and SOS continued their crusade to save Ahmanson. Discovering that the federal Land and Water Conservation Fund had been stockpiling cash, she announced an effort to crack it open so that the Ahmanson property could be purchased by the Park Service or the Conservancy. Mainstream environmentalists in Washington hadn't been able to crack open the Land and Water Conservation Fund despite years of trying, but that didn't dissuade Weisbrock from thinking she could do it. She and her fellow SOS members remained bitter about VanderKolk. "She took our principles," Weisbrock said afterwards, sounding a little like a priest who lost a member of the flock, "but they weren't in her heart."

There was no question that Mary Weisbrock and her fellow eco-activists wanted Jordan Ranch saved. But giving the eco-activists what they said they wanted wasn't enough. That was what Maria VanderKolk didn't understand, having grown up in Colorado instead of Calabasas. Saving Jordan wasn't a goal; it was a symbol, a metaphor for keeping the growth machine out.

Maria VanderKolks come and go in the Santa Monica Mountains, and sometimes they do some good. But the growth game goes on: Developers try to build projects; Mary Weisbrock complains; Joe Edmiston makes a deal; everybody reaches for the nuclear weapon of litigation. An outsider, a flatlander, may be able to save a piece of land now and then and feel good about it. But an outsider can't change this little world.

CHAPTER 8

The Politics of Extinction

The California gnatcatcher is a small songbird that ranges across thousands of square miles of land in the rapidly developing areas south and east of Los Angeles. Whether or not the gnatcatchers found in Orange, Riverside, and San Diego counties are a separate species or not depends on who you talk to; there are many similar birds in Baja California. But no one disputes that there aren't very many in Southern California, probably only around two thousand pairs.

As it happens, this same area south and east of Los Angeles is also an important habitat for the California Republican. Ordinarily this species is far more numerous than the gnatcatcher. It has appeared in vast numbers over the years in both affluent and working-class suburbs, providing big electoral margins for candidates like Ronald Reagan, Richard Nixon, and Pete Wilson. In 1992, however, the California Republican appeared to be endangered too. Amid the region's dismal economic climate, suburban Republicans, including many important real estate developers, deserted George Bush in droves and flew instead to Bill Clinton, who promised them a return to prosperity. The endangered Republicans in Orange County and elsewhere helped Clinton win California in 1992, and it was generally agreed that Clinton needed to hold them in order to have any chance of re-election in 1996.

The common habitat of gnatcatchers and Republicans explains why Bruce Babbitt, the new Interior Secretary, turned up at the Hyatt Regency in Irvine in June 1993, just a couple of weeks after Clinton had fielded an angry question about the gnatcatcher at a town meeting in San Diego.

Shortly after taking office in January, Babbitt had stepped into the middle of a brewing controversy in Southern California by declaring the California gnatcatcher a "threatened" species under the Endangered Species Act, a move that held the potential to shut down dozens of building projects throughout the region. With this announcement, he was trying to force Southern California's landowners to sit down at the negotiating table and reach a compromise with state and federal biologists and with local environmental groups—not just to save the gnatcatcher, but to save the Endangered Species Act itself.

For more than two years prior to Babbitt's appearance in Irvine, both state and federal wildlife officials had been considering whether to place the gnatcatcher on their endangered species lists. "Listing" doesn't sound like much of a weapon, but listing carries with it the power to shut down most economic activity, including real estate development and highway construction projects, in areas where the species is found. Though very few people had heard of the gnatcatcher before this controversy began, the bird's range was so great—and overlapped so much with the brush and grasslands developers coveted for homebuilding—that listing it seemed likely to disrupt the economy of the entire region.

Coming on the heels of a huge controversy over the listing of the spotted owl in the Pacific Northwest, the gnatcatcher accelerated the national debate over the Endangered Species Act. In Congress, business interests used the bird to help bolster their case for changing the law. In response, Babbitt defended the Endangered Species Act as written, pointing to the gnatcatcher—and to a promising set of negotiations initiated by the Republican governor, Pete Wilson—as proof that the law could be made to "work" without being weakened by Congress.

Now, at Clinton's prompting, Babbitt had come to a meeting of business executives in Irvine to reassure them that Orange County was not the Northwest, and that the gnatcatcher situation would not be the "train wreck" that the spotted owl had been. Having declared to Congress that the gnatcatcher negotiations represented the best hope for making the Endangered Species Act work, Babbitt now had to keep Orange County's developers at the negotiating table.

"The outcome is by no means clear," he told them. "But we're going to be writing history in the process, and I want to do everything in my power to make certain that the federal government is doing everything that it can to make this thing work. We have to make it

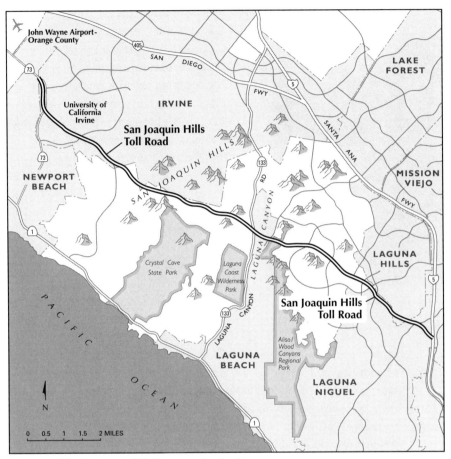

The route of the San Joaquin Hills Transportation Corridor.

work. And the reason is simply this: We have an Endangered Species Act, and it is a permanent part of the environmental structure of American law."

Once he had served up the rhetoric, however, Babbitt made it clear he was willing to sacrifice something in return for the developers' participation in the gnatcatcher negotiations. "Lastly," he said, "a word about the San Joaquin Hills Transportation Corridor." A controversial toll road that would slice through an undeveloped portion of south Orange County, the San Joaquin was the largest construction project affected by the gnatcatcher. Environmentalists hated the road and wanted it stopped, but three months earlier Babbitt had issued a ruling that gave

Old Laguna Canyon Road (Highway 133) prior to construction of the San Joaquin Hills toll road.

it a green light under the Endangered Species Act—a so-called no-jeopardy ruling, meaning that construction of the road would not jeopardize the survival of the species. Now Babbitt, a highly regarded environmentalist himself, was being pressured by environmental groups to reverse the ruling. At the Hyatt Regency in Irvine, Babbitt gave his answer.

"Our word, once given, has got to be kept," he said, "because we're going to be asking all of you...to act the same way. We can't make that request of all of you unless we first say to you our word is good. And that non-jeopardy opinion is our word, and it's good, and we're going to keep it."

In other words, Babbitt was saying, the federal government was willing to play ball on Orange County's most controversial road—if the county's developers would help him preserve the Endangered Species Act in return. As it happened, Babbitt had chosen to play ball on a road that was, symbolically, almost as important to environmentalists as the gnatcatcher itself. It was a road all of them were against, a road that represented to them everything bad that Southern California was or would become if rampant development were allowed to continue.

〜

"Stop the road!"

Earth First! founder Dave Foreman stepped back from the microphone and raised his fist. Two thousand protesters standing amid the movie-set green of Laguna Canyon raised their fists too, and the timing was perfect, because at that exact moment the Channel 11 news helicopter emerged from behind a nearby hill.

With the helicopter still whirring overhead, the protesters picked up hundreds of blankets and white sheets they'd brought from home and began walking south. Helped by white-shirted volunteers, the protesters headed down Laguna Canyon Road and across an open field, where they began to lay down their sheets. Within a few minutes, five hundred sheets were on the ground, forming the outline of the eight proposed lanes of the San Joaquin Hills Transportation Corridor and its massive cloverleaf interchange with Laguna Canyon Road.

Never before had Orange County seen such a large, dramatic, and heavily publicized environmental protest as the Laguna Canyon rally on Leap Day (February 29) 1992. But never before had Orange County's environmental activists felt so close to such a major victory.

Only a few years earlier, a countywide growth control initiative had been crushed by the political power of developers. (See chapter 2, Perestroika Co-opted.) Since then, however, a whole cadre of environmental activists had emerged in Orange County, especially in Laguna Beach, the beautiful onetime art colony that stood along the Pacific Ocean at the mouth of Laguna Canyon. One was Norm Grossman, a diminutive, bearded aerospace engineer, who brought his disappointing experience in the slow-growth initiative to bear on new problems, especially in the Laguna Beach area. Another was Elisabeth Brown, an articulate Ph.D., who brought a calm, reasoning presence to Laguna Greenbelt, the leading environmental organization in the area. And there were many others.

It was easy to call them NIMBYs, and a desire to keep development out of local backyards clearly was part of the motivation behind the burgeoning movement. But success was coming. In 1990, Laguna Greenbelt had scored a major victory by stopping The Irvine Company from building a housing project in Laguna Canyon and winning a commitment from the Laguna Beach City Council to buy the land in question (for $78 million). The next year, the environmentalists had forced an astonishing deal with The Irvine Company to preserve seventy percent of the land in the ten-thousand-acre "Irvine Coast" tract just north of Laguna Beach, the last large undeveloped piece of property along Orange County's coast.

So when Grossman, Brown, and other Laguna Beach environmentalists asked Dave Foreman to headline the rally, he came, and so did the TV helicopters. Laguna Canyon and the gnatcatchers nesting there had become extraordinarily important symbols, because environmentalists had never had any true political power in Orange County. They had always been out of the loop.

Given the size and political influence of Orange County's major landowners (see chapter 6), this was no surprise. From the 1960s through the 1980s Orange County served as the staging area for sophisticated real estate development techniques and clever community planning models developed in response to the staggering pace of growth. With their ability to hire top architectural and planning talent and their skill at marketing one generation after another of suburban communities, the big Orange County developers had dominated local politics for decades.

To be sure, they fought their share of local political battles. As small cities popped up around the county—largely the result of their own development activities—landowners had to cut the size of the projects, jack up their affordable housing quotient, and deed over land for public open space. And when a rare head-on challenge to the county's growth ethic emerged, as when a countywide growth control measure made it to the ballot in 1988, the big developers simply hired the political skill necessary to bat it down and go about their business. Maintaining enough political clout to develop land in Orange County was becoming harder and harder for the growth machine, but it was still possible.

To complete the buildout, the landowners needed the San Joaquin Hills and two other toll roads through the southern part of the county. The same suburban planning ideas that the Irvine Company and others had marketed so successfully—cul-de-sacs, isolated neighborhoods, quiet local streets—had also robbed Orange County of the transportation flexibility a growing metropolis required. To go anywhere, you had to use a freeway; and the county, mostly developed after California's postwar freeway building boom, didn't have very many freeways. (San Diego County, with the same population, had a hundred more freeway miles than Orange County.) As early as 1976, the county's planning documents called for a locally funded highway along the San Joaquin freeway corridor that Caltrans had once identified.

Grading along the right-of-way for the toll road, 1992.

Supporters said that toll roads would relieve Orange County's overburdened freeway system, and on its face this argument was hard to contest. Yet there was more to it than that. The tollways were being constructed by a government agency—actually three entities known as the Orange County Transportation Corridor Agencies—funded primarily by fees the big developers paid to the county. (Fees were necessary because tolls alone couldn't cover the cost of the roads, especially up-front costs.) The proposed roads, while making important connections in Orange County's transportation, also opened up important new territory owned by the big developers.

Local environmentalists weren't crazy about the Foothill or Eastern toll roads, but the San Joaquin was the one they really despised. The route began in Irvine, hooking off Interstate 405, and sliced through beautiful, rolling hills, the last undeveloped hills in coastal Orange County. Then it slipped down into Laguna Canyon.

More than any other, Laguna Canyon was the place that defined the environmental movement in Orange County. Beautiful and dramatic, it was the gateway to Laguna Beach, a community that still stood out as distinctive in a sea of suburban subdivisions. Over the years Laguna Canyon had managed to evade the bulldozers, and it was still served only by a winding two-lane road, State Route 133, that meandered through the canyon toward the beach.

Some of the land in the Laguna Canyon area was part of the $78 million deal between Laguna Beach and The Irvine Company. But most of it was still up for grabs. The environmentalists thought that stopping the tollway was the key to controlling the future of south Orange County. Even though large projects had been approved along the route, those developments were scarcely viable without the tollway. Stop the road, the environmentalists believed, and you could stop the developers.

In the months leading up to the Laguna Canyon rally, the Orange County environmentalists had been gearing up to use every tool at their disposal to stop the road. They had legal tools, principally the federal Clean Air Act and the California Environmental Quality Act, that could be used to stall. And they had resources at their disposal from renegade cities like Laguna Beach and from environmental groups. But they were still searching for an organizing principle—something that would symbolize what was at risk in Laguna Canyon, galvanize public opposition, and carry with it enough legal clout to stop the road. Then along came the bird.

↩

The California gnatcatcher is only two inches long, and—as reporters never tire of pointing out—when it sings it sounds much like a kitten mewing. It is one of perhaps a dozen or so similar birds that range across a common natural setting in Southern California: the low-lying brush-like areas that stretch from the ocean inland, petering out where the ocean breezes begin to dry up. Scrub is a familiar sight throughout the region, and even far beyond; among other things, it's the background foliage appearing in *Gidget*, Frankie Avalon movies, and a thousand other surfer flicks and television shows.

For decades, developers, road-builders, and homeowners have been pulling coastal sage scrub out of the ground and hauling it to the local dump. The effect on the gnatcatcher and on other birds that nest in the scrub has been devastating. Unlike the mountain lion or the sea lion or the California condor, no one noticed when the gnatcatcher began to disappear. Indeed, hardly anyone had ever heard of it, even within the environmental community, until one day in 1989 when a Ph.D. student at UCLA named Jonathan Atwood approached the Natural Resources Defense Council and asked for help in placing the bird on the endangered species list.

At the time, the Endangered Species Act was becoming one of the most controversial laws in America, and one that threatened to turn Southern California inside out. As the spotted owl controversy had made abundantly clear, the Act was the biggest weapon in the environmental arsenal. Unlike other environmental laws, the Endangered Species Act had no wiggle room, no escape hatches, and no trap doors. It was, as environmentalists liked to say, the pit bull of American environmental laws; once it sunk its teeth into something, it did not let go. Throughout the 1980s, the Endangered Species Act sunk its teeth into more and more areas of private business in America. That's why it was widely reviled by business generally, and by landowners in particular.

Congress passed the law in 1973, at the tail end of a burst of environmental legislation. Building on previous laws designed to protect vanishing high-profile species, the Endangered Species Act was envisioned as a law of last resort. Traditionally, states have taken on most of the task of protecting wildlife by setting up preserves and refuges. The purpose of the Endangered Species Act was to protect individual species that had somehow slipped through the state's safety nets and were now hurtling down the chute toward extinction.

For this reason, the Endangered Species Act is an extreme law, deliberately designed to bring the federal government into the fray extremely late in the process. In most cases, the U.S. Fish and Wildlife Service has no formal regulatory power over real estate development or other activities that might affect the welfare of wildlife. But once a species is designated as endangered or threatened—that is, virtually on the brink of extinction—the Fish and Wildlife biologists wield tremendous power.* Suddenly, those same biologists have virtually total authority to stop all economic activity on the land where the species in question resides.

In California, the issue of endangered species is even more complicated. The state's own Endangered Species Act not only parallels the federal law, but is tougher—because unlike the federal law, it blocks development even while a species is being studied for possible listing. Thus, when a species is placed on the endangered list in California, local officials and developers usually find themselves facing angry stares from not one but two sets of biologists: those from the U.S. Fish and Wildlife Service, and their counterparts (wearing a different set of uniforms) at the California Department of Fish and Game.

The federal Endangered Species Act has always been controversial, but for many years those controversies—the snail darter, the spotted owl—were limited to activities occurring on federally owned land. In the 1980s, however, private real estate developers began to push farther and farther into previously undisturbed natural areas. As they did so, they began running into endangered species on their land, especially in California, where the concentration of new homes is matched only by the concentration of biological diversity. Thus began a whole new area of contention over how private land is used and how it can be regulated.

In Southern California, the alarm bell rang on Halloween of 1988, when the Fish and Wildlife Service suddenly threatened to send the Riverside County Board of Supervisors to jail for approving one hundred thousand new houses (see chapter 4). The reason was that the Service had just placed on the endangered species list a tiny rodent, the Stephens' kangaroo rat, which thrived in the flat grasslands of western Riverside County favored by developers who built starter homes. The Service had written many letters warning Riverside County that the new housing projects would harm the rat's habitat. But because the rat hadn't yet been listed, the county was under no obligation to respond. Once the species

* "Endangered" is a category meaning that a species is about to become extinct. "Threatened" is a category that indicates a species is in trouble, but not quite close enough to merit endangered status. However, Fish and Wildlife's regulatory power for each category is similar. Fish and Wildlife declared both the spotted owl and the gnatcatcher threatened, even though biological evidence probably would have supported an endangered listing in both cases.

was listed, the Service had the power to impose criminal penalties on those who disturbed its habitat, including the Board of Supervisors.

Riverside County really had only one option. Under the law, the county could obtain a special permit from the Service to allow some development if all sides could agree on a "habitat conservation plan," a plan to establish a preserve of up to forty thousand acres that would ensure plenty of room for the kangaroo rat to thrive. A permanent plan would take years to prepare. But even a temporary plan came at tremendous cost: a $1,950-per-acre mitigation fee for developers and a new county agency to administer the funds.*

By this time the Fish and Wildlife Service (and its counterpart, the state Department of Fish and Game) had caught the attention of politicians, developers, public works agencies, and everyone else who was part of the Southern California growth machine. And the kangaroo rat was merely the first species heading down the chute toward extinction in Southern California. In a region blessed—or cursed—with unparalleled biological diversity, the Service had identified more than twenty other species approaching extinction. Every one of them held the same potential as the kangaroo rat to disrupt the local economy. And this fact was not lost on Southern California's environmental activists, nor on their friends at the Natural Resources Defense Council.

Founded in 1969 by a group of newly minted graduates of Yale Law School, NRDC was unique among environmental groups, serving as both a membership organization and an aggressive environmental law firm. Like many environmental groups, NRDC had always run its West Coast operations from San Francisco, where many environmental activists preferred to live. By the late 1980s, however, national environmental groups like NRDC had to establish a beachhead in L.A. The boom times of the 1980s had produced too much growth, too many new environmental problems, and too big a base of donors to ignore.

The office immediately attracted a talented staff of experienced lawyers and scientists.† One of the best was Joel Reynolds. Reynolds looked like the classic environmental lawyer: tall, thin, bearded, and

---

* A final plan was not approved until 1996, but even then controversies continued to rage, especially on the question of the $1,950-per-acre mitigation fee. Local officials cut the fee to $500 and attempted to get the state and federal governments to make up the difference.

† The staff was put together by the office's chief, Mary Nichols. An air pollution specialist, Nichols had been chair of the California Air Resources Board under Governor Jerry Brown. In 1993 President Clinton appointed her assistant administrator of the Environmental Protection Agency in charge of air pollution issues.

intense. And he was not afraid of contentious public disputes or feisty litigation. As a lawyer for the Western Center for Law and Poverty, a nonprofit law firm in Los Angeles, one of his chief tasks had been to try to stop construction of the Diablo Canyon nuclear power plant in central California. When Jonathan Atwood, the ornithologist, turned up with the gnatcatcher on his mind, Reynolds had already sized up the situation in Orange County. In fact, he had already taken on the task of trying to stop the San Joaquin Hills toll road.

How this occurred is the subject of considerable speculation. The NRDC has always maintained that the two issues came in the door coincidentally: Orange County environmentalists brought the toll road to the group's attention, while Atwood sought help in listing the gnatcatcher as endangered. It's also true, however, that Laguna Beach, where the toll road was universally despised, served as an important fundraising base for the NRDC. The Los Angeles office received important seed money from the Homeland Foundation, a virtually anonymous foundation operated by a former World Wildlife Fund biologist and his wife, a granddaughter of J. Paul Getty.* The couple lived in Laguna Beach and was known to be opposed to the road.

While insisting that the gnatcatcher and the toll road were separate projects, Reynolds, like his environmentalist clients in Laguna Beach, was not blind to the power of the Endangered Species Act and its potential to kill the road. By 1991, his office in the historic Oviatt Building in downtown Los Angeles had become the nerve center for the toll road/ gnatcatcher operation. Joining with Laguna Greenbelt and the City of Laguna Beach, Reynolds sued Orange County in state and federal court, challenging the environmental documents prepared for the toll road. At the same time, Reynolds directed the NRDC's efforts to have the gnatcatcher listed as endangered by both the U.S. Fish and Wildlife Service and, under state law, by the California Fish and Game Commission. Intentionally or not, the NRDC had launched an all-out war on development in south Orange County, using the road as its major target and the bird as its major weapon.

⌒

* According to Internal Revenue Service records, the Homeland Foundation donated $100,000 per year to the Natural Resources Defense Council beginning in 1989. Apparently financed with a small portion of the Getty fortune, Homeland contributes approximately $1.5 million annually to various environmental causes.

While NRDC was pushing forward in its drive to list the gnatcatcher, another player entered the scene: Pete Wilson, who was elected governor of California in November 1990 and took office in 1991. Though a Republican, Wilson had a reputation as a conservationist. And in staffing his new administration, Wilson turned for advice to his friend William Reilly, the longtime head of the World Wildlife Fund who was then serving as the head of the Environmental Protection Agency in the Bush Administration. Reilly, in turn, recommended that Wilson hire two of his WWF colleagues: Douglas Wheeler, a former Interior Department official who was running WWF in his absence, and Michael Mantell, WWF's general counsel.

Within a month of Wilson's election, Wheeler and Mantell were in Sacramento setting up shop as Secretary and Undersecretary of the state's Resources Agency, the parent agency of the Department of Fish and Game. They were, at first glance, an unlikely pair. Wheeler was a large, outgoing man, an Easterner with a hale-and-hearty Chamber of Commerce manner. He was the only Republican who ever headed the Sierra Club, a brief experiment that quite predictably hadn't worked out. By contrast, Mantell was a native Southern Californian with an intense manner and a sincere personal interest in the state's natural environment. This Mutt-and-Jeff combination became, for better or worse, the embodiment of the environmental movement's high hopes for the Wilson Administration.

They faced a difficult task. Like most Southern California Republicans, Wilson had strong political ties to the land developers of Orange County and especially to Donald Bren, the billionaire owner of both the Irvine and Mission Viejo Companies. And Wilson came into office at the beginning of a long recession in California which, as it turned out, produced tremendous pressure to streamline environmental regulation. Wending their way through this political thicket would be tricky, to be sure. But coming from Washington, where a white-hot debate was going on, Wheeler and Mantell brought their own agenda for the Endangered Species Act.

Like many other conservationist critics of both state and federal law, Wheeler and Mantell did not like the fact that the whole culture of endangered species regulation revolved around the listing of individual species. Instead, they argued, wildlife agencies and local officials should move toward protecting entire ecosystems—whole swaths of natural areas that provided habitat for dozens of species, not just one. The coastal sage scrub was an example, for it served as the habitat not just for the gnatcatcher, but for many other species that were likely to be listed in the near future.

Wheeler and Mantell immediately proclaimed a doctrine of "bioregionalism" and made the gnatcatcher situation their highest priority. To craft a solution, they wanted to organize a massive negotiation in which landowners sat down with local, state, and federal bureaucrats, and with environmental groups, to hammer out a plan. The result would be a multi-species preserve that would probably look like a patchwork quilt: vast in size but weaving around subdivisions, roads, military bases, and the rest of the Southern California urban infrastructure. During their first few months on the job, they gave this process a name—the Natural Communities Conservation Planning process, or NCCP—and they pushed through state legislation authorizing it to move forward.

Environmentalists, of course, didn't trust the process. And neither did the state and federal biologists, at least at first. Trained to think in terms of listing individual species, biologists had a hard time grasping the broader approach. They worried about exceeding their legal authority, and didn't want to bargain away their power to regulate later on. This, in turn, created a problem for the landowners. Unless the state and federal biologists were willing to give iron-clad guarantees about the future, the landowners had little reason to negotiate.

Of course, there was one possible way to force the landowners to the table, and that was to list the bird first. If the gnatcatcher were placed on the endangered species list, all the landowners would be paralyzed, just as they had been in Riverside County, and they would be forced to negotiate.

To list the bird, Wheeler and Mantell had to be willing to risk a lot. They had to be sure that listing wouldn't be bad politics for Pete Wilson—a tough assignment, considering who his political friends were. They had to be sure that the whole thing wouldn't backfire, causing a firestorm of attack on the Endangered Species Act in Washington or Sacramento. And they had to be sure it would bring the landowners to the table, rather than driving them into court.

All of which may explain why they didn't do it.

⌐

While Reynolds' petition to list the gnatcatcher under federal law languished in the Fish and Wildlife Service's biological bureaucracy, the state petition moved forward quickly. By the summer of 1991, the California Fish and Game Commission was ready to hear the NRDC's request to classify the gnatcatcher as a candidate species—kicking off a study period during which there would be no grading, no development, and most of all no toll road, without the permission of the Department of Fish and Game.

The Fish and Game Commission had long been a political reward for well-connected duck-hunting enthusiasts.* At the time, the commission was still controlled by holdovers from the administration of Wilson's predecessor, George Deukmejian, who cared deeply about hunting and fishing and showed little enthusiasm for endangered species.

There was little question that the gnatcatcher qualified for candidate status at least. Even before the Fish and Game Commission hearings began, however, the building industry began to mount a major assault. Some of it was an attack on the environmentalists' science. But much of it was pure public relations. For example, rumors began to circulate that "cowboy" property owners would start plowing up coastal sage scrub in the middle of the night if the gnatcatcher became a candidate species. And the landowners claimed they would sue if the Fish and Game Commission voted in favor of candidacy.

The first Fish and Game Commission hearing, in Newport Beach on August 1, was raucous but inconclusive. Environmentalists were incensed when Fish and Game wardens prevented them from bringing protest placards into the hearing room. After lengthy testimony on both sides, the Commission decided to wait a month before making its decision. At the second hearing, on August 31 in Long Beach, the environmentalists evaded the sign prohibition by dressing their children up as gnatcatchers—and the game wardens didn't dare throw out the kids along with the placards. Other than that, the meeting was entirely controlled by Mantell.

---

* California's Progressive-era state government deliberately decentralizes power in a confusing way. The Department of Fish and Game, which is part of the Resources Agency, implements state policy and makes biological assessments. The Fish and Game Commission is a separate and theoretically independent body, with its own small staff, that makes policy decisions on wildlife issues, including whether to list species under the state's Endangered Species Act. In the federal government, these functions are consolidated in the U.S. Fish and Wildlife Service, which is part of the Interior Department.

In an unusual epilogue to the staff report, Mantell recounted all the steps the Wilson Administration had taken to set up the NCCP negotiation. Though a halting public speaker, Mantell tried to inspire the group with a quote from John Muir—"Everything is hitched to everything else"—but the duck-hunters on the commission seemed thoroughly uninterested. Then he dropped the bomb: The Administration was formally requesting that the gnatcatcher not be listed as a candidate species.

Amid a chorus of "Ugh!," "Geez!," and other cries of dismay, Mantell went on to say that he would establish milestones for progress in the NCCP negotiation—for example, an interim set of controls to prevent the destruction of coastal sage scrub. If the milestones were not met, the gnatcatcher would automatically return to the commission for reconsideration. Mantell was practically laughed out of the room by the environmentalists, and he was skewered on the local television news that night. But he got what he came for: a two-to-one decision by the Fish and Game Commission to "try this NCCP thing" and a resulting commitment from the building industry to sit down at the negotiating table instead of tearing up scrub in the middle of the night.

What Mantell didn't get was progress. As negotiations convened, environmentalists insisted that the bird be listed, while the landowners wanted interim controls to be voluntary. And local governments did not want to stick out their necks politically by advocating preservation. A team of biologists hired by the state concluded that good scientific information about the coastal sage scrub species might take several years to accumulate.

Some movement did occur. Many local governments and landowners enrolled voluntarily, agreeing not to disturb any coastal sage scrub until the end of 1993, when the negotiations were supposed to be complete. The Orange County Transportation Corridor Agencies enrolled the land for the Eastern and Foothill toll roads. But it held out the land for the San Joaquin, leaving open the possibility of a side deal with state and federal regulators.

By the spring of 1992, the interim controls were not in place and, despite Mantell's promise, the gnatcatcher issue did not go back to the Fish and Game Commission. The federal Fish and Wildlife Service reported that in six months more than two thousand acres of coastal sage scrub had been destroyed.

Though other environmental groups stayed, NRDC dropped out, preferring instead to focus on listing the bird under federal law. Two weeks after the state Fish and Game Commission's meeting in Long Beach, the Service announced that it was designating the gnatcatcher as a candidate for the endangered species list. While carrying no gnatcatcher protections, the announcement did kick off a one-year deadline for the Service to determine whether to list the bird. A final decision was due in September 1992, two months before the presidential election.

NRDC lobbied heavily to list the gnatcatcher under federal law, and helped coordinate the testimony of local environmentalists as well. NRDC also sued the state Fish and Game Commission, demanding candidate status for the gnatcatcher under state law. And the environmentalist lawsuits challenging the toll road were coming to a head.

All through 1992, the balance of power seemed to swing back and forth. The NRDC and other environmental groups lost the toll road case, and made little legal headway against the Fish and Game Commission. The building industry filed a mound of paper with the Fish and Wildlife Service demanding additional studies and access to more information on the proposed federal listing, essentially hoping to slow down the process. Momentum grew among Republicans in Congress on revising the Endangered Species Act to include economic issues.* And in south Orange County, near Laguna Canyon, the big landowners began to build. As fast as possible, they threw up houses along both sides of the toll road corridor. Among the homebuilders in the area was Kathryn Thompson, developer of the comically named Laguna Audubon subdivision, who became one of Orange County's key Republicans for Clinton.

In September 1992, the Service decided not to decide whether to list the gnatcatcher as an endangered species. Instead, the Service took advantage of a little-used provision in the law allowing it to study the gnatcatcher for another six months, punting the bird past the presidential election.

By the time the Fish and Wildlife Service had to make a decision, the gnatcatcher problem had fallen squarely in the lap of Bill Clinton's new Interior Secretary, Bruce Babbitt. A former governor of Arizona, a lawyer, and a geologist, Babbitt came from a longstanding ranching

---

* This charge was led by Representative William Dannemeyer of Orange County, who introduced a bill to declare American workers an endangered species.

family in Flagstaff, yet his environmental credentials were unparalleled. And he had a rare ability to forge consensus among warring factions in the West on a wide range of seemingly intractable issues.

Local sentiment about the toll road.

Having defended the Endangered Species Act in his confirmation hearings, Babbitt now had to find a way around the listing conundrum on the gnatcatcher. As he pondered what to do, the landowners turned up the heat. Shortly after Clinton's election, the Building Industry Association of Southern California and the Transportation Corridor Agencies had filed a potentially devastating lawsuit seeking to overturn the entire listing process for the gnatcatcher. The suit was filed in Washington, D.C., where the Fish and Wildlife Service was headquartered, and where Congress wouldn't be able to ignore it.

And in February, just a few weeks before Babbitt's deadline for a decision on listing the gnatcatcher, the BIA and the TCA raised the stakes. Going into federal court in Washington, the builders and the toll road agency sought a pre-emptive strike, asking a judge to find the process defective even before the gnatcatcher was listed. They lost, but clearly pressure on Babbitt was mounting. At the same time, the clock was ticking on the eighteen-month NCCP enrollments, which were due to expire at the end of 1993. Pummeled by the House Natural Resources committee in mid-February, Babbitt reiterated his commitment to ecosystem planning.

Then, on March 25, a week after the deadline established by law, Babbitt finally revealed his plan. It was a clever idea, and one typical of Babbitt's consensus-building approach. Instead of declaring the gnatcatcher endangered, he chose instead to declare it threatened. This designation carried with it all the same protections: no development, no disruption of coastal sage scrub without the permission of the Service.

But the threatened designation also allowed Babbitt to do something no Interior Secretary had ever done before. Under Section 4(d) of the Endangered Species Act, when a species is listed as threatened rather than endangered, the Fish and Wildlife Service is authorized to create a special regulation permitting real estate development, and other economic activity, under certain circumstances.

Babbitt's proposed 4(d) rule for the gnatcatcher simply stated that any landowner who wanted to develop under the rule had to participate in the California NCCP negotiation. Then, the following day, the Wilson Administration released a proposed set of guidelines under which landowners could develop while the NCCP negotiation continued. It would take three to five years to complete a full scientific investigation. In the meantime, the coastal sage scrub area had been divided into twelve subregions; and up to five percent of the scrub in each subregion could be destroyed for new development. Since all scientific information wasn't known, the biologists couldn't draw maps. So anyone who wanted to develop would be required to produce additional scientific surveys to determine whether or not gnatcatchers lived on the property.

Of course, under the law, individual landowners could still go to the Fish and Wildlife Service and try to cut an individual deal to develop on gnatcatcher property under Section 7 of the Endangered Species Act, just as they could before. All the pronouncements by Babbitt and others that day made it clear that the Service would not be receptive. That was supposed to be part of the inducement to play the NCCP game. But the San Joaquin toll road had already slipped through this supposed blockade.

〜

In late 1991—around the time, coincidentally, that the NCCP process was set up—Rob Thornton began talking to the Interior Department about a Section 7 deal for the San Joaquin toll road. A red-haired, fortyish man of intelligence and persistence, Thornton was widely recognized as the best endangered species lawyer in Orange County, and maybe the best in the entire western United States. Other species lawyers were better known to the general public; still others had a wider range of experience in environmental law. But no one could match Thornton when it came to working the Endangered Species Act itself.

As a Democratic House staffer, he had helped rewrite the law in 1978; as a lawyer representing industry, he had helped draft further changes in 1982. He had helped invent, and then shaped, the whole concept of ecosystem planning. Thornton knew the law inside-out. He had connections in Washington, and he had the experience and savvy to put his knowledge and connections to work for his clients.

Beginning in 1989, Thornton's law firm—the well-known Irvine-based firm of Nossaman, Guthner, Knox, and Elliott, which usually represented developers—received about $600,000 a year to act as general counsel to the Orange County Transportation Corridor Agencies. Nossaman, Guthner's chief job was to take the agency through a minefield of environmental laws so that the three toll roads could actually be built. What that meant was that wherever Joel Reynolds went, Rob Thornton was not far behind. Thornton and his partners defended the TCAs against state and federal environmental lawsuits; they challenged the listing of the gnatcatcher in federal court in Washington; they helped draft the conservation guidelines released along with the listing of the bird. But none of that mattered as much as their Section 7 consultation on the San Joaquin Hills toll road.

By the time Clinton was elected president, the San Joaquin toll road was ready to go. Substantial grading had already been done, albeit under the auspices of the big landowners. The transportation agency was putting together a billion-dollar bond package to take to Wall Street, but the bond market was jumpy about a road that had become so entangled with the gnatcatcher. If the San Joaquin wound up under the thumb of the listing, it might never get built.

By that time, however, Thornton had already laid the legal groundwork for a Section 7 exemption for the San Joaquin. He had begun doing so in December 1991, when the TCA and the Federal Highway Administration requested a Section 7 consultation—not for the gnatcatcher, which was not yet listed, but for Bell's vireo, another bird in the area already listed. In the spring of 1992, after Thornton had submitted volumes of biological information, the Fish and Wildlife Service issued a "no-jeopardy" opinion, stating that construction of the San Joaquin would not jeopardize the bird's future survival. Then, during the winter of 1992–93, as the Clinton Democrats began unpacking their bags at the Interior Department, Thornton lobbied the Service to expand this Section 7 exemption to the gnatcatcher. At the end of February, a month before Bruce Babbitt announced he wouldn't be making any deals like this, the Fish and Wildlife Service agreed to expand the San Joaquin no-jeopardy opinion to the gnatcatcher and the cactus wren.

Thornton subsequently insisted that he did not throw around any political weight in order to win this change. "The only time any representatives of the agency [meaning TCA] spoke with the policy levels of the Fish and Wildlife Service concerning the gnatcatcher opinion was *after* the February 1993 conference opinion was issued, and then only after the NRDC and its clients had put on full court political pressure (including contacting the Secretary of DOI, the Assistant Secretary..., and Senator Boxer) in an attempt to change the opinion previously issued by the Fish and Wildlife Service biologists," he later recalled.*

This may well be true, because part of Thornton's skill as a lawyer was to work the intricate legal niceties of the Endangered Species Act to his clients' advantage. And the no-jeopardy opinion was a model of bureaucratic hedging.

The key question in environmental law is often to determine whether an action like construction of the San Joaquin will have a "significant impact" on the species involved. The no-jeopardy opinion tacked around the significance question with extreme skill, largely navigating in waters Thornton himself had charted. Ordinarily, for example, destruction of "critical habitat" for an endangered species would be a significant impact. Some one hundred fifty-five acres of gnatcatcher habitat would be destroyed by the project, but—because of the NCCP process, which did not include the toll road—the Service had uncharacteristically chosen not to designate critical habitat for the gnatcatcher. Thus, habitat loss, normally a huge issue in species disputes, was not an issue here.

A second example of this hedging came regarding proposed greenbelts around Laguna Canyon and other development in the area. The developers had argued all along that, because the county had already approved all the private development to be served by the toll road, building the road itself would not be a big deal—especially since The Irvine Company had promised to sell local agencies critical pieces of land to preserve as open space. The no-jeopardy opinion accepted this reasoning, stating that the federal biologists, "currently lacking sufficient data to the contrary," believed that the planned open space would be sufficient to permit the birds to survive. (Subsequently, in fact,

* Because the gnatcatcher and the wren were still merely proposed for listing at the time, this opinion was called a "conference" opinion—an opinion resulting from a conference with the Fish and Wildlife Service at TCA's request. Later, when the gnatcatcher was listed as threatened, this opinion was changed in status to an official "biological" opinion.

Laguna Beach, Laguna Greenbelt, and other local entities had difficulty raising enough money to buy all this land from The Irvine Company.)

In short, the Fish and Wildlife Service said, "a population or populations of these species likely will not be extirpated as a result of the proposed project as presently conceived and described"—a statement assuming the implementation of a whole variety of land purchases and mitigation measures that had not yet occurred.

Coming in the midst of the huge national battle over the bird and the Endangered Species Act itself, the no-jeopardy opinion did not generate much publicity. But the environmentalists understood that it was the beginning of the end. At a rally ten days later, the day $1 billion worth of tax-exempt bonds were taken to Wall Street to build the San Joaquin, grim reality began to set in. "We're losing," lamented Laguna Beach councilwoman Lide Lenney. "We're really losing."

After the gnatcatcher was listed, environmentalists lobbied to have the no-jeopardy opinion overturned. In a lengthy letter to the Fish and Wildlife Service in April, Joel Reynolds pleaded for a change in policy. "Adoption of the toll road conference opinion," he said. "would undermine literally every NCCP interim conservation strategy." The conservation strategy called for development to be concentrated in areas with few gnatcatchers; the toll road would be built in an area where they were abundant. The conservation strategy called for protection of linkages; the toll road would bisect an important greenbelt. The letter was signed by high officials from, among others, the Environmental Defense Fund, Greenpeace, the World Wildlife Fund, and the National Audubon Society. Many were old friends of Bruce Babbitt.

In June, of course, the NRDC got its answer at the Hyatt Regency in Irvine when Babbitt said: "Our word, once given, has got to be kept." If that was not clear enough, the answer was repeated early in 1994, when the Service reaffirmed its no-jeopardy opinion, even though one hundred forty-four pairs of gnatcatchers—eight percent of the total— had been killed in the Laguna Beach fires the previous fall. And Babbitt repeated the answer yet again in March 1994 at yet another speech at yet another Hyatt Regency, this one in San Diego. (So tenuous was the commitment of local officials to the NCCP process that Babbitt had to fly out once every couple of months to hold their hands.) As usual, he floated lofty rhetoric about changing the way the politics of extinction works. But when it came to the toll road, he simply reiterated what he had said before: "The toll road was in the Fish and Wildlife pipeline, and it has been there for a long time."

~

A few days before Christmas 1994, a Dana Point psychologist named Cris Scaglione drove to Laguna Canyon, got out of her car, and stood in front of the bulldozers that were preparing to grade the path of the San Joaquin Hills Transportation Corridor—the path that had been outlined by environmentalists with white sheets almost three years before. "I was the only person here for a while," she said later. "Then the bulldozers started coming down the hill. I stood there in front of the bulldozers, and I stopped them for about ten seconds. Then they just went around me."

Cris Scaglione was the second-to-last person who tried to stop the San Joaquin toll road from being built through Laguna Canyon. The last was Joel Reynolds, who filed a frantic end-run legal brief two days later with the Ninth U.S. Circuit Court of Appeals in Pasadena. Reynolds was able to stop the bulldozers for two weeks, while the court considered his argument. But then word came to send the 'dozers forward.

These final efforts came after almost two years of legal chess moves stretching through courtrooms from California to Washington. At one point during 1994, Rob Thornton convinced a federal judge in Washington to "de-list" the gnatcatcher, while at the same time Reynolds persuaded a federal judge in Los Angeles to enjoin the transportation agency from building the road through Laguna Canyon. The more one side pushed, the more the other side pushed back, until the cost and delay took on an almost comical cast.

In the end, however, the toll road assumed an inevitability that even Reynolds knew could not be reversed. By the time the 'dozers really began to roll, Republicans had taken control of Congress and the Endangered Species Act was under direct attack. Some landowners even thought, rightly or wrongly, that it might be repealed.

The Laguna Beach councilwoman had been right: The environmentalists really were losing. Laguna Canyon would not be their Gettysburg but their Waterloo. And the turning point had been February 28, 1993, when the Fish and Wildlife Service had issued its no-jeopardy opinion.

In 1991, Doug Wheeler and Michael Mantell had stared the Orange County growth machine in the face and backed off. In order to make any progress at all, they felt, they had to play ball and not alienate the big landowners. Two years later, Bruce Babbitt reached the same conclusion. He wanted to protect the Endangered Species Act in Congress, and he wanted to keep all those endangered Republicans in Bill Clinton's column in 1996.

Over time, the whole conservation planning process began to produce results on a broader scale across gnatcatcher country. The Irvine Company and other large land developers eventually agreed to set aside significant chunks of land in an attempt to protect a whole range of species. And, discouraged by the contentious experience of the San Joaquin, both the TCA and the environmentalists agreed to an impressive set of mitigations on the Foothill toll road. In order to make this kind of progress, however, Babbitt had to make a tough choice: he had to let the growth machine build the road, and hope that the bird could take care of itself.

On November 5, 1996, Bill Clinton didn't carry Orange County. But he held Bob Dole to fifty-one percent of the vote there—a key factor in his landslide victory in California as a whole.

PART FOUR

Money

There are a lot of myths about "golden years" of postwar prosperity in Los Angeles, the years from the 1940s to the 1970s. It was a small town. Schools weren't crowded. There was no crime. There was no race problem. You could drive sixty miles an hour on the freeway anytime, day or night. And the taxpayers were happy to provide the money that growth required—money for new schools, new roads, and the new governments that popped up all over the region as suburb after suburb "incorporated" during the 1950s and 1960s.

Like all myths, most of the Los Angeles myths contain a kernel of truth but little more. Schools went on double-sessions all over Los Angeles after the war. The race problem was hidden by the city's extreme segregation. The new freeways simply provided a brief respite from congestion as the stop-and-go nature of the city's traffic was being transferred from city streets.

But the money myth did have some truth to it. Postwar Los Angeles generally proved willing to invest in the infrastructure required to support growth. In part, this generosity grew from the prosperity of an expanding economy. Millions of people rising into the middle class created an ever-broadening tax base capable of increasing tax revenue without raising tax rates, as the history of California's gas tax revenues suggests. And in part, this generosity emerged from the fact that the great Los Angeles middle class could see what it was getting. The California aqueduct might mean higher state income taxes, but it also meant more water flowing to Los Angeles. Nobody wants higher property taxes, but suburban homeowners in postwar Los Angeles were often willing to pay this price in order to have a neighborhood school for their kids. The cliché that postwar Los Angeles invested in its future is correct.

In time, however, the kids grew up, water was taken for granted, the freeways got crowded, and property taxes rose because real estate prices went out of sight. As a result, middle-class Angelenos began to question the old equation. Why should they pay for more freeways if the result is simply more people competing for available asphalt? Why should they pay for schools after their kids have grown up? Why should they pay huge property tax bills to support hospitals and welfare systems for the poor? All this growth, Angelenos concluded, should have to pay for itself.

And so in June 1978, voters in Southern California—and their counterparts elsewhere in the state—turned the relationship between growth and money upside down by passing Proposition 13, a citizen initiative that cut property tax rates and touched off the national "tax revolt." They did so mostly to lower their own property tax bills, but also to send a very clear message about government and growth: They would not support big government spending if they did not see how all that spending would benefit them.

Proposition 13 ushered in a new era characterized by financial desperation. It was partly because of financial pressures created by Proposition 13 that Robert Citron, the Orange County treasurer, engaged in high-flying investment schemes that eventually led to the county's bankruptcy. It was these same pressures that led the county and other agencies to rely on Citron's stratospheric financial yields to finance their normal operations when they should have known better.

For the growth coalition, the post-Proposition 13 era was littered with Rube Goldberg mechanisms designed to raise enough money to pay for the hard infrastructure and soft services expected from still-expanding local governments. Throughout the metropolis, little revenue mechanisms popped up that could operate outside of Proposition 13: developer fees, recreation and arts fees, "Mello-Roos" taxing districts, parcel taxes, excise taxes on new development—even a revival of little-used "assessment districts" originally authorized by state legislation seventy years before.

Just as important, Proposition 13 forced government agencies of all kinds to scramble for money however and wherever they could find it. And the source of all this "new money" usually had something to do with land and with the urban development that land could accommodate. Because the raw material of a municipality is land. In the days when local government was financed mostly by property taxes, this link was obvious. Even after Proposition 13 restricted property taxes, however, towns were defined by their land and how it was used, a fact that was just as obvious to the budget director as it was to the planning director. The cost of government services—police, fire, trash, even welfare—was determined in large part by whether a city's territory was devoted to houses or apartments, office buildings or stores. Similarly, even after Proposition 13, the sources of a city's or county's revenue—whether Rube Goldberg assessment schemes or sales taxes or business license taxes—were determined almost entirely by how the land was used.

Thus, the post-Proposition 13 era in Los Angeles has been an era during which, more than ever before, growth patterns have been driven by money—and not just by the desire for private profit, but by the desire for public profit as well. If a city or county owned a choice piece of real estate, the property's fate was usually determined not by what was best for the town but what was best for the treasury. And if a local government sought to open up new territory controlled by private landowners, the principal concern was usually how to develop the land in a way that would maximize revenue—and minimize cost—for the town.

The concept of a town as a well-balanced mixture of homes and businesses that provided everything a resident might need went out the window, sacrificed to the public's bottom line. The result, not surprisingly, was a dismal urban landscape. Towns designed by bean-counters are rarely towns that anyone would want to live in.

CHAPTER 9

The Taking of Parcel K

The standard joke urbanists make about denizens of the Los Angeles metropolis—the joke that is intended to single them out for ridicule as people who truly live on Mars and not in a real city—is that most of them have never been downtown.

Downtown Los Angeles is not an insignificant place. It is California's largest business center, with two hundred thousand people working there every day and more office space than any other concentrated area in the state. Yet since its peak in the 1920s, downtown has eroded in most Angelenos' mental maps from the center of civic life to little more than a footnote.

You might go downtown if you are in some kind of hassle with City Hall, or if you want to buy cheap jewelry, or if you are going to a car show at the Convention Center. You might go there if you want to gawk at the lawyers entering the Criminal Courts building for the O.J. Simpson trial, or if you want to see where the real-life *L.A. Law* skyscraper is located. You might even think you've been downtown if you have merely driven on the loop of freeways that surround it, which make up the core of the region's transportation spiderweb. But you would never, ever mistake downtown Los Angeles for an actual place that has significance in your life.

Unless, that is, you are somehow connected to L.A.'s blueblood elite, such as it is. For the law firms, the banks, the old corporations, the Jonathan Club, the Chandler family of *Los Angeles Times* fame, and many others who trace their roots back to the engineers of the Los Angeles growth machine, downtown still remains the center of civic life. It is the place where the old power brokers have their offices and do their deals. It is the place where money from all across the region funnels in so that it may be transferred and re-invested in new ventures. And, perhaps most important for the bluebloods' image of themselves, it is the place where the allegedly vibrant cultural life of a world-class city is supposed to be headquartered.

To the bluebloods, downtown revolves around Bunker Hill, a prominent bulge in the earth that covers fifteen or so city blocks on the northern end of downtown. Though it has a sordid past, Bunker Hill has always been surrounded by monuments to L.A.'s urban pretensions. At the north end lies the Civic Center Mall, where the county government offices are located, as well as the Los Angeles Music Center, downtown's major nod to the cultural elite. At the south end stand those twin icons of 1920s Los Angeles, the Central Library and the Biltmore Hotel. On the east side of the hill are the shabby remains of the city's magnificent office and retailing districts from the 1910s and 1920s; on the west side are their pale, overgrown counterparts from the 1970s.

And in the middle, straddling Bunker Hill, runs Grand Avenue, the greatest urban street Los Angeles has never quite figured out how to build. Grand Avenue was once the colorful locale of shabby boarding-houses and sleazy novels—the kind of place where hotels were "built on a hillside in reverse, there on the crest of Bunker Hill," as novelist John Fante once described it, "built against the decline of the hill, so that the main floor was on the level with the street but the tenth floor was downstairs ten levels." These days, however, Grand Avenue is the boulevard of blueblood dreams in Los Angeles: the Park Avenue, the Michigan Avenue, the Champs-Élysées wannabe that is supposed to silence those joking urbanists from the East Coast and Europe once and for all.

Beginning in the early 1970s, when downtown-booster Tom Bradley was elected mayor, the bluebloods used all their political muscle to transform downtown in general and Grand Avenue in particular into a sophisticated urban locale. Under federal urban renewal programs, the flophouses had been demolished and their residents forcibly removed in the 1960s. After his election as mayor in 1973, Bradley wooed major developers, and encouraged them to invest in the area. On either side of Grand Avenue, famous architects built grand office skyscrapers,

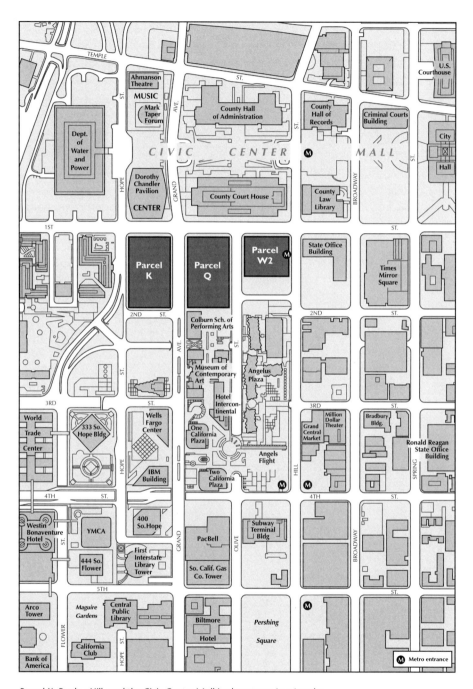

Parcel K, Bunker Hill, and the Civic Center Mall in downtown Los Angeles.

punctuating them with distinguished smaller buildings such as the Museum of Contemporary Art. At the southern tip of Bunker Hill, Bradley swung a deal with developer Rob Maguire to invest more than $100 million to renovate the Central Library, and in return permitted Maguire to build the First Interstate World Tower, the tallest building on the West Coast. Underneath Bunker Hill, the city's power brokers dug a subway, since no world-class downtown can be taken seriously without one.

And gradually, during the 1970s and 1980s, these new edifices began to shape the outlines of the kind of a downtown that the blue-blood elite thought a world-class city should have. Whatever damage the original urban renewal project might have done to the lower-class urban fabric, by the mid-1980s the entire Bunker Hill area was becoming an upscale, pedestrian-oriented district with cultural activities, employment centers, housing, and easy access via public transit to surrounding neighborhoods. It was one of the few places in Los Angeles where you could hail a taxi instead of calling for one on the telephone.

In urban design terms, however, Bunker Hill didn't really hold together, and the reason was obvious to anyone who visited the area. At the corner of First and Grand—the absolute epicenter of Bunker Hill, where yuppie-skyscraper downtown met cultural-governmental downtown—stood three lonely parcels of virtually empty land. Two were used as surface parking lots, while the third featured a comical erector-set parking structure. These three parcels were the hole in the middle of this emerging donut, and how they were developed would go a long way toward determining whether Bunker Hill would become a true urban core, or would stand as yet another half-successful redevelopment effort.

The Grand Avenue corridor. The Dorothy Chandler pavilion is at the bottom right, just across the street from the site of the Walt Disney Concert Hall.

The three parcels—known locally as Parcel K, Parcel Q, and Parcel W-2—totalled nine acres, a huge amount of land for a downtown area. They were wanted by the downtown blueblood elite, which needed to expand its burgeoning complex of cultural monuments. But they were owned by the Los Angeles County government, one of the nation's leading social service providers and, for this reason, chronically cash-poor. Their worth at the time was probably in the vicinity of $200 million. Partly because of their value, partly because of their location, they were coveted by both the bluebloods and the cash-strapped county government. But each had a very different idea of what the future of these parcels should be. And in the hot real estate market of the 1980s, it was this covetousness, not their crucial role as a piece of urban design, that dictated the terms of the struggle over how they should be used.

⌐

Los Angeles County is the nation's largest local governmental unit, larger even than New York City. Covering more than four thousand square miles, an area almost the size of Connecticut, the county is home to more than nine million people. And unlike New York, it is still growing fast; Los Angeles County added more than one million new residents during the 1980s, mostly immigrants from Asia and Latin America and their children.

Under California's byzantine governmental structure, the county does not control all this territory, but it is responsible for most of its social problems. Its main task, carried out by an eighty-thousand-member army of bureaucrats, is to oversee sprawling social service, health, and criminal justice systems. And since 1978, when Proposition 13 cut property taxes throughout the state by more than half, Los Angeles County has not been able to raise enough money to keep its bureaucracy fed. The result has been a chronic mismatch between the revenue it receives and the job it is supposed to do.

Throughout the 1980s, there was a growing political mismatch in the Los Angeles County government as well. Though burgeoning inner-city social service problems were consuming the county government, the five county supervisors relied for electoral support mostly on conservative, middle-class suburbanites who favored Proposition 13 and low taxes. Beginning in 1980, a conservative faction led by Pete Shabarum and Michael Antonovich controlled the Board of Supervisors, and these conservatives undertook to cut spending, tame the bureaucracy, and find creative ways to pay for and deliver government services.*

Throughout the 1970s and 1980s, the sprawling bureaucracy had been presided over by the genial Harry Hufford, a well-liked and respected veteran bureaucrat who had worked his whole life for the county and rose to the position of chief administrative officer, the top staff job in county government. The CAO's job was not an enviable one. To survive, Hufford had to operate in a world constrained by the political agendas of the five county supervisors, the undeniable power of the county labor unions, the independent authority of the sheriff and district attorney, and the sheer size of his work force. Low-key and conciliatory, Hufford had been able to keep relations between the bureaucrats and the politicians on a more or less even keel. But managing the county under the political mismatch of Proposition 13, lurching constantly from one financial crisis to another, was no fun. In 1985, Hufford moved down Grand Avenue to one of the new skyscrapers on Bunker Hill, where he became the administrator of the city's largest law firm, Gibson, Dunn, and Crutcher.

In ordinary times, Hufford would have been replaced by another insider, someone who knew and understood the county bureaucracy and who could be trusted to manage it efficiently, if not creatively. Seeking to shake things up, however, Antonovich and Shabarum wanted someone different—an outsider who could infuse the system with private-sector efficiency and entrepreneurial zeal. The man they chose was Jim Hankla.

Then in his early forties, Hankla was a lifelong public servant, but he could not have been more different than Hufford. Impatient with bureaucrats, Hankla was the very prototype of a hard-driving, entrepreneurial dealmaker who had emerged from the crucible of Proposition 13. As redevelopment manager in Long Beach, Hankla had wooed both Wall Street and the White House to put together an economic stimulus package for the city following the closure of a large naval base in 1974. (He had also succeeded in hastily restructuring the deal after Proposition 13 undermined his financial assumptions about property tax

---

* Local elections in Los Angeles County are technically nonpartisan, but Antonovich and Shabarum were both partisan Republicans. In 1980 they helped engineer the election of their ally, Deane Dana, thus ending liberal rule of the board. The liberals regained power in the 1990s when Gloria Molina, a Latina, won Shabarum's Eastside seat. By then, however, even the liberals had to confront the county's budget problems.

revenue.) At the time he was tapped for Hufford's job, Hankla was serving as the head of the county's Community Development Commission, a crazy-quilt of development and housing agencies located six miles southeast of downtown in the City of Commerce.

At the county, Hankla joined forces with other entrepreneurial bureaucrats to figure out how to squeeze new revenue from the county's existing assets, and especially from its real estate holdings. As the nation's largest local government—and the steward of an enormous health, social service, and criminal justice operation—Los Angeles County may have been cash-poor, but it was land-rich. Of course, most of the real estate in the county's impressive portfolio was being used by county agencies. But much of it was not being used for anything at all. So Hankla and his colleagues decided to exploit the real estate value of these properties in order to make money for the county.

Expanding on its fledgling "asset management" program, Hankla and his managers inventoried the county's surplus land, rated it according to its market value, and convinced the State of California to change its longstanding ban on the sale or lease of surplus government property for the purpose of raising revenue.* Advising a group of local government officials in 1985, Hankla said: "Real estate economics is what counties and cities must learn."

Though Hankla's real estate deals were time- and labor-intensive, they soon bore fruit. When the county needed almost $15 million to construct a new hospital in his hometown of Long Beach, Hankla and his managers negotiated a sixty-six-year ground lease with private developers for the surplus land underneath two old hospitals that the new facility was going to replace. Supervisor Dana, the conservative who represented the Long Beach area, called the action "a milestone in county government" that would "change the way the county does business." Other deals were in the works, and Hankla's star was rising.

When Hankla arrived at the county Hall of Administration in 1985, he was faced, as Hufford had been before him, with the impossible task of navigating between Proposition 13 on the one hand and the county's sprawling bureaucracy on the other. He hoped his asset management program could help bridge this gap permanently. Indeed, Hankla

* Bill Kreger, an aide to Harry Hufford, had begun this effort before Hankla arrived, but Hufford, an old-school bureaucrat, was not enthusiastic about it.

boasted that the county owned so much valuable real estate that the asset management deals could yield tens of millions of dollars a year— not a huge amount, but enough to help solve the problem the county faced in funding its social service programs. Seeking to jump-start the asset management program, Hankla and his assistants turned to what was potentially the most lucrative deal of all: development of the three county parcels at the corner of First and Grand. But they would soon discover that, Harry Hufford notwithstanding, Grand Avenue was a two-way street.

⌐⌐

Along the east side of the Los Angeles Music Center, the side that affords the view down the hill through the Civic Center Mall to City Hall, four hundred names are chiseled into the wall. Ahmanson. Taper. Wasserman. Hawley. Keck. Zanuck. These are famous names in Los Angeles, the names of the wealthy and powerful who donated the money, in the early 1960s, to build the Music Center in the first place. It is an understatement to say that these names represent L.A.'s ruling elite. Quite simply, there *was* no ruling elite—that is to say, there was no such elite in the cohesive and powerful form conveyed by the chiseled names— until the Music Center was built. The Music Center was the vehicle by which one powerful woman—Dorothy Buffum Chandler, daughter of an important retailer and wife of the publisher of the *Los Angeles Times*— brought most of the wealth and power in Los Angeles together for the first time. The Music Center was also the vehicle through which the city announced, upon its opening in 1964, that Los Angeles had undeniably become a great city, a city of culture and taste and refinement as well as a city of wealth and growth. For this reason, the Music Center has attained reverential status among many of L.A.'s most powerful figures as a symbol of its maturity and its ability to get things done.

Dorothy Chandler's one-woman effort to build the Music Center is an achievement of legendary proportions in Los Angeles history. Indeed, all by itself this episode explains the Music Center's importance to Los Angeles society, and the importance that the Music Center crowd came to place on a particular parcel of land at First and Grand that Hankla had his eye on for private development.

When the Los Angeles Music Center opened in 1964, Dorothy Chandler appeared on the cover of *Time* magazine, having accomplished what *Time* described as "the most impressive display of virtuoso money-raising and civic citizenship in the history of U.S. womanhood." In the early 1960s Chandler was virtually unparalleled as what was once called "a society woman." Blessed with natural competitiveness and drive, and wed to the most powerful name in Los Angeles, she had single-handedly raised $18 million in private funds for the Music Center itself, and twisted Los Angeles County's arm to float $13 million in bonds to build the necessary parking structures.

In the process, however, Dorothy Chandler did more than create an important cultural institution. She brought the disparate elements of Los Angeles society together for the first time. She knew the old-guard downtown elite might not be able to provide her with enough philanthropy to achieve her dream. So she began to look around for other sources of wealth, and noticed that new money was popping up all over Los Angeles, though in a fragmented way. Realizing that the postwar boom had created a new generation of real estate barons—a phenomenon she could hardly overlook, since her father-in-law Harry Chandler had been the prototypical L.A. real estate tycoon—she wooed the nation's two largest savings-and-loan kings, Howard Ahmanson, of Home Savings, and Mark Taper, of American Savings and Loan, until they made million-dollar contributions.

Most important, as it turned out, Dorothy Chandler was the first downtown cultural figure to reach across town to the other center of wealth and power in Los Angeles: Hollywood. She aggressively courted the "Hillcrest Country Club" crowd—the wealthy Jewish circles with close ties to the entertainment industry—and secured major donations even though Jews were not allowed in the downtown clubs that served as her traditional power base. And she sought the help of Walt Disney, who came up with the idea of the "buck bag," a shopping bag designed to encourage average people to donate a dollar apiece to the cause. Disney also helped her woo Supervisor Kenneth Hahn's support for a county-financed parking garage by inviting him to the Disney box at the Hollywood Bowl.

So complete was Dorothy Chandler's power in the 1960s that she was able to hand-pick the site of the Music Center, and in the process dislodge the city's most powerful government agency. The site she chose was a beauty: the top of First Street hill, at the northern terminus of the Civic Center Mall, looking down on the county government

buildings, City Hall, and even the *Los Angeles Times*. The site was originally supposed to serve as the location for the Los Angeles Department
of Water and Power building—the very symbol, both literally and figu-
ratively, of the power that built Los Angeles into a great city. But at her
insistence, the DWP building was pushed one block to the west, behind
the Music Center, and the commanding lot at the top of the mall was
leased to the Music Center organization for one dollar a year. Ironically,
the DWP building, designed by the prominent Los Angeles architecture
firm of Albert C. Martin and Associates, is a far more imposing structure
today than the prosaic Dorothy Chandler Pavilion, designed by Welton
Becket. But there is no mistaking the fact that the Music Center, not the
DWP building, occupies the prize parcel at the top of the hill.

Just as there was no question where it would be built, there was
never any question—not, at least, until the 1980s—where the Music
Center would expand when the time came. Parcel K lay just across First
Street, south of the Music Center. Like the Music Center parcel itself, it
commanded the high ground. In 1968, before the original complex was
even completed, the Los Angeles County Board of Supervisors made a
formal commitment that Parcel K would be used for the Music Center's
eventual expansion, which was then expected to take the form of a
music academy. Almost twenty years later, Daniel Frost, who succeeded
Dorothy Chandler as president of the Music Center's Board of Governors,
still spoke of Parcel K in the same reverential tone that he and his colleagues used to describe the Music Center itself. "Lot K," he said, "was
and is considered to be the crown jewel property up there."

Frost, like Dorothy Chandler before him, was a force to be reck-
oned with in the power elite of downtown Los Angeles. As managing
partner of Gibson, Dunn, and Crutcher, he was credited with trans-
forming a stately old downtown institution into one of the largest and
most profitable law firms in the country. As the longtime outside counsel for the Times Mirror Corporation—and, at the time, the husband of
Dorothy Chandler's daughter—Frost was a key advisor to downtown's
most important family. In early 1985, just about the time Jim Hankla
became chief administrative officer of Los Angeles County, Frost took
over as president of the Music Center's Board of Governors, and began
to implement its long-delayed expansion.

The original Music Center had consisted only of the Dorothy Chandler Pavilion. In 1969, two smaller theaters, named for major donors

Howard Ahmanson and Mark Taper, were completed. But by the mid-1980s, competition for performance space had become a problem. So the Board of Governors began planning a new concert hall exclusively for the Los Angeles Philharmonic, as well as two other live theaters. Indeed, anticipating Hankla's entrepreneurial ideas, the Music Center had proposed, as early as 1980, that some of the county property be developed in order to raise money for Music Center operations and expansion.

For the Music Center, there was no question as to where the expansion would take place. Other parcels could be developed for revenue purposes, but the concert hall and the other theaters would be built on Parcel K. And there was no question about the terms by which the Music Center would obtain the property. Even a blueblood non-profit organization like the Music Center could not afford to pay the county tens of millions of dollars for the property. As with the original location across the street, the county would lease Parcel K to the Music Center for a dollar.

⌒

The question of how to design a solution that accommodated all these conflicting demands fell to Barton Myers. An architect of mid-level prominence and strong opinions, Myers had made his name in that paragon of urbanism, Toronto, before moving to Los Angeles in the 1970s. Like many architects, Myers was viewed as brilliant but quirky. He had, for example, always maintained his office on Hollywood Boulevard, an architecturally magnificent but seedy location. And he had worked on any number of outstanding, never-built visions of urban Los Angeles, including a now-legendary proposal by developer Rob Maguire for the redevelopment of Grand Avenue.

Myers was called into the Parcel K project by the Community Redevelopment Agency, the powerful and semi-autonomous city agency, controlled by Mayor Tom Bradley, that was redeveloping the whole Bunker Hill area. Under the CRA's land use plan at the time, Los Angeles County could build only 1.7 million square feet of space on the three parcels—the equivalent of two thirty-five-story office buildings. But Hankla and his assistants hoped to produce $32 million a year in annual revenue for the county by the late 1990s. To achieve that goal, they planned about four million square feet of development, or the equivalent of two Empire State Buildings. To work out a design solution, the CRA and the county agreed to hire Myers.

Myers understood the main advantage of placing the concert hall and the other theaters on Parcel K: It would create an almost continuous string of culture along Grand, beginning with MOCA and stretching northward to the Music Center. Also, he recognized, as did the CRA staffers, that a low-rise cultural institution would be less likely to overwhelm Grand Avenue than the type of tall office building the county had in mind.

But he also saw a problem. If the Music Center took up all of Parcel K, then the county's four million square feet of private development would have to be stacked into taller and bulkier buildings on the other two lots—especially on Parcel Q, the larger of the two. This strategy would make the buildings more expensive to build, and, just as important, more difficult to bring on line. Smaller buildings could be built cheaply and quickly, and could easily be leased to lawyers, accountants, and other tenants. A couple of monster skyscrapers, however, couldn't be built unless the downtown office market was so hot that big tenants would be easy to find. This meant that if the real estate market went into a tailspin, Parcel Q might not be developed for many years, perhaps not until after the year 2000.

Civic Center Mall, with the Music Center above it and the Department of Water and Power Building at the top of the picture.

As an urban designer, Myers was also concerned about the failed design of the existing Music Center and the adjacent Civic Center Mall. The remnant of a once-inspired effort to create a distinguished governmental complex, the Civic Center Mall ran perpendicular to Grand Avenue along a three-block east-west axis from Los Angeles City Hall to the Music Center. But the results were a hollow disappointment. One of the three blocks remained a surface parking lot. The other two were heavily landscaped, but were cut up by streets and parking ramps. And the government structures lining each side, including Richard Neutra's County Hall of Records, were severe Modernist buildings from the 1950s.

The design relationship of the Music Center to the mall was especially disappointing. It was possible to look down the mall's vista, such as it was, from the plaza of the Music Center. But this view was interrupted by Grand Avenue itself—whose street-level treatment by the Music Center was done in the typical 1960s walling-off style—and by the parking ramps emerging from the ground on the other side of the street.

Myers also believed that the configuration of the Music Center itself did not create an exciting urban fabric. Because the block was long and thin, the three theaters (the Chandler, the Taper, and the Ahmanson) had been laid out railroad-flat style—one behind the other behind the other—and, in design terms, operated in separate spatial zones. Myers feared that building the concert hall across the street on a separate site would further dissipate an already diffuse cultural institution. Los Angeles would have four theaters in close proximity to one another, all run by the same organization, but it would have no cultural district.

One day in mid-1985, during a break in a meeting at the county offices, Myers pulled Hankla aside and said: "What about this?" Then he drew a quick sketch which proposed actually building the concert hall on the Civic Center Mall itself. The Music Center plaza would be extended on a platform across Grand Avenue to the east, and the concert hall would be built on the other side of Grand, facing west. Thus, the concert hall, the Chandler, and the Taper would all empty into the same plaza, similar to New York's Lincoln Center, opening up the possibility of an exciting pedestrian environment on the plaza itself. At the same time, the concert hall would cover up the unsightly parking ramps on the mall.

Myers's idea played perfectly into Hankla's agenda. With Parcel K freed up for commercial development, Hankla would be able to meet the CRA's design and circulation concerns much more easily. Hankla told Myers to go ahead and draw up the plans for a concert hall on the Civic Center Mall.

The week before Christmas, 1985, Barton Myers left his office in Hollywood and drove the short distance over Cahuenga Pass to Universal Studios. He was greeted by Frost, Hankla, and Hollywood legend Lew Wasserman, the chairman of MCA/Universal and a Music Center board member. The trio personified the power structure that controlled the Grand Avenue cultural institutions: the downtown elite, the Hollywood elite, and the county elite. Excited, Myers produced a model detailing his plan to build the concert hall on top of the parking ramps along Grand Avenue, at the west end of Civic Center Mall. He described the way the concert hall would create a pedestrian atmosphere in conjunction with the other theaters, and the way the buildings would relate to, and improve, the moribund mall.

He expected a positive response. Instead, he got an angry confrontation. According to all accounts, both Frost and Wasserman exploded with anger, demanding to know why they hadn't been presented with a site plan for construction of the concert hall on Parcel K. To Myers' surprise, they wanted nothing to do with the Civic Center Mall. They wanted the concert hall to have no relation to other buildings on the mall, which they called "an architectural joke." In response to Myers' proposal, Frost said later: "If your agenda was to free up Lot K for some other use, that's one thing. But that wasn't our agenda."

The Music Center's agenda, as became abundantly clear over the following eighteen months, was to build the concert hall on Parcel K. Throughout 1986 and 1987, Myers drew up a dozen or more different site plans, playing around with all the different building elements— putting some on the mall, others on Parcel K, hoping to find a combination that would win the support of all concerned.* The Music Center hired a real estate consultant, who concluded that the mall site would be prohibitively expensive, requiring, among other things, an additional $14 to $16 million just for the underground parking garage.

The Music Center still had the ear of the Board of Supervisors, but the county still had budget problems, and the prospect of tens of millions of dollars in additional revenue remained an attractive alternative. If the Music Center had major donor dollars in hand, breaking the stalemate might be possible. With mere promises instead of dollars, however, even the Music Center heavyweights could not persuade the supervisors to give up altogether on the mall site.

$$\backsim$$

On Sunday, February 22, 1987, the dispute over the Music Center received wide public attention for the first time, when the *Los Angeles Times* published an article on page one of the Metro section documenting the entire story. Among the Angelenos who read the story was Lillian Disney.

* Myers claims he began to win support among Music Center insiders, but no one at the Music Center remembers it that way.

Walt Disney was one of the best-known public figures in Los Angeles for decades before his death in 1966. His wife, on the other hand, was one of the most anonymous. Even book-length biographies of Walt Disney barely mention her. But she was not unknown to L.A.'s cultural elite. Along with her husband and her daughters, she had been active in the Music Center since its inception. And Ronald Gother, Lillian Disney's lawyer—like Dorothy Chandler's son-in-law and lawyer, Dan Frost—was a partner at Gibson, Dunn, and Crutcher.

In 1987, Lillian Disney was considering the possibility of becoming a little less anonymous, largely because she wanted to commemorate her late husband with a large philanthropic gift. Thanks to takeover wars and the early success of Michael Eisner, she was sitting on Disney stock worth $250 million over and above the estate that her husband had left her. Lillian regarded this money as "Walt's money," and after a four-for-one stock split she decided to find a philanthropic outlet that would create, quite literally, a monument to Walt Disney.

After reading the *Times'* story about the Music Center dispute, eighty-seven-year-old Lillian Disney asked her lawyer to come to her house and discuss the possibility of using some of Walt's money to make a substantial gift for the concert hall. Gother recalled that she came down and walked the site herself, concluding that it would be a better site than the mall. On May 12, 1987, some ten weeks after she originally broached the subject, Lillian Disney offered the Music Center $50 million toward the construction of the concert hall. But she imposed several important conditions that, coincidentally or not, dovetailed perfectly with the Music Center's agenda.*

First, she said, the concert hall must be built on Parcel K, and it must be connected to the Music Center via a pedestrian bridge across First Street. Second, the Music Center would retain the option to use all of Parcel K if necessary, and Mrs. Disney would retain veto power over all other private development on the parcel. Third, the county would be required to build the parking garage and be responsible for operations and maintenance of the new concert hall. And finally, Lillian

---

* After the Disney gift was made public, persistent rumor claimed that, in order to break the stalemate over the concert hall, the Music Center went looking for a donor who would insist on Parcel K, and came up with Lillian Disney. But Ron Gother insists that Frost did not persuade him to whisper in Mrs. Disney's ear. In fact, Gother recalls that when he relayed the news of a possible Disney gift, "Dan about fell off his chair."

Disney would select the architect and all other contractors on the concert hall project. She gave the L.A. County Board of Supervisors thirty days to accept or reject the offer.

The prospect of bringing the revenue to the county through speculative real estate projects was one thing, but $50 million in the bank was something else again. The Board of Supervisors readily accepted the offer, and all its conditions, within the thirty-day deadline. Regardless of the urban design potential of placing a concert hall on the mall, the Music Center's power brokers had won.

Almost immediately, they moved to the next step: securing a world-class architect who would validate L.A.'s claim to being a world-class city. To manage the process of designing and building the Concert Hall, the Music Center selected Fred Nicholas, a veteran Beverly Hills shopping center developer with close ties to the board, as head of the Walt Disney Concert Hall Committee. Meanwhile, with Lillian Disney's blessing, the Music Center board members went on a highly publicized tour of European concert halls, saying that their intention was to build the best orchestral facility in the world. But they also seemed interested in proving that local boys could compete with the big guns. Early in 1988, Nicholas announced that the competition among architects had been reduced to four. Three were from Europe. The fourth was L.A.'s own postmodern master Frank Gehry. Gehry was rapidly moving into the architectural stratosphere after winning a local reputation with designs that featured materials like chicken wire. Recently he had produced a magnificently creative design (with no chicken wire) for the campus of Loyola Law School. But he had never attempted anything so monumental as the Disney Hall.

And the structure would be monumental, both physically and culturally. There was no question that, having fought so hard to place the Disney Hall on a prime piece of downtown real estate, the Music Center board was going to make sure that it was the most significant architectural event in recent Los Angeles history, something similar to the opening of the original Music Center in 1964. "The advent of the Disney Concert Hall reinforces Los Angeles' transformation from a suburban to an urban culture," architectural critic Joseph Giovannini swooned some years later in the *L.A. Times* Magazine. "The city is now one of the two poles of the United States, and it has had few public buildings commensurate with its status as a world capital." This kind of

big talk was exactly what the Music
Center people had in mind when
they undertook the selection process.

So it was something of a surprise
in architectural circles, but not in Los
Angeles, when the Music Center designated Gehry as the Disney Hall
architect at the end of 1988.

Characteristically, Gehry had submitted a daring and unconventional
design which he said would provide
"a lush garden oasis nestled among the towers." The design was dominated by a huge conservatory/foyer that Gehry called "an outdoor
room" and was filled with complex design elements that seemed to
harken back to an underlying floral theme. According to *Times* architectural critic Leon Whiteson, the concert hall was "a giant walk-in
Easter lily," and the outside of the building would be covered with "suc-
culent" layers of irregular limestone. Gehry himself said the design
would look "like a beautiful rose for the city."

A model of Frank Gehry's rose for the city.

But one critic called it a shoebox that had been left out in the rain
too long. Another complained that while it fronted nicely on Grand
Avenue, the design turned a blank face to the other three sides, including the First Street connection with the original Music Center.
Whatever its merits, Gehry's selection allowed the Music Center to
announce to the world that Los Angeles had arrived, not just as a cultural center willing and able to construct such an important building,
but as a creative center capable of breeding an architect who could
beat out the Europeans in a stiff competition to design it.

↩

While the architectural world was toasting Frank Gehry and the Music
Center, Los Angeles County's leaders were faced with the challenge of
how to shoehorn Jim Hankla's four million square feet of private development around Disney Hall onto the county-owned land. Furthermore,
they had to do it without Jim Hankla.

Apparently frustrated with his inability to bend the county
bureaucracy to his will, Hankla jumped ship in late 1987 when he was
offered the opportunity to return to Long Beach as city manager, a job

he had long wanted. Nevertheless, the fate of the county parcels would continue to be dictated, as during Hankla's tenure, largely by the personality and approach of the county's chief administrative officer.

Hankla's successor was Richard Dixon, Los Angeles County's long-time treasurer. Whereas Hankla sought to solve financial problems with entrepreneurial zeal, the curmudgeonly Dixon sought to achieve the same objective through financial cunning. A nationally recognized innovator in the area of public finance, Dixon would try to keep the county's finances—and the Disney Hall project—afloat with a succession of clever bond issues. Among other things, as both treasurer and CAO, Dixon led the county's efforts to raise cash by bonding against virtually all of the county's real estate holdings, including the Hall of Administration.

When he arrived in the CAO's office, Dixon concluded that the four-million-square-foot scenario was possible. But he realized it would also require construction of a hotel and a four-hundred-thousand-foot office building on Parcel K, and that was a scenario the Disney people had to approve.

Fred Nicholas recognized that the Music Center might need an elegant luxury hotel, not just to add to the project's cosmopolitan flavor but also to add to the financial coffers. By this time, it was clear that the $50 million Disney gift wasn't going to be nearly enough to build the Concert Hall. In 1989, that figure was looking more like $90 million, and Nicholas acknowledged in an interview that the hotel "could reduce our costs by $15 million" by paying for offices and banquet facilities that the Music Center would otherwise have to fund.

But Nicholas was not willing to consider an office building on Parcel K. So Dixon and other county officials removed one four-hundred-thousand-square-foot office building from their pro forma and resigned themselves to a 3.6-million-square-foot scenario that would generate $26 million a year. Thus began the county's "slippery slope." Bit by bit over the next three years, its revenue goals were completely undermined.

In 1989, having concluded that a hotel was necessary, Nicholas and the Music Center asked Gehry to go back to change his design to accommodate it. But this task didn't prove nearly as insurmountable as actually trying to get the hotel built. The CRA and the county agreed on a hotel developer, Gemtel Corporation, on the promise that Ritz-Carlton would be brought in as the operator. But when the agreement was submitted to the CRA in 1991, the redevelopment agency rejected it. With the backing of Mayor Tom Bradley and local labor unions, the CRA board (chaired by an AFL-CIO leader appointed by Bradley) demanded that Gemtel provide service workers with prevailing union wages. Gemtel refused and eventually sued.

Faced with a seemingly insurmountable problem, the county and the Music Center dropped the hotel idea altogether. That left Frank Gehry free to sculpt his concert hall on Parcel K with no interference from other structures. But it also robbed the county of another profit center on Parcel K.

Then there was the question of what to do on the other parcels. Although the county still wanted three million square feet of new development on Q and W-2, the Community Redevelopment Agency had to approve any project over 1.7 million square feet. As it happened, Bradley and Dixon were locked in a longstanding dispute over the distribution of downtown property tax revenues between the city and the county. With that dispute pending, the CRA was unwilling to consider anything larger than 1.7 million square feet.

This meant limiting development to the ill-fated hotel on Parcel K plus a 1.4-million-square-foot office building on Parcel Q. (Nothing would be built on W-2, where the subway portal was being constructed.) This single skyscraper of sixty or so stories could be expected to bring the county $6 million a year in revenue—less than twenty percent of Hankla's original dream.

When the county went looking for a developer for the office building in 1988, the downtown real estate market was still robust. But only two development firms responded to the proposal, and county officials spent well over a year trying to decide between them—even hiring the future mayor, Richard Riordan, to help negotiate the deal. (The problem was that the developer the county wanted, Rob Maguire of Maguire Thomas Partners, had not made the more lucrative financial offer.)

Finally, in 1990, the county formally selected Maguire Thomas, but by then the downtown real estate market was going down the tubes. A year later, when it was clear that no one would need another downtown skyscraper anytime soon, Maguire Thomas gave up the option on Parcel Q, and the county lost any hope of developing, or selling, the First Street parcels in the foreseeable future. Property that had once been valued at $200 million, and had once held out the prospect of providing the county with $30 million a year in cash, was now for all practical purposes worthless.

⌒

Meanwhile, the projected cost of Frank Gehry's design was going up fast. By 1991, the cost of the building alone was estimated at well over $100 million, far more money than the Music Center had available for the project. Even worse for the county, however, was the fact that the parking garage, which was the county's responsibility under the deal, might also cost $100 million or more. So from 1989 to 1991—a period of time during which the Southern California real estate market crashed and burned—the Disney Hall project bogged down in a protracted negotiation over who would pay for what. In particular, Dixon did not want to float the county bond issue for the parking garage until the Music Center had raised enough money to actually build Disney Hall.

At the end of 1991, the Music Center and the county reached an agreement. The cost of Disney Hall itself was estimated at $110 million, and at the time the Music Center had $78 million in hand. According to the deal, the county would not have to begin construction on the garage until the Music Center had raised eighty-five percent of the funds necessary for Disney Hall. Thus, the Music Center had to raise an additional $15.5 million. The county, in turn, agreed to float $110 million in bonds for the twenty-five-hundred-car parking garage, to be paid back from the garage's projected revenue. Six months later, in June 1992, Lillian Disney came to the Music Center's rescue once again by contributing another $17.5 million to the Disney Hall construction fund.

By now, however, the Music Center was running up against one of Lillian Disney's additional conditions. Now in her nineties, she wanted Walt's monument finished soon. This meant that the required construction on the parking garage had to begin by the end of 1992. Hurriedly, both the Music Center and the county scrambled to meet the deadline. The Disney Concert Hall Committee prepared a set of cost estimates, as required by the agreement with the county. The whole project was now estimated at $131 million, including $91 million for the actual construction of the building.

But they based their cost estimates on preliminary drawings, because the architects had not yet prepared final drawings for the complicated design. It was a calculated risk, and some members of the Music

Center Board resisted the idea. But, as Nicholas said later, "We had to do that or else we wouldn't get the gift, and we didn't want to lose the gift."

In December 1992, a ceremonial groundbreaking occurred. And beginning in 1993, Grand Avenue was blocked off in between Parcels K and Q as construction on the garage progressed, and Gehry's office continued to work on the Concert Hall design. But by the end of the year it was becoming obvious to everyone that the financial situation was spinning out of control.

The problem was that constructing such a complicated design was going to cost a lot more money than anyone anticipated. Fees for architects and other specialists were expected to be $56 million, thirty percent higher than original estimates. The limestone exterior alone was expected to cost $22 million, though this appeared to be within budget. Even drywall costs were $5 million higher than anticipated— because, according to Nicholas, the Disney Hall drywall "has curves and movement that don't have any comparison to anything else that's been built in this city." Altogether, the Disney Concert Hall was now expected to cost $160 million, $30 million more than anyone had previously guessed.

All during the spring and summer of 1994, the Disney Concert Hall Committee, which included representatives of both the Music Center and the Disney family, met to decide what course of action to take. In November, the committee finally announced that all construction-related activity on the Concert Hall itself would be stopped, and that a big-name real estate firm, the Gerald Hines Interests of Houston, would be hired to analyze how to get the project done.

When the Hines estimates came in a few months later, they revealed an even more desperate situation than anyone imagined. The overall cost for the project, the company estimated, was not $110 million or $130 million but $255 million, including $170 million for the building itself and $64 million in "soft costs," such as architectural and consulting fees. The Hines company recommended construction cost savings of some $27 million, including the use of metal rather than limestone on the outside of the building. Even with these savings, the cost of Disney Hall was now estimated to be $227 million, or almost double any previous estimate.

⤺

At this point, the course of events was once again shaped by the personality and approach of Los Angeles County's chief administrative officer. In 1992, Dixon's prickly personality had led to his ouster. He was replaced the following year by Sally Reed.* Like Hankla and Dixon before her, Reed brought her own distinctive approach to solving the county's chronic budget problems. It was this approach, and the force of her strong personality, that set the terms for the final phase of the Disney Hall deal.

A tall woman in her fifties, Reed had a reputation as a tough administrator who ruled with a warm smile and a tight fist. She had served as CAO of Santa Clara County, in Northern California, for a dozen years, where she cut the budget mercilessly. And even though the Los Angeles County Board of Supervisors was once again controlled by liberals in 1993, the budget problems had grown so severe that the board chose Reed to succeed Dixon in the CAO's job. They hoped she could balance the budget and, in so doing, tame the sprawling bureaucracy at last—the very task that had eluded Hufford, Hankla, and Dixon before her.

Reed was a controversial figure—most people either loved her or hated her—and the reason was that, unlike some of her predecessors, she never shrank from confrontation. She seemed to enjoy nothing more than forcing the county's power structure to make a hard financial decision when its natural political inclination was to skate around the problem. So it was not surprising that when Sally Reed looked at the Disney Hall situation she decided to take a hard line that would require the Disney Concert Hall people to, as it were, face the music.

"Fairly early on," Reed recalled later, "it became clear to us that there wouldn't be any money to spend." She was alarmed to discover, for example, that about fifty percent of the original Disney gift had already been spent, even though the Disney committee still did not have completed architectural plans. She feared that the committee would simply run out of money, and that the unbuilt Concert Hall project would somehow drag down the parking garage and the county's bonds with it.

---

* In the interim, Harry Hufford had left Gibson, Dunn and returned to the county as interim administrator. But because of his work at the law firm, he recused himself from all work on Disney Hall while working for the county.

In late November, just three weeks after the Disney committee announced its plan to bring in Gerald Hines, Reed wrote a letter to Ron Gother demanding that the parking garage be redesigned to function as a stand-alone building. She also demanded assurance that the garage be completed by February 1996 "to enable the county to receive parking revenue to service the debt issued to pay for the garage." It was the first time anyone involved in the Disney Hall situation had ever publicly talked about what might happen if the Concert Hall were never built.

For three weeks, Reed heard nothing back from Gother. So on December 16, she dropped the bomb. In a second letter to Gother, she demanded "a serious, bona fide response and suggested program promptly." Otherwise, she said, she would have "no choice" but to declare the Music Center in default of its lease for Parcel K. In essence, she was saying it was time to get on with actually constructing the Disney building or forget the whole thing. No one, not even Hankla, had ever challenged the Music Center so directly.

Gother responded by saying he was concerned about the "alarmist" tone of Reed's letters, but there was no question that the warm smile and the tight fist had the desired effect. Before long, Fred Nicholas was gone from the scene, the Disney committee had been restructured, and Harry Hufford, willing as always to step into the breach, had been recruited as the new volunteer executive director of the Disney project and charged with "getting the ball over the goal line," as he put it.

So Hufford rolled up his sleeves and tried to make a deal with the county. It took five months of negotiating, until May 1995. And when it was made, the deal reflected the undeniable fact that, as Hufford later put it, "Sally was in the driver's seat."

There were two important components to the deal. The first was that the parking garage would be redesigned so that it could be topped out and opened for business in 1996—no matter what. Reed's purpose was to ensure that there was at least some revenue flowing from the garage to pay off the county bonds.

The second was an agreement that the Disney committee would have four years to raise enough money to build the project. Under this schedule, additional fundraising costs and construction delays would increase the cost of the Disney project from $227 million to $264 million, and the Disney Committee only had $115 million available, including additional Disney family gifts that brought the Disneys' own contribution to more than $100 million. According to Hufford's analysis, this meant the Disney people had to raise another $149 million by 1998. The agreement also included several fundraising milestones to be met—such as a thirty-five-percent commitment, or about $50 million, by the middle of 1997.

The deal represented an embarrassing but inevitable compromise by both sides. For the Disney Hall Committee, it meant having to admit the possibility that the hall might never be built. Indeed, Hufford readily admitted that the fundraising schedule required the Disney committee to quickly find another big donor, willing to throw in as much as or more than the Disneys. There were such people in Los Angeles, including Hollywood mega-producers like Steven Spielberg. But such a donor might have to share top billing with Walt Disney, a tough condition to meet in ego-driven Hollywood.

For Los Angeles County, the compromises were less publicized but no less embarrassing. Reed had to acknowledge that without Disney Hall in operation, and with a soft real estate market downtown, the county garage wouldn't generate sufficient revenue any time soon to pay off the bonds. In a year when the county government was already flirting with bankruptcy and laying off thousands of people, Reed had to agree to cover the county bonds out of the general fund. Instead of making money for the county, as Hankla had envisioned a decade earlier, Parcel K would now cost somewhere between $7 million and $18 million a year.

Furthermore, Reed also had to agree to build the parking structure in such a way that it would support the Disney Hall, as designed, on top of it—meaning, among other things, permanently retaining a series of posts that would form the Disney Hall's foundation. As Harry Hufford said, "Their concession was to keep the little guys sticking out of the roof so that we could build the Concert Hall on top of it."

This was, perhaps, the county's biggest concession, because it limited its future options if the Disney Hall were not built. The garage and the hall had been designed together; building something else on top of the garage would be shoving a square peg into a round hole at best. No sixty-story office building would ever occupy the site, even if the real estate market came back. If Disney Hall were not built, the county would have to propose something that was designed very much like it, and nothing like this design had ever been built anywhere. When Reed asked one of her aides what else they could build there someday, the aide answered, with a sardonic nod to Frank Gehry's architectural vision, "An office building that looks like a rose."

～

Today, the hole in downtown's urban design donut is still there. Parcel W-2, located at the bottom of the east side of Bunker Hill, is vacant except for a subway portal. Parcel Q, at the corner of First and Grand, still contains the erector-set parking structure, and its primitive steel shell provides a stark contrast to the rich texture of the Museum of Contemporary Art behind it. And Parcel K now features a subterranean parking structure with nothing on top—nothing, that is, except a couple of temporary structures needed to run the parking garage and Harry Hufford's "little guys sticking out of the roof," hinting at the possibility that someday, somehow, Frank Gehry will be able to plant his rose.

The bluebloods still believe Disney Hall can be built. To keep up morale, L.A.'s growing community of artists and architects occasionally speaks out with passion about its significance to downtown and to the metropolis at large. "Disney Hall is not about steel and concrete," wrote Esa-Pekka Salonen, director of the Los Angeles Philharmonic, in one op-ed piece. "It is not about budgets or sociology.... It is an investment in the heart of Los Angeles." In particular, the Disney Hall defenders frequently draw parallels to the Sydney Opera House, which was such a financial disaster that it had to be rescued by an Australian nationwide lottery, yet today is regarded as a worldwide architectural masterpiece.

There is little question that these pieces of punditry are in fact fragrant messages lobbed in the general direction of the Hollywood elite, hoping that one of them, as Lillian Disney once did, will read the paper and begin to feel philanthropic. But it is a race against time—not only against Sally Reed's deadlines, but against the continued fragmentation of the already sprawling arts community in Los Angeles. While the battle over Parcel K was going on, the Orange County Performing Arts Center grew in prestige and importance, and two small suburban cities, Thousand Oaks and Cerritos, opened their own performing arts centers as well. Indeed, the Disney Hall debacle is already being cited as an example that the get-things-done cultural elite fused together by Dorothy Chandler no longer exists—or, at the very least, no longer gets things done. In the arts, as in everything else, Los Angeles continues to splinter apart.

Meanwhile, the plight of Los Angeles County becomes more and more grim. At the same time that she was negotiating the Disney Hall deal in 1995, Sally Reed proposed draconian budget cuts that called for laying off eighteen thousand county workers and shutting down the health care system, including County-USC Hospital, one of the busiest public hospitals in the country. Though federal aid eventually rescued the county budget, some three thousand workers were laid off. A few months later, even Sally Reed apparently decided that some things weren't worth the trouble: She quit the Los Angeles County job and took a $70,000-a-year pay cut to become head of the California Department of Motor Vehicles, which had never been anyone's idea of a plum assignment. The last chapter in the Disney Hall story would be written by yet another county CAO.

In the end, after a decade of maneuvering over the control of Parcel K, Los Angeles has gained nothing from the Disney debacle. The pauperized county government is forced to subsidize the Parcel K parking garage even as it lays off employees. The bluebloods are in disarray, having won control of the parcel and then blown the opportunity to build what they wanted. And the idea of downtown as a compelling common experience for everyone in the reluctant metropolis has suffered most of all.

All these goals have been sacrificed to L.A.'s conceits. There was conceit of power on the part of the bluebloods, who believed that Parcel K belonged to them no matter what was good for the community. There was the artistic conceit of Frank Gehry, who designed the building without much regard for its cost. And there was the financial conceit of Jim Hankla and his successors, who believed, albeit from desperation, that they could somehow manipulate the private real estate market in order to alter the unbalanced mathematics left behind by the passage of Proposition 13. To any observer standing at the hole in the downtown donut, there can be little doubt that the rest of Los Angeles is poorer as a result.

CHAPTER 10

Welcome to Sales Tax Canyon

One Sunday in June 1994—just when the recession was ending, and they began thinking about going shopping again—readers of the *Los Angeles Times* opened their paper and discovered a colorful surprise falling out of it. It was a special advertising supplement showing off the opening of a new factory outlet shopping center along Highway 101 in Ventura County just inside the Oxnard city limits, about a half-hour west of the San Fernando Valley.

It was a surprise to see such a sophisticated advertisement, because most factory outlets weren't much to look at. Traditionally they had been nondescript places, relegated to rural highways, where manufacturers could dispose of excess inventory at low prices. But in the fickle world of big-time retailing, factory outlets were now hot. "Saving Money Is Now In Fashion," one discount retailer boasted in its advertisements. As shoppers abandoned traditional malls, a building boom in factory outlets and other discount shopping centers resulted that could not have been predicted just a few years before.

The Oxnard Factory Outlet supplement didn't have the look of a typical shopping center insert. It wasn't cluttered with cutout photos of various retail products, nor did it hammer readers with sale prices in large type. It looked, more than anything else, like a clever variation of an early Southern California fruit-and-vegetable postcard. The ad depicted the rolling hills of Ventura County in verdant green, and it showed a seemingly endless expanse of citrus land across the Oxnard Plain. Through this pastoral setting wound Highway 101, which appeared as a charming country road. And along the highway, the ad showed only one collection of buildings: a quaint assortment of barns, windmills, packing houses, and agricultural structures called the Oxnard Factory Outlet. Catering to Southern California's anti-urban bias, the ad made a visit to the outlet seem as peaceful and relaxing as a trip to the country to pick the lemons that were prominently featured in the foreground.

The Oxnard Factory Outlet is, indeed, located in one of Southern California's most important agricultural areas. But it's not exactly in the country. Highway 101 isn't a pastoral, winding road. It's a modern six-lane freeway carrying some one hundred seventeen thousand cars per day past the shopping center at sixty-five miles per hour, creating a deafening roar in the middle of the mall's "food court." And even though some farm fields still operate nearby, the Oxnard Factory Outlet is really located at the epicenter of a cutting-edge, asphalt "sellscape" that stretches for several miles along the freeway in both directions.

Right across the freeway is the Oxnard Auto Center, a collection of twelve auto dealerships and other discount retailers (such as Price Club) that's also designed to tempt shoppers from a forty- or fifty-mile radius. To the west, shopping centers are lined up along Highway 101 like airliners waiting to take off. Only a few hundred yards west of the Oxnard Factory Outlet is that superstar of retailing, Wal-Mart—another retail chain that's cashing in handsomely on the shoppers' infatuation with discount stores. A little farther west, where 101 makes a big sweeping turn north toward Santa Barbara, the old Esplanade regional shopping mall is still doing brisk business on the left-hand side of the road. On the right-hand side of the freeway is the proposed site of a "supermall" called Oxnard Town Center. Just over the Santa Clara River bridge in the City of Ventura stands Ventura's own auto mall, and a couple of miles farther up the road is the Buenaventura Mall, traditionally the area's leading regional shopping center.

And to the east, it's more of the same. In the City of Camarillo, a half-dozen or more small shopping centers stand alongside the freeway. Four miles east of the Oxnard Factory Outlet—four miles closer to the one-million-plus people who live in the San Fernando Valley—lies the site of the Camarillo Factory Stores Center, which is bigger and more upscale than the Oxnard center, and has been luring shoppers from throughout Ventura County. In fact, the only reason that the Camarillo

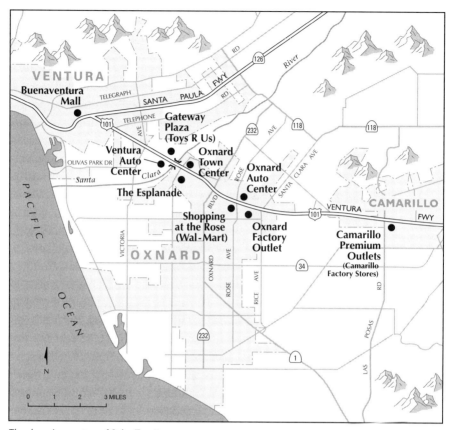

The shopping centers of Sales Tax Canyon.

center wasn't up and running when the Oxnard ad supplement came out was that the president of the Oxnard Chamber of Commerce had tied up the Camarillo center in court.

In other words, advertising notwithstanding, the Oxnard Factory Outlet doesn't stand in the middle of a lush rural plain. It stands instead in the middle of a powerful emerging regional shopping district—a kind of Sales Tax Canyon, about ten miles end to end, where shopping centers of all shapes and sizes line both sides of the freeway, crossing three city boundaries in the process. And however congested, however ugly, however out of place it might appear, Sales Tax Canyon isn't there by accident. It has been created quite deliberately by the three cities in the emerging sub-metropolis.

In keeping with their agricultural traditions, these three cities have "planted" stores along the freeway in hopes of reaping a rich harvest of sales tax revenue. They have wooed big retailers, cut red tape, arranged for the acquisition of land, and even given retail chains cash payments from tax funds. They have done all this because under California's peculiar taxation laws—made all the more peculiar by the property tax initiative Proposition 13—a retail store is a city's best cash crop.

⌐

The Oxnard Plain was not always the home of Sales Tax Canyon, of course. A broad, flat land that lies between the Santa Monica Mountains and the ocean, this territory has been defined for most of the last century by the way settlers have exploited its rich and fertile soil. For decades, Ventura County has been one of the richest agricultural areas in all of California, leading the state in orchard crops such as lemons and supplying the entire country with strawberries and winter vegetables.

Over time, several towns grew up around the fields and the packing plants where the fruit was prepared for shipment. Along a railroad siding near the ocean, the Oxnard Brothers built a sugar beet plant at the turn of the century. The plant soon drew Chinese and Mexican laborers to create a town that eventually became known, even though the brothers never lived there, as Oxnard. A few miles north, near the mouth of the Ventura River, another town had grown up around the local Franciscan mission and was eventually named for it: San Buenaventura, or Ventura for short. Ventura became the county seat and the headquarters for the county's agricultural and oil financiers. Along the stage lines and rail lines elsewhere in the plains and valleys of Ventura County, small settlements sprang up, but none was very big. As late as 1940, the entire population of the county was only sixty-nine thousand, or about one-fortieth the size of its massive neighbor, Los Angeles County.

Then came the freeway, and as with so many outlying areas in the Los Angeles region, the freeway altered life in a fundamental way. The county's population tripled between 1950 and 1970. By 1980 this rural farming county had a population of more than a half-million, about the same as the population of Cleveland or New Orleans or Boston.

Oxnard had grown to a city of more than one hundred thousand people, a diverse place with a large Latino and Asian population, a growing business and financial community, and high-end condominiums by the beach. Ventura, still the county seat, was now a mostly white enclave of more than seventy thousand people. Both had burgeoning new suburban tracts and decaying but important old downtowns. Meanwhile, along Highway 101 a few miles east of Oxnard, the freeway had greatly expanded the small community of Camarillo, making it a classic Southern California freeway suburb of low-slung office buildings, neighborhood shopping centers, and red-tile-roof subdivisions. Incorporated as a city in 1964, only six years after the freeway arrived, Camarillo by 1980 had a population of almost forty thousand.

To any geographer looking at a map, it was obvious that these three cities constituted the disparate elements of an emerging mini-metropolis of a quarter-million people, as big as Rochester or Jersey City or Tampa. They were separated from Los Angeles by the mountains, but linked to it by the freeway. They were separated from each other by farmland, but lined up, one after the other, along the Oxnard Plain.* And all three cities were undeniably part of the same subregional economy.

Yet to residents of the three cities, and to the political leaders they elected, this was not how things looked. All three cities had a long history of rivalry with one another. Traditionally wealthier and more powerful, Ventura looked down on Oxnard as a poor farming community with a large minority population—a "muscle place," as Oxnard City Councilman Manuel Lopez once said. Oxnard, in turn, viewed Ventura as snooty and elitist and took pride in its more diverse character. Meanwhile, Camarillo was concerned about establishing a squeaky-clean suburban image, partly because it lived in the shadow of a state mental hospital that had been located there since the 1930s. Its mostly white suburban residents feared being swallowed up by annexation from Oxnard; indeed, this was the major reason for incorporation in the first place.

By the late 1970s, then, all three cities were reaching maturity, yet all three were struggling to maintain their own identity. They wanted to grow in ways that benefited their towns, but didn't want growth to overwhelm them. They wanted to remain separate from one another, yet they were drawn together by an increasingly interdependent economy.

* Another component of this mini-metropolis was the Port Hueneme Navy "seabee" base and the neighboring city of the same name, which had seventeen thousand residents and was completely surrounded by Oxnard and the ocean. This area also had a "hinterland" that depended on it, including many farm areas around such towns as Ojai and Santa Paula.

Most of all, like all cities, they struggled to create the right combination of homes, businesses, and shops that would provide a solid tax base to keep their towns solvent. But then along came Proposition 13.

⌐

Proposition 13 was the culmination of two decades of growing voter unrest in Southern California about rising property taxes. Conceived by longtime tax-fighter Howard Jarvis, then in the employ of the Apartment Owners of Los Angeles, it was sold to voters as a way for typical homeowners to strike back against big government. And when it was passed in June 1978, Proposition 13 was widely—and, as it turned out, correctly—viewed as the first rumblings of a nationwide tax revolt.

As drafted, the measure reduced property tax rates all around the state by imposing an annual cap of one percent of assessed value. Furthermore, Proposition 13 permitted reassessment only when property was sold, which meant that property owners of modest means didn't have to worry about being hit with a big tax bill if the market value of their property happened to increase. Given the rapidly rising property values in Southern California at the time, Proposition 13 was a godsend to the average homeowner.

But for Southern California's municipal governments, the effect of Proposition 13 was devastating—at least at first. Not only had they lost half their property tax revenue, but they had no way to increase taxes on existing houses and businesses in the future. Layoffs and cutbacks quickly ensued, which was, of course, exactly what Jarvis and his fellow tax-cutters wanted to see.

Over time, however, the cities of Southern California learned how to work the angles. They increased fees on all services and scoured the legal books for assessment districts and other revenue-raising methods that didn't require voter approval. Most important, they learned how to manipulate the process of urban planning to take advantage of the financial opportunities that lay hidden within Proposition 13's anti-government rhetoric. In this way, Proposition 13 has provided the architecture on which Southern California's urban landscape has been built ever since.

Fees and assessments aside, there were only two ways a city could dramatically increase its revenue under Proposition 13. One was to encourage new real estate development, because the construction of new buildings also triggered a reassessment of property. But this strategy didn't always work. After Proposition 13, property taxes were so low that many new development projects, especially housing tracts, were money-losers, unable to pay the cost of police, fire, and other services they required.

The second way to raise money—far more preferable in the view of most city managers—was to focus on retailing.

Retail sales tax has always been important to cities in California, but after Proposition 13 it was like gold. Property tax may have been bound and gagged by Proposition 13, but sales tax lay outside its purview. As a result, after Proposition 13, the traditional balance of sales and property taxes was turned upside down.

In 1978, the year before the proposition passed, the three major cities on the Oxnard Plain collected about $8 million in property tax and $10 million in sales tax.* In 1979, when the Proposition 13 tax limitations kicked in, the three cities collected almost $12 million in sales tax and only $3.7 million in property tax. Suddenly, sales tax was now three times as important as property tax. It was obvious that, to survive, the Oxnard Plain cities—like a couple of hundred other cities in the Southern California megalopolis—would have to focus on sales tax.

Under California's tax laws, typical of tax laws nationwide, the way to bring in more sales tax was not to find more residents who buy things or more factories that make things, but to bring in more stores that sell things. Every city in the state received one penny of sales tax for every dollar of retail sales made at any store inside the city's boundaries, no matter where the purchaser lived. If a resident of Camarillo bought a Honda in Oxnard for $15,000, then Oxnard got $150 in sales tax and Camarillo got nothing, even if the car buyer drove straight back to Camarillo and never returned to Oxnard again. With this kind of gold at the end of the rainbow, most cities understood what they had to do to survive. "If I were a city manager," one California local government expert said in the 1980s, "I'd be out getting every Buick dealership I can find."

But in many cities, including those on the Oxnard Plain, this required a complete reversal of local planning policies.

* This figure was slightly skewed because Camarillo, like many conservative Southern California suburbs incorporated during the 1960s, had never levied a property tax. In most parts of the state, the sales and property tax figures were very close.

In the years after Proposition 13 passed, retailers in all three cities were landlocked along the older postwar boulevards and avenues, and they pretty much catered to a local clientele. Oxnard's car dealerships and newer retailers were lined up along Oxnard Boulevard, leading out of downtown north toward The Esplanade Mall. Ventura's situation was almost identical, with the dealerships and shops lined up along Main Street from downtown south to Buenaventura Plaza. In Camarillo, the old retailing core lay right along the freeway in the center of town.

Planners in these cities—Ventura and Oxnard in particular—were focused on downtown redevelopment efforts and viewed the strips and the malls as damaging competition. Though politically powerful landowners sometimes got their way, official public policy discouraged such development. Indeed, Oxnard operated at the time under a master plan from the 1960s, drawn up by the respected architectural firm of Gruen Associates, that called for suburban residential development near Highway 101.

Yet even as Ventura, Oxnard, and other cities were looking inward, the retailing business was exploding outward. In business after business—from autos to drugs to hardware and even books—the big chains started building superstores that were two, three, or even four times as big as their old local stores. Far from being friendly operations on a typical Main Street, these stores were usually housed in a windowless three-hundred-by-four-hundred-foot box standing by itself surrounded by several hundred parking spaces. Sometimes called "big-box retailers" or "category-killers" (because of their ability to kill off all other retailers in their category), these operations looked a lot more like warehouses than stores. To draw shoppers from many cities, these retailers needed accessible, high-traffic locations, usually near freeway interchanges. And to accommodate the huge scale of their operations, they needed lots of cheap land.

In order to play this high-stakes game, the cities on the Oxnard Plain had to break out of the downtown-and-boulevard-strip thinking in which their planners were mired. With a half-million people or more in a thirty-mile radius, they had the market. Gradually, they altered their thinking in order to free up the necessary land as well.

In fact, each city controlled several miles of open land along the freeway, more than enough to build a Sales Tax Canyon. While continuing to pay lip service to the need to strengthen their downtowns, and to preserve agricultural land, all three cities began to figure out how to set up the large-scale retailers at strategic locations along the freeway. And so they went into competition with one another for stores.

⤸

The first city that caught on to the need to build along the freeway was Ventura. Ventura was traditionally the strongest retail market in the county, because it was a solid working-to-middle-class city that had historically served as the area's center of political and financial power. The 1970s, however, had been a somewhat sluggish time for business growth—partly, perhaps, because a pro-environment city council had been in place during much of that period. Throughout the 1970s, Ventura had consistently lagged fifteen to twenty percent behind Oxnard in total sales tax.

In the recession year of 1981, however, Ventura voters swept in a new, business-oriented council. Searching for ways to expand the city's business base and its tax revenue, the new team realized that Ventura had one asset that could be exploited: a precious three-mile stretch of farmland running along Highway 101 from the existing Buenaventura Plaza mall east to the Santa Clara River. Determined to capitalize on this asset, the new council went to work. "We were in a decision-making mode," says John Sullard, an urban planner who was elected to the council in 1981.

The council opened up one thousand acres of land near the free-way for commercial and industrial development, and designated several key parcels near Highway 101 interchanges for shopping centers. These changes attracted such solid retailers as Gemco, Mervyn's, and the Feder-ated electronics chain. Along the Santa Clara River, the traditional divid-ing line between Ventura and Oxnard, the city approved another series of retail developments. On one side of the freeway, several of the Main Street auto dealers were set up in a new auto "mall." On the other side, the city approved a multiplex theater, a Toys R Us store (a category-killer if ever there was one), and an adjacent retail center. On top of all that, Buenaventura Plaza, the city's largest shopping center, expanded and be-came an enclosed mall in 1983, changing its name to Buenaventura Mall.

Not all of these developments were popular, and eventually a slow-growth backlash began to build. Traffic problems quickly mounted, and in 1985 the council was forced to impose a moratorium in certain areas. Political support for the pro-business council eroded, and the city began to take its retail development for granted. The planning commission rejected the shopping center next to Toys R Us twice because the commissioners were dissatisfied with the uninspired "strip" design. When the developer complained that he had never had so much trouble getting a project approved, one city council member simply stated, "We certainly don't need the extra tax dollars."

At the time, the arrogance was well founded. In 1980, Ventura and Oxnard both had about eight hundred retail businesses. By 1987, Ventura had more than twelve hundred, while Oxnard had about nine hundred. And Ventura reaped a windfall as a result. By 1985, Ventura was bringing in $10 million a year in sales tax revenue, an increase of seventy-two percent since the recession began four years earlier. Sales tax in Oxnard, by contrast, had grown by only twenty percent and stood at less than $8 million.* More than ever, Ventura was rich and Oxnard was poor.

Oxnard's politicians were not blind to this trend. Oxnard had also experienced a period of lethargy toward business in the 1970s. But in the early 1980s, the city council was taken over by an aggressively pro-business faction led by Mayor Nao Takasugi. Mild-mannered and extremely popular, Takasugi later became the only Asian-American member of the California legislature. But his politics had nothing to do with ethnicity. They had to do with business. Having run his family's grocery store for decades, Takasugi was naturally oriented toward business concerns. In the 1970s, Takasugi once said, "the attitude of the city was to not be aggressive about economic development." He was determined to change this attitude.

Oxnard critics always complained that Takasugi and other pro-development council members were too close to developers—taking their money for political campaigns, for example—but there was no question that in the early 1980s things were changing. As the economy revved up, the city left the old Gruen Associates' plan in the dust.

With impressive speed, Oxnard sought to change its image by approving upscale developments of all kinds: beachfront hotels and condominiums, red-tile-roofed subdivisions, a high-rise financial center designed to lure stockbrokers and lawyers from Ventura. Seeking to put Oxnard on the national sports map, the city even subsidized construction of a new golf course and Raddison Hotel and installed the Los

---

* The statewide increase during this period was thirty-two percent.

Angeles Raiders' training camp. (The idea of the Raiders as a tourist attraction evaporated when Al Davis, the team's secretive owner, wrapped a black tarp around the field to keep out possible spies.)

This aggressive pro-development strategy was not focused on retail development at first. But Oxnard's strategic location halfway between the affluent communities of Santa Barbara and Thousand Oaks was tailor-made for the big-boxers. The beginning of Sales Tax Canyon in Oxnard can be traced back to 1985, when the Price Club approached the city with a plan to plop down a big box right at the bend in Highway 101 in north Oxnard, about a mile from the Ventura city line.

At the time, Price Club was playing a critical role in shaping the post-Proposition 13 landscape in California. By pioneering warehouse-style retailing around the state, Price Club expanded into almost every market. For cities, a Price Club was a gold mine. A single one-hundred-thousand-square-foot Price Club might generate $600,000 to $700,000 a year in sales tax, almost as much from one store as a city would reap from a much larger regional mall. Well aware of this fact, the company frequently played neighboring cities off against one another in order to get a better financial deal, and even made up a brochure for cities, extolling the sales tax benefits of having a Price Club in your town. To bring in a Price Club, Oxnard quickly made a deal to facilitate a crucial land swap at a below-market rate.

The next building block of Sales Tax Canyon came shortly after that, when Oxnard turned its attention to the city's single most important source of sales tax: its auto dealers.

Languishing off the freeway on the declining Oxnard Boulevard strip, Oxnard's auto dealers were not happy, especially since Ventura had moved its auto dealers into a new center along the freeway only two miles away. To mollify the Oxnard auto dealers, the city's political leaders made a deal with developer Viggo Boserup to set them up along Rose Avenue on the north side of the freeway, about three miles east of the Ventura Auto Center. At the same time, Oxnard approved an adjacent discount shopping center proposed by a different developer.

To assure that the two new centers had high-quality landscaping and streets, Oxnard established a special assessment district. But in order to keep the auto dealers happy, the city made a deal, one that came to be viewed as the standard against which all future Sales Tax Canyon deals would be measured. Ordinarily the auto dealers would have had to pay the land assessment out of their own pockets, footing the bill for semi-annual bond payments to Wall Street investors. But Oxnard agreed to take half the auto center's sales taxes (estimated at about $600,000 a year) and use those funds to cover the assessment. Thus, money that otherwise would have flowed into the general fund—to pay for police officers, the fire department, and so on—was instead diverted for handsome new roads and landscaping at Rose and Highway 101.

By 1987, the first auto dealerships were moving into the Oxnard Auto Center. And when the adjacent Plaza del Norte broke ground later that year, Mayor Takasugi called it "a great milestone in the forward progress of the city." Not long after, Price Club moved to Plaza del Norte, to be replaced at its old location by another big-boxer, the Home Depot. Soon the Oxnard Price Club gained a reputation as one of the highest grossers in the chain; even Santa Barbarans surreptitiously slipped down the coast for discount purchases. Sales Tax Canyon had established a firm foothold on the Oxnard side of the Santa Clara River.

It was not long, however, before the retail warfare reached the banks of the river itself.

⤿

One of Oxnard's most crucial assets in the sales tax competition was a two-hundred-sixty-five-acre swath of farmland along Highway 101 on the south bank of the Santa Clara River, just over the boundary from Ventura. In the mid-1980s, Ventura was heavily fortifying the north side of the river by building the Toys R Us shopping center and the Ventura Auto Center. But there was no doubt that the large parcel across the river was also valuable. It was Oxnard's best hope of building something—retailing, industry, offices—that would draw the traditionally reluctant Venturans across the river into their city.

In 1984, the Robert P. Warmington Company, a well-known Orange County developer, drew up a high-flying plan for this site far beyond anything ever proposed for the Oxnard Plain. Warmington proposed some four million square feet of space—as big as the World Trade Center in New York. More than half of the project would be devoted to office and research and development uses—enough space, altogether, to support eleven thousand employees. Warmington also proposed a one-thousand-room hotel, a restaurant, a bank, a cultural arts facility, and a two-acre neighborhood park. But most important, from Oxnard's point of view, was what Warmington described as a "super-regional mall."

A super-regional was the category-killer of malls, an attempt to eliminate the competition by creating an outsized shopping center anchored by three, four, or even five department stores. The Warmington mall would be a one-million-square-foot enclosed shopping center, almost twice as big as Buenaventura Mall or The Esplanade. In a retail market where Sears and J.C. Penney's predominated, the mall would be capable of attracting high-end department stores like Nordstrom, Macy's, or Bloomingdale's—and, in the process, vacuuming up $170 million retail dollars a year from the surrounding area.

Warmington called the proposal Oxnard Town Center. After looking at the renderings, Oxnard's planners jokingly nicknamed it The Emerald City, a gleaming group of expensive buildings clustered together in an area traditionally best-known for farming, quarrying, and a county maintenance yard. But neither the staff nor the politicians were blind to the possibilities. If successful, Oxnard Town Center would bring in almost $4 million a year to the city treasury, half of it in the form of sales tax from the mall. And it would force other cities to pay a little respect to the municipality that had always been the Rodney Dangerfield of the Oxnard Plain.

With a hot real estate market in progress, Oxnard worked quickly. In May 1985, the city's environmental impact report, or EIR, was released, and all through the summer the staff, the planning commission, and the city council pushed the project toward approval. It did not take long, however, for Ventura's politicians to begin worrying.

There was no question that the Town Center project was a threat to Ventura's retail dominance. But the Town Center proposal also came right at the time when politics in Ventura was turning against growth. The Town Center EIR was released in the middle of Ventura's controversy over whether to approve the shopping center adjacent to Toys R Us, just across the river from the Town Center site. Ventura was already considering a moratorium in certain areas because of traffic. And the Town Center EIR predicted that the project would send twenty-seven thousand cars per day across the Santa Clara River bridge.

Ignoring the fact that its own branch of Sales Tax Canyon had been attracting shoppers from Oxnard across this same bridge, Ventura began to complain. The EIR had not been broad enough, city officials said. The potential fiscal impact on existing malls such as The Esplanade and Buenaventura Mall hadn't been analyzed. And most of all,

the EIR hadn't evaluated the impact of Town Center traffic on interchanges in Ventura. "Thirty percent of the traffic will travel upcoast
and across the Santa Clara River bridge," Ventura's public works director, Shelley Jones, complained at one hearing. "The EIR makes no
further mention of those cars, but they surely don't drop off the end of
the bridge. They have to go somewhere."

Warmington's response was, essentially, to laugh. "I think it is
highly unusual that the city of Ventura would comment on the inade-
quacies of the interchanges in their city... in light of the fact that they
have hundreds of acres of commercial and industrial projects that impact
on those same interchanges," said Warmington executive Michael
Mackin. Meanwhile, Oxnard's response was to ignore Ventura's complaints. The planning commission approved the project in mid-August,
and Ventura officials complained that Oxnard was stonewalling them
by not providing all available information.

"I want to make it clear that this is not an Oxnard versus Ventura
thing," Ventura Mayor Dennis Orrock said in an appearance before the
Oxnard City Council. But, of course, it was. While insisting that they
actually favored the project, Ventura's officials nevertheless sought
to slow down the approval process. Meanwhile, Oxnard's leaders tried
to appear open-minded while still keeping things on schedule. In September, the Oxnard City Council conducted an all-day hearing on a
weekday specifically to listen to Ventura's complaints. Not surprisingly,
the council rejected Ventura's appeals and approved the project. Also
not surprisingly, Ventura then filed a lawsuit.

The Ventura lawsuit wasn't designed to actually kill the Town
Center project. Instead, since a neighboring city never has any direct
influence over a development proposal, it was merely a way for Ventura
to gain some leverage over the process. For several months, Oxnard and
Ventura negotiated in private, trying to find a way for both cities to save
face. Finally, in March 1986, six months after Oxnard's approval, the
mayors of the two cities held a dramatic press conference on the steps of
the Ventura County Courthouse and announced a settlement that theoretically allowed the project to go forward, but tied it to the expansion
of the Santa Clara River bridge on Highway 101.

Under the terms of the deal, the two cities agreed on a 55–45 split
for the local share of the bridge project. Oxnard's share was expected to
be $3.8 million, Ventura's $3.4 million. But the entire cost was expected

to be much more: around $25 million. Only the state had that kind of money. So the deal specified that the retail portion of Oxnard Town Center wouldn't be built until Caltrans committed the funds to expand the bridge.

Oxnard had extracted an important concession: an admission by Ventura that forty-five percent of the traffic problem on the bridge had been created in the Ventura portion of Sales Tax Canyon. But Ventura got something which turned out to be more important: an indefinite delay in the Town Center project while a cumbersome and financially strapped state bureaucracy tried to come up with a large sum of money.

Confident nevertheless that the Emerald City would be built, Oxnard moved forward with a plan to float a $15 million bond issue—backed by the land values at Oxnard Town Center—to build the up-front infrastructure. Soon the site was filled with wide access roads and handsome rows of palm trees leading to the locations of the soon-to-be-constructed buildings.

In fact, however, Warmington had missed its chance to build the center. Nineteen eighty-six was the high-water mark for new real estate development during the 1980s' boom. But the tax reform laws passed by Congress that year cut out most tax breaks for real estate invest-ment, and the money available to invest in projects like Oxnard Town Center began to dry up. One office building was constructed in 1989, and a second in 1991. But Warmington never lined up a shopping cen-ter developer before the real estate recession hit in 1991.

At the end of 1991, Warmington missed a $1 million tax payment on the infrastructure bond. Oxnard foreclosed on the property, touch-ing off a lengthy and unpleasant lawsuit over who would wind up with the Oxnard Town Center property once the dust had settled. And at a council meeting in early 1992, Oxnard Finance Director Rudy Muravez reported to the city council, "The Oxnard Town Center, as an entity, has ceased to function."

The boom of the 1980s was over. Oxnard had come out of it with $11 million a year in sales tax. But Ventura had come out of it with $14 million a year and a pretty sure bet that the retail fortress on the north bank of the Santa Clara River wasn't likely to be pierced.

⌐

During the depths of the California recession, however, a funny thing happened in the world of retailing. While regional malls slumped and department store chains vanished, discount retailers became the hottest trend in real estate. Eager developers often grouped two or three category-killing discounters together into a mutant version of the old strip shopping center now known as a "power center"—so-called because of the immense power the discounters could wield over the local marketplace. Sometimes the big manufacturers and retailers cut out the discount middlemen and opened their own low-priced stores in factory outlet centers.

Weary of high prices and ever-expanding malls, shoppers loved the discount trend. "I buy just about everything from outlets," one shopper told *Business Week* at the beginning of the discount boom. "When I get desperate, I go to a department store." And so in the space of only a few years, the entire world of retailing was turned upside down. A whole new kind of retail animal was emerging, and real estate investors were tripping over themselves to get this animal built. It wasn't long, therefore, before Sales Tax Canyon was back in business, and the cities were at each other's throats once more.

On the Oxnard Plain, the beginning of this new era can be precisely pinpointed to the day Wal-Mart arrived. In mid-December 1991, about a week after Warmington had defaulted on the Oxnard Town Center bonds, Oxnard City Manager Vern Hazen made the dramatic announcement that Oxnard had made a deal to bring Wal-Mart to town.

Arkansas-based Wal-Mart was, of course, the ultimate big-box category-killer: a highly efficient nationwide chain with enough financial muscle to undercut everyone else's prices and stay open twenty-four hours a day at any location. Preferring rural areas, Wal-Mart had avoided California during the 1980s. But when the recession began to harm other discount retailers, Wal-Mart moved into the state with plans to build two hundred stores.

On a fifty-five-acre strawberry field along Highway 101 at Rose Avenue, just a mile east of the Santa Clara River bridge, Wal-Mart and Los Angeles developer Stan Rothbart proposed a five-hundred-thousand-square-foot power center called Shopping At The Rose. The Rose project would feature a Wal-Mart and a Sam's Club, Wal-Mart's sister retailer, as well as other stores. When completed, the project was expected to bring the city $2.5 million a year in sales tax.

For Oxnard, still reeling from the Town Center debacle and other reversals, the deal looked great, and the city rammed the project through the permitting process in only a few months. When the project came before the city council in July 1992, more than one hundred residents from an adjoining neighborhood came to complain. But the council was not sympathetic. "We need revenue," Councilman Manny Lopez told them. "We're at a situation where we can't even keep our restrooms open in the park."

Of course, not all the sales taxes reaped from the Rose project were earmarked for park restrooms. In a deal that went beyond the Oxnard Auto Center arrangement, the city agreed to give $2.4 million back to Rothbart and Wal-Mart. Every year, half of the Rose sales tax revenue would go back to Rothbart, who would use the funds to pay off fees and assessments imposed by the city for traffic improvements. Once Rothbart was paid $1.4 million, then the "developer half" of the sales tax money would flow straight back to Wal-Mart headquarters in Bentonville, Arkansas. For the privilege of having this store inside its city limits, Oxnard was going to pay one of the nation's most successful companies $1 million out of its own tax money.

But Oxnard was not yet done with Sales Tax Canyon. The same week that the city council approved the Wal-Mart project, Oxnard announced a developer's plans to construct the Oxnard Factory Outlet, a discount shopping center to be situated only one hundred yards down the freeway from Shopping At The Rose. The project was expected to generate an additional $850,000 a year in sales tax.

Still panting from the Wal-Mart project, Oxnard sprinted to approve the factory outlet. Although the proposal involved squeezing two-hundred-eighty-thousand square feet of buildings and fifteen hundred parking spaces onto twenty-five acres adjacent to an outdated freeway interchange, the city did not write up a full environmental impact report. Instead, at the end of August, just five weeks after the project was announced, Oxnard released a lengthy "mitigation" document claiming that

The garish architecture theme of Oxnard Factory Outlets.

the project would have "no significant environmental effects." On October 2, a little over two months after it was announced, the Oxnard Planning Commission approved the project 6–0.

Indeed, about the only thing Oxnard held firm on was the design. Fearing just another prosaic suburban project, Oxnard's staff planners demanded something innovative and suggested an architectural theme that reflected the city's roots. Soon the developer's architect was also racing to come up with agricultural-looking buildings to squeeze onto the narrow site, which ran right along the freeway.

The reason Oxnard was sprinting was that Camarillo had recently entered the race to build Sales Tax Canyon as well. The previous year, citizen opposition there had killed one giant factory outlet proposal. But Camarillo's leaders were clearly tantalized by the $2 million in sales tax that had been dangled in front of them. In 1992, they began to work on a second factory outlet project with local landowner Tom Leonard and the Koll Real Estate Company of Orange County, one of the biggest developers in the region.

The location was just off Highway 101 near Las Posas Road, about four miles east of the proposed Oxnard Factory Outlet. The city had approved an office/industrial park on the site in 1985, and had even formed a special taxing district, known as a Mello-Roos district, to construct roads and handsome landscaping. But the office/R&D market fell apart, and only one building was constructed. So Koll and Leonard proposed building a factory outlet center on twenty-two of the project's ninety-two acres.

During the summer of 1992, while Oxnard was fast-tracking its factory outlet project, Camarillo worked out a deal. In exchange for building the Camarillo Factory Stores, the city agreed to return to the developers fifty percent of the sales tax the project generated. (The total sales tax was estimated to be between $700,000 and $1 million.) The money would then be used to pay off the Mello-Roos bonds that were floated to pay for the roads and landscaping.

There is no question that this deal was motivated by the fear that Oxnard would get a jump on Camarillo in the factory outlet war. The Mello-Roos tax, the city later explained in court papers, "causes an economic disadvantage in leasing potential for the property as compared to the Oxnard project, which is not subject to any special tax levies." As Assistant City Manager Larry Davis told the *Los Angeles*

Times, "This is the first time we've considered such a tax change, but the times have changed."

On October 7, the Camarillo City Council approved the tax-sharing agreement with Koll and Leonard, even though the city had not yet acted on the formal development application. A week later, the Oxnard City Council approved the Oxnard Factory Outlet project. "It looks like we're in a horse race," said Oxnard Mayor Takasugi, "but we're now in the pole position."

The pole position was strengthened on October 20, when Stephen J. Maulhardt, the president of the Oxnard Chamber of Commerce, sued Camarillo in an attempt to block the deal to share sales tax revenue. Camarillans thought Maulhardt was a stalking horse for the City of Oxnard, attempting to slow down the Camarillo project just long enough for the Oxnard project to be built first. Maulhardt simply said that an industrial park he owned in Oxnard would be harmed economically by the Camarillo deal.* Whatever his motivation, both sides were now playing for keeps, each trying to upstage the other.

After Maulhardt filed his suit, Camarillo hurriedly prepared a set of environmental mitigation measures and approved the project in January 1993. Then Oxnard upped the ante again. The city had already agreed to freeze development fees on the Oxnard Factory Outlet. Now Steve Kinney, Oxnard's economic development director, went back to the council for more.

"The Oxnard developer cannot compete on even terms with the Camarillo developer in offering leases to prospective tenants which are economically supportable by the project," he wrote in his staff report. He asked the council to provide the developer with "a limited amount of financial support" and concluded, "Not more than $1 million would be sufficient support for him to be able to make competitive lease offers." The council agreed not just to freeze the level of the fees, but to defer their collection for five years.

---

* One little-noticed aspect of these deals is that sales tax-sharing sometimes benefits other properties in the same development that have no retailers on them. The Camarillo sales tax rebate actually covered the entire Mello-Roos tax bill for the whole project, even the industrial and R&D portion. This reduced the developer's cost, and the saving was passed on to the tenants. Maulhardt, whose industrial project was in an assessment district in Oxnard, claimed he was therefore placed at a competitive disadvantage. In fact, Maulhardt's project eventually went into bankruptcy because of his inability to pay the land assessments.

Meanwhile, Maulhardt's lawsuit moved forward in dramatic fashion. In May, Superior Court Judge Melinda Johnson in Ventura ruled that Camarillo's deal with Koll and Leonard constituted a gift of public funds to a private entity, an arrangement prohibited by the California constitution. The city, she said, had not proven that the Koll-Leonard subsidy would lead to a public benefit. The subsidy was "a benefit to the developer which may produce a benefit to the city in the future." She ordered the city to nullify the deal with Koll and Leonard.

Reluctantly, Camarillo rescinded the agreement. But the factory-outlet developer working with Koll—a national leader known as GCA Chelsea Inc.—agreed to go forward without the subsidy. Fearing more lawsuits from Maulhardt, Camarillo also prepared a full environmental impact report. After the city approved the project again, in April 1994, Maulhardt again sued, this time only on environmental grounds.

By then, however, the Oxnard Factory Outlet project was almost completed. On Memorial Day Weekend of 1994, a year after Judge Johnson's ruling, Phase One of the Oxnard mall opened amid great hoopla. "I got Revlon nail polish for $1.25," explained one local shopper who previously trekked to an outlet center near Palm Springs, almost two hundred miles away, for bargains such as these. Three weeks later, the Camarillo Factory Stores held a ceremonial groundbreaking and pledged to donate computer equipment to the local school district. In August, Camarillo settled the lawsuit by giving Maulhardt $150,000, mostly for attorney fees.

The Camarillo project opened for business early in 1995. A typically handsome, suburban-style Camarillo project, complete with red tile roofs, the center quickly attracted high-end discounters like Jones of New York and Saks Fifth Avenue, and during Christmas season 1995 the city reported that sales tax revenue was up almost twenty-five percent. A twelve-screen cinema complex was built next-door. (The name of Camarillo Factory Stores was later changed to the lyrical "Camarillo Premium

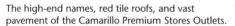
The high-end names, red tile roofs, and vast pavement of the Camarillo Premium Stores Outlets.

Outlets," giving the whole project both an upscale and downscale touch.)

Meanwhile, the more garish Oxnard project, hard against the freeway with its agricultural-style buildings, had a more difficult time wooing high-end tenants. Both citizens and members of the city council ridiculed the agricultural theme, which the staff planners who dreamed up the idea agreed had been poorly executed. Ironically, going first and subsidizing the project had not spelled success for Oxnard. But each city's frantic race to build such a project had permanently altered the landscape of Sales Tax Canyon.

A billboard for Camarillo Premium Outlets.

⌒

Back on the north bank of the Santa Clara River, Sales Tax Canyon's latest additions were causing problems. Some of Ventura's retail developments from the early 1980s were still performing well. Increasingly, however, Ventura was losing retail traffic to the other side of the river. After peaking in 1990 at around $14.3 million, Ventura's sales tax revenue dropped ten percent over the next two years—and in 1993, Ventura slipped behind Oxnard in sales tax receipts for the first time since 1981. Meanwhile, thanks to Sales Tax Canyon, Oxnard's sales tax receipts grew by sixty percent between 1985 and 1992.

To Ventura's leaders, there was little doubt about what the problem was. The Buenaventura Mall, once the county's leading shopping center, had ceased to be competitive. In the new world of 1990s' retailing, shopping centers either had to be cheap (like Wal-Mart or the factory outlets) or they had to be "experience-based," providing shoppers with restaurants, entertainment, and lots of other experiences that would make them want to return.

Buenaventura Mall was neither. Tucked onto a sixty-acre parcel of land at the very western edge of Sales Tax Canyon, it was nothing more than a typical 1970s shopping mall. It had a middle-market department store at each end (The Broadway and J.C. Penney's) with small stores in between. One end of the property also included a drugstore, and other stores lined up, shopping-center style, outside the mall. Like its counterpart in Oxnard, The Esplanade (which was anchored by Sears and

Robinson-May), Buenaventura Mall was based on a twenty-year-old idea of what shoppers wanted.

No one was more aware of this problem than the mall's owners. The mall had been purchased, for a high price, by two international banks in 1988, and it was run by a retail management firm from Los Angeles, the MaceRich Company. Beginning in 1991, MaceRich tried to double the size of the mall. Hemmed in on all sides by residential area, however, the mall was vulnerable to neighborhood opposition. Given the lingering anti-growth sentiment that still existed in Ventura in 1991 and 1992, and the doubtful outlook on Wall Street for old-fashioned malls, the MaceRich proposal died.

As the 1990s recession wore on, pro-business forces once again secured control of the Ventura City Council. And when the sales tax dip hit hard in 1992, the mall issue seemed more important than ever. By churning out $1 million a year, Buenaventura Mall was the city's most important single source of sales tax revenue. The city's economic consultants were predicting disaster if nothing was done.

With Wal-Marts and factory outlets in abundance, the consultants said, the Oxnard Plain didn't have room for two old-fashioned regional centers like The Esplanade and Buenaventura Mall. What the retailers wanted was one mall where the remaining three or four department store chains could hunker down together. Sooner or later, the consultants said, one mall would expand, and the other would die.

In 1994, The Esplanade's owners announced that they would try to double the size of their mall. In addition, Oxnard officials occasionally announced that they were talking to shopping mall developers about going ahead with Oxnard Town Center. This put Ventura in a tough spot. Unlike Oxnard, Ventura had no other options, having chewed up its freeway frontage during the 1980s. For Ventura, it was expand Buenaventura Mall or nothing.

Frustrated with MaceRich's inability to get things done, the mall's owners turned to a different developer—a well-known national firm named LaSalle Partners. Ventura, in turn, hired a Berkeley economist, Walt Kieser, to represent the city. In May 1995, after about six months of negotiation, both sides called a press conference at Ventura City Hall to announce that they had made a deal.

On the face of it, the deal was a victory for Ventura and a defeat for Oxnard. The new mall would simply be a larger version of the current mall, with four anchors instead of two. And it was pretty obvious who those two additional anchors were. Robinson-May had already committed to moving from The Esplanade to the expanded Buenaventura Mall, and Sears made a similar announcement two weeks later.

But this victory did not come without a price. Faced with disaster scenarios about future sales tax revenue from the Buenaventura Mall if it didn't expand, the city had played defense. City Manager Donna Landeros, who was new to the job, had made preservation of the existing $1 million her highest priority. In order to get it, she gave up a lot.

To accommodate the expanded mall on a tight site in an existing urban area, LaSalle agreed to bankroll a parking garage and a series of road improvements with a price tag of approximately $30 million. The biggest difference about this deal, which the city never failed to crow about, was that Ventura did not have to risk floating tax-exempt bonds to build these improvements, which was a typical concession cities made to developers. But to make the deal, Ventura agreed to give LaSalle all of the increases in sales tax revenue over a fifteen-year period. Thus, even though the mall would double in size, Ventura wouldn't see any increase in sales taxes flowing into the general fund in the foreseeable future. This was not a typical concession, though it was necessary if LaSalle was to front the money for the improvements.*

Landeros called the deal "win-win" because "it preserves our current sales tax revenue stream while providing an opportunity to substantially upgrade our public infrastructure." Her financial advisors insisted that it was "low-risk," because the city didn't have to front any money and because LaSalle had to absorb the cost of the garage and roads if sales taxes from the mall didn't increase.

All this was true. As a defensive move—low risk and preservation-oriented—the Buenaventura Mall deal was a good one. Ventura wouldn't profit if the mall succeeded, but it wouldn't be squeezed if the mall failed. And the tax subsidy would finance public improvements—a far cry from Oxnard's Wal-Mart deal, with its $1 million flowing directly back to Wal-Mart's corporate headquarters.

---

* There would be an increase in property taxes. The project's construction costs were estimated at $50 million, meaning property taxes would increase by approximately $500,000 per year—an amount which, under Proposition 13, the city would have to share with the county, the school district, and other local government agencies.

When the Ventura City Council approved the initial financial agreement, lawyers for The Esplanade threatened to file suit, claiming the city had violated the state's open-meetings law by not providing sufficient notice. Reluctantly, the council rescinded the agreement and then adopted it again after following more stringent notice procedures.

Then an anti-mall petition drive was mounted, led by a gadfly tax-payer activist and a longtime Ventura merchant. Calling themselves Citizens Against the Sales Tax Giveaway, and insisting that their organization was "a grassroots effort," they began collecting signatures to place an initiative on the March 1996 ballot to prohibit sales tax-sharing agreements with private developers. Incensed, Ventura politicians accused the two men of being a front for The Esplanade—which turned out to be true, as campaign finance reports eventually proved. Nevertheless, the group had no trouble collecting thirteen thousand signatures to place the measure on the ballot.

Anxious to approve the mall expansion before the March 1996 vote, Ventura began to move quickly, just as Oxnard and Camarillo had done countless times before when sales tax revenue hung in the balance. The project moved through the planning commission in the fall of 1995, and then on to the city council in January 1996, just a few weeks before the scheduled election. In December, two Ventura council members went on a three-city tour to assure retailing chains that the mall would proceed.

At this point, Oxnard city officials stepped forward in an attempt to short-circuit the whole debate. Steve Kinney, the city's economic development director, said Oxnard developers were talking to the department store chains about going into a new mall at Oxnard Town Center. Then Councilman Andres Herrera proposed building the mall at Oxnard Town Center and sharing the tax revenue between Oxnard and Ventura.

Tax-sharing was something policy wonks had been discussing for a long time, but this was the first time any politician on the Oxnard Plain had uttered the idea in public. It may well have been a negotiating ploy, rather than a sincere offer. Whatever the motivation, the idea fell on deaf ears. A decade before, Ventura Mayor Dennis Orrock had pleaded with the Oxnard City Council to take Ventura's concerns into account on the Town Center, only to be ignored. Now it was Herrera's turn. All through December and January, as Ventura officials rammed the Bue-naventura Mall project through despite mounting opposition, Herrera sat forlornly at the back of the Ventura City Council chamber, watching the latest drama unfold.

In the spring, the campaign rhetoric heated up. "This is not about creating new business," said Oxnard councilman Tom Holden. "This is about spending $30 million to move two stores three miles." When it became clear that the Ventura City Council would approve the mall expansion before the March initiative, The Esplanade bankrolled a second signature-gathering campaign, this time for a ballot measure that would specifically scotch the deal. Ventura's political leadership responded with a stinging flyer titled "There They Go Again" and blaming "the outside interests."

Even so, when the election came in March 1996, Ventura voters overwhelmingly defeated The Esplanade's initiative (the measure got a thirty-five percent yes vote), and the second measure never found its way to the ballot. Then Oxnard turned its attention to the legal front, filing two lawsuits against the mall project similar to the lawsuits Maulhardt had filed against the Camarillo Factory Stores. The lawsuits alleged, among other things, that the mall deal involved an illegal gift of public funds and violated environmental laws. The two cities immediately started fighting over who the judge should be, and two judges withdrew within a month. Meanwhile, the Buenaventura Mall vacancy rate rose, as more and more stores shut their doors. Upscale shoppers headed for the Camarillo Factory Stores. And when Ventura announced plans to make a deal with a developer for a downtown multiplex cinema, Oxnard followed suit shortly thereafter.

⌒

Whatever else Sales Tax Canyon may be, it is not a place. Though created by the three cities it runs through, it is completely divorced, deliberately, from the daily life of these communities. The ten miles of pavement and big-boxes that run alongside Highway 101 from Ventura to Camarillo is nothing more than what Richard Moe of the National Trust for Historic Preservation calls a "sellscape." It's a bleak, relentless, lifeless zone designed not to encourage or facilitate community, but simply to empty passing wallets. Sales Tax Canyon exists because in post-Proposition 13 Southern California, cities have proven that they can be just as ruthless about exploiting the consumer culture as the real estate developers and retailers they subsidize.

There's nothing wrong with stores and shopping centers like these. Clearly, people love them—or, at least, use them. But there is something perverse about municipalities falling all over each other, overturning their own planning priorities, and providing subsidies in order to create them. Over the past fifteen years, the cities of the Oxnard Plain have, time after time, sprinted and subsidized in the hope of quickly exploiting whatever this year's retailing fad happens to be. It's understandable why they do this: Proposition 13 has forced them to view the urban landscape not as a place where people live and work and die, but as a cash register. Yet in the end, it's a losing game.

Retailing has become such a volatile business that it's impossible to keep up with it anymore. "The trouble with retailing these days," one real estate marketing expert says, "is that nobody has any idea what the next T.J. Maxx's is going to look like in five years." Subsidizing this year's fashion may seem like good politics or even good budgeting, but there's no guarantee it will be successful next year. Just look at the Oxnard Plain's factory outlet sprint: Oxnard's speed and depth of subsidy turned out to be no advantage at all. Camarillo had a better location, a stronger developer, and a higher-end, if more prosaic, architectural theme—all of which turned out to be more important.

Furthermore, the short-term approach of retail-oriented urban planning is fundamentally at odds with the long-term view that communities must adopt to thrive and prosper. The long view makes it clear that if you hurt your neighbor, sooner or later you'll get hurt too. In 1985, Oxnard needed the Santa Clara River bridge expanded to lure shoppers across the river from Ventura—while Ventura, needless to say, wasn't very interested. A decade later, the reverse was true: Now Ventura needed additional lanes to bring shoppers to Buenaventura Mall, while Oxnard, sitting in the middle of Sales Tax Canyon, had no particular desire to help. And at the same time that Oxnard was trying to stymie the Buenaventura Mall expansion, the city was fighting a rearguard action against a local school district complaining about Phase Two of Shopping At The Rose. What goes around come around.

The inevitable result of such short-term financial lust by cities is a breach of faith with their own citizens. In Camarillo, the arrival of a twelve-screen cinema adjacent to Camarillo Factory Stores was hailed as a great step for the city—until the theater chain began showing the NC-17 film *Showgirls*. Local residents complained, and the same city council that have enthusiastically approved the project then demanded that the theater chain stop showing the film. Similarly, in Ventura, city officials could never quite understand the citizenry's skepticism about the financial deal involving the Buenaventura Mall. At one public meeting, the city's economist explained that his financial analysis revealed that a subsidy was needed because no private developer would consider the project otherwise. But he was tongue-tied when a local gadfly asked, simply, "But have you looked for one?"

In the end, as cities up the ante on one another, City Hall just becomes part of the Sales Tax Canyon sellscape. Politicians, city managers, and consultants have to use a hard sell to explain to their residents why tax money must be used to subsidize huge out-of-town retailers out by the freeway. But even the least informed citizen knows that towns are more than cash registers—or at least they were until Sales Tax Canyon was built.

PART FIVE

Consequences

The consequences wrought by a sprawling and fragmenting metropolis—a metropolis flying apart almost before it is cobbled together— are vast indeed. In many ways, a metropolis like Los Angeles is nothing more than a churning bundle of consequences, a "growth machine" throwing off side effects left and right. Most of this book has been little more than a description of what has resulted, good and bad, from a century of unfettered growth following two decades of tentative questioning about it. Pieced together into a few overarching themes, however, these consequences paint a bleak picture indeed: a relentless flight from responsibility by anybody who can afford to flee; an unshakeable belief in the piety of the suburban pioneers who stake out new territory, no matter what they leave behind; a grueling struggle for daily survival by those who remain in the old neighborhoods.

The consequences of today's Los Angeles are no different than the consequences the metropolis has been spinning off for decades. Since the 1920s at least, some people have successfully escaped the hurly-burly of urban life while others have been left behind, forced to confront the problems others fled. Indeed, as the historian Daniel Boorstin has written, American life has been "attenuating" for a century and a half or more. Americans have fled their geographical communities and sought to bind themselves together with what we today would call "virtual" communities, such as common demographics and consumer preferences. All along the way—not just in Los Angeles but elsewhere as well—our sense of ourselves as complete citizens, bound together by a common set of interests and a shared commitment to a specific piece of geography, has been attenuating as well.

Yet today's consequences are starker, more vast, and harder to ignore—not just in Los Angeles, but in all American cities. It is one thing to flee the slums for the suburbs; it is quite another for suburbanites to shield their eyes so completely from a hundred square miles or more of bleak urban desolation that such places all but cease to exist in the public consciousness. It is one thing to start over again with the pioneer spirit; it is something else again to use that pioneer energy to recreate exactly the same "growth machine"—headed toward exactly the same fate—in a desert three hundred miles away. And, finally, it is one thing to be actively engaged in building our new suburban cocoons. But there is something different, something sadder and scarier, in devoting all our civic energy to protecting that cocoon from the larger metropolis. Because while that larger metropolis may sometimes be scary and alienating, it clearly shapes and nurtures who we are, and we ignore it, or abandon it, at our own peril. There is a difference, in other words, between a sense of community that is attenuating and one that is disintegrating altogether.

CHAPTER 11

Whose Riot Was This, Anyway?

Vermont Avenue is one of the longest streets in Los Angeles—so long (about twenty-five miles) that it exceeds the length of several of the area's most important rivers. This comparison is appropriate, because in many ways Vermont is more like a river than a street. It encompasses an entire urban ecosystem along its length, and in the process reveals the whole breadth of the metropolis to anyone who cares to look.

Vermont begins with babbling tributaries in Griffith Park in the Hollywood Hills, then cascades gently past the bookstores and art houses of the Los Feliz district. It rushes through Hollywood and the once-elegant Wilshire district with increasing speed, passing L.A. City College and pausing at Vermont and Wilshire, the busiest bus transfer intersection in the city. Vermont then moves past the University of Southern California, the Coliseum, Manual Arts High School, and an eclectic mixture of neighborhoods in South Central L.A. before opening up to a graceful one-hundred-eighty-foot width at Gage Avenue. After a lengthy run across the rest of South Central, Vermont hurdles quickly through the working-class suburbs of Gardena and Carson, passing the County-UCLA Harbor Medical Center before its confluence with Normandie Avenue in Wilmington, two miles short of the Pacific Ocean.

Vermont has always had its ups and downs, its rocky shoals and its smooth stretches. But between April 29 and May 2, 1992, everything changed for the street, or at least for that portion of it that runs through South Central.

Located just a half-mile east of the flashpoint of violence at Florence and Normandie, Vermont became one of the riot's leading victims. Having already suffered the ravages of disinvestment for decades, the five-mile stretch of Vermont from the Santa Monica Freeway to Manchester Boulevard—the five-mile section running through what is commonly referred to as South Central Los Angeles—suffered the additional loss of some fifty structures with a value of $40 million. "On some blocks," the *Los Angeles Times* later reported, "the voracious flames left only charred storefronts opening onto debris and sky." The commercial center at Vermont and Florence was especially hard-hit, with the riots claiming not just retail stores but also such buildings as the local branch of the Bank of America, one of the few banks left in South Central.

The torching of Vermont Avenue was a tragedy in one sense, but viewed from a different perspective it offered an unexpected opportunity. It was a rare chance to reinvent an entire commercial corridor—to figure out how to restore this stretch of Vermont to its former greatness, while still accommodating the neighborhood's rapid social and demographic change.

Everyone in town knew Vermont was a great opportunity, and maybe that's why things seem to be turning out the way they are. Ever fractious, L.A.'s sprawling centers of political and economic power could never quite agree on the right approach. After the civil unrest of 1992, almost every constituency claimed that the riot was somehow theirs, to be appropriated for their own political ends. Similarly, in the years that followed, almost everyone laid claim to the recovery, with the power and money flowing toward it appropriated for whatever political purpose they happened to be pursuing. Nowhere in Los Angeles was the recovery-belongs-to-me phenomenon more apparent than along Vermont Avenue, and especially on a rundown, mostly vacant acre-and-a-half lot at the corner of Vermont and 81st Street, adjacent to one of the area's nicer residential neighborhoods.

⤸

That part of Los Angeles now popularized in the media as the crime-ridden urban hardscape called South Central is actually a sprawling area of more than fifty square miles that consists of dozens of neighborhoods—some of them "good," some of them "bad," and more often than not a little of both. In sociological terms, some are middle- and even upper-middle-class in character. Others can be accurately described as slums. For decades, they have suffered from poverty, high crime rates,

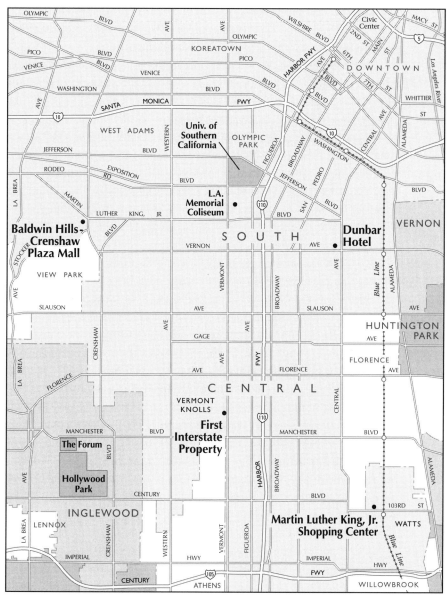

South Central Los Angeles and the First Interstate site on Vermont Avenue.

and an almost total lack of interest from private real estate and business investors. Yet even the worst neighborhoods rarely conform to the popular image of a ravaged inner-city ghetto, because South Central, like the rest of Los Angeles, is a city of homes. Turn off even the most decimated commercial boulevard, and you are likely to find a row of neatly kept houses and at least a few proud homeowners.

For a while after the riots, the definition of South Central seemed to be expanding every day to include any area where damage and violence had occurred and, more broadly, any area where nervous white people were reluctant to venture. Latino neighborhoods near downtown were deemed part of South Central; so were middle-class black neighborhoods in the Crenshaw district and predominantly Korean neighborhoods just south of the Wilshire corridor. No matter what their nuances and personalities, all these neighborhoods were lumped together by the media as poor and dangerous—an image that persists in the popular culture, thanks to a thousand TV news shows, violent movies, and rap videos.

What this broad and often inaccurate term was really trying to characterize was the cluster of historically black neighborhoods located south and southwest of downtown Los Angeles. These were the neighborhoods where both the Watts riots of 1965 and the broader civil unrest of 1992 took place. These were the neighborhoods with nearly unsolvable social and economic conditions. In short, these were the neighborhoods viewed in the popular imagination as L.A.'s biggest problem.

The South Central neighborhoods arrived at this position in the popular imagination after a century-long cycle of segregation, neglect, and bad publicity. Though sprawling, these neighborhoods stand as a testament to the rigid racial segregation that emerged early in the twentieth century as the city's black population grew. Initially, Los Angeles was more open to African-Americans than other cities. However, at the apogee of L.A.'s "national suburb" era in the 1920s, when the white population exploded, blacks were gradually segregated into several large but sharply defined areas.*

The largest of these was the original South Central area, straddling Central Avenue from downtown southward to Slauson Avenue, a distance of about four miles. A couple of areas farther west were also open

---

* Most, but not all, of L.A.'s historically black neighborhoods are located in the City of Los Angeles. A few, such as Florence, Willowbrook (south of Watts), and parts of the affluent Baldwin Hills and View Park neighborhoods, are located in unincorporated Los Angeles County. As the black community expanded, blacks assumed political control of a few outlying cities with high black populations such as Inglewood (to the west) and Compton (to the south). This chapter discusses the City of Los Angeles neighborhoods almost exclusively.

to blacks, as was Watts, a more rural, independent city farther south. (Indeed, the annexation of Watts to Los Angeles in 1926 has been interpreted by some historians as an attempt to block the creation of an independent political power base for African-Americans.) Blacks were prevented from moving outward, or even into the white areas in between black districts, through the use of deed covenants that allowed blacks to own property but prohibited them from living there.

Most African-Americans migrated to Los Angeles from Texas and Louisiana, which had good rail connections to California. As the black population grew, the original black districts became more crowded and more diverse with, as one historian has put it, "poverty and prosperity existing side by side." This was true in all "Northern" cities, but it was particularly striking in Los Angeles, where homeownership was a real possibility for working- and middle-class blacks. Central Avenue emerged as the center of black life in Los Angeles, featuring everything from an elegant hotel, the Dunbar (a local icon where all black celebrities stayed), to overcrowded rental apartments and an impressive row of jazz clubs and nightclubs.

The racial lines held until after World War II, during which some two hundred thousand African-Americans had migrated to L.A. in search of work after President Roosevelt desegregated the defense plants. In 1948, the U.S. Supreme Court struck down racial covenants, and the black population began to expand outward, largely to the west and south. (The eastern dividing line at Alameda Street, separating black neighborhoods from working-class white cities such as South Gate and Huntington Park, never fell, and those cities shifted mostly to Latino populations in the 1980s without ever absorbing many African-Americans.)

The outward expansion had two effects. First, it segregated L.A.'s black residents by economic class. More affluent residents moved westward, toward the ocean and the hills, while poor blacks remained in the eastern sectors along Central Avenue and in Watts. This movement was not uniformly true, of course, as many working- and middle-class blacks remained in eastern neighborhoods, providing stability that continues to this day. But it had the effect of dispersing the common energy of the black community that had been focused along Central Avenue.

Second, as it decentralized the black population, this shift effectively segregated the city even more severely. Most new areas that opened up to blacks after the war became virtually all black within a few years as a result of white flight, and new suburbs such as the San Fernando Valley remained completely off limits. Thus, even as affluent blacks were leaving the traditional ghetto behind, the entire black community was being ghettoized into a larger geographic area by the mostly white metropolis.

Despite these limitations, most black Angelenos believed Los Angeles was a "promised land" compared to Texas and Louisiana and even compared to cities in the North. One powerful lure was no different for blacks than for whites. Los Angeles offered the ability to attain a middle-class lifestyle, with a single-family home, a backyard, and a car— the simple pleasures depicted by Walter Mosley in *Devil in a Blue Dress* and in other detective novels about postwar black life in L.A. Black homeownership was always much higher in Los Angeles than in Northern cities like New York and Chicago, and housing conditions in general were far better. Lois Medlock, an anti-redevelopment activist who has owned a home in South Central for almost fifty years, wistfully recalls that when she and her husband moved to Watts from New Orleans in 1946, they could live in a single-family home and yet still "we could walk to the show on 103rd Street."

After the Watts riots in 1965—an event that was, in large part, caused by pent-up frustration about the limits of black life in L.A.—the problems of the city's historically black neighborhoods just got worse. The poorer neighborhoods, such as Watts and the areas along Central, fell into steep decline with the accelerated departure of the black middle class. Even in the developing middle- and upper-middle-class black neighborhoods, the city failed to provide the same level of services that equivalent white neighborhoods received. There was more than a little truth to the comic ending of Charles Burnett's film, *To Sleep with Anger*, in which Danny Glover's dead body lies in the doorway of a middle-class black family's Los Angeles home for an entire day until the coroner finally arrives to pick it up. The persistent view in the black neighborhoods was that they did not get a fair shake from the city no matter what their economic class—even when Tom Bradley was mayor. And this view simply fed the alienation that appeared time after time during L.A.'s racial tensions—in the Rodney King trial, the O.J. Simpson trial, and other similar situations—in the 1990s.

Faced with these conditions, many blacks, like their white counterparts, simply fled the city for the fringes of the metropolitan area. Geographer James Johnson found that during the 1980s, Los Angeles blacks migrated in large numbers to areas like Riverside County, Oxnard-Ventura, and Las Vegas. "Blacks are no longer choosing the region's largest black population centers as migration destinations, but are moving instead to small- and medium-sized metropolitan areas within the region," Johnson concluded in 1990.

Meanwhile, the old black neighborhoods continued to change dramatically, leading to what UCLA social scientist Eugene Grigsby has called "a competition for race and space." The entrepreneurial Korean immigrants began buying up liquor stores throughout South Central, and "Koreatown" expanded geographically from the Wilshire District to encroach on neighborhoods that were historically black and historically white. One of the crucial events leading up to the 1992 riots was the controversy surrounding LaTasha Harlins, a young black woman who was shot by a Korean grocer during an argument. The grocer received a light sentence, touching off great resentment in the black community.

Just as significantly, the historically black neighborhoods were transformed during the immigration boom of the 1980s and 1990s. As the city's Latino population exploded, new immigrants from Mexico and Central America began settling all over South Central. By 1990, they made up more than forty percent of the population, a figure that had doubled in only a decade. While these numbers were growing fast, the black population was stagnant. However, because they were not politically active (indeed, many were not citizens), South Central's institutions remained in African-American hands. As political scientist (and former South Central political operative) Rafael Sonenshein has pointed out, the black leaders in South Central, like the Jews in the Bronx, are now in the unaccustomed position of controlling an area now occupied largely by someone else.

〜

These roiling conditions were hardly a secret before April 1992, but rarely did they appear to be high-priority items on the broader public agenda. City Hall's "iron triangle" of politics, real estate development, and the Democratic Party focused on the high-stakes development fights on the Westside and in fashionable parts of the San Fernando Valley. (See chapter 2, Perestroika Co-Opted.) And the administration of Mayor Tom Bradley, who grew up along Central Avenue, focused on redeveloping the downtown—also part of the high-stakes real estate game that dominated city politics.

Occasionally a police brutality case might bring attention to conditions in South Central. And community activists sometimes joined forces to good political effect—as when Westside environmentalists and South Central community groups successfully opposed a trash incineration plant in South Central in 1987. But these were the exceptions. Although internal politics in South Central were thick with machinations, citywide attention for the area's problems was hard to come by.

When the 1992 civil unrest rocked the city, then, it came as a shock to many affluent residents all over the city, who couldn't understand how such a thing could have happened. The riots erupted in the wake of a decision by a Ventura County jury to acquit the four police officers who had beaten Rodney King, the black motorist whose arrest had, by happenstance, been captured on amateur videotape. The disturbance went on for four days, characterized by spontaneous riots and beatings of innocent bystanders, by looting, and especially by a seemingly well-planned arson attack on retail centers across a large portion of the city. The riots spread out of South Central into the Wilshire District and Hollywood. By the time it was over, the 1992 riot was the largest civil disturbance in the history of the United States. More than fifty people had died, and more than one thousand structures had been destroyed. Damage was estimated at more than $450 million.

The Bradley Administration proved almost totally unprepared to deal with the riot's consequences. Even before the fires were doused, the mayor created a high-profile recovery organization called "Rebuild L.A."—and then took the odd step of naming Peter Ueberroth, the Orange County business executive and former commissioner of baseball, to head it up.

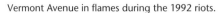

Vermont Avenue in flames during the 1992 riots.

One pundit quipped that the Ueberroth appointment simply revealed that Bradley, after nineteen years in office, had developed "boundless faith in rich white businessmen to solve problems." (Ueberroth's "get-things-done" approach to the 1984 Olympics, which he also headed, helped make that event one of the highlights of Bradley's career.) But it soon became apparent that leaders like Ueberroth, and even Bradley himself, were ill-equipped to handle the political bonfire that the riots had ignited.

Assuming that Rebuild L.A. would be a rich and powerful organization dispensing money, black political groups began demanding more control over it. Ueberroth's response was to insist that Rebuild wasn't going to dole out cash but, instead, would simply put the arm on private corporations to invest in business growth in South Central. (When Ueberroth named all the corporations he said he was leaning on, the *Los Angeles Times* discovered that most of them didn't remember talking to him.)

Meanwhile, Bradley's predictable political response to black demands was to dig up a rich *black* businessman, Stan Sanders, and make him co-chair of Rebuild L.A. with Ueberroth. But this move brought more groups out of the woodwork. Latino leaders, pointing out that more Latinos had been arrested in the riot than blacks, demanded their own co-chair; so did the Koreans, who emphasized the fact that they had suffered the most property damage. Pretty soon Rebuild L.A. had a rainbow coalition of five co-chairs and an increasingly vague mission of what it was supposed to do.

Of course, there was already a whole network of people and organizations, both in City Hall and in the South Central neighborhoods, devoted to revitalizing the city's long-neglected neighborhoods. This was the interconnected web of city agencies, nonprofit organizations, and "for-profit" developers operating under the broad heading of "community development." And the people who ran these organizations were not particularly happy with the general public perception that the process of solving the area's problems had begun with Peter Ueberroth in May 1992. "The whole idea of rebuilding L.A. is a joke," Anthony Scott, a young urban planner working to create a historic district around the Dunbar Hotel on Central Avenue, said shortly after the riots. "What have we been doing all these years?"

Yet as Rebuild L.A. fell deeper and deeper into a political muddle, the community development network began to sense an opportunity. Never before had the attention of the entire city—indeed, the entire nation—been so focused on the neglected neighborhoods where they operated. Thanks to the efforts of Rebuild L.A., some corporations (supermarket chains, for example) were making an investment in South Central. And with both presidential and mayoral elections coming up, a considerable amount of political attention, and public money, was sure to flow toward the area. To take advantage of this opportunity, the network began to mobilize.

The community development network had many different components, but it was tied together by a common desire to create new building projects in neglected neighborhoods and a special skill in using various sources of government money to make the pro formas on these projects work. The people making up this network came from all backgrounds and belonged to all races. Some were homegrown residents; others were highly educated outsiders who planted themselves in neighborhoods where they wanted to work, either in neighborhood-based nonprofits or in for-profit development companies. Still others operated from central locations, including City Hall, consulting firms, and private fund-raising organizations.

The most obvious, if least trusted, vehicle for rebuilding the South Central neighborhoods was the Community Redevelopment Agency, which Bradley controlled. The CRA was a powerful if somewhat ambivalent component of the community development network. It had originally been formed as an urban renewal agency, using federal funds to clear out inner-city slums and replace them with new structures. Later, the CRA financed redevelopment efforts by using a state law allowing the diversion of property tax revenue that would otherwise go into the city treasury and to the county, the school district, and other local agencies. At the time of the riots, the CRA had an annual budget of more than $300 million a year.

Under Bradley's leadership, the Community Redevelopment Agency had focused most of its attention on rebuilding downtown, neglected since the 1920s, so the city could compete as an international financial center. But the CRA had never completely forgotten about South Central. The agency had created three redevelopment project areas scattered throughout South Central, including a small (two-hundred-acre) area along 103rd Street, the epicenter of the 1965 Watts riots. Initially, the agency replaced some burned-out stores with apartment buildings. Bringing in new stores, however, took more than twenty years. It wasn't until the mid-1980s that Bradley succeeded in making a development deal to build a new shopping center. When it finally opened at 103rd and Compton, the Martin Luther King Center was a commercial success. But it required deep city subsidies and a fortress-like security system later ridiculed by social critic Mike Davis in his book *City of Quartz*.

The CRA also undertook several other projects, including the renovation of Baldwin Hills Crenshaw Plaza, an upscale shopping center in the Crenshaw District which had originally been the first regional mall built in Los Angeles. In general, however, the three small project areas meant that CRA's overt presence in South Central was small. To a much greater degree, CRA's reputation in South Central was established by its support for constructing "affordable housing" projects—subsidized housing projects for people of modest means.

Under state law, the CRA was required to devote at least twenty percent of diverted property tax money to affordable housing. And these projects could be constructed anywhere in the city, not just in the small designated redevelopment zones the city had created. Unlike an earlier generation of "public housing" (built under a separate program with federal funds), these developments were not owned and operated by the city. Instead, they were usually subsidized by the CRA, but owned and operated by nonprofit organizations that functioned in the neighborhoods themselves.

The nonprofits were the other end of the revitalization effort in South Central, and they represented the tail end of a national trend that took a long time to get to Los Angeles. During the 1960s and 1970s, neighborhood protest groups had popped up in poor neighborhoods all across the country—New York, Boston, Chicago, Cleveland—often as a result of federal funding for these programs. Wanting to take positive steps to improve their neighborhoods, these groups gradually transformed themselves from protesters into nonprofit developers. Building on such diverse organizations as social service groups, settlement houses, ethnically oriented organizations, and civil rights groups, they became experts at patching together financing from a variety of sources (some governmental, some philanthropic, some private) to build needed housing and commercial buildings in poor neighborhoods.

Among other things, these groups relied on a federal law, the Community Reinvestment Act, requiring banks to make loans in inner-city neighborhoods from which they accept deposits but which they've historically neglected. (Many banks have separate "community banking" sections to handle these loans.) And as they grew in size and significance, the nonprofits established a national network of organizations to train personnel and raise money. One group in particular that sought to raise equity for real estate projects from foundations and corporations was the Local Initiative Support Corporation, a national organization based in New York that was formed by the Ford Foundation in 1979.

With its general dearth of political action, Los Angeles was almost the last major American city to undergo this transformation. By the mid-1980s, a few such groups had sprung up throughout the city. But in the five or so years before the riots, their numbers began to grow. In the 1980s, LISC opened a field office in Los Angeles, filled it with motivated and ambitious people, and soon carpet-bombed South Central and the Eastside with nonprofits.

Some of these organizations were strongly rooted in the community and did good work. Others were thin and inexperienced. And they sought to undertake a wide variety of activities. Anthony Scott's Dunbar Economic Development Corporation was a good example. Operating along the formerly glorious Central Avenue corridor, Scott's group—which included people interested in the city's black history—sought to revive the area by undertaking a loving, historic restoration of the Dunbar Hotel. The Dunbar group hoped to create an historic district that reinforced black ties to the neighborhood and still worked together with its growing Latino residential and business community.

But the first step for the Dunbar group, as for most of the other groups, was to convert at least part of the hotel into an affordable housing project. This was a typical step. As Nicholas Lemann, author of the book *The Promised Land*, has pointed out, although these groups often say that their goal is economic development, usually their primary business is to construct and manage affordable housing projects. Lemann calls this phenomenon "the myth of community development." The community development network will often focus on affordable housing projects because the whole structure of public policy is based on the assumption that the biggest problem in inner-city neighborhoods is poor housing. In Los Angeles, the nonprofits were driven toward housing by the availability of funds: the Community Reinvestment Act loans, the redevelopment agency's twenty-percent housing set-aside, and federal low-income housing tax credits and rent subsidies. And they were driven to affordable housing because in a city with so many poor people, these projects are almost always financially successful. As long as the right deal is put together, low-income tenants will always have an affordable place to live, investors will always make a profit, and non-profits will have a continuing revenue stream from managing the project.

In South Central's poor neighborhoods—with their overcrowded houses, a chronic lack of employment, and the rapid influx of Latino immigrant families—there was never any lack of clientele for the afford-able housing units produced by the community development network. There was, however, less than a clear consensus about whether building affordable housing was the right thing to do. South Central was scattered with longtime homeowners, most of them African-American, who took great pride in their neighborhoods and resented the construc-tion of affordable housing units. These unhappy homeowners were a vocal group, and they had a deep distrust of politicians from down-town, whom they accused of attempting to exploit their neighborhood at every turn.

When the Blue Line station opened at 103rd Street and Mayor Bradley proposed a dramatic expansion of the Watts redevelopment project area in 1990, some local homeowners opposed the project, fearing that the CRA would take their land via eminent domain and build high-rise condominiums for yuppies commuting to downtown by rail. The attitude of anti-redevelopment activist Lois Medlock was typical. A longtime homeowner who lived near the Dunbar, she lumped the nonprofits and the CRA together, saying, "These people are all land-grabbers. They come in to take out single-family homes and put in boxes." This was a distrust borne of fifty years of disap-pointment that the American dream had never quite worked out in L.A.'s historically black neighborhoods. The CRA's project manager in Watts once described it this way: "People around here say, if the city's talking about bringing in something good, it must be because some-body else wants it."

Not everyone in South Central held this view. The area was filled with influential pastors, business owners, and other community leaders who wanted the CRA and other city agencies to come in after the riots and help rebuild. But the vocal homeowners had influence—especially when they teamed up with mostly white homeowners from other areas who also disliked redevelopment. The Watts homeowners actually persuaded Bradley to back away from the redevelopment proposal in 1990 even though most local business and church leaders were supportive.

After the riots, Bradley and the CRA again attempted to expand the role of the redevelopment agency in South Central. Working with Assemblyman Curtis Tucker, Jr., the son of a legendary South Central politician, Bradley proposed a bill in Sacramento to streamline the process required to create redevelopment project areas in South Central. The bill would have limited environmental review and lifted some requirements for community participation in the creation of redevelopment zones. Bradley and Tucker leaned heavily on other legislators to pass the bill, which was similar to other bills that had routinely sailed through the legislature after earthquakes, fires, tidal waves, and other natural disasters. But in the summer of 1992, the anti-redevelopment activists joined together with like-minded souls around the state, and even enlisted the support of the Paul Gann Taxpayers Association to kick up a ruckus in Sacramento.

Facing a storm of protest, Tucker unceremoniously withdrew the bill. This development didn't kill the CRA's plans to expand its role in South Central; eventually, the agency created seven new "post-riot" project areas. But because the Tucker bill died, the agency was unable to set up the new redevelopment zones quickly. (Indeed, at the time this book went to press in early 1997, almost five years after the riots, some of these zones were still being created.) What this meant was that, in the super-charged political atmosphere that prevailed in 1992 and 1993, the city's leading vehicle for the renewal of these devastated neighborhoods didn't have the political credibility to step in—and the opposition of black homeowners to affordable housing projects was alive and well.

There was, however, another city agency with close ties to the community development network that viewed the devastation of South Central as an opportunity: the city's Housing Department. Unlike the county's Public Housing Authority, the city Housing Department did not build and manage public housing projects, and therefore wasn't tainted by the bad reputation that dogged public housing. Instead, the Housing Department was an agency that doled out millions of dollars per year in grants and loans—federal money, state money, and CRA set-aside money—to nonprofits and for-profit developers all over town.

Along with LISC, the Housing Department was the "big daddy" of L.A.'s community development network.

At the time of the riots, the Housing Department's director was Gary Squier, a trained urban planner with shrewd political instincts who had gradually accumulated more bureaucratic power as the CRA (and the city's planning department) had floundered. Like most of the housing activists, Squier viewed the housing situation in Los Angeles as a crisis. Despite the boom economy of the 1980s, housing costs were high, and the number of poor people was increasing. The result was not just homelessness, but overcrowding in apartments and houses all over the city, and even a dramatic increase in the number of families renting garages as living space. At the time of the riots, Squier's department estimated that the city had to produce fourteen thousand new affordable units per year to meet demand. This notion of housing-as-crisis led Squier to see the riots differently from most observers. Reporters, sociologists, and policy wonks looked at the devastated commercial strips of South Central, such as Vermont Avenue, and wondered how any retail stores could ever be induced to return. Gary Squier looked at these same strips, all covered with L.A.'s typically over-generous zoning, and saw more places to build apartments.

Within a few months after the riots, Squier was promoting the idea that the South Central commercial strips, and Vermont in particular, would be an ideal place to test out a strategy of mixed-use development. The mixed-use idea, long an ideal of urban planners, simply meant building new projects along the commercial strips that could accommodate stores on the streetfront and also provide affordable housing—either above the stores or behind them, adjacent to the residential neighborhoods. In the summer of 1992, Squier, along with Mayor Bradley and several other high-ranking city officials, brought in a special advisory team of developers from around the country, specifically to look at possible development scenarios along the devastated five-mile stretch of Vermont from

The intersection of Vermont and Manchester, which sustained heavy damage during the 1992 riots.

the University of Southern California south to the Century Freeway. The group came in under the auspices of the Urban Land Institute, a national developers' organization.

In November 1992, the ULI panel reported back to the city. Amid a slew of recommendations, the panel proposed that the city "develop a new heart" for Vermont between Slauson and Manchester, and specifically in the Vermont/Manchester area, by developing a new town hall, retail stores that could serve local needs, and housing. New housing units, the ULI panel suggested, could be built above the retail stores along Vermont, either as townhomes for sale or apartments for rent to middle-income residents. The report received widespread publicity as the kickoff for a new mixed-use development strategy along Vermont.

Among the Angelenos who read the Vermont Avenue report was John Gray, a vice president in the community banking section of First Interstate Bank, the largest bank headquartered in Los Angeles. First Interstate had recently announced a $2 billion commitment to make loans in South Central under the Community Reinvestment Act. Like Squier, Gray was white. He was an earnest man with do-gooder tendencies and close ties to the community development network, and he was looking for opportunities. An architecture and planning aficionado, Gray was intrigued by the mixed-use idea, and he was appalled by the massive and sterile design of most affordable housing projects. Starting in late 1992, therefore, Gray hatched the idea of sponsoring a competition among architects and planners to design a high-quality, affordable housing project somewhere in South Central.

Gray took the idea to Squier and to Mark Ridley-Thomas, the young civil rights activist who had been elected to the city council from a South Central district in 1991. Both responded enthusiastically, and throughout 1993 Gray and Squier trolled South Central, and especially the Vermont Avenue corridor, looking for a good site. By the end of the year they found one.

What they found was a one-and-a-half acre parcel of land on the west side of Vermont at the corner of 81st Street, just six blocks north of the Manchester Boulevard intersection that the ULI panel had identified as the heart of the Vermont corridor. Located along Vermont's gracious (if somewhat rundown) one-hundred-eighty-foot median, the area had originally been developed by George Pepperdine, the founder of Pepperdine University. The Vermont and 81st parcel was adjacent to the original Pepperdine campus, now owned by a religious organization. Most of the site was vacant, and had been since the early 1970s, when Pepperdine pulled up stakes and moved to a new location in Malibu. On the corner of 81st was an attractive art deco building (complete with a small cupola) with pull-up doors that had originally served as a neighborhood market and was later used as Pepperdine's administration building.

What's more, the property backed up to one of the nicest neighborhoods in South Central L.A.—the Vermont Knolls neighborhood, a community of Spanish-style houses and red tile roofs originally developed by George Pepperdine as faculty housing. Most of Vermont Knolls consisted of single-family homes, but the Vermont Avenue parcel backed up to an alley that also had some apartments on it. The apartment dwellers looked out over the alley and the litter-infested vacant lot on Vermont. The owner of the property had recently proposed that the parcel be used for a swap meet.

In January 1994, First Interstate took an option on the property and announced a statewide architectural competition for an affordable housing project that would include up to one- hundred thirty affordable units and retail shops along Vermont. "We want to show," said Gray's boss, Charles Cline, the head of community banking at First Interstate, "that affordable housing and potential mixed-use projects like this can enhance and strengthen neighborhoods."

To manage the competition, the bank selected the same Oregon-based expert who had handled the architectural competition for the Walt Disney Concert Hall. To judge the entries, First Interstate picked a jury of seven people, including Councilman Ridley-Thomas; Denise Fairchild, the Los Angeles field director for LISC (and a key member of

The 1.5-acre site of First Interstate's proposed housing project at the intersection of Vermont Avenue and 81st Street.

L.A.'s community development network); black architect Michaele Pride-Wells; black artist John Outterbridge; and a Vermont Knolls resident named Naomi Nightingale, who worked for the Metropolitan Transportation Authority. For its part, the bank promised to provide up to $15 million in construction financing—the initial loan required to build the project—though help from the city would probably be required as well.

By June, the bank had picked three teams of architects and developers to draw up final plans. All three included members that were part of the community development network. Hoping to pick a winner by the end of 1994, bank officials asked the finalists to talk to the neighbors and draw up plans that would meet the goals of the bank, the community, and the city. In a newspaper ad featuring photos of most of the judges, the bank proudly proclaimed, "This is one competition we can all win." But as First Interstate and the judges soon learned, not everyone in the Vermont Knolls neighborhood thought they'd be winners if a one-hundred-thirty-unit affordable housing project was built at Vermont and 81st.

⌐

The organized group that represented the Vermont Knolls neighborhood was known as the Vermont Knolls/Vermont Manchester Vicinity Improvement Association. The group actually covered an area larger than Vermont Knolls, including a number of residential neighborhoods farther south, near the intersection of Vermont and Manchester. Like many other groups in South Central, this one was dominated by longtime African-American homeowners who had lived through South Central's sad decline. They were proud of their own neighborhood, however, and resentful of the way people lumped all of South Central together in pejorative terms.

The Vermont Knolls neighborhood around the corner from the Vermont and 81st site.

"There are many nice neighborhoods in South L.A.," the association's president, Julie Simmons, once pointed out, deliberately choosing not to use the tainted moniker "South Central." "The myth that it's a blighted neighborhood and we must be saturated with low-income housing *is* a myth."

As an example of the general public misperception about the Vermont/Manchester area, Simmons sometimes pointed to an incident that occurred in late 1995, just as the Vermont and 81st battle was heating up. Three men who held up a store in Fontana led police on a sixty-mile freeway chase that ultimately led into, and ended in, this neighborhood. As is commonly the case in Los Angeles, the television stations broke into regular daytime coverage to carry the chase live— complete with closeup shots, via helicopter, of the three men jumping backyard fences in the vicinity of Vermont and 83rd before being apprehended. "The anchorman kept saying, 'This is a poor neighborhood in South Central Los Angeles, this is a poor neighborhood'," Simmons recalled with anger. "This is not a poor neighborhood." As Julie Simmons never tired of telling reporters, the particular census tract where Vermont Knolls was located had a median household income in 1990 of $32,000.

Like everyone else, the Vermont-Manchester homeowners saw the devastation of the 1992 riots, in an odd way, as an opportunity. With Vermont reduced to little more than a string of swap meets, neighborhood auto shops, and vacant lots, the homeowners dreamed of attracting retailers who would revive it as a shopping street. No longer would they have to go to the Target store in Gardena or to Fox Hills Mall in Culver City to buy what they needed. "We used to have See's Candies right around the corner," Julie Simmons said. "Now I have to drive seven miles to go to See's Candies." After the riots, the members of the Vermont Knolls/Vermont Manchester Vicinity Improvement Association believed they had a better-than-even chance of making this dream come true, because they knew it was a dream shared by their most famous neighbor: Maxine Waters.

After Tom Bradley stepped down as mayor of Los Angeles in 1993, the general consensus was that Maxine Waters, U.S. Representative for the 35th district of California, was the most powerful African-American politician in Los Angeles. Strong, vocal, and stylish, Waters had devoted her long career in the California legislature and Congress to championing the rights of minority groups in general and African-Americans in partic- ular. She had been Jesse Jackson's campaign co-chair in 1988, and had

Maxine Waters, the powerful South Central politician who lived in the Vermont Knolls neighborhood.

worked tirelessly to advance the cause of inner-city neighborhoods—challenging, among other things, banks like First Interstate to live up to their legal obligations under the Community Reinvestment Act. She was protective of homegrown activism in inner-city neighborhoods, suspicious of people from the outside who said they wanted to help, and usually maintained a take-no-prisoners approach to politics. "Righteous anger is a constant companion," writer Kay Mills once explained, "a tool she is not afraid to use."

Waters lived in the Vermont Knolls neighborhood, around the corner from the site First Interstate chose for its affordable housing demonstration project. Like her neighbors, she recalled the glory years of South Central's commercial strips. "I knew about Vermont when I first moved to L.A.," she once said. And after the riots, she began working to try to bring retail back. She had, for example, arranged a $200,000 federal planning grant for the community groups along the Vermont corridor. "If I could live to the time when I can walk out of my house and walk down Vermont and sit at a sidewalk cafe or go listen to some blues or just buy me some hose," she once said, "I'd be happy."

For obvious reasons, the Vermont/Manchester homeowners presented a political problem for First Interstate; they did not particularly want to see one hundred thirty units of affordable housing in their neighborhood. But Maxine Waters' presence made the whole issue far more political, and the politics involved were tangled indeed.

Chief among these complications was the fact that Waters and Mark Ridley-Thomas, who represented the area on the city council, were not political allies. Some years earlier, Waters had broken politically with Bradley and allied herself with more activist African-American politicians such as Jesse Jackson. Bradley had supported the candidacy of Ridley-Thomas in 1991, while Waters had opposed it.

Furthermore, Ridley-Thomas was an ambitious young politician—many said his ultimate aim was to be mayor—and this meant he was a challenge to Waters' stature as a leader in African-American politics. Twenty years her junior, Ridley-Thomas was never afraid to attack Waters on the record, frequently referring to her "gargantuan ego" and her desire for complete control of their common turf. Waters, for her part, was usually too smart to take this bait, and merely said she was sorry that he spoke of her that way. But the animosity between them was palpable.

Once in office, Ridley-Thomas proved to be an enthusiastic supporter of the community development network and its projects, including affordable housing; he frequently recited the number of projects being constructed in his district and the amount of investment this represented. Waters, though she frequently approved of government action to stimulate investment, was more cautious in her support of some of these efforts, partly because they were carried out by Squier and other members of the community development network outside the neighborhood, whom she didn't really trust.

Further complicating the politics of Vermont Avenue was the election of Richard Riordan to succeed Bradley as mayor in 1993. A white lawyer and businessman with long-established connections to the downtown power structure, Riordan had worked hard to build bridges to South Central even before he ran for mayor. (He invested his own money in a South Central supermarket, for example.) But his election one year after the riots was widely viewed as having been induced by racial fears. In contrast to the Bradley years, the 1993 mayoral race was badly split along racial lines, with whites supporting Riordan and minorities supporting his main challenger, Michael Woo. Riordan had no particular reason to court the black politicians, and even when he tried his attempts always seemed awkward.

Virtually every African-American politician in the city endorsed Woo, and in winning the election Riordan received only fourteen percent of the mostly black vote in Ridley-Thomas's council district. Bucking the trend, Maxine Waters never endorsed Woo, and although she didn't endorse Riordan either, they remained cordial. Thus, Waters had a close connection to a white mayor that other African-American politicians in Los Angeles lacked, and in Waters the Vermont/Manchester neighborhood had a powerful advocate who could attract publicity and political attention to the proposed affordable housing project at Vermont and 81st.

⌐

Almost from the beginning, First Interstate ran into trouble with the neighbors and with Maxine Waters. By the end of February 1994, less than two months after the competition was unveiled and even before the finalists were announced, Waters was publicly leading the charge against the project. "I've got low-income housing to the south of me, and to the north of me. We just don't need any more piled up on us," she told a reporter. "What we need to do is spread low-income housing throughout the greater Los Angeles area." Writing in the *Los Angeles Times* two weeks later, she insisted, "this is not a 'not-in-my-backyard' kind of attitude" but "a question of allowing the community to make judgments on the kind of development most appropriate to this particular property."

A week later, *Times* columnist Ron Harris, who is African-American, also came out against the project. What's more, Harris reported a tense interview with Ridley-Thomas, who can sometimes be prickly, which concluded with Ridley-Thomas saying, "Go to hell, Ron....I said, go to hell! Now put that in your damn newspaper." By mid-April, the *Los Angeles Sentinel,* the city's leading black newspaper, was pleading with Waters and Ridley-Thomas to "work together at 81st and Vermont." In May, the Vermont/Manchester homeowners picketed the First Interstate headquarters downtown, carrying placards with phrases like "WE NEED BUSINESS ON VERMONT" and "FIRST INTERSTATE STOP REDLINING BLACK COMMUNITY."

Throughout 1994, First Interstate winnowed the competition from sixty-six entrants to ten semi-finalists and then to three finalists. (Teams included both architects and developers.) At the bank's instruction, the finalists talked to the neighbors frequently in shaping their final proposals. As a result of these talks, the number of housing units kept going down, and the idea of providing these units exclusively for low-income residents vanished completely.

In December, the bank announced the winning team. Though no nonprofit developers were on the team, the team's leaders were all key members of L.A.'s community development network. Rodney Shepard of Caleb Construction had built small housing projects in Watts. Bill Witte of The Related Group, a former housing deputy to San Francisco Mayor Dianne Feinstein, was an expert in the financial aspects of affordable housing. Dan Solomon of Berkeley was widely regarded as the best affordable housing architect in California. Shepard was black; Witte and Solomon were white.

What they proposed was radically different from the original idea of one-hundred-thirty low- and moderate-income units, but it was still dominated by housing. Six storefronts would face Vermont. The old market building would be used to house a business incubator program set up by the University of Southern California. Above and behind the stores, facing Vermont Knolls, would be thirty-six middle-income townhomes offered for sale at prices between $88,000 and $132,000 each. In an interview, Solomon admitted that the neighbors had been "agitated" by the one-hundred-thirty unit idea and said he had changed the project because "it is important for Vermont Knolls to reinforce homeownership." Solomon's resulting design, most experts agreed, was a stunning piece of architecture.

Throughout 1995, Waters and her neighbors continued to fight the project, and as the matter was headed for city council approval, they found another weapon against it: the deep city subsidies that would be required to make the project work—deep subsidies made necessary, in part, by the changes that the neighbors themselves demanded. The elimination of low-income units meant that Shepard and Witte couldn't use federal low-income housing tax credits. And cutting the project down to thirty-five units (while still maintaining low townhome prices) meant it was harder for the project to absorb the site's high land cost.

The final proposal, which involved financing from both First Interstate and the city, estimated that each townhome would cost $188,000 per unit to build—more than the average cost of a home for sale in the Vermont Knolls neighborhood, and about twenty percent above the city's typical cost for constructing housing in South Central. In order to keep the townhome prices down to moderate-income levels, each unit required a city subsidy of about $89,000, double the maximum subsidy typically provided by the city. All these subsidies arose in part from the fact that the property's owner was holding fast to a price of $1.7 million, or about $1 million per acre, and saying he would simply put in a swap meet if his price wasn't met.

On November 3, 1995—a Friday—the Housing Department's $1.7 million loan to Shepard's company came before the Los Angeles City Council. Ridley-Thomas lined up a long list of speakers in support of the project, including John Gray of First Interstate, Bill Witte, Rodney Shepard, and several South Central business owners. When these speakers were done, Ridley-Thomas proclaimed that "the community" wanted this project to go through. Maxine Waters did not speak, but five Vermont/Manchester homeowners did. Testifying in pre-arranged order, they raised a series of questions about the subsidies and other financial aspects of the deal, and when they were done *they* claimed that "the community" was *opposed* to the project.

On the floor of the Los Angeles City Council, however, individual council members usually get what they want—everyone is interested in protecting his or her own fiefdom—and Ridley-Thomas's motion to approve the loan passed with no opposition.

Despite the unanimous vote, the complaints about the subsidy created an oddly shaped political opening for Richard Riordan, the business-oriented mayor who had been elected with Valley votes. Mayors of Los Angeles are "weak mayors" under the city charter, meaning they have little executive power. For this reason, among others, they rarely tangle with individual council members on pet projects in the council districts. But in two years as mayor Riordan had accumulated a lot of bad blood with Ridley-Thomas over affirmative action, Riordan's treatment of LAPD Chief Willie Williams (an African-American), and other issues.

Riordan had ten working days to decide whether to approve or veto the city loan for the Vermont project. Waters claimed she did not intervene on her neighbors' behalf, but there is little doubt she assisted them in orchestrating the lobbying effort for a veto. Letters and petitions flooded the mayor's office. The mayor's aides, who prided themselves on their orientation toward business and finance, began questioning many small points in the deal—not just the amount of the subsidy, but the possibility that the loans from the city might not be paid back.

Still, Riordan did not tip his hand until November 16, the deadline for action. On that afternoon, a Thursday, he invited Julie Simmons and the other Vermont/Manchester homeowners to a meeting at City Hall. Dramatically, Riordan invited reporters to sit in on the forty-five-minute meeting while he listened to homeowners' complaints. Asked by one of the reporters what he was going to do, he answered, "I'm going to make up my mind in the next ten seconds." Then he pulled out a veto letter and signed it, while the homeowners applauded.

In the veto letter, he recited all the financial reasons to oppose the project, and then added, "Interestingly, this community and neighborhood opposition is not 'anti-development' or 'not in my backyard' in nature. On the contrary, those in opposition to the project cite their strong desire to see *business and entrepreneurial development* along Vermont Avenue, and retention of Vermont Avenue as a commercial corridor."

But Riordan's veto was not the end of the Vermont project. Instead, it touched off a peculiar backlash, and gradually the conventional wisdom around City Hall came to view the veto as a political mistake—yet another awkward move by Riordan in his relations with the black power structure. Most remarkable was criticism from Bradley. Characteristically, the former mayor had made no comment of any kind on city issues since leaving office. But cornered by a *Times* reporter the next day after leaving (ironically) a meeting of the Rebuild L.A. board, Bradley said, "Dick Riordan, just because he has a hatred for Mark Ridley-Thomas, vetoed it...and

Richard Riordan at his inauguration as mayor of Los Angeles, 1993.

we were stunned." He said the project "demonstrated his insensitivity" to South Central. Though Bradley later took back the remarks, the damage was done. Riordan might as well have been criticized by the Pope.

The Vermont/Manchester homeowners held a public meeting to celebrate, which Riordan attended. But Ridley-Thomas quickly recovered. He held his own public meeting a few days later, and then orchestrated a pressure campaign on the mayor complete with phone banks and pre-printed postcards. In early December, he mustered another unanimous council vote to override the veto.

After that, there was little the mayor could do but backtrack. Soon enough he and Ridley-Thomas had reached a compromise he could sign off on calling for First Interstate to put more money into the deal so that the city's subsidy dropped to $70,000. Yet even after losing the veto override and seeing the project move forward, Riordan claimed victory, and identified himself as the only politician in City Hall willing to listen to "the community" along Vermont Avenue.

"A community came to me and said, 'No one is listening to us'," he said in a television interview a couple of weeks later. "I became the spokesman and the change agent." In the end, Richard Riordan, the rich white businessman elected with Valley votes, seemed to conclude that somehow this had been his riot too—that he was the one who had come to the defense of a neglected neighborhood that really needed help.

⟿

Rebuilding L.A. does not begin and end at Vermont and 81st, of course. All during the battle over the First Interstate project, revitalization efforts went on all over South Central, and especially along the Vermont Corridor.

At the time of the Vermont/81st debacle, a dozen other development projects were under way along Vermont, including such diverse projects as a new supermarket, a library renovation, and the Berry Gordy Center for the Performing Arts. Four other projects can be found in the immediate neighborhood of Vermont and 81st alone. Seeking to overcome its longstanding reputation, the Community Redevelopment Agency has moved forward with seven new redevelopment zones in the riot area, including one along the Vermont and Manchester corridors that includes the Vermont and 81st property. The city and the banks have put together a Community Development Bank to provide lending in the area, and the community development network continues to drum up investor interest. Even Rebuild L.A. (now known as RLA) stuck around until its five-year charter ran out, doing useful work in identifying business sectors and sites that can help revive neglected neighborhoods. Los Angeles is not lacking in efforts to bring back South Central.

What may be found at the corner of Vermont and 81st, however, is an understanding of just how hard it really is to rebuild these neighborhoods, especially when the larger metropolis has fragmented almost beyond any hope of reconciliation. Ironically, after decades of neglect and ignorance, Vermont suddenly found itself with several competing ownership claims from groups with different political agendas.

Gary Squier and the community development activists thought Vermont Avenue belonged to them, to reshape according to the idealistic principles of good urban planning and the undeniable need to boost the city's housing stock. The bankers at First Interstate thought Vermont Avenue belonged to them as a way of winning recognition for investing in the inner city they have ignored for so long. Having won it electorally, Mark Ridley-Thomas thought Vermont belonged to him; so did Maxine Waters and her neighbors. So too do the business owners and immigrant renters who live on the other side of the boulevard; and so, undoubtedly, did the people who torched the street during the riots in the first place. Even the mayor thought Vermont somehow belonged to him—although Dick Riordan, awkward, white, and wealthy, is about the most unlikely savior of South Central anyone can imagine.

In fact, revitalizing South Central is a lot more difficult than any one of these agendas suggests. Vermont and South Central's other commercial boulevards cannot magically revert to their glory days, if only because L.A.'s African-Americans have many other choices when they shop today. In this way, Vermont's fate is not so different from the fate of older, quaint commercial strips in all of the neighborhoods of Los Angeles, which have lost lots of business to shopping malls or to high-powered entertainment-oriented downtowns such as Santa Monica and Pasadena. It is not only the residents of Vermont Knolls who must drive seven miles to a See's Candy store; many suburbanites must do the same.

Similarly, South Central can't be revived solely by the construction of affordable housing projects, however laudable these projects may be. As Nicholas Lemann has pointed out, it is never easy to stabilize poor or neglected neighborhoods, if only because of the constant turnover. In most cases, people will leave as soon as they have the means to do so, and making these people feel that they still have a stake in the old neighborhood is a big problem—the biggest problem, in fact, in the history of suburban flight.

In the end, South Central can't be brought back until everyone lays some kind of claim to it—not to further their own political ends, but because they see the fate of these neighborhoods as inextricably tied to the fate of their own neighborhoods. Vermont Avenue may be a twenty-five-mile river, but it cannot flow smoothly from its headwaters to the ocean until people all over town see how the five-mile stretch through South Central is part of the larger urban ecosystem from which they all drink.

CHAPTER 12

Cloning Los Angeles

It should be no surprise, really, that Summerlin looks like Irvine.

Irvine began as a two-hundred-square-mile ranch some forty miles from Los Angeles in Orange County, and in little more than thirty years it's been transformed into the prototypical Edge City—a "master-planned" community of more than one hundred thousand people that has set the standard for real estate development nationwide.

Summerlin is a forty-square-mile piece of real estate stretched across the side of a mountain near Las Vegas, a five-hour drive east through the desert from Los Angeles. It was purchased more than forty years ago by Las Vegas's most famous Los Angeles transplant, Howard Hughes. And now it's being developed by Hughes's company in the grand tradition of master-planned Southern California communities like Irvine.

When completed, early in the next century, the community will probably contain somewhere around one hundred eighty thousand people. Like Irvine, Summerlin is mostly auto-oriented—with a large collection of sealed-off villages (with names like "The Trails") connected by sweeping and handsome roads that serve as marketing tools as well as transportation arteries. Summerlin even has a few circular roadways around commercial areas, a land planning homage to Irvine's chief designer, architect William Pereira. Irvine was an Orange County development laid out in Pereira's Los Angeles office; Summerlin is a Las Vegas development that was laid out in the Orange County office of Phillips Brandt Reddick, a prominent land planning firm.

Like Irvine, Summerlin is big on high-quality amenities, such as jogging trails. And in a manner that Southern Californians understand, Summerlin creates this suburban-style quality of life not by accentuating the natural environment but by nearly obliterating it. Though mountains provide the backdrop and some jogging areas are adorned with native plants, the general approach is the highly manipulated Florida-in-the-desert look so popular in Orange County and Palm Springs. "They're blasting for the new golf course up the road," a Summerlin publicist said during a tour one day, apparently oblivious to the irony of destroying the real desert in order to make way for a fake one.

In fact, it's tempting to think of Summerlin as a little slice of Southern California on the edge of the Nevada desert. Except the truth is that everything in Las Vegas looks like an import from Southern California. The famous "Strip," named after L.A.'s equally famous Sunset Strip, has always served as a kind of mutant theme park for Angelenos, and from the beginning it has adopted L.A.'s roadside architectural styles. Meanwhile, in emerging suburban areas throughout Las Vegas, cheaper subdividers use red tile roofs (real ones and fake ones) as a pseudo-Los Angeles iconography, as if trying to prove that while these subdivisions may not be Irvine, at least they might be Moreno Valley.

As Los Angeles becomes increasingly crowded and expensive, Las Vegas is holding itself out as the last frontier of the California dream. Las Vegas has always prospered by skimming the Los Angeles tourist trade, but these days it's different. Now, Las Vegas is grabbing not just tourists but also L.A.'s factories and homebuilders and working class, in hopes of replicating in Nevada the powerful success that L.A.'s expansion-oriented growth machine has created three hundred miles to the west along the Pacific Coast. In short, Las Vegas is deliberately cloning Los Angeles.

⌐⌐

The Clark County Planning Commission meets twice a week, on alternate weeks, at the spanking-new Clark County Government Center, located at the end of a long, sweeping driveway just on the edge of downtown Las Vegas. Like Los Angeles County before it, Clark County is the driving force behind the growth of the surrounding metropolis. Geographically, the City of Las Vegas is quite small; at fifty-five square miles, it is one-ninth the size of Los Angeles, one-sixth the size of

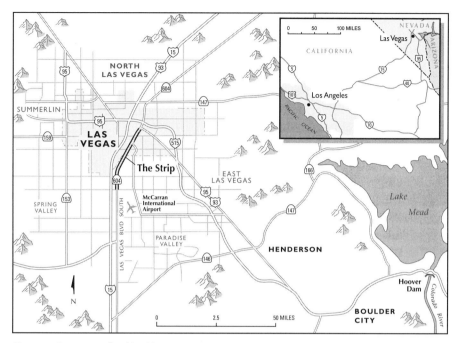

The emerging metropolis of Las Vegas.

Phoenix, and smaller even than the city limits of Lincoln, Nebraska. By contrast, the county government controls most of the famous Las Vegas Strip, as well as most of the fast-growing outlying territory.*

The technology of the planning commission chamber is impressive—maps are projected onto video monitors, and the commissioners' votes are recorded on the monitor as soon as they are cast. Not that there is ever much doubt about the outcome. The planning commission handles sixty or so items on each agenda, so the commissioners have to move quickly.

Staff planners must read the staff reports Federal Express-style—so fast that almost no one in the room can actually make out the words. If the applicant is not standing at the mike, map in hand, when the staff report is done, he or she is dressed down by the planning commission chairman, whose main goal seems to be to keep things moving.

---

* The surrounding cities of North Las Vegas, Henderson, and Boulder City also control some territory, and they are similarly pro-growth.

Half of all the planning commission meetings are devoted exclusively to "variances"—special requests to be exempted from regular zoning and planning regulations. In most jurisdictions, variances are frowned upon because they undermine local planning policies. But in wide-open Clark County, planning pretty much amounts to governance by variance. (The Las Vegas area is a veritable museum of mismatched land planning; paradoxes like houses and apartments adjacent to enormous power lines are the rule rather than the exception.)

In their rapid-fire reports, the staff planners dutifully record their opposition to the use of variances and note that the case at hand does not meet the conditions required by the county code to grant a variance. Before this idea can sink in, however, the staff report has moved on to listing the conditions the commissioners might want to impose—just in case they want to approve the variance anyway, which, invariably, they do. Opposition is rare, and in those unusual instances when an opponent demands that the applicant work out a compromise, the commissioners usually agree. Sit down and talk it over, they suggest, just as soon as we've approved the applicant's request.

This is the kind of meeting that has made Las Vegas the fastest-growing metropolis in America today. The population has doubled—from a half-million to a million—just since Ronald Reagan was elected president, and throughout the 1990s the burgeoning city has had to accommodate something on the order of six thousand new arrivals per month. The newcomers are all kinds of people, and they come for all kinds of reasons. Many come because of job opportunities in the gaming industry, because the casinos are still the biggest economic players in town by far. And an increasing number of arrivals are retirees from colder climates, for whom Las Vegas is a stimulating combination of warm weather, cheap housing, and interesting diversions.

But most of these newcomers aren't arriving, *Showgirls*-style, to find fame and fortune in the casinos. Most of them are just ordinary people looking for steady work and a house they can afford. Somewhere between a third and half come from Los Angeles, where the remnants of the growth machine, stuck in its traditional orientation of endless outward expansion, can no longer deliver the middle-class dream.

This fact—that Las Vegas is a place where ordinary people want to live—has caused an image crisis in the mass media, which have traditionally turned sinful depictions of the city into a profitable product line. In

1991, *The New York Times Magazine* signalled that this trend had become apparent even on the East Coast by publishing an article titled, "From Vice to Nice." Most other major national publications have done the same.

Similarly, the city's recent boom has caused a crisis among leading architects and urban planners, for whom Las Vegas has come to occupy a very specific place in their folklore. Las Vegas and its gaudy commercial architecture were mostly ridiculed up until the publication of a landmark book, *Learning from Las Vegas*, by architects Robert Venturi and Denise Scott-Brown, in 1972. In their re-interpretation, these distinguished Yale professors concluded that Las Vegas was the prototypical expression of American urbanism as it was emerging in the Southwest—"a New Florence to the New Rome of Los Angeles," as urban historian Carl Abbott has put it. Its sprawling, auto-oriented, amusement-driven nature was really not so awful after all.

Since then, Las Vegas, far from being ridiculed, has been celebrated as the prototypical American city of the future—gaudy, breathless, vital. Typical is the view of architectural critic Alan Hess, who celebrated the history of the architecture of the Las Vegas Strip in his recent book, *Viva Las Vegas*. The very first sentence of Hess's book reads, "Las Vegas and Disneyland are the two most potent urban models in twentieth-century America."

Such books have defined Las Vegas in the world of architecture and urban planning, just as sleazy television shows and movies have defined it in the parallel universe of popular culture. But they don't quite get it right. There is something more to what's going on in Las Vegas today than the construction of giant casinos. At its core, Las Vegas is not about glitz but growth.

As in Los Angeles, the mega-monuments of self-amusement are simply highly visible metaphors for the city's underlying vision. Like Angelenos before them, Las Vegans believe in a kind of manifest destiny. They believe they are destined to build a great city in the desert. Indeed, far more than that, they believe that the whole future of the Southwest will be urban.

And this future won't be shaped by the needs of farmers, who will be superfluous, or the requirements of the natural environment, which can be kept at bay. Instead, it will be built on the foundation of a vast urban economy with two poles, one in Southern California and one in Southern Nevada.

Most other cities in the West, and especially in the Southwest, have this same idea in mind, and they are pursuing it with equal fervor. Indeed, as Denver author Ed Quillen has written, every city in the West today is a knockoff of Los Angeles, just as every city in the West a century ago was a knockoff of Chicago. But only Las Vegas, with its historical ties to Southern California, is building so obviously on the Los Angeles model. And only Las Vegas is being built so literally by people from Los Angeles. More than anything else, today's Las Vegas is a monument to the power of the idea of Los Angeles. As the architectural critic Morris Newman has said, Las Vegas is "the last wriggling spermatozoa of the primal energy that was once Los Angeles."

⌒

It is probably not too much of an exaggeration to say that if Las Vegas did not exist, Los Angeles would have been obliged to invent it. Indeed, to a remarkable degree, Las Vegas *is* an invention of Los Angeles—or, rather, an invention of the Los Angeles growth machine, which needed it to help realize L.A.'s own manifest destiny.

Like Los Angeles, Las Vegas was not historically the center of power within its own state. As in California, power in Nevada was traditionally concentrated in the north, where silver mining had created riches and proximity to San Francisco banks was an important advantage. Even after the state set up its aggressive strategy to pursue "sin revenue" from divorce and gambling, Nevada's economy revolved around Reno, which lay only a dozen miles from the California border.

Located in a desert valley almost four hundred miles southwest of Reno, Las Vegas seemed, if anything, a less likely place for a major city than Los Angeles. The town wasn't even laid out until 1905. As late as 1930, it was a tiny railroad stop with a population of about five thousand. At just about this time, however, the federal government began construction of Boulder (now Hoover) Dam, thirty miles away—a mammoth project made necessary largely by the mammoth dreams of the Los Angeles metropolis. (See chapter 4, Redefining Chinatown.)

Though the government built Boulder City adjacent to the dam to house the construction crew, Las Vegas immediately boomed as a resort town, not only for construction workers but for gawking tourists who came to see this modern wonder. In the Depression-wracked year of 1932, Las Vegas drew more than two hundred thousand tourists. Most came for

The El Rancho hotel, the first
Los Angeles-style motor hotel
on the Las Vegas Strip.

the dam, of course, but many came to gamble—and, setting a pattern, most of them came from Los Angeles, the nearest sizeable city. Nevada legalized all forms of gambling in early 1931, and within three months the notorious Los Angeles gambling king Tony Cornero (who had once operated gambling boats offshore from Santa Monica) had established a high-end casino on the road from Las Vegas to Boulder Dam. Four years later, Las Vegas hosted its first major convention—five thousand shriners from Southern California, "with Union Pacific ferrying the delegation up from Los Angeles," reports Las Vegas historian Eugene P. Moehring.

By the 1940s, Las Vegas had become a resort suburb of Los Angeles, a kind of wide-open Palm Springs, combining the allure of a desert climate with the titillations of gambling and prostitution. After World War II, the great Las Vegas Strip emerged. Not surprisingly, it emerged along the edge of town, on the Los Angeles Highway, where California motorists could be picked off before they hit the established downtown. And, of course, the Strip drew its name from the Sunset Strip, apparently because it had the same kind of approach to nightclubbing and entertainment—an "anything goes" mentality that nevertheless aspired to be classy.

All the early resort-hotel builders were from Southern California, including the famous gangster Bugsy Siegel, who opened the Flamingo in 1947. The pioneer was California hotel operator Tom Hull, who came to Las Vegas in 1940 to build the El Rancho. Hull was lured in part by the defense boom he saw coming in Los Angeles because of World War II, which he believed would create amusement opportunities in Las Vegas. He became the first hotel operator to buy property on the Los Angeles Highway, rather than downtown.

To design his pathbreaking hotel, Hull hired the Los Angeles firm of McAllister and McAllister, with whom he had worked in California. The McAllister firm produced a low-rise Spanish Colonial complex that sprawled across seven acres in a very Los Angeles-like manner. The edge-of-town location allowed plenty of land for convenient parking, and the McAllisters even included a gas station in hopes of luring motorists arriving from L.A. to stop. "Hull knew Angelenos liked these low-rise motor-court type buildings," says Moehring, the Las Vegas historian. "He liberated casinos from riverboats and railroad hotels and put them into the resort hotel."

The casinos that followed in the 1940s and 1950s were similarly geared toward the preferences of Angelenos. In his book on Las Vegas architecture, Alan Hess points out that Siegel's elegant, low-rise Flamingo Hotel, designed by Los Angeles architect George Vernon Russell, was quite literally borne from the school of Los Angeles Modernism pioneered by R.M. Schindler and Richard Neutra. The intent, of course, was to appeal to the discerning tastes of the Los Angeles film crowd, which was accustomed to such designs.

With the advent of jet travel in the 1960s, Las Vegas became more cosmopolitan. It drew more tourists from other parts of the country, and began to look less and less like L.A. In particular, the influence of Miami hotel designers became more pronounced as the hotels became skyscrapers. But as Hess points out, the roots of Las Vegas were not in Miami or New York or anywhere else except Los Angeles. "It is a western phenomenon, tied to the car, the suburban strip, and a postindustrial society emerging after World War II," he writes. "Los Angeles, providing many of Las Vegas's architects and most of its customers in this period, was its model."

Of course, Las Vegas paid a price for this colonial status. It remained a resort town even as its competitors throughout the West began to grow into diversified cities able to challenge Los Angeles directly rather than feeding off of it. The area did prosper from defense investment, especially at the Nevada Test Site just sixty miles away. But typical of Las Vegas, even atomic weapons were turned into a tourist attraction, with mushroom clouds rising over the Golden Nugget on local postcards.

The city's history contrasts dramatically with the history of Phoenix, which aggressively pursued industrial development after World War II. Among other things, Las Vegas suffered from an inade-

quate water system—even though
Lake Mead was only thirty miles
away—and the state did not make a
major commitment to a university
in Las Vegas until the 1960s. Even
after these problems were solved,
Las Vegas still had to overcome its
negative image as a racy resort town.

And it might never have turned
into anything more than a weekend
playground for L.A., except that a

The classic postcard photo of Las Vegas.

peculiar thing happened. Los Angeles itself changed, and could no
longer be the city that its visionary growth brokers and its ambitious
working-class residents wanted it to be. Suddenly, there was an opening
for a new Los Angeles, and Las Vegas stepped into the position willingly.

⌇

North Las Vegas isn't much to look at. It's a hot and windy stretch of
desert along Interstate 15 just a few miles north of downtown Las Vegas—
an area filled with truck-clogged freeway interchanges, unadorned
industrial buildings, railroad sidings, and modest residential tracts
perched a little too close to the factories. And from the outside, a plant
owned by Potlatch Corporation doesn't add much to the scenery. Though
new, it's a utilitarian building down a long side road near the freeway,
surrounded by a parking lot and the desert.

There is, however, one interesting addition to the landscape alongside the Potlatch factory: Row upon row of large truck trailers, bearing
the names of famous Los Angeles supermarket chains, waiting to be
filled and sent back to California. At this factory, Potlatch manufac-
tures "private-label" paper products—toilet paper, napkins, and paper
towels that will be sold in Southern California bearing the name of the
supermarket chain that sells them. Open only since 1993, the plant is
efficient and profitable for Potlatch, a Fortune 500 company headquartered in San Francisco.

But it's not a Las Vegas factory. It's a Los Angeles factory—displaced
three hundred miles to the east, across the state line, where local officials
are eager for new plants and factories can pick up good shipping rates
by "deadheading" their products back to California.

A generation ago, Potlatch would not have needed to put a Los Angeles plant in Las Vegas. The plant could easily have fit into Los Angeles itself. It might have been built somewhere along the vast industrial corridor southeast of downtown, between Alameda Street and Interstate 5. Or else it could have gone into one of the developing industrial areas to the south in Orange County or to the east in San Bernardino County.

Today, however, things are different. The Alameda Corridor is mostly full, and although public officials around Los Angeles have made redeveloping the corridor a high priority, it's more crowded and expensive than the spacious "greenfield" sites that industrial companies love. And while they still have land available, the industrial parks around Ontario and San Bernardino come with the California-style regulation that has grown up over the past thirty years in response to the wide-open practices of the growth machine.

Las Vegas, on the other hand, comes with no such impediments. Unlike California, Nevada has no environmental laws requiring lengthy analysis of real estate development projects, and, as the practices of the Clark County Planning Commission demonstrate, lengthy planning delays are unheard of. Even raising the concept of "impact fees"—the special fees levied on new development in California to pay for the cost of growth—is enough to cost a Las Vegas politician an election.

Furthermore, Las Vegas is now trying to make up for lost time in proving itself a respectable location for business. The Nevada Development Authority, financed by the state government and local businesses, operates a classic economic development shop, identifying businesses in other states interested in moving and then trying to sell them on coming to Las Vegas.

When these business headhunters talk about what it's taken to make Las Vegas a respectable location, most of them focus immediately on how they lured Citibank's western credit card processing center in the early 1980s, a move that required a special session of the state legislature in order to eliminate the state's usury laws. But what really turns the headhunters on is California. Almost a third of all their leads are California businesses looking to relocate, and many more are East Coast companies craving proximity to the California market. Low deadheading rates in trucking are part of the reason Las Vegas is so attractive. Las Vegas is a national capital of consumption, but, as one business headhunter says proudly, "we don't make anything." Trucks full of merchandise barrel into the city constantly, but the truckers are desperate to scrape up any kind of payload in return.

The poster boy for Las Vegas industry is Donald Staley, owner of Basic Food Flavors—a company that makes soy concentrates and other food flavorings, much of which is shipped to Asia out of the Port of Long Beach. Staley's company, which has about twenty-five employees, used to be located in Pomona, thirty miles east of Los Angeles. He ran into such regulatory trouble trying to expand that he was featured in a special issue of *Forbes* magazine in 1990, which lamented California's poor business climate. First, air pollution officials gave him the runaround, he says; then he ran into trouble with the local sanitation department. His attempt to expand his operations in the Pomona area went on for years.

Finally, he moved to North Las Vegas, just a couple of interchanges north of the Potlatch factory, where local officials gave him a building permit in three weeks. And the deadheading helps him. "Even today," he says, "we can ship from here to the Port of Long Beach cheaper than from Pomona to the Port of Long Beach." Staley's twenty-thousand-square-foot building is little more than a concrete bunker along a major arterial, and it's located across the street from a working-class residential subdivision. But Staley's employees say they're happy; two-thirds of them moved from California when the company moved.

If the workers who follow Los Angeles companies across the desert to Las Vegas feel at home once they get here, part of the reason is that the homes available for them to buy look pretty familiar. Though they don't have a stranglehold on the local market, California's home-builders have realized no less than California's industrial companies what a gold mine Las Vegas has become.

The main headquarters of Lewis Homes is in the San Bernardino County bedroom suburb of Upland—ironically, not far from Don Staley's former headquarters in Pomona. The Nevada operation is located amid the characteristic jumble of a typical Las Vegas neighborhood, just on the other side of Interstate 15 from the Strip. It's housed in a small office that's partly a standard-issue, California-style tilt-up industrial building. Within a block of the Lewis office is the Howard Johnson casino, apartment buildings, an E-Z 8 hotel, the high-rise Rio hotel and casino, and warehouses.

In Southern California, where assembly-line construction of suburban tract homes was perfected, Lewis Homes is consistently one of the market leaders. The company has been so successful that its founders, Ralph and Goldy Lewis, have made separate $5 million donations to the urban planning schools at both UCLA and the University of Southern California.

But the Lewises also began building houses in Las Vegas more than thirty years ago, and now one of the Lewis sons, Robert, runs the Las Vegas operation and has become an integral part of the city's business community. (Among other things, he's on the board of the Nevada Development Authority, the outfit that headhunts California companies.)

In 1995, the Lewises sold 789 new houses in Southern California, ranking fifth in the local marketplace. In Las Vegas, they sold 1,170 and ranked first. And Lewis is not alone; four of the top five Southern California homebuilders now operate in the Las Vegas market. Some, like the Lewises, have been there a long time. But most of them arrived after the Southern California real estate crash of the early 1990s, looking for a new gold mine.

It's no big surprise that the California companies are successful. After all, they're selling to many of the same buyers in Las Vegas that they've sold to in California. Wayne Laska, the Lewis sales manager in Las Vegas, reports that of the seventeen thousand people who looked at a Lewis home in Las Vegas in 1994, fifteen percent were people then living in California; and he estimates that another twenty percent or so were Californians who had moved to Las Vegas within the last few months.

"We're starting to see more East Coast people," Laska acknowledged recently, and he pointed out that retirees have become a driving force as well. Some twenty-five percent of Las Vegas residents are retired, and at least one "places-rated" study found it to be the best retirement location in America. No matter who they are or where they come from, however, the new Las Vegans are affected by Californians. Despite an astonishing rate of construction, Laska says prices are rising—driven up, he says, by the equity refugees arriving from Los Angeles every day.

It is no wonder that the Los Angeles homebuilders love Las Vegas. Not only can they tap into a Los Angeles-style market with Los Angeles-style products, but they can do things the way they used to do them in the good old days in L.A. The people moving to Las Vegas love living there. Like Los Angeles refugees elsewhere in the country, they feel as though they've dodged a bullet. Yet unlike Angelenos in exile in Portland or Seattle, most of these refugees are content with the way Las Vegas is growing. In fact, they're even willing to tax themselves to keep growing. While the developers pay absolutely no fees toward new infrastructure, in 1994 the taxpayers approved a $600 million bond issue to build new schools in the new neighborhoods, including Summerlin.*

The Howard Hughes Corporation's Summerlin project.

Where Las Vegas has had trouble getting ahead of the growth curve is in creating the regional organizations required to fulfill its destiny. Partly because it has always been a colony of Los Angeles, Las Vegas has not always had L.A.'s vision in building for the future. Often it has been hard enough just to build for next week. This has been a problem in Las Vegas in many areas, including transportation and flood control. But in the current growth boom, no issue has been more of a problem than water.

Sitting behind her massive desk at the offices of the Las Vegas Valley Water District, not far from the Strip, Patricia Mulroy, the general manager, insisted in 1995 that her main concern was that "we are managing water on a cliff." What she meant by this statement is obvious. While six thousand people a month arrive in town, and the Clark County Planning Commission races through project approvals like drivers at the Indy 500, and the casinos along the Strip build ever-larger monuments to amusement, Las Vegas is running out of water. The valley has perhaps fifteen years of water supply at current growth rates—a blink of an eye in the world of infrastructure planning.

Her solution, consistent with the view of most of Las Vegas's growth brokers, isn't to rethink what Las Vegas should become. Rather, her solution is to turn Western water rights upside down in order to ensure that Las Vegas achieves its manifest destiny as the Los Angeles of

* In most cases, including Summerlin, it is true that the developers contribute land for the schools. But in the Los Angeles area, the developer of a project like Summerlin would likely be expected to bear at least some of the cost of actually constructing the schools as well.

the desert. Her strategy is to use Los Angeles-style tactics—and, indeed, L.A's own political muscle—to do it.

Mulroy is a strong-minded and straightforward woman who minces no words. She's often referred to as Las Vegas's "water czarina," and, like a lot of entrenched bureaucrats, she is sometimes regarded as more powerful than the politicians she serves. (On the Las Vegas Valley Water District's letterhead, her name appears in large type at the top; the board members' names appear in small type at the bottom.) Since 1989, she has been pursuing a water strategy so aggressive—so filled with the chutzpah of manifest destiny—that it's been breathtaking to watch.

Though Las Vegas has always grown rapidly, the area's population exploded in the late 1980s after reaching a low during the recession of 1981–82. In 1987, Las Vegas added about forty thousand people, the vast majority of them arriving from elsewhere. In 1988, that figure jumped fifty percent, to more than sixty thousand, and by 1990 Las Vegas was adding close to eighty thousand new residents per year. Water use skyrocketed as well. Just between 1987 and 1989, water demand rose by almost a third, from one hundred seventy thousand acre-feet to two hundred twenty thousand acre-feet. And all this occurred as the West was gripped by a lengthy drought that was causing huge cutbacks in California water supplies. "In 1989 we were in the beginning of a growth spurt," Mulroy recalled later. "And as far as water is concerned, we were coming out of a state of 'virtual reality'."

This rapid increase strained Las Vegas's water supplies almost to the breaking point. Despite its proximity to Hoover Dam, Las Vegas has very little claim to water from Lake Mead, a fact that most Las Vegans have a hard time believing. "You try telling people," Mulroy once said, "that they don't have water when they have been out boating on Lake Mead." Nevada's whole entitlement from the Colorado River basin is only three hundred thousand acre-feet per year—one-tenth of Arizona's claim and one-fourteenth of California's. The reason is simply that Nevada had very little political power when Colorado River water was divvied up in the 1920s.

Beginning in 1989, the year of the biggest spurt in water use, Mulroy tried to maneuver Las Vegas into a more muscular position. She hinted that Las Vegas might divert water from the Virgin River, which flows through Zion National Park and cuts through Arizona before it enters

Nevada and empties into Lake Mead. If it couldn't get the water from Lake Mead itself, Las Vegas would grab the water before it got there.

Mulroy also filed a claim with the state engineer for all the unappropriated water in Nevada. The claim covered some 23 hydrological basins, including a huge underground aquifer running from Death Valley in California into rural Nevada. This part of the claim touched off angry rhetoric from politicians in these rural counties. Many of them compared the Las Vegas move to William Mulholland's famous diversion of Owens Valley water at the turn of the century, which destroyed farming in that area. It is an unfortunate coincidence—unfortunate for Las Vegas, at least—that the Death Valley underground aquifer stretched underneath a good portion of California's Inyo County, home to most of the Owens Valley.

In response to the rhetoric, Mulroy consistently claimed that there would be plenty of water to go around and she would be happy to work out a deal so that the rural counties could use the groundwater supplies too. But there was no question that the claim had achieved its purpose: It had captured everyone's attention and placed Las Vegas in a stronger position.

During 1990 and 1991, Mulroy took a number of other steps designed to emphasize the severity of Las Vegas Valley's water situation and further strengthen her position. In 1990, a series of new regulations imposed more water conservation requirements on new development—banning, among other things, artificial lakes in new subdivisions, which had become a source of political embarrassment and undermined Mulroy's argument that a water crisis was at hand. Low-flow toilets were required, and a restructuring of water rates called on bigger users to pay higher rates. Eventually Las Vegas even imposed a connection fee of about $3,000 per house to finance construction of necessary facilities, the first time that infrastructure costs had been placed directly on Las Vegas developers.

Then, in 1991, Mulroy took another page from L.A's book and helped to organize the Southern Nevada Water Authority, Las Vegas's version of the Metropolitan Water District of Southern California. The new agency brought together Mulroy's water district with other local water and sewer districts and the cities in the Las Vegas area. The intent was to stop parochial bickering and pursue new water supplies together. But there was little question who ran the new operation; Mulroy's district was by far the largest water agency in the group, and the Southern Nevada Water Authority was headquartered at her office.

With local agencies unified behind her, Mulroy was then able to begin pursuing a dramatic rearrangement of water rights on the Colorado River to benefit Las Vegas. Though the city had staked dramatic claims to the Virgin River and the underground supplies, these maneuvers were merely bargaining chips. And while her agencies had promoted water conservation, it was clear that these moves had been meant merely to buy a little time and avert political attacks on the city's high water consumption. Like the Met's water engineers before her, Mulroy consistently rejected the idea of solving the Las Vegas water problem through conservation as "ridiculous." What she really wanted to do was get more water out of Lake Mead to fuel the city's future growth, a strategy that would require a reversal of seventy years of water rights on the Lower Colorado.

Unbuttoning the water rights on the Colorado would seem to be an almost impossible task. The Colorado River Compact dated back to 1922. The Compact had divided water rights among California, Arizona, and Nevada. Any attempt to rearrange those rights was usually perceived as a zero-sum situation—one state would win and other states would lose—and for this reason challenges to water rights usually led to decades-long litigation between states. (The California-Arizona dispute was a classic example.)

But it was Mulroy's genius to see, just as Carl Boronkay at the Met had seen, that traditional water alliances in the West were breaking down. The future would be dominated not by the states, which had to accommodate a whole series of water interests within their own borders, but by growing cities with a lot of money to spend chasing after more water.

In this insight, she was sustained by a typical Las Vegan's sense of manifest destiny—the notion that the future economic prosperity of the entire region would emerge from the city's stupendous growth. "The Southwest is an urban economy," she once said in an interview. "It's the most urbanized area of the country. And Las Vegas is the only city that sits on the river." She stated, as she has frequently, that the problem of Colorado River rights should be decided in a "non-court" forum. And perhaps most tellingly, she added, "There is plenty of Colorado River water for Southern California and Southern Nevada."

What all this means is that Mulroy is pegging the future of Las Vegas not on Nevada's ability to litigate water rights in court, but on the ability of the metropolis to buy them up.* And all along, she has understood that her most important potential ally in turning the Colorado upside down is not anyone in her own state, but the Metropolitan Water District of Southern California.

During the whole period between 1991 and 1995—as the Carl Boronkay era at the Met was giving way to the John Wodraska era—Mulroy negotiated with the Met on a pathbreaking agreement to join forces. Finally, in November 1995, both sides gave their approval. The agreement had three components. First, the two agencies would work together to pursue long-term water supplies. Second, the Met would share with Las Vegas a portion of the Colorado River "surplus"—water allocated to Arizona under the Colorado River Compact but used by California. And third, Las Vegas would kick in $50 million toward a Met project to line the earthen canals of the All-American Canal in California's Imperial Valley, and share in the resulting water. "This is something," one of Mulroy's commissioners said, "that will benefit Nevada probably when we're all gone."

Predictably, everyone else on the river hated the idea. So did some people who weren't even on the river, like environmentalists in Northern California. In the peculiar world of Western water, geographic regions are tied together by the web of relationships that revolves around the Met. Every drop of Colorado River water the Met can squeeze out of neighboring states is one less drop that Southern California needs from the State Water Project—and, therefore, one more drop available to restore the fragile ecology of the San Francisco Bay and the Sacramento Delta. If the Met had so much Colorado water that it could give some to Caesar's Palace, the environmentalists screamed, then something must be wrong.

Arizona Governor Fife Symington threatened to sue. Arizona even began to talk about building additional water facilities, in order to take water it didn't need from the Colorado so that Las Vegas and Los Angeles wouldn't get it. California Governor Pete Wilson dressed down the

* Mulroy has said that she believes water disputes ultimately must be resolved by negotiations among the states, which is probably true in strictly legal terms. But she clearly believes that Nevada's negotiating position will be enhanced by the economic power of Las Vegas and its relationship to the Met.

Met for assuming that the agency had more legal power than he had. In the Las Vegas deal, the Met had agreed to transfer Colorado River water across state lines. Wilson reminded the agency that the Met is a creation of California state legislation, and the power to move Colorado River water across state lines resides in Sacramento, not in Los Angeles. It did not take long for the Met to see the light. In March 1996, three months after the Las Vegas officials popped champagne, John Wodraska told a California legislative committee, "Is the Met selling water to Las Vegas? The short answer is NO."

Still, there was an air of inevitability about the Met-Las Vegas alliance—brought about, among other things, by the determined attitude of Pat Mulroy. For example, Interior Secretary Bruce Babbitt, who would have had to approve the deal, said, "If California and Nevada can agree, who's going to second-guess that? I think there's a good chance this thing could play out in a positive way." (Babbitt's Bureau of Land Management, one of the biggest landowners in the Las Vegas Valley, was already helping urban growth in Las Vegas through a series of land trades and land releases designed to facilitate the city's outward urban expansion.) There is little doubt that sooner or later Los Angeles and Las Vegas will restructure the Colorado. And when that happens, Patricia Mulroy's sense of manifest destiny will seem more than justified.

↝

If the water problem can be solved, the machine will likely continue to crank out growth in all directions until the Las Vegas Valley is full of undifferentiated suburban sprawl—following the model of the San Fernando and San Gabriel Valleys and L.A.'s coastal plain, if not learning their lessons. It is no coincidence that the most common metaphor used to describe Las Vegas's growth opportunities is a "gold mine." Because mining is what the brokers of growth in Los Angeles and Las Vegas are doing in Southern Nevada, just as they have done for decades in Southern California.

The history of the American West is the history of extractive industries. Miners, loggers, oil and gas drillers, and others have grown rich by removing the region's natural resources and then moving on to another location when there's nothing left to mine. The result, predictably, has been a volatile boom-and-bust economy in every town, where local prosperity depends on this year's commodity prices and the entire community can vanish once the mine is played out.

To a Western city, the seduction of an urban/suburban vision based on the Los Angeles model is that it can theoretically break this cycle by providing a more stable long-term economy. In some ways this is true. Yet in its own peculiar way, the Los Angeles-style urban/suburban economy is just as dependent on mining as the traditional extractive industries. Like Los Angeles before it, Las Vegas is banking its future on cheap houses and cheap land. But as the Los Angeles experience shows, cheap houses and cheap land don't last forever.

Like a mine or a forest or underground oil, land is a limited commodity in any geographical location. The more you chew up, the less is left. So what remains becomes more expensive and more difficult to transform into a usable commodity. When the mine is played out, the community is usually left in turmoil, because the underpinnings of the local economy have been knocked away. This is not a problem for the miners, who simply take their money and go someplace else. But it is a problem for the people who stay behind, usually the working- and middle-class residents who were lured by jobs in the extractive industries.

When the Los Angeles mine began to play out, the growth miners simply pulled up and staked a new claim over in Nevada. Los Angeles is not a ghost town, of course. It is a vibrant city with a diversified economy that could easily stand on its own without the growth machine. But Los Angeles is in crisis now because land is expensive and life in these formerly pastoral suburbs has become such a hassle that people have begun to take political action. That, in short, is the problem of L.A.'s growth machine.

Like Los Angeles, like the silver mines in Tonopah—like all the extractive industries in the West over the last century—Las Vegas will play out. The place has twenty, maybe thirty years before the land starts getting really expensive. And already the backlash is beginning. It's a minor undercurrent now, but its components are familiar. Schools are holding double sessions, just as they did in the 1950s in Los Angeles. Transportation is, increasingly, a mess. Opposition to taxes in order to finance new development is growing, especially among the senior citizens who play a larger and larger role in the city's political life. And in a few isolated cases, Las Vegas has even come face to face with actual California-style anti-growth sentiment. As the number of

Californians increases, and as the hassles mount, it's inevitable that California-style anti-tax, anti-growth fervor will rise sooner or later. In the end, there is little doubt that Las Vegas will become another Los Angeles—not just in the short-term economic opportunity it will provide for working- and middle-class refugees from Los Angeles, but also in the eroding quality of life those refugees sought to escape by leaving California in the first place.

CHAPTER **13**

Cocoon Citizenship and
Toon Town Urbanism

Toward the middle of June in 1993—when Carl Boronkay was retiring from the Metropolitan Water District, and Maria VanderKolk was struggling to hold the Ahmanson Ranch deal together, and John Gray and Gary Squier were touring South Central looking for affordable housing sites—one of L.A.'s few truly regional controversies came to a head.

At the time, a consortium of eleven oil companies was promoting a plan to build a new oil pipeline from offshore rigs at Gaviota Point (past Santa Barbara) to refineries in El Segundo and Wilmington. To the oil companies, the Pacific Pipeline was a vital piece of economic infrastructure, allowing them to leave behind the constant environmental controversies associated with shipping the oil by tanker through the Santa Barbara Channel. But everyone else had an opinion too.

The pipeline snaked along a circuitous one-hundred-seventy-one-mile route through Santa Barbara and Ventura Counties, around Bakersfield, way out past Riverside, and finally back in through urban Los Angeles. Along this route, the pipeline stirred up every conceivable emotion. Oil and construction workers spoke frequently about the pipeline's potential to create jobs, and environmental consultants with connections to the oil industry also looked forward to more work. Ever protective of the natural environment near the Pacific Ocean, Santa Barbara environmentalists were critical of the project. And local officials along the pipeline's route in urban Los Angeles came out strongly against the pipeline for a somewhat different reason: they claimed that plowing yet another major project through their neighborhoods constituted "environmental racism."

The climax of the debate on the Pacific Pipeline came during the week of June 14, when the California Public Utilities Commission conducted four hearings in Southern California—one in Santa Barbara, one in Ventura, one in downtown Los Angeles, and one near the refineries in Carson. Sometimes tedious and occasionally boisterous, the meetings were never without drama. Sober Santa Barbara environmentalists presented their case. Crowds of unemployed union members shouted their support in Ventura and Los Angeles.

Most dramatically, the minority neighborhoods turned out in force at the Los Angeles hearing on Monday, June 14, to object to environmental racism. They complained about a lack of translators, and cheered when L.A. City Councilman Mike Hernandez, who has lived all his life along the proposed route, stepped forward to complain. "You need to understand that this pipeline goes through the most densely populated area of Los Angeles," Hernandez shouted into the microphone. "I say this as someone who has been evicted twice from my house!" "*Gran trabajo*, Mike!" Hernandez's inner-city constituents exclaimed. Good job!

You wouldn't have learned this entire story, however, just by reading your local edition of the *Los Angeles Times*, especially if you lived in the northern and western suburbs in the San Fernando Valley and Ventura County. With a daily circulation of more than 1.1 million, the *Times* is the second largest metropolitan daily in the country, and one of the few institutions in the Los Angeles area with enough breadth and scope to bring regional issues like the Pacific Pipeline into clear perspective. Yet in covering the pipeline, sometimes the *Times* seemed to be covering two different stories. Because what you read depended on where you lived.

If you lived in inner-city Los Angeles, you found the kind of heavy-duty, in-depth coverage you'd expect from one of the nation's best newspapers. In particular, the paper's acclaimed "City Times" section covered the pipeline and inner-city opposition to it. (City Times was a special section devoted to local news in the inner-city neighborhoods and nearby suburbs; it was eliminated, along with some suburban sections, in a 1995 cutback.)

On Sunday, June 13, City Times published an impressive four-page spread by reporter Lucille Renwick, complete with color maps and diagrams, outlining the project and the environmental racism angle. (The article was also printed, more or less in its entirety, in the paper's South

Bay and Long Beach editions.) After attending the Los Angeles hearing on Monday, June 14, and the Carson hearing on Tuesday, June 15—which was heavily attended by labor union supporters of the pipeline—Renwick produced a shorter follow-up story covering both sides of the issue. The follow-up article appeared under the headline "RESIDENTS JEER, UNION CHEERS" in the South Bay edition on Friday, June 18, and in the weekly City Times edition on Sunday, June 20.

If you lived in the suburban areas of the San Fernando Valley and Ventura County, however, you got a somewhat different story. These editions were put together not at the *Times* headquarters downtown, but in a suburban printing plant in Chatsworth, in the western San Fernando Valley. No one in these areas ever read one word of Lucille Renwick's comprehensive twenty-three-hundred-word story. In fact, these readers barely knew that inner-city environmental racism was an issue. The only time this aspect of the story was mentioned in their zoned editions was when the *Times* ran a one-hundred-eighty-word summary in May reporting that the Los Angeles City Council had taken a formal position against the project. (This was true even though the City of Los Angeles encompasses the San Fernando Valley, including Chatsworth, within its borders.)

Instead, what *Times* readers in the Valley and Ventura County got was a completely different spin, which ignored the inner-city angle and reflected the local values and political dynamics of their own communities. The Pacific Pipeline didn't run through the populated areas of Ventura County, but the county stood to benefit from it economically. Like many oil industry supply companies, Pacific Pipeline Systems Inc. was based in the City of Ventura, as were many of the unionized workers who would be hired if the pipeline were built.

When the PUC conducted the June hearings, Valley and Ventura readers were not given a well-rounded view of the debate. Instead, all they got from the *Times* was a straightforward news story reporting on the PUC's hearing in Ventura, held on Thursday, June 17, where testimony was stacked by union leaders supporting the project. Headlined "WORKERS PACK HEARING TO SUPPORT OIL PIPELINE PLAN," this story appeared in the Ventura edition on Friday, June 18—the same day that the South Bay edition ran Lucille Renwick's four-page spread reporting on the two hearings in the Los Angeles area. But the Ventura story carried no account of inner-city opposition to the pipeline, or of the controversy over translators, or of Mike Hernandez's *"gran trabajo"* in appearing before the PUC in Los Angeles four days earlier. In fact, the Ventura version of the *Times* story did not mention the other three hearings.

The *Times* did not begin to tell its Valley readers much about the Pacific Pipeline until three years later, when a somewhat different proposal came before the Public Utilities Commission and Richard Alarcon—a Latino member of the Los Angeles City Council who represents parts of the Valley—made it an issue. In April 1996, the PUC approved the project and its environmental documentation, and the City of Los Angeles sued. This story was covered by the Valley edition of the *Times*. By then, however, its Ventura County edition had stopped writing about it altogether.

The reporters and editors of the *Los Angeles Times* did not deliberately set out to deceive their readers, or to deprive them of the full story about the Pacific Pipeline proposal. Rather, the pattern of coverage on this issue (and others) is the result of editorial practices deeply imbedded in the newspaper's approach to "targeting" its readers. And that approach, in turn, is derived from the desire of typical Southern Californians to disassociate themselves from the metropolis in which they live.

More than most metropolitan dailies in America, the *Times* has had to decentralize in order to retain readers and advertisers that have fled from the city. The paper has opened local editions in outlying areas, offering "partial run" advertising to local businesses, and has built satellite printing plants in Costa Mesa and Chatsworth. All these are common practices among metropolitan dailies. But in adapting them to an especially reluctant metropolis, the *Times* has fundamentally altered the way it covers news. In the process, this venerable institution has embraced anti-urban, parochial thinking wherever it is expedient, just as L.A.'s growth promoters have done for a century or more.

Much of the *Times*'s thinking has been shaped by its lengthy, costly, and (so far) unsuccessful war with the Orange County *Register*. When Orange County boomed in the 1970s, the *Times* moved in, thinking that it could dominate the market simply because it was the *Los Angeles Times*. Despite a substantial investment, however, the *Times* has never caught up with the *Register*, and the reason is obvious. From the beginning, the *Register* has respectfully treated its readers as Orange County residents first and as citizens of the great Los Angeles metropolis only incidentally.

In the columns of the *Register*, L.A. is portrayed as a distant metropolis of passing interest, much like San Francisco or London, while Orange County emerges as an independent metropolitan power hurtling toward inevitable greatness. The resulting success in the market-place is indisputable. Once a small newspaper with a libertarian phi-losophy that spilled over into the news columns, the *Register* is now the twenty-fifth largest paper in the country, and usually ranks second (only to the *L.A. Times*) in ad lineage. It's also far ahead of the *Times* in Orange County circulation.

In order to compete, the *Times* has now adopted the *Register*'s philosophy, not just in Orange County but in all suburban areas. Most of the paper's local news appears not in a unified Metro section produced downtown, but in the special zoned sections (or reconfigured Metro sections) put together in Chatsworth and Costa Mesa. In essence, sub-urban *Times* editors now produce a series of separate newspapers dis-tributed under the *Times* banner.* And *Times* marketing reinforces this idea. Newsrack posters advertise not "*Los Angeles Times*" but "*Times* Valley" or "*Times* Ventura County," and reporters introduce themselves the same way. Freeway billboards feature local images and emphasize that the *Times* is deeply committed to whichever suburb the freeway driver happens to be passing through.

In short, the *Times* has decided that the way to remain a great metropolitan newspaper is to deny that there is a great metropolis. If suburbanites are determined to wrap themselves up in little cocoons—social, economic, or political—then *the Los Angeles Times* is determined to make sure that those cocoons are manufactured of newsprint pro-vided by Times Mirror Inc. But the *Times* is not completely at fault here. The newspaper may be pandering to the "cocoon citizens" of the suburbs—but the *Times* didn't invent them.

⌢

The suburb, as the great urbanist Lewis Mumford once wrote, emerged from the chaos of the nineteenth century industrial city as its antidote, a saner and more humane way of life. Where the city enveloped residents in a coffin of concrete and asphalt, the suburb would release them into a

---

* In some cases this is literally true. After closing several suburban sections in 1995 as part of a cost-cutting program, the *Times* contracted with a community newspaper group to produce special supplements for those zones, which the *Times* distributes as part of its own newspaper. Predictably, these supplements do not have the same editorial depth and insight that even the *Times*'s own suburban zones contained.

green expanse of open space. Where the city poisoned people with foul air, the suburb would allow them to breathe free. Where the city produced mechanized noise, the suburb would provide a natural quiet.

There is no denying the suburb's appeal, and for more than a century the Los Angeles metropolis has served as the real-life American city that has come closest to a suburban ideal. Originally, of course, Los Angeles was meant as a suburb for the whole country, and even after it industrialized the city provided a comfortable suburban way of life for many people (African-Americans, the working class) who could not achieve it anywhere else.

Yet Mumford also pointed out that suburbs are only partial communities, and suburbanites themselves only partial people. Removed from the fully rounded reality of urban life, suburbanites find themselves succumbing to "the temptation to retreat from unpleasant realities, to shirk public duties, and to find the whole meaning of life in the most elemental social group, the family, or even in the still more isolated and self-centered individual."

"What was properly a beginning," he concluded, "was treated as an end."

Close to forty years have passed since Mumford wrote those words, and in that time the suburbs have changed. They are more diverse; they have skyscrapers and mega-malls, not just houses and neighborhood stores. Some have mutated almost beyond recognition into what Joel Garreau has called "Edge Cities," while others are aging ungracefully into little more than single-family slums. Much more of the real work of living (and dying, both naturally and violently) occurs in suburbs nowadays.

Suburbanites are often driven, and bound together, not so much by what they are heading toward as by what they are running from, and what they are running from is their perception of the ugly realities of urban life. This has always been the case, of course, but today there is a different and more desperate quality to this escapism—all across America, but especially in Los Angeles.

Ironically, as historian Greg Hise has shown, L.A.'s neighborhoods were originally designed to be a different kind of suburb—not the "economically inert bedroom community populated predominantly by middle- and upper-income white families" but "complete communities for balanced living, affordable for workers and families." In a way, they were intended to fulfill Mumford's dream of a garden metropolis, with small, balanced communities serving as stars in a metropolitan constellation. Yet the result in Los Angeles has been, if anything, attitudes more intensely suburban. In Los Angeles you could leave everything behind—not just your old house in the inner city, but your old job as well. Now there was nothing at all connecting you to the rest of the metropolis.

Coccon Citizenship: Entrance to the Rancho Conejo subdivision in Thousand Oaks.

Whatever its faults, the early postwar suburb at least was a place where new residents were eager to build a community. Indeed, as Alan Ehrenhalt pointed out in *The Lost City*, the pressure to participate in community life was so great that many suburbs developed a social structure every bit as rigid and unforgiving as the crowded ethnic wards that the new suburbanites had left behind. Whether they were inclined to or not, these suburbanites were literally forced into building their community.

Today the hard work of community-building is left mostly to the developers, who are called upon to create not just houses and streets but also parks and schools and shopping centers and even homeowner associations that will govern the community long after the developers have finished their work. For the new suburban residents buying into this prepackaged set of amenities, the task of citizenship consists mostly of making sure that the walls keeping the metropolis at bay remain in place—in other words, that outsiders do not pierce the cocoon.

More than ever, of course, the cocoon is literal. As any real estate developer will tell you, the hottest idea in new suburbs these days is the gated community, the subdivision not merely surrounded by a wall but protected by a gate that residents control. Whether secured by a guardhouse or operated by remote-control, the gate offers suburbanites a sense of security and exclusivity. Indeed, the idea of a gate is so compelling that it is literally impossible to sell a suburban subdivision to homebuyers above a certain income category—upper-middle-class and up—if it comes without a gate.

Nowhere is the phenomenon of the gate more pronounced than in suburban Los Angeles, where fear and snobbery are so prevalent that gates are *de rigueur* even in the safest suburbs, especially in upscale areas like south Orange County and the ring of second-generation suburbs surrounding the San Fernando Valley. The tiny city of Hidden Hills is entirely behind gates. Forty percent of the residents of Calabasas live behind gates, including many prominent local politicians who began their careers as homeowner association activists. One tract in Santa Clarita attracted national attention in 1992 by installing hydraulic ballards originally developed to stop terrorists at embassies and airports. Try to "run" the gate, and your car is impaled on two three-foot-long steel cylinders. Predictably, it wasn't long before those impaled began to sue and residents themselves were impaled because of accidents and malfunctions.

Once the gate is up, making sure that it is operative and performing the task of keeping others out becomes the major focus of community activity. "There isn't a week goes by,"one homeowner activist in Camarillo told me in an interview, "that I'm not down there fixing the gate or putting in a new gate or calling the gate people." And whatever political power residents can muster is devoted to assuring that only the right suburbanites are permitted behind the gate. When one prominent developer in Thousand Oaks sought to build an apartment building behind his gate—an apartment building everyone knew about, because it was called for in plans approved by the city—the new residents who had just bought houses came unglued. "It's not that I have anything against people who live in apartments or that they are unwelcome," one homeowner said. "It's just that what's the point of having a gated community when it's going to be a free-for-all?" The apartment building is now being built behind a separate gate. And all this controversy took place in a city regularly rated by the FBI as one of the two or three safest cities in the country—so safe that many FBI agents choose to live there themselves.

The suburban cocoon can be figurative as well, keeping outsiders away through financial and political means. Special taxing districts established by cities and developers after the passage of Proposition 13 have woven financial cocoons around many suburban subdivisions. Unable to pay for roads, parks, and schools out of property tax revenue, the cities essentially bill the residents of new subdivisions for the cost. Also since

Proposition 13, suburbanites have turned increasingly to the practice of seceding from the surrounding metropolis by creating new cities.

It should not be surprising, then, that people living inside these suburban cocoons become cocoon citizens, defining the common good as that which benefits only those inside their particular cocoon. Far from identifying themselves as citizens of a region or a metropolis, they often have trouble identifying themselves even as citizens of the small suburban cities of which they are a part.

In Calabasas, even some politicians who live behind gates lament the fact that residents feel isolated from one another and appear united more by what the city is not—it is not the San Fernando Valley—than by a positive vision of what it is or could be. At the same time, many suburbanites who live in special taxing districts understandably develop a proprietary attitude about the pieces of public infrastructure they are funding. Why should others be permitted into their parks and schools, even if they are technically public, when only those inside the cocoon are footing the bill?

At bottom, of course, cocoon citizenship is built on the foundation of L.A.'s traditional anti-urban bias, and cocoon citizenship, in turn, forms the basis for the slow-growth and no-growth attitudes that are prevalent all across the region. Because once inside their cocoon, the suburbanites see no butterfly-like value in emerging. They only seek to stay inside forever, petrified in their tracts, like ancient fossils.

So removed are cocoon citizens from the totality of metropolitan life that they can no longer see the full range of activities a metropolis encompasses, or that they are part of it no matter what they do. All they can do is try to define the breadth of metropolitan life by what they've observed inside their cocoon. "We're diverse!" a former member of Agoura Hills City Council once stated, a little defensively, at a public meeting. "We have custom homes *and* tract homes." It is no wonder that even a great regional institution like the *Los Angeles Times* would rather pander to this attitude than challenge it.

↜

Of course, even cocoon citizens must draw upon the larger metropolis every now and then—for jobs, for goods, for recreation and amusement and stimulation. In a more traditional city, this broader understanding of the interconnectedness of metropolitan life would be called "urbanism." But in Los Angeles, this term cannot be applied unvarnished. Angelenos do leave their cocoons to conduct all these activities: to work, to shop, to play. But it is not their intention to engage themselves with the full range of urban life. Instead, they simply trade one cocoon for another, leaving a residential cocoon for a working cocoon or a spending cocoon. In this way, they don't practice real urbanism, but a kind of Toon Town Urbanism, a fantasy version of the real thing—with few of the risks, and few of the rewards.

Toon Town, of course, is the mythical, cartoonish part of town that was overlaid on live-action reality in the Disney movie, *Who Framed Roger Rabbit?* Now it's also a real-life fake neighborhood in Disneyland, complete with doorknobs that squeal, a tiny roller-coaster, and Mickey Mouse's house. Toon Town is good fun as far as it goes. But you're less likely to think of the place as fake if you've emerged from your residential cocoon and paid to enter Disneyland to experience it. There's something about the audible thunk of $26 at the entry booth that makes Toon Town seem more real—and, in the process, makes every so-called urban experience in Los Angeles feel like a knockoff of Toon Town.

In 1993, for example, MCA-Universal unveiled, with great fanfare, another exercise in Toon Town Urbanism: the highly publicized City-Walk on the Universal Studios' property in Universal City, a mountaintop location in between Hollywood and Burbank. In point of fact, CityWalk was simply a shopping center, carrying with it the usual pointless array of consumer items, that filled the space between the Universal parking lot and the gate to the studio tour. But thanks to the clever vision of architect Jon Jerde, a leading devotee of Toon Townism, CityWalk actually touched off a lengthy and serious debate about urbanism in Los Angeles.

Toon Town Urbanism at University CityWalk.

Collecting and reassembling certain physical Los Angeles icons—Hollywood Boulevard, for example—Jerde managed to make City-Walk into a *faux* version of real life (if, indeed, it is possible to make a *faux* version of Los Angeles at all). And he cleverly interspersed real-life activities at City-Walk to further blur the line between the actual city and the virtual one. It wasn't long, for example, before UCLA Extension, the adult education division of the university, leased space in a building along CityWalk and began offering classes there. At first glance, it's unclear what's real and what's not. Is UCLA Extension really located here? Or has Jerde simply appropriated it as an icon?

All this is clever enough—urbanism with mirrors—but as Jerde himself knows it is not a substitute for a real-life urban experience. In fact, Jerde's CityWalk is actually a knockoff of an unbuilt concept he proposed for the area two miles away around the Mann Theater on Hollywood Boulevard—a real urban place, for better or worse. But most people in Los Angeles don't seem to know the difference. As the Boston architect Steven Cecil once pointed out, only in Los Angeles would CityWalk be taken seriously enough to spark a public debate about urbanism. In Boston everyone would understand that it's nothing more than a theme park with stores. There's a fundamental difference between how people feel about a park, a downtown, a public space, and how they feel about a theme park or a shopping mall. Urbanism means taking responsibility as a citizen for the public areas in your town, feeling like you are connected to them and care about them. Toon Town Urbanism involves surrendering yourself to the commercial forces that are in control of the spending cocoon.

It's not simply that people in Los Angeles are missing something by choosing spending cocoons over street life. All successful public spaces are cocoons of some sort, places where people feel comfortable because they are protected by gates, by entry fees, or simply by social customs enforced with a stern glance. Central Park in the 1860s, at the height of the carriage-trade promenades, was no less a cocoon than CityWalk is today. And there's nothing inherently wrong with surrendering yourself to a commercial cocoon like Disneyland or CityWalk every now and then. But there is more at stake when everything becomes a cocoon, when the citizens of a metropolis spend their entire lives protecting themselves from the full range of urban experience. Because it is inside these cocoons that citizenship, pride of ownership of a larger community, breaks down.

Life in Los Angeles today is little more than an exercise in Cocoon Citizenship and Toon Town Urbanism. It's a constant caravan between the residential cocoon, where citizenship is exercised only in narrow, self-interested ways, and the spending and working cocoons, where citizenship is totally surrendered to the commercial forces that run the place. The result is an erosion of real citizenship, a disintegration of common ownership of the metropolis, just when real citizenship is needed most.

⌒

A century ago, the historian Frederick Jackson Turner declared the closing of the American frontier in a now-famous paper delivered to the American Historical Association. Turner's paper had a somewhat narrow purpose—he was challenging the biases of the Eastern establishment in historical scholarship—but it had a powerful impact on the popular imagination. The frontier had shaped American individualism and democracy in the West, Turner argued, and now the frontier era was at an end. Henceforth there would be no uncharted territories to explore and conquer, no new land on which Americans could pursue the dream of self-reliance and agrarianism that dated back to the founding of our country.

Confronting the closing of the American frontier required a radical shift in American thinking. Back to the founding of our colonies—indeed, back a thousand years to medieval Europe—the progress of our civilization had been built on the assumption that if life got too expensive or complicated or difficult, some people could simply start over by creating a new place.

In *The City in History*, Lewis Mumford pointed out that many of Europe's now-venerated older cities began as "new towns" designed to accommodate spillover population and the speculative financial dreams of kings and noblemen. European colonization of North America, Australia, and other continents furthered this pattern. And as Daniel Boorstin has so eloquently explained in his synthesis of American history, eighteenth and nineteenth century Americans extended this pattern still further, often simply abandoning played-out land in the East or the South in order to pursue new dreams farther West.

In the century since Turner delivered his paper, we have simply transferred the pioneer spirit from the fringe of our country to the fringe of our metropolises. Generation after generation of suburban pioneers has left the familiar confines of central cities and struck out onto the suburban prairie, hoping to wrest middle-class happiness from its newly developing terrain. As we did so, we impoverished the communities left behind by robbing them of their most affluent, motivated, and productive citizens. But it has not been in the nature of Americans to dwell on what we have left behind. Instead we dream of what is ahead. Los Angeles, the eternal suburb, was quite literally built from this dream. And it is this dream—however debased, however hobbled—that we cling to as we spin our suburban cocoons, hoping to keep the realities of the larger metropolis at bay.

Yet we cannot keep them at bay. That is clearly the message drawn from the collapse of the Los Angeles growth machine over the last thirty years. Reluctant or not, a metropolis is woven tightly together and cannot be easily unraveled. It is possible for us to escape or hide, but sooner or later our connections to the metropolis pull us back to it—and it to us. Slow down growth in Santa Monica or Agoura Hills, and that growth goes somewhere else. Abandon South Central, and the ring of neglect and violence will grow. Build a Sales Tax Canyon on the edge of the metropolis, and you bring the metropolis to the edge. Try to build a pipeline, and you'll run into people all along the route who don't want it in their backyard. Sooner or later, there is no place left to go.

During the suburban boom of the last half-century, we have extended the promise of a peaceful and pastoral suburban life to working people who previously couldn't afford one. But to keep the suburbs serene, we have practiced a domestic version of the containment policy our national government used against Communism during the Cold War. Inner-city neighborhoods were increasingly impoverished and dangerous, but as long as we kept the bad guys and scary people contained inside them, they couldn't do us any harm.

The urban riots of the last thirty years have done nothing to dispel this idea. When civil disorder erupts in an inner-city neighborhood, its target is usually close at hand. Even the 1992 Los Angeles riots, though broad in geographic scope, reinforced this notion for many suburbanites. Vermont Avenue was firebombed by local residents, but no one bothered to drive thirty miles to the Simi Valley courthouse and burn it down. And after the riots, the impulse of residents and business owners alike— black and white, Korean and Latino—was to move as far out as possible.

Yet the social problems that once characterized the inner city alone now afflict all communities and, to a lesser but still significant extent, all neighborhoods. Divorce and family instability is rampant everywhere. The thirty-percent illegitimacy rate that led Daniel Patrick Moynihan to declare a crisis among black families a generation ago has now spread to all families everywhere, black or not, urban or not. Crime may rise or fall depending on the year or the place, but it strikes in cities, in suburbs, even in small towns where, according to conventional wisdom, it has no business going. In Los Angeles today—in America today—the containment policy has failed. There are no suburbs here. There is only a mirror reflecting the pathology of our society into every community.

And there *is* nowhere else to go. Today we are seeing the closing of the suburban frontier, just as we saw, a century ago, the closing of the American frontier. Today's sprawling megalopolises, Los Angeles chief among them, have become too big and unwieldy to accommodate much more in the way of outward expansion.

The core members of the growth machine don't believe this, of course. To the land developers and homebuilders, there will always be another Orange County or Moreno Valley. And so there may be, at least for a while. But not forever. It might be possible to squeeze another generation of suburban sprawl out of Las Vegas (or Phoenix or Fresno or even Moreno Valley), but sooner or later the day of reckoning will come for the growth machines there as well. In purely environmental terms, the fragile ecology of the West may not be able to withstand this onslaught. And in a world dominated by instant communication and rapid travel, sixty miles—or three hundred—is an insufficient barrier to protect these emerging suburban paradises from urban social pathologies. A punk with a gun can find Moreno Valley and Las Vegas just as easily as a thirty-year-old couple with a down payment.

And so we are left with ourselves, with each other, and with all those neighborhoods and communities we seek desperately to escape. Instead of escaping, we must confront them, help them tackle their problems. We must redefine the American dream so that it does not rest on the assumption that we can throw old places away and create new ones in the middle of nowhere.

To do this we need not surrender the basic components of the American dream, any more than we needed to surrender them when we transformed the dream from an agrarian to a suburban vision. Privacy, self-reliance, choice—all these can and must remain core American values. Yet so too must we remember that other core American value, the value of community. And we must redefine community more broadly to include not just our street or our tract, but our town, our metropolis, our region.

To do this we need not move from our own neighborhoods, but simply find ways to puncture the cocoon and reconnect with other people and other towns. No matter which edition of the *Los Angeles Times* we read, we must find ways to make other places—places different than our own—meaningful to us once again, so that we care about them and provide the political will required to nurture them. Simply put, we cannot afford to practice Cocoon Citizenship and Toon Town Urbanism anymore. We can no longer afford to be suburbanites, no matter where we live. We must, instead, learn once again to become citizens of the metropolis, no matter how reluctant a metropolis it may be.

Acknowledgments

I wrote this book because writers love to tell good stories and Los Angeles is hands-down the best story I ever ran across. I arrived in Los Angeles sixteen years ago, knowing no one, without a job—without even a car—and expected to stay a few months at most. The main reason I'm still in Southern California today is because I'm still fascinated by watching the story unfold. That and Vicki.

For almost all of those sixteen years, Victoria Torf Fulton has been my Los Angeles tour guide. My wife understands it and appreciates it as only a native can, and her insights have broadened and deepened my understanding of Los Angeles far beyond anything I could have hoped to discover on my own. That is one of the many reasons why I love her so much. My daughter, Sara, also teaches me a great deal about the urban environment every day with her wide-eyed wonder, and both have been more than patient with me during the writing of this book. Most of the time spent writing this book was really time that belonged to them.

My greatest editorial debt is to Morris Newman, who has been my colleague, my partner, my friend, and my main kibbitzer for almost a decade now. As the Notes indicate, I have relied on his research and observations frequently throughout this book. But such acknowledgments do not adequately describe Morris's role in shaping my thinking. The truth is that Morris's sensibility and understanding of Los Angeles drenches every page of this book, and I cannot thank him enough for that.

Many other people have played an important role in shaping this book. My publishers, Warren Jones and Jaimie Levin of Solano Press Books, stuck with me during many missed deadlines and crises of faith, as did my editor, Pat Shell. Keith Breskin has provided me with my most important friendship over the past sixteen years, as well as keen insights into Los Angeles politics. Steve Svete has also provided me with special friendship, criticism, and assistance that has helped to sustain me during this effort. Steve Schafer of Schaf Photo in Ventura did a great job of capturing the reluctant metropolis on film.

Research for chapter 7 was conducted in part under a grant to UCLA Extension from the John Randolph Haynes and Dora Haynes Foundation, which originally resulted in a public-policy research report in 1993. The research for chapters 9 and 10 was supported in part by a grant from the now-defunct Design Arts Program of the National Endowment for the Arts dealing with the impact of municipal revenue needs on urban design. Many thanks to both organizations.

I owe many debts to individuals for their assistance on specific chapters. I literally could not have written chapter 3 without the research assistance of Andrea Figler, who also helped doublecheck facts, gather photos, and prepare the manuscript for publication in a thousand little ways. As my research assistant on chapter 7, Janice Mazurek provided much-appreciated help, as well as support and encouragement from far-flung places in the succeeding years. On chapter 4, Carl Boronkay was very generous with his time. On chapter 6, Mark Pisano provided me with access not only to his memory but also his filing cabinet, for which I am very grateful. Michael Mantell has provided me with invaluable assistance in chapter 8 and enduring friendship as well.

Numerous other people have spent many hours talking to me about Los Angeles and/or providing special assistance for this book. To name just a few, these include Steve Cecil, Lou Cherene, Aaron Curtiss, Peter Detwiler, Denise Fairchild, Gay Forbes, Will Fleissig, Joanne Freilich, David Gay, Madelyn Glickfeld, Dolores Hayden, Timm Herdt, Bob Gomperz, Dorothy Peyton Grey, Anna-Lisa Hernandez, Con Howe, Lenora Kirby, Steve Mattas, Dennis McClendon, Jamie McCormick, Lisa Picard, Michael Pittas, Adam Relin, Mike Ruane, Greg Salvato, Arnie Sherwood, Paul Silvern, Woodie Tescher, Rudy Torres, Carol Whiteside, Mark Winogrond, Jack Wong, Dennis Zane, and especially Phil and Milly Torf and all their relatives, who have endured endless interrogations over the years about what Los Angeles used to be like. I miss the influence and generous spirit of the late Harvey Perloff very much. To these and to the many I have failed to mention, I am most grateful.

I must also acknowledge the important influence of many writers who have chosen Los Angeles as their subject over the years. They are listed in the Notes, especially for the Introduction. Special thanks are due to Mike Davis, whose work has helped to prove all over again in the 1990s that Los Angeles is a compelling subject that people want to read about.

I am also very grateful to the hundreds of people who were interviewed as part of the research effort of this book, which stretched over a great many years. Finally, thanks to various newspaper and magazine editors who have given me the opportunity to write about Los Angeles over the past few years. These include Tom Brom, Greg Critser, Alan Ehrenhalt, Sam Gwynne, Ruth Knack, Sylvia Lewis, John Martin, Dirk Olin, Allison Silver, and Gary Spiecker. Despite the many contributions of these and others, all errors are my own.

William Fulton
Ventura, California
February 1997

Notes

In many ways this book is an amalgamation of political science, history, sociology, and urban planning, but ultimately it is meant to be an act of journalism. As such, I have used a variety of research methods designed to assist me in telling good stories and ferreting out their meaning.

Almost every chapter in this book contains a fair amount of history, but for this history I have almost always relied on secondary sources such as books and dissertations. Primary historical research was beyond the scope of this book, and in most cases excellent work had already been done anyway. All books are listed in the accompanying Bibliography, while other sources are fully identified in the Notes.

To construct chronological narratives and get a sense of contemporary feeling about my topics, I have relied heavily on newspaper reports. In most cases I have used the *Los Angeles Times* but where possible I have also relied on other newspapers in Southern California. As a veteran of five different newsrooms, I am well aware of the shortcomings of newspaper accounts; they are often hurried, incomplete, and even occasionally inaccurate. Nevertheless, they are invaluable source of the "running history" of any topic, and I have not hesitated to put them to use for that purpose.

The guts of the book's research consists of personal interviews and eyewitness accounts of events from 1981 to 1996. The interviews number in the hundreds and are listed in the Notes with each chapter. The eyewitness accounts will be evident in the narrative. The eyewitness accounts are all mine with three exceptions—two in chapter 3 and one in chapter 13—which are listed in the Notes below.

Finally, wherever possible, I have supplemented the interviews and eyewitness accounts with documentary evidence, especially government staff reports, correspondence, and material contained in lawsuit files.

Introduction: The Collapse of the Growth Machine

1–2: For more information on Moreno Valley, see William Fulton, "The Long Commute," *Planning*, July 1990, pp. 4–8.

4: "Monster" Cody Scott: Mark Horowitz, "In Search of Monster," *The Atlantic Monthly*, December 1993, pp. 28–37.

5: Geological instability of San Gabriel Mountains: John McPhee, *The Control of Nature*, Part 1: "Los Angeles Against the Mountains."

5: "a remarkable victory of human cunning": John R. Logan and Harvey Molotch, *Urban Fortunes: The Political Economy of Place*, p. 55.

5: "growth machine" theory: Logan and Molotch, chapter 3: "The City as Growth Machine."

6: Henry Huntington's fortune: William B. Friedrichs, *Henry E. Huntington and the Creation of Southern California*, p. 162.

6: Ninety growth barons: Friedrichs, *Henry Huntington*, p. 11.

7: "Harry Chandler wanted to move it": "Who's Who—and Why: Serious and Frivolous Facts about the Great and Near Great," *Saturday Evening Post*, June 5, 1926, p. 52.

7: Sioux Falls immigrants: Perhaps the most vivid source of information about the consequences of the growth machine on Los Angeles is the writing of mystery novelist Raymond Chandler, especially his novels *The Big Sleep*, *Farewell, My Lovely*, and *The Lady in the Lake*. Chandler had a great eye for detail of all kinds, and the details he provides us with about the Southern California landscape and its people are filled with insight. In *Farewell, My Lovely*, published in 1940, detective Philip Marlow visits a neighborhood busybody living in a transitional section of what we would now call South Central. Seeking to gain her confidence, he admires her carved sideboard and says: "I bet that side piece was the admiration of Sioux Falls." She answers: "Mason City. Yesser, we had a nice home there once, me and George. Best there was." Just in that one exchange Chandler manages to convey volumes about the hopes and the realities of Midwestern migrants living in Los Angeles in the 1930s.

7: Planned decentralization: Greg G. Hise, "The Roots of the Postwar Urban Region: Mass-Housing and Community Planning in California, 1920–1950," Ph.D. dissertation, University of California, Berkeley, 1992.

7: "By 1940 virtually every family had a car": Interview with Pete Hathaway, California Transportation Commission.

8: Description of William Pereira: Douglas Frantz, *From the Ground Up: The Business of Building in the Age of Money*.

8: "Like earlier generations of English intellectuals": Reyner Banham, *Los Angeles: The Architecture of Four Ecologies*, p. 23.

9: Black population in the San Fernando Valley: Robert Conot, *Rivers of Blood, Years of Darkness: The Unforgettable Classic Account of the Watts Riots*, p. 107.

10: More than 20 percent of Riverside County's employment base was tied to construction: Ben Bartolotto, Construction Industry Research Board, Burbank, California.

11: If all Americans lived and worked so close, they would fit inside Missouri: Calculation of real estate consultant Alfred Gobar.

12: Los Angeles had become a kind of national suburb for old-line Protestants: Kevin Starr, *Material Dreams: Southern California through the 1920s*, chapter 6: "The People of the City: Oligarchs, Babbitts, and Folks."

12: Lakewood System: Gary L. Miller, *Cities by Contract: The Politics of Municipal Incorporation*, especially chapter 1: "The Political Origins of the Lakewood Plan." Also Joan Didion, "Trouble in Lakewood," *The New Yorker*, July 26, 1993, p. 46.

13: Explosion in the sale of Japanese pickup trucks: David Halberstam, *The Reckoning*, p. 427.

14: "Come to Irvine and hear the asparagus grow": Comments of Thomas Neilsen, Urban Land Institute conference, Los Angeles, October 1987.

15: Dairy City, Dairyland, Dairy Valley: William Fulton, "Keeping 'Em Down on the Farm," *California Lawyer*, August 1986, p. 29.

15: A decade earlier, the homeowner groups in the area had organized: Mike Davis, *City of Quartz, Excavating the Future in Los Angeles,* pp. 71–73.

16: "Plains of Id": Banham, *Los Angeles: Architecture of Four Ecologies*, chapter 8, "Ecology 3: The Plains of Id."

Chapter 1: The Beachhead

Most of this chapter is based on first-hand research I conducted in Santa Monica between 1981 and 1984 and then again in 1992. During this time I interviewed dozens of people, attended dozens of public meetings, and even accompanied Dennis Zane in walking precincts.

Significant interviews: Dennis Zane, Ruth Goldway, Derek Shearer, Herb Katz, Frank Hotchkiss, Ken Edwards, Robert Myers, Christine Reed, James Conn, Vivian Rothstein, John Alschuler, Mark Tigan, Larry Fondation, Ken Genser, Susan Cloke, Paul Silvern, Ernesto Flores, Richard Knickerbocker, and David Shell. I also drew heavily upon the files of the *Santa Monica Evening Outlook* (mostly 1976 to 1984), to which I had access when I worked there in 1983 and 1984.

24: Tents and subdivisions: Fred E. Basten, *Santa Monica: The First Hundred Years,* pp. 3–5.

24: Deep-harbor port: Lanier Bartlett, "The Battle for South Pacific Ports," Part II, *Westways,* 27: 8 (August 1935), pp. 26–29.

24: Stood three-deep at local newspaper offices: *Evening Outlook,* September 28, 1981.

24–25: Housing construction, 1960–72, and increase in renter population: Mark Forster, "Revolt of the Renters in Once-Staid Santa Monica," 10 *California Journal* 365–367 (October 1979), p. 366.

25: Tom Hayden's arrival in Venice: Tom Hayden, *Reunion: A Memoir,* pp. 425–428.

27: History of Venice and Ocean Park: Tom Moran and Tom Sewell, *Fantasy-by-the-Sea.*

27: Switching from Goldwater to McGovern: Shearer, Derek, "Santa Monica: How the Progressives Won" (University of California, Los Angeles, School of Architecture and Urban Planning, undated working paper), p. 3.

28: Economic democracy: Martin Carnoy and Derek Shearer, *Economic Democracy.*

28: Removal of residents to make way for Santa Monica Shores: "A Short History of Ocean Park" (Ocean Park Community Organization pamphlet, undated); Edward Soja and Derek Shearer, "Urban Self-Management in Santa Monica" (UCLA School of Architecture and Urban Planning, undated working paper).

28: Plans for 1,400 apartment units and subsequent litigation: *Evening Outlook,* December 13, 1979 (part of special series on Ocean Park).

29–30: Hayden 1976 Senate campaign: Robert Scheer, "Tom's Common Sense for the Seventies," *New Times,* July 9, 1976, p. 8.

30: Yannatta campaign: Shearer, "How the Progressives Won," p. 3.

30: "Hoarding houses": Adam Smith, *Paper Money,* pp. 87–99.

30: Five percent of city's apartments demolished: Shearer, "How the Progressives Won," p. 5.

31: 1978 rent control campaign: *Evening Outlook,* June 7, 1978; Shearer, "How the Progressives Won," p. 5.

31: New, tougher rent control initiative: "Petition for Submission to Voters of Proposed Amendment to the Charter of the City of Santa Monica," undated.

31–32: Renters rights campaign tactics: Zane interview; also, information gathered by the author in accompanying Zane in walking precincts, 1984.

32: "We dug our own grave": Interview with Joe L. Walling, president, Santa Monica Bank.

32: Three electoral victories in 1979: Shearer, "How the Progressives Won," pp. 6–9.

33: Reformers opposed to rampant growth: Katz, Edwards, Hotchkiss, Reed interviews.

33: Account of 1981 election: Shearer, "How the Progressives Won," pp. 11–17.

33: "We're not going to be taking trips:" Los Angeles Times, June 15, 1981.

33: "Revolt in Reagan's Backyard": Alexander Cockburn and James Ridgeway, "Revolt in Reagan's Backyard," Village Voice 26:17 (April 22–28, 1981), p. 1.

34: "People's Republic of Santa Monica," Los Angeles Times, June 15, 1981.

34: "Suburban radicals": Wall Street Journal, July 1, 1981.

34: "Really just a coincidence": Los Angeles Times, June 15, 1981.

35: Ice-skating rink at $80 per square foot: Evening Outlook, July 29, 1980.

35: Office space approved, 1976–79: Hall Goodhue Haisley and Barker, "City of Santa Monica General Plan Land Use and Circulation Elements: Background to the Issue Papers" (undated, c. 1983), p. 7.

35: Sixty-one development projects: Evening Outlook, April 30, 1981.

35: Six-month building moratorium: Evening Outlook, April 22–23, 1981.

35: One developer sued: Evening Outlook, April 30, 1981.

36: Other left-leaning cities: William Fulton, "'Frisco Hotel Builders Settle with Tenderloin," Washington Star, July 19, 1981; Joel Werth, "Tapping Developers," Planning (January 1984), pp. 21–23.

36: Welton Becket design of Santa Monica Civic Auditorium: James Lunsford, Looking at Santa Monica, pp. 27, 33.

36: Welton Becket background and O'Malley quotes: Los Angeles Times, December 19, 1982.

36–37: Becket development proposal specifics: Evening Outlook, June 1, 1981; Cecilia Flanagan, "Changes in the Architecture Environment," unpublished master's thesis, UCLA Graduate School of Architecture and Urban Planning (1983), pp. 22–24.

37: $7 million: Ibid.

37: O'Malley came to the council in June: Evening Outlook, June 3, 1981.

37: "I'm not impressed at all": Evening Outlook, June 14, 1981.

37: Commercial and industrial task force hearing in July: Evening Outlook, July 30, 1981.

37: Task force recommendations: "Recommendations of Citizens Task Force on Developers in Commercial and Industrial Zones on Parameters for Development of Three Sites," report to the Mayor and City Council of Santa Monica from the city staff, August 11, 1981.

37: "By God, the developer will": Evening Outlook, July 30, 1981.

38: Delays nearly bankrupted Welton Becket: David O'Malley and Richard F. Davis, "Case Study on Legislation to Protect Vested Rights," manuscript dated April 2, 1984, prepared for Urban Land Institute "Handbook on Improving Developer and Community Relations in the Development Process," p. 10.

38: Zane background: Zane interview.

38: Zane-O'Malley deal details: Ibid.

39: Goldway refusal to vote: Goldway interview.

39: Development agreement details and approval: "Development Agreement Between Colorado Place Ltd., a California Limited Partnership, and the City of Santa Monica," and Santa Monica City Council Ordinance No. 1231, dated Oct. 27, 1981.

40: Subsequent history of Colorado Place: Interview conducted by Andrea Figler with Kenyon Webster,

Current Planning Manager, City of Santa Monica.

40: 1992 departure of Robert Myers: William Fulton, "Saint Bob," *California Lawyer,* February 1993, pp. 51–55.

Chapter 2: Perestroika Co-Opted

This chapter was written mainly from written reports, including newspaper reports, and interviews.

Significant interviews: Carlyle Hall, Jane Blumenfeld, Mark Fabiani, Cal Hamilton, Ken Topping, Con Howe, Dan Garcia, Gordon Murley, Robert Gottlieb, Laura Lake.

43: Bradley remarks, library deal: Remarks of Tom Bradley at groundbreaking for Library Tower, June 19, 1987.

43–44: *Atlantic* article: Charles Lockwood and Christopher B. Leinberger, "Los Angeles Comes of Age," *The Atlantic Monthly,* January 1988, pp. 31–56.

44: Los Angeles gobbled up Hollywood: William Fulton, "'Those Were Her Best Days': The Streetcar and the Development of Hollywood Before 1910," *Southern California Quarterly,* Fall 1984, pp. 235–255.

47: Eras in Bradley mayoral tenure: Rafael J. Sonenshein, *Politics in Black and White: Race and Power in Los Angeles,* chapter 11: "Political Hegemony, 1963–1985."

47: Forty percent of Braude campaign contributions from developers: *Los Angeles Times,* June 29, 1986.

48: "Homestead exclusivism," Davis, *City of Quartz,* p. 159.

48: Calvin Hamilton's 1974 General Plan: Hamilton interview; William Fulton, "Los Angeles: Prime Time," in *American Planning Association, The Best of Planning,* pp. 348–352.

49: Despite Hamilton's efforts, it was possible to...: See *Friends of Westwood Inc. v. City of Los Angeles,* 191 Cal.App. 3d 259 (1987).

50: In the 1970s, the California Supreme Court...: See, for example, *Arnel Development Co. v. City of Costa Mesa,* 28 Cal.3d. 5 11 (1980).

50: The result was an explosion of initiatives restricting growth: This trend was documented in Madelyn Glickfeld and Ned Levine, *Regional Growth...Local Reaction: The Enactment and Effects of Local Growth Control and Management.*

51: "Many of the homeowner groups": Carlyle Hall interview.

51: Judge's ruling in 1985 against City: *Ibid.*

51–52: Account of Braude/Yaroslavsky press conference announcing Proposition U: *Los Angeles Times,* February 26, 1986.

52: Yaroslavsky background: Sonenshein, *Politics in Black and White,* pp. 131–133.

52–53: Bradley background: Sonenshein, pp. 58–60.

53: "from the day I walked into office": *Los Angeles Times,* June 29, 1986.

54: Yaroslavsky raised $1 million from developers: *Ibid.*

54: Yaroslavsky's support for skyscrapers: *Los Angeles Times,* February 21, 1988.

54: Number of ballot measures in 1985 and 1986: *California Planning and Development Report,* December 1986.

54: Braude and Yaroslavsky used campaign funds to attack "greedy developers": *Los Angeles Times,* June 29, 1986.

54: Pat Russell took the lead in ramming through exceptions: *Los Angeles Times,* October 1, 1986.

54–55: Other background on exemptions: *Los Angeles Times,* September 9, 1986; September 17, 1986; September 19, 1986.

55: San Francisco's office restrictions passed: *California Planning and Development Report,* December 1986.

55: Proposition U results: *Los Angeles Times,* November 4, 1986.

55: Less than a month later: *Los Angeles Times,* December 3, 1986.

55: Creation of citizen planning committee: *California Planning and Development Report,* December 1986.

55: Appellate court overturned city approval of skyscraper: *Friends of Westwood Inc. v. City of Los Angeles,* 191 Cal. App.3d 259 (1987).

56: Fundraising and other details in Galanter-Russell campaign: *Los Angeles Times,* April 15, 1987.

56: A week after Galanter forced Russell into a runoff: *Los Angeles Times,* April 23, 1987.

56: Account of Galanter stabbing: *Los Angeles Times,* May 6, 1987.

56: Galanter endorsed by Braude: *Los Angeles Times,* May 12, 1987.

56: Failure of Hyperion plant: *Los Angeles Times,* May 20, 1987; see also Davis, *City of Quartz,* pp. 196–203.

56: Galanter victory in runoff: *Los Angeles Times,* June 3, 1987.

57–58: Defeat of LANCER project: William Fulton, "A Neighborhood Says No: The Defeat of LANCER," *Architecture and Planning,* 1988–89 issue.

58: Shearer op-ed piece: *Los Angeles Times,* June 5, 1987.

58: San Diego housing restrictions: *California Planning and Development Report,* July 1987.

58: Developers identified growth control as number one issue: *California Planning and Development Report,* November 1987.

58: Orange County slow-growth initiative and poll: *Los Angeles Times,* February 21, 1988.

58: "We will continue to grow": *Los Angeles Times,* March 16, 1988.

58–59: Gage background: Gage interview. See also William Fulton, "Going with the Flow," *California Lawyer,* May 1993.

59: Bradley announced that the city would comply: *California Planning and Development Report,* August 1988.

60. During early 1988, with Gage's assistance: *Los Angeles Times,* March 16, 1988.

60: In early May of 1988: *Los Angeles Times,* May 3, 1988.

60: Yaroslavsky fundraising and "riding the issue all the way": *Los Angeles Times,* February 3, 1988.

61: Background on Orange and Riverside ballot measures: *California Planning and Development Report,* June and July 1988.

61: In April, slow-growthers convened in Riverside: *Los Angeles Times,* April 10, 1988.

61: "I just hope they were whoever the good guys are": Rogers interview.

62: Orange County ballot measure campaign and results: *California Planning and Development Report,* July 1988; *Los Angeles Times,* June 8, 1988.

62: Riverside initiative: *California Planning and Development Report,* December 1988; *Los Angeles Times,* November 8, 1988.

62–63: Bradley appearance at Gilbert Lindsay Community Center: *Los Angeles Times,* April 6, 1988.

63: Bradley raises $1 million: *Los Angeles Times,* July 30, 1988.

63: Bradley tightens up review of liquor stores: *Los Angeles Times,* September 13, 1988.

63: Bradley reopens comment on Ma Maison: *Los Angeles Times,* September 15, 1988.

64: Bradley endorses regional growth management proposal: *Los Angeles Times,* November 2, 1988.

64: Bradley press conference on Westside Pavilion and Yaroslavsky quotes: *Los Angeles Times,* December 23, 1988.

64: Yaroslavsky agrees to Bradley demand: *Los Angeles Times,* January 4, 1989.

64: Yaroslavsky withdraws from mayoral race: *Los Angeles Times,* January 6, 1989.

64–65: Bradley vulnerability and 1989 election: Sonenshein, *Politics in Black and White,* chapter 12.

65: Two urban planning professors concluded: Chien-Hwa Chen and Charles M. Hotchkiss, "When Is Growth Management Not Growth Management? Prop. U, Land Use Regulation, and Development Intensity in Los Angeles," undated, unpublished paper (c. 1994).

Chapter 3: Suburbs of Extraction

This chapter was written largely from personal interviews, attendance at public events in the Hub Cities, and various books and background documents. This chapter owes a great debt to Andrea Figler, who tracked down many important pieces of source material and conducted most of the interviews in Bell Gardens, as well as some in Huntington Park. She also provided eyewitness accounts of Bell Gardens and Huntington Park City Council meetings.

Significant interviews (some conducted by Andrea Figler): Raul Perez, Ric Loya, Jessica Maes, Sam Chew, Tom Jackson, Rosario Marin, Carlos Parros, Steve Skolnick, Jack Wong, Claude Booker, George Deitch, Maria Chacon, John Robertson Jr., Father Rody Gorman.

68: "It used to be quiet here": David Bacon, "Moving Mountains," *Environmental Action Magazine,* Spring 1995, pp. 27–29.

69: Greater Eastside: Victor Valle and Rodolfo D. Torres, "Latinos in a 'Post-Industrial' Disorder," *Socialist Review,* Vol. 23, No. 4, 1994, pp. 1–28.

69: "Laboratories of democracy." This phrase was first used by David Osborne in his book of the same name to describe states engaged in innovative economic development efforts. I have appropriated it here for a very different purpose.

70: "We thought when we finally elected Latinos": *Los Angeles Times,* March 20, 1996.

72: Planned decentralization of Los Angeles industry: Greg G. Hise, remarks at Society for Commercial Archaeology conference, Los Angeles, April 19, 1996.

See also Hise, "The Roots of the Postwar Urban Region."

72: Suburbs of production: See Chauncy D. Harris, "Suburbs," *American Journal of Sociology* 49 (1943) pp. 1–13. Also Fred H. Viehe, "Black Gold Suburbs: The Influence of the Extractive Industry on the Suburbanization of Los Angeles, 1890–1930." Quoted in Hise.

72: Vernon and Huntington Park incorporations: James Kilty, *Leonis of Vernon*; Carson B. Hubbard, *History of Huntington Park.*

72: Samson Tire: Charles Elliott, *City of Commerce, An Enterprising Heritage,* pp. 73–74.

73: "The suburban ideal of moderate decentralization": *Huntington Park Signal,* May 15, 1929, quoted in Elliott, *City of Commerce,* p. 72.

73–74: Otto Claire Beck and the development of Bell Gardens: Madelina Barberena, "Otto Clair Beck: Developer of Bell Gardens," unpublished manuscript, no date; Charles Spaulding, "The Development of Organization and Disorganization in the Social Life of a Rapidly Growing Working-Class Suburb Within a Metropolitan District," Ph.D. dissertation, University of Southern California, 1939.

74: "We had to live on goat's milk": Booker interview.

74: "For children of the Dustbowl": Mike Davis, "The L.A. Inferno," *Socialist Review,* January–March 1992, page 61.

75: Lawrence Walsh background: Lawrence E. Walsh Oral History interview, conducted in 1990 by Donald P. Seney, California State University, Sacramento, for the California State Archives, State Government Oral History Program, pp. 1–30.

75: Incorporation of Southeast: Richard Bigger, and James D. Kitchen, "II: How the Cities Grew: A Century of Municipal Independence and Expansionism in Metropolitan Los Angeles," pp. 87–93; in "Metropolitan Los Angeles: A Study in Integration," Haynes

Foundation, 1952. Also, Elliot, *City of Commerce*, pp. 122–128.

75: Bell Gardens incorporation: Madeline Barberena, "Bell Gardens: After Incorporation—Growth of a New City," unpublished manuscript, pp. 1–2.

75: Cudahy incorporation: Robertson interview.

76: Walsh calling Southern Pacific during riots: Walsh oral history, p. 59.

77: Pacific Boulevard decline after Watts riots: Jackson interview.

78: Twenty-five percent of Hub Cities territory in redevelopment: "Annual Report of Financial Transactions Concerning Community Redevelopment Agencies of California, Fiscal Year 1991–92," State of California, Gray Davis, State Controller. A vivid appreciation of the situation can be gleaned from *Huntington Park Redevelopment Agency v. Martin*, 38 Cal.3d 100 (1985), and *Huntington Park Redevelopment Agency v. Duncan*, 142 Cal.App.3d 17 (1983).

78: Fifteen hundred houses demolished: Jackson interview.

79: "We liked each other," Jackson interview

79–80: Bicycle Club background: Booker interview; Sam Gideon Anson, "House of Cards," *L.A. Weekly*, April 12–18, 1996, p. 22+; L.J. Davis, "Card Club Shuffle," *California Lawyer*, December 1995, p. 42+; *Bell Gardens Bicycle Club v. California Department of Justice*, 42 Cal.Rptr. 730 (1995).

81: Four hundred thousand immigrants per year: Hans Johnson, "Undocumented Immigration to California, 1980–1993," Public Policy Institute of California, September 1996.

81–82: Immigration trends: Douglas Massey et al., *Return to Aztlán: The Social Process of International Migration from Western Mexico*.

82: History of Mexican-Americans in Los Angeles: Acuña, *Anything But Mexican*; Gloria E. Miranda, "The Mexican Immigrant Family: Economic and Cultural Survival in Los Angeles, 1900–1945," in Norman M. Klein and Martin J. Schiesl, editors, *Twentieth Century Los Angeles: Power, Promotion, and Social Conflict*.

82–83: Population changes: U.S. Census Bureau estimates, 1975; official Census counts, 1980 and 1990.

83: Mexican touches like fences: James Rojas, "The Enacted Environment: The Creation of 'Place' by Mexicans and Mexican Americans in East Los Angeles," unpublished master's thesis, Department of Architecture, Massachusetts Institute of Technology, 1991.

83: "It is heartbreaking": *Los Angeles Times*, April 7, 1990.

84: Perez background: Perez interview.

84: Perez said Jackson couldn't represent Latinos: *Los Angeles Times*, April 10, 1988.

84: Jackson response: *Ibid.*; Jackson interview.

85: April 1990 election results: *Los Angeles Times*, April 11, 1990.

86: Account of December 1990 City Council meeting: *Los Angeles Times*, December 20, 1990.

86: Appointment of Rosa Hernandez: *Los Angeles Times*, April 11, 1991.

86: Recall election results: *Los Angeles Times*, December 11, 1991; *Long Beach Press Telegram*, December 12, 1991.

87: Special election results: *Long Beach Press Telegram*, March 11, 1992.

87: Scene at first Bell Gardens council meeting: *Long Beach Press*, Telegram, March 19, 1992.

87: "If we cut off the head": *Long Beach Press Telegram*, March 16, 1992.

87: "It was a great honor": *Los Angeles Times*, March 26, 1992.

87: "This is the first time": *Long Beach Press Telegram*, December 12, 1991.

88: Account of chair-throwing incident: *Los Angeles Times*, January 13, 1993.

88–89: 1994 election results: *Los Angeles Times*, April 17, 1994.

89–90: "Fucking old woman" and other notes from Bell Gardens City

Council: Eyewitness account of Andrea Figler, May 13, 1996.

90: Maes and Marin background: Maes, Marin interviews.

90–91: Chew background: Chew interview.

91–92: Account of UNO and CBE attempts to resolve *La Montaña* dispute: Perez, Parros, Marin, Gorman interviews.

93–95: Huntington Park City Council meeting on *La Montaña*: Eyewitness account of Andrea Figler, May 6, 1996.

94: Jackson toys with idea of taking city job: Wave newspapers, February 28, 1996.

94: "Why make the guy do an EIR?": Jackson interview.

95: *La Montaña* public nuisance hearing: Skolnick interview; eyewitness account of author at hearing, September 17, 1996.

95–97: Perez funeral: Eyewitness account of author, October 30, 1996.

97: "I can't imagine anywhere in the U.S.": *Los Angeles Times*, April 20, 1995.

Chapter 4: Chinatown Redefined

The story of water in Los Angeles is, of course, one of the great stories in American urban history, and it has been told many times in many ways by many writers, including historians, journalists, novelists, and screenwriters. Much of the journalism and history produced about water in Los Angeles is among the most insightful writing about California anyway.

Nevertheless, historically there was little on the Met except its own official publications. In the last ten years, however, this has begun to change. A great deal of the credit for this change goes to Robert Gottlieb, a journalist and environmental planning professor at UCLA who served on the Met board from 1980 to 1987 and subsequently wrote two books about its inner workings. An environmental activist, Gottlieb is an unabashed critic of the old Met and an advocate of reform, but his critique and insight were very helpful in informing this chapter.

Significant interviews: Carl Boronkay, Mike Gage, Bob Gottlieb, Chris Reed, Tim Brick, George Miller, Bob Will, John Wodraska, Dan Silver, Jason Peltier, Greg Taylor, Don Cox, Ardon Moore, Mike Clinton, Rici Peterson, Tom Graff.

102: "Eastside will be so big… " "As a Reservoir, Rose Bowl Fumbles; But Domenigoni Valley Doesn't Have Parade," MWD Press Release, December 17, 1992.

105: The story of Los Angeles's water grab from the Owens Valley is best recounted in William L. Kahrl, *Water and Power: The Conflict over Los Angeles' Water Supply in the Owens Valley.*

106: Most of the description of the Colorado River and Hoover Dam is drawn from Marc Reisner, *Cadillac Desert: The American West and Its Disappearing Water,* especially chapter 4, "An American Nile (I)."

106–107: The formation of MWD is described in Joel Schwarz, *A Water Odyssey: The Story of the Metropolitan Water District of Southern California,* p. 43.

107: "The presence of scores of cities": Hundley, *The Great Thirst,* p. 285.

107: Opening of Colorado River Aqueduct: Schwarz, *A Water Odyssey,* p. 78.

107: Postwar Met annexation: Robert Gottlieb and Margaret FitzSimons, *Thirst for Growth: Water Agencies as Hidden Government in California,* p. 13.

108: "Land is just land": Robert Gottlieb, *A Life of Its Own: The Politics and Power of Water,* p. 8.

108: "The term of office": Irwin Cooper, *Aqueduct Empire: A Guide to California, Its Turbulent History, Its Management Today,* p. 88.

108: Average age of MWD board: Gottlieb, *A Life of Its Own,* p. 3.

108: "Mostly they were white": Reed interview.

109: Oroville Dam description: Author's eyewitness account; Reisner, *Cadillac Desert*, pp. 368–370.

110: Met has paid 70 percent of State Water Project Cost: Figure confirmed by Met spokesman Bob Gomperz.

111: Pat Brown's support for State Water Project: Reisner, *Cadillac Desert*, chapter 10, "Chinatown."

112: Threats to dam Eel River: Ted Simon, *The River Stops Here.*

113–114: Account of Peripheral Canal campaign: Gottlieb, *A Life of Its Own*, chapter 1, "Unholy Alliance"; also Gottlieb and FitzSimons, *Thirst for Growth*, pp. 17–20.

114: Boronkay background: Boronkay interview.

114: "The Met had a one-track mind": *Ibid.*

115: B.C. and A.C.: Gottlieb and FitzSimons, *Thirst for Growth*, p. 22.

116: Background on Won Yoo's purchase of and development plans for Santa Rosa Plateau: *Los Angeles Times* and *Riverside Press Enterprise*, January 6, 1991.

116: Met commitment of $15 million to save Santa Rosa Plateau: MWD press release, March 12, 1991.

117: Met purchase of Shipley Ranch in between Lake Skinner and Domenigoni site: MWD Press Release, October 8, 1991.

118: "To me, the most important question is": Silver interview.

118: "We got nervous": Boronkay interview.

119: Met-IID deal: Hundley, *The Great Thirst*, 393–395; Boronkay interview; Graff interview.

120: "Substantial increases in water transfers: MWD Press Release, May 30, 1991.

120: "I'm sitting in the second row": Boronkay interview.

120: "vigorously pursue": Met press release, December 10, 1991.

120: A few months later: Met press release, March 10, 1992.

121: "It's an odd organization": Anonymous source, U.S. House of Representatives staff.

121: By the fall of 1992: MWD Press Release, October 8, 1992.

121: Congress approves bill: MWD Press Release, October 30, 1992.

121: "There's not a representative": Peltier interview.

121: "I told the farmers": Boronkay interview.

121–122: Kahrl article: *Sacramento Bee*, March 24, 1993.

123: So in Boronkay's wake the agency belatedly undertook a wrenching re-examination: Much of this re-examination was stimulated by the release of a critical task force by a blue-ribbon task force appointed to examine internal problems in January 1994. This task force was chaired by Nelson Rising, the prominent developer and political insider who had engineered the construction of Library Tower (described in chapter 2).

123–124: Threat from San Diego over Imperial Valley deal: Wodraska, Cox, Moore, Clinton interviews.

Chapter 5: The Money Train

This book was written based on interviews, historical documents, and contemporary accounts. The assistance of Dorothy Peyton Gray, the MTA's librarian, was invaluable.

Significant interviews: Pete Hathaway, Judy Wilson, Marv Holen, Jim Ortner, Franklin White.

125: "As you acquire the special skills involved": Banham, *Los Angeles: The Architecture of Four Ecologies*, p. 214.

126: Transportation palimpsest: Banham, chapter 4: "The Transportation Palimpsest."

128: From the 1880s onward: Fulton, "'Those Were Her Best Days': The Streetcar and the Development of Hollywood Before 1910."

128: "It would never do...": Robert

M. Fogelson, *Fragmented Metropolis: Los Angeles, 1850–1930*, p. 85. Quoting the *Los Angeles Herald*, December 12, 1904.

129: As Robert Fogelson pointed out: Fogelson, pp. 142–43.

129: Most people continued to work and shop: Scott M. Bottles, *Los Angeles and the Automobile,* chapter 3: "The Democratic Impulse and the Automobile."

129: $60 million real estate fortune: Friedrichs, William B., *Henry Huntington and the Creation of Southern California,* p. 162.

129–130: In 1911, Huntington consolidated: Bottles, *Los Angeles and the Automobile,* p. 29. Even today this event is known around the MTA as "The Great Merger."

130: It would often take a PE Red Car longer: Bottles, p. 45.

130: When the Progressive movement took over: Bottles, chapter 3: "The Democratic Impulse and the Automobile."

130–131: Statistics about growth of auto ownership and traffic in the 1920s: Starr, *Material Dreams,* pp. 79–80; Bottles, p. 93.

131: "The individual citizen": Bottles, p. 53.

131–132: Emergence of Wilshire Boulevard shopping district: Starr, *Material Dreams,* pp. 81–83.

132: Kelker-DeLeuw plan: "Recommendations on a Comprehensive Rapid Transit Plan for the City and Council of Los Angeles," Kelker, DeLeuw and Company, 1925 .

132–133: Controversy over construction of Union Station: Bottles, *Los Angeles and the Automobile,* chapter 5: "The Union Station Controversy."

133: Auto Club's 1937 proposal: "Traffic Survey, Los Angeles Metropolitan Area, Nineteen Thirty-Seven," Automobile Club of Southern California, 1937.

133: Collier-Burns Act: Bottles, pp. 232–233.

134: "In the mid-1960s": Joseph C. Houghteling, "Some of Our Freeways

Are Missing." In John Hart, *The New Book of California Tomorrow: Reflections and Projections from the Golden State.*

134: "As the end result: David Brodsly, *L.A. Freeway, An Appreciative Essay,* p. 13.

134: "Actual participation": Joan Didion, *The White Album,* p. 83.

134–135: Still others saw: William Bronson, "Home Is a Freeway." In Hart, *The New Book of California Tomorrow.*

135: Diamond lane and decline in freeway construction: Houghteling, "Some of Our Freeways Are Missing"; Hathaway interview.

136: The politics of transportation nostalgia: This viewpoint is perhaps best reflected in Spencer Crump, *Ride the Big Red Cars: How Trolleys Helped Build Southern California.*

136: Downtown lost 20 percent of its traffic. Coverdale and Colpitts, "Report on Estimated Traffic and Revenue of the Backbone Route," June 30, 1962.

136: Creation of RTD: Reviewed in: Assembly Committee on Transportation, Subcommittee on Southern California Regional Transportation, "Review of the Southern California Rapid Transit District," transcript of hearing, December 13, 1974, Los Angeles.

136: Shutdown of Red Cars and streetcars: "Die Day in L.A.," 22 *Interurbans Magazine* 1, Spring 1964.

137: RTD ridership doubled from 1966 to 1978: "Facts at a Glance," Los Angeles Rapid Transit District, published annually.

137: Ninety percent of RTD employees unionized: *Ibid.*

137: 1968 sales-tax campaign: Thomas H. Shanks, *From Horse Car to Red Car to Mass Transit: A Century of Progress,* pp. 126–127 (this is the RTD's official history); Jonathan Richmond, "Transport of Delight: The Mythical Conception of Rail Transit in Los Angeles," Ph.D. dissertation, Massachusetts Institute of Technology, June 1991.

138: 1974 and 1976 campaigns: Richmond, pp. 142–143.

138: RTD's Red Line proposal: *Los Angeles Times*, October 12, 1978.

138–139: 1980 sales-tax proposal and political maneuvering: *Los Angeles Times*, August 21, 1980; Richmond, pp. 143–145.

139: "I've written dozens of stories": *Los Angeles Times*, January 3, 1990.

141: Hiring of John Dyer: *Los Angeles Times*, May 21, 1981.

141: Dyer typically spent part of each week in Washington: Author's recollection. I remember this vividly because it made it very difficult for journalists in Los Angeles to obtain an in-person interview with Dyer.

141: Unable to secure funding from Reagan Administration: See, for example, *Los Angeles Times*, April 10, 1984.

141: Completion of San Diego Trolley: The most insightful analysis of this project is contained in Calvin Trillin, "U.S. Journal: San Diego," *The New Yorker*, December 14, 1981. Among other things, Trillin said: "The San Diego Trolley, which went into service last summer, has been widely praised for not being any number of things.... One of the lessons of its reception may be that we have come to the point where a large public project in an American city can be celebrated simply for not being a disaster."

141: "San Diego has pointed the way:" Comments of Chairman Bruce Young, Assembly Committee on Transportation, "Light Rail Transit in Southern California—Return of the Red Cars," transcript of hearing, August 14, 1981, Long Beach, California.

141: "We've been dilly-dallying": *Los Angeles Times*, September 10, 1981.

142: Blue Line proposal: *Los Angeles Times*, March 28, 1985.

142: Dyer did not obtain funding until 1986: *Los Angeles Times*, August 28, 1986.

142: Red Line groundbreaking: *Los Angeles Times*, September 30, 1986.

142: Problems with bus drivers: *Los Angeles Times*, May 12, 1986; June 27, 1986; October 11, 1986; January 28, 1987.

142: Dyer quits: *Los Angeles Times*, October 10, 1987.

143: "Automated is an idea whose time has come": *Los Angeles Times*, May 26, 1988.

143: Schabarum held RTD bus subsidy hostage: *Los Angeles Times*, October 29, 1988.

143: Bradley intervenes to resolve dispute: *Los Angeles Times*, December 9, 1988

144: Patsouras tirelessly paraded: For example, Patsouras made such a presentation to an all-black Assembly committee hearing in South Central after the 1992 riots. Author's eyewitness account.

145: Passage of Proposition C in 1990: *Los Angeles Times*, November 5, 1990.

145: Fending off Sherman Block: Wilson interview.

145: In 1992, the Transportation Commission approved: "Los Angeles County Transportation Commission 30-Year Integrated Transportation Plan," adopted April 1992.

142: Opening of commuter rail system: *Los Angeles Times*, October 27, 1992.

142: Peterson spending scandal: See, for example, *Los Angeles Times*, March 10, 1992.

146: Four months after he arrived: *Los Angeles Times*, May 15, 1993.

147: Relentlessly, they attacked: See, for example, *L.A. Weekly*, April 8, 1994.

147: Even the new mayor: *Los Angeles Times*, June 30, 1994.

148: "This is politics as usual": Remarks of Chris Niles on "Which Way L.A." radio program, May 3, 1994.

148: "There can be no deviation": *Los Angeles Times*, May 15, 1993.

148: Tunnel joints plugged with wood: *Los Angeles Times*, October 5, 1994.

148–149: "There's going to come a point": Remarks of Zev Yaroslavsky at Metro Investment Report/Chamber of

Commerce symposium on rail transit in Los Angeles, February 10, 1995.

149: In the spring of 1995: Los Angeles County Metropolitan Transportation Authority, "A Plan for Los Angeles County Transportation for the 21st Century," adopted March 1995.

149: "The original long-range plan": "A Vision for the MTA," undated document attributed to White, distributed at February 10, 1995, symposium.

150: Shifting MTA funds to County: *Los Angeles Times*, September 17, 1995.

150: "This is a money train": *Los Angeles Times*, December 21, 1995.

Chapter 6: The Reluctant Metropolis

Very little has been written about SCAG and regional planning in Southern California over the years, especially in the journalistic context. Newspaper coverage of the turf wars over regional planning and regional governance has been spotty. In my view, this lack of coverage is largely because journalists and researchers have viewed SCAG as a boring and toothless bureaucratic entity—which, in some respects it is—rather than the reflection of infra-regional political jealousies.

Much of the material about SCAG itself is derived from my own experience there and acquaintances with those who work there. My first and only public-sector planning job was a six-month stint at SCAG in 1981 as a transportation planning intern. During that period, I not only got the feel of the place but made many lasting friendships with people who worked there then. Some of them still work there today. I am grateful to these acquaintances for their impressions.

I am especially grateful to Mark Pisano, who shared his time and views with me generously and also opened SCAG's files to me unhesitatingly. I could not have reconstructed the events in this chapter without his cooperation.

Significant interviews: Mark Pisano, Jim Lents, John Flynn, Marshall Kaplan, Christine Reed, David Stein, Peter Detwiler, Paul Silvern, Harriett Wieder, Arnie Sherwood, Stan Oftelie, Jim Ortner, Bill Hodge, Janet Huston, Sandy Genis, Mike Ruane, Bev Perry.

151: At three o'clock in the morning: *Los Angeles Times*, December 7, 1994.

156: "SCAG's biggest accomplishment...": *Los Angeles Times*, April 8, 1991. The comment is from Norton Younglove, a Riverside County supervisor for many years.

157: Pisano personal background: *Los Angeles Times* Home Magazine, August 24, 1980.

157: Pisano's rhetoric on regional planning: See, for example, Mark Pisano, "Federal Policy and Community Involvement: Responding to National Economic and Social Trends," *National Civic Review*, Winter 1995, p. 30.

157–158: Background on Lents and Air Quality Management District: William Fulton, "Mr. Clean," *California Business,* September 1989.

161: "A major new freeway for Orange County...": Letter from Harriett Wieder to Don Griffin, February 1, 1989.

161: As early as 1973: This history is traced in Orange County RAPC staff report, June 1995.

162: 1989 attempt at liberation: This history is outlined in SCAG Government and Public Affairs Department memo to Executive Committee, March 2, 1989.

162: Orange County withdrawal from SCAG: *Los Angeles Times*, October 29, 1991. Account of City of Garden Grove's withdrawal: *Los Angeles Times*, April 21, 1992.

162: 1989 legislative bills attacking SCAG: *Los Angeles Times*, March 8, 1989.

162: Attempt to withdraw from SCAG squelched by Bradley: *Los Angeles Times*, August 11, 1992.

163: Description of L.A. 2000 Report:

California Planning and Development Report, December 1988.

164: "Time to reassess SCAG's mandate": Memo from Pisano to SCAG staff, December 1, 1988.

164–165: Flynn committee final report: Final Draft Report, Intra-Regional Restructuring Task Force, May 21, 1990.

166: Willie Brown insisted he was not going to back off growth management legislation: *California Planning and Development Report*, March 1991.

167: "This proposal reads like an attempt:" Letter from Roy Paul to John Flynn, February 25, 1991.

167: Simi Valley threat to withdraw: Letter from Greg Stratton to John Flynn, February 25, 1991.

167: "There is an undeniable feeling": Letter from Dana Reed to John Flynn, March 6, 1991.

167: Description of Fall 1991 proposal: Memo from Abe Seabolt, chairman of SCAG's Redefinition Task Force, to SCAG Executive Committee, October 3, 1991.

168: "I look at San Diego": *Orange County Register*, November 2, 1991.

170: "Why should the mayor of Brawley...": Ortner interview.

170: Bollens recommendations: Scott A. Bollens, "Metropolitan Transportation Governance in Orange County," Final Draft, November 1993.

170: Sitting and voting as a bloc: Stein, Sherwood, Pisano interviews.

171: Bev Perry comments: Perry interview.

171: "Whenever they needed the votes": Hodge interview.

172: Final lunch in Santa Ana: Stein, Hodge interviews.

172: "do not contain actions or policies": *Around the Region*, Vol 7:3,4; Fall, Winter 1994.

173: Number of government agencies affected by bankruptcy: Drawn from list published in *Los Angeles Times*, December 7, 1994.

174: Orange County Council of Governments proposal: Minutes of Orange County Council of Governments meeting, Irvine City Hall, September 19, 1996.

174: Orange County COG Proposal: Letter to Pisano from Janet M. Huston, executive director, Orange County Division, League of California Cities, March 13, 1995.

174: "days as a land baron": *Los Angeles Times*, October 1, 1995.

174: Orange County Council of Governments proposal: Minutes of Orange County Council of Governments meeting, Irvine City Hall, September 19, 1996.

Chapter 7: The Education of Maria VanderKolk

This chapter was drawn primarily from research I conducted as part of an in-vestigative team examining land-use and intergovernmental relations issues in the 101 Corridor under a grant from the John Randolph Haynes and Dora Haynes Foundation. My telling of the Ahmanson-Jordan story relies heavily on newspaper accounts from the *L.A. Times, Daily News,* and *News Chronicle* (Thousand Oaks) over a seven-year period, from 1986 through 1993. In addition, I interviewed more than 30 people about the Ahmanson-Jordan situation and related issues, including key players such as Joseph Edmiston, Maria VanderKolk, David Gackenbach, Donald Brackenbush, Mary Weisbrock and other board members of SOS, and local officials in Calabasas. Finally, I was present at several key public events in the Ahmanson-Jordan story, including the court hearings for the Ahmanson lawsuits and the formal dedication of Palo Camado Canyon on the Jordan Ranch on April 3, 1994.

178–180: Account of Jordan Ranch dedication: Author's eyewitness account.

181–182: History of Santa Monica Mountains National Recreation Area and land purchases between 1978 and 1984: Land Protection Plan, Santa Monica Mountains National Recreation Area, U.S. Department of the Interior-National Park Service, June 1984.

182–183: Confusing web of interlocking agencies and organizations: For example, the Conservancy had joined with two parks districts in Ventura County to form the Mountains Recreation and Conservation Authority, which was the financial conduit for much of the Conservancy's activity but had the benefit of being independent of direct state oversight.

184: 160-acre zoning: *News Chronicle,* November 14, 1986.

185: Strong-arming National Park Service in 1987: See, for example, letter from William Fairfield to William P. Horn, Assistant Secretary, Department of the Interior, April 30, 1987.

185: Keuhn rejection of Potomac proposal: Letter from Keuhn to Potomac, April 4, 1987.

185: Potomac proposal to National Park Service: Letter from Kyros to Keuhn, May 9, 1988.

186: Under intense lobbying pressure: Statement of Stanley Albright, Regional Director, National Park Service, July 11, 1988.

186: Writing a letter to a Ventura County Supervisor: Letter from Edmiston to Maggie Erickson, December 14, 1987, regarding General Plan Amendment for Jordan Ranch.

186–187: They bickered with him constantly: See, for example, letter from Sue Nelson, Friends of the Santa Monica Mountains, to Edmiston, July 30, 1992, which thanks Edmiston for help in securing a piece of land but rails at length about "kited" land prices and reviews the history of the park back to 1963.

187: Through sheer will: See, for example, "Excerpts from Public Hearing re: Proposed land exchange between NPS and PIA," May 17, 1989. This document includes comments from Rosemary Woodlock, who eventually became SOS's lawyer; Elois Zeanah, who eventually became an SOS-sympathetic member of the Thousand Oaks City Council; Margot Feuer, a longtime Malibu activist who had forged an alliance with Weisbrock; and Siegfried Othmer, a key member of SOS. See also profile of Mary Weisbrock, *Country and Canyon,* July 19, 1990.

187–188: "a raid on the federal treasury": Letter from George Frampton to *Los Angeles Times,* April 25, 1990.

188: Synar investigation: *Los Angeles Times,* February 28, 1990.

188: "It bugs the hell out of me": *News Chronicle,* March 10, 1990.

188: Potomac came to the table: "Agreement Between Bob Hope and the Santa Monica Mountains Conservancy to Preserve Parkland and Create a Wildlife Corridor from the Pacific Ocean to the Santa Susana Mountains," Santa Monica Mountains Conservancy, June 1990.

188: On April 19 he signed: *Ibid.*

189: Weisbrock courts VanderKolk: Weisbrock, VanderKolk interviews.

189–190: VanderKolk background: VanderKolk interview.

190: Less than two weeks after: *Ibid.*

190: Arrival at toy company and level of ignorance: *Ibid.*

191: Hope's lawyer wrote a letter: Letter from Payson Wolff to City of Simi Valley, July 19, 1990; *Los Angeles Times,* July 30, 1990; Simi Valley staff report, July 30, 1990.

191: The Conservancy hosted tours: *Los Angeles Times,* August 20, 1990.

191: Jordan Ranch EIR: *News Chronicle,* August 28, 1990.

191: Potomac offered a new development deal: *News Chronicle,* January 16, 1991.

191–192: March 1991 meeting with Wilson: VanderKolk interview; meeting summary in VanderKolk office files.

192: Lujan letter: Letter from Manuel Lujan, Secretary of the Interior, to Pete Wilson, Governor of California, March 6, 1991.

192: Weisbrock and others often pointed to the meeting as a turning point: Interview with Weisbrock and other SOS board members.

192: She wanted a permanent solution: VanderKolk interview.

193: Beginning in 1986, Home Savings had proposed: *News Chronicle*, November 14, 1986.

194: Ahmanson's development proposal: *Ibid.*

194: Calabasas and Los Angeles political opposition: *News Chronicle*, August 17, 1990.

194: Ahmanson proposed a much smaller project: Brackenbush interview; *News Chronicle*, January 16, 1991.

194: Secret meetings: VanderKolk, Kirby, Brackenbush interviews.

194: VanderKolk press conference: *News Chronicle* and *Los Angeles Times*, October 15, 1991.

195: "park deal of the century": Press release from Richard Sybert, director, Governor's Office of Planning and Research, October 15, 1991.

195: "like, wow, a miracle"; "thrilled'; "I am going to do whatever I can": *News Chronicle* and *Los Angeles Times*, October 15 and 16, 1991.

196: Expedited schedule: *News Chronicle*, December 6, 1991; *Los Angeles Times*, December 9, 1991.

196: Approval pushed back to December 1992: *News Chronicle*, July 15, 1992.

196: Native grasses: *News Chronicle*, May 19, 1992.

197: County Planning Commission votes against: *Los Angeles Times*, December 11, 1992.

197: Board of Supervisors approval and VanderKolk and Weisbrock comments: *Los Angeles Times*, December 16, 1992.

198: "Talks in Ahmanson Land Swap Snarled": *Los Angeles Times*, March 6, 1993.

198: But he said if he failed to spend the money: Gackenbach interview.

198: Gackenbach withdrew the offer: *Los Angeles Times*, April 17, 1993.

198: Hope finally folded: *Riverside Press Enterprise,* June 5, 1993.

199: "I don't have much courage": VanderKolk interview.

191: "She took our principles": Weisbrock interview.

Chapter 8: The Politics of Extinction

This chapter was written largely from interviews, background documents, and eyewitness accounts of key events such as the February 1992 protect at Laguna Canyon. I have occasionally used newspaper accounts as well.

Significant interviews: Jonathan Atwood, Michael Mantell, Douglas Wheeler, Mike Ruane, Norm Grossman, Elisabeth Brown, Mary Nichols, Michael Fitts, Joel Reynolds, Rob Thornton, Lisa Telles, Brian Loew, Dan Silver, Don Berry, Michael Bean.

201–204: Babbitt appearance in Irvine: Transcript of Bruce Babbitt remarks to *Orange County Forum*, June 6, 1993.

204–205: Laguna Canyon protest: Author's eyewitness account.

205: Background on Orange County environmental protests: Grossman, Brown interviews.

205–206: Background on role of landowners in Orange County politics: For further information, see Martin Schiesl, "Designing the Model Community: The Irvine Company and Suburban Development, 1950–1988," in Rob Kling et al., editors, *Postsuburban California: The Transformation of Orange County Since World War II.*

206: As early as 1976: Ruane interview.

207: $78 million deal between Laguna Beach and the Irvine Co.: Among other things, Laguna Beach voters approved a sales tax to pay for property but it did not cover the full cost. *Cali-*

fornia Planning and Development Report, December 1990.

208: Jonathan Atwood approached NRDC: Atwood, Reynolds interviews.

208: Background on Endangered Species Act: Berry, Bean interviews.

210: Riverside County's $1,950 mitigation fee: Loew interview.

210: NRDC Background: Nichols interview.

211: Homeland Foundation contributions to NRDC: Homeland Foundation federal tax returns, 1989–1991.

211–213: Wheeler and Mantell strategy and goals: Wheeler, Mantell interviews.

213–215: Account of Fish and Game Commission meeting: Author's eyewitness account, August 31, 1991.

215: Interim controls were not in place: California Planning and Development Report, March 1992.

216: NRDC sued state Fish and Game Commission: Orange County Register, September 1, 1992.

216: Fish and Wildlife Service decides not to decide: California Planning and Development Report, September 1992.

217: Shortly after Clinton's election: "BIA Joins TCAs in Lawsuit Challenging Listing Process," Building Industry Association press release, December 1, 1992.

217: Pre-emptive strike: Los Angeles Times, December 3, 1992.

217: On March 25, Babbitt revealed his plan: "Gnatcatcher to Be Listed as Threatened," Interior Department Press Release, March 25, 1992.

218: Thornton background: Thornton interview.

219: $600,000 per year: Figure provided by TCAs press liaison Lisa Telles.

219: Section 7 consultation for Bell's vireo and expansion to include gnatcatcher: Letter from Jeffrey D. Opdycke, Field Supervisor, U.S. Fish and Wildlife Service Carlsbad office, to Roger Borg, Federal Highway Administration, California Division, April 7, 1992. (Conference Opinion on the San Joaquin Hills Transportation Corridor.)

219–220: Thornton subsequently insisted: Letter from Robert D. Thornton to the author, February 6, 1996.

220–221: Details of Conference Opinion: Opdycke letter, April 7, 1992.

221: "We're losing": Orange County Register, March 8, 1993.

221: Adoption of the Toll Road Conference Opinion: Letter from Joel Reynolds and Michael Fitts to John Turner, director, U.S. Fish and Wildlife Service, April 8, 1993.

221–222: The NRDC got its answer: In addition to Babbitt's remarks at the Hyatt Regency in Irvine, the Fish and Wildlife Service officially converted its "Conference Opinion" to a "Biological Opinion" on May 24, 1993. Fish and Wildlife Service letter to Roger Board, May 24, 1993.

222: "The toll road was in the pipeline for a long time": Remarks of Bruce Babbitt, Hyatt Regency La Jolla, March 3, 1994.

222: "I was the only person here for a while": Orange County Register, December 12, 1994.

Chapter 9: The Taking of Parcel K

I researched the Disney Hall story in 1987–88 and again in 1995, partly under a grant from the Design Arts program of the National Endowment for the Arts to examine the conflicts between local government goals in urban design and revenue production. I am very grateful to many people who assisted me in my research, but especially to Harry Hufford, who was always courteous and helpful and provided me with much significant documentation about the final deal between the Disney Committee and the county.

Significant interviews: Dan Frost, Ron Gother, Harry Hufford, Sally Reed, Sharon Yonashiro, Bill Lewis, James Hankla, Barton Myers, Joanne Kozberg, Charles Loveman, John Spaulding, Mark Fabiani.

230: "built on a hillside in reverse": John Fante, *Ask the Dusk*, p. 15.

233: $200 million value of First and Grand parcels: Calculated by the author based on a probable value at the time of $500–600 per square foot. Comparable sites around down sold for between $450 and $1,000 per square foot at the time.

234–235: Hankla's role in the Long Beach economic stimulus deal: Hankla, James, "Federal Interagency Coordination And Economic Development in Long Beach," *Public Administration*, September 1979, pp. 6–8.

235: Background on L.A. County Asset Management Program: "Asset Management," by Bill Kreger, Chief, Capital Projects Division, L.A. County; presented at "Building on Local Assets: Development Strategies That Work"—Council on Urban Economic Development Technical Seminar, Long Beach, January 30–February 1, 1985.

235: "Real estate economics is Hankla remarks at Utilizing the Wealth in California's Public Real Estate: Can Joint Development Projects Help to Offset Federal Budget Cuts?" UCLA Faculty Center, May 10, 1985.

235: Long Beach hospital deal: *Los Angeles Times*, June 2, 1985.

236–237: Background on Dorothy Chandler and the Music Center: "Brightness in the Air," *Time*, December 18, 1964, p. 46; Robert Gottlieb and Irene Wolt, *Thinking Big: The Story of the Los Angeles Times, Its Publisher, and Their Influence on Southern California*, pp. 309–313.

238: Music Center expansion plans: *Los Angeles Times*, February 14, 1987.

239: $32 million in annual revenue: Memo from Alan Kotin to Bill Kreger, October 13, 1987.

239–241: CRA concerns and urban design details: Spaulding, Loveman, Myers interviews.

241: "What about this?": Myers, Hankla interview.

242: Account of meeting in Lew Wasserman's office: *Los Angeles Times*, May 10, 1987; Myers, Hankla, Frost interviews.

242: Myers claims he began: Kozberg, Fleishman interviews.

243: Lillian Disney's assets: Richard Schickel, *The Disney Version: The Life, Times, Art, and Commerce of Walt Disney*, pp. 31–32; John Taylor, *Storming the Magic Kingdom: Wall Street, the Raiders, and the Battle for Disney*.

243: After reading the *Times'* story: Gother interview.

243–244: Disney conditions to county: Lillian Disney letter to Dan Frost, May 12, 1987.

244: County acceptance of conditions: Memo from Bill Lewis to Bill Kreger, June 19, 1987.

244: Background on Disney Hall competition: *Los Angeles Times*, May 18, 1988; April 29, 1988; December 13, 1988.

244: "The advent of the Disney Concert Hall": Giovannini, Joseph, "Scissors, Paper, Rock," *Los Angeles Times* Magazine, November 22, 1992.

245: "a giant walk-in Easter lily": *Los Angeles Times*, December 8, 1988

245: "like a beautiful rose for the city: *Los Angeles Times*, June 20, 1991.

246: Reduced county development scenarios: Memo from Alan Kotin to Richard Dixon, October 13, 1987

246: Fred Nicholas recognized: *Los Angeles Times*, October 12, 1989.

246–247: Labor dispute over hotel: *Downtown News*, May 6, 1991 and October 21, 1991. Much of the Gemtel story is recounted in the Ninth U.S. Circuit Court of Appeals ruling, *Gemtel Corp. v. Community Redevelopment Agency*, 23 F.3d 1542 (1994). Gemtel argued that by redesigning the project without the hotel because of the question over labor policy, the CRA had violated the Employee Retirement Income Security Act and the National Labor Relations Act. The Ninth Circuit ruled in favor of the CRA.

247: Bradley and Dixon were locked in a longstanding dispute: Fabiani interview.

247: When the county went looking for a developer: "Request for Development Proposals, First Street Properties, Downtown Los Angeles, Corporate Office Tower," Los Angeles County Chief Administrative Office, March 4, 1988.

248: At the end of 1991, the Music Center and the county reached an agreement: Memorandum from DeWitt Clinton, County Counsel, to Board of Supervisors, December 6, 1991; *Los Angeles Times*, December 14, 1991.

249: "We had to do that or else we wouldn't get the gift": *Los Angeles Times*, August 27, 1994. In general, Nicholas's comments were substantiated by Hufford interview.

251: Exchange of letters between Reed and Gother: *Los Angeles Times*, December 21, 1994; Reed interview.

251: Harry Hufford, willing as always: *Los Angeles Times*, February 27, 1995; Hufford interview.

251–252: Cost estimates: June 1992 cost estimates for Disney Hall and Gerald Hines Interests 1995 costs estimates were taken from "Walt Disney Concert Hall Project Cost Estimate," undated comparison provided by Harry Hufford.

252: 1995 deal points: Hufford, Reed interviews.

252: Timetable and other information about fundraising: "Walt Disney Concert Hall Plan," document provided to Los Angeles County by Walt Disney Concert Hall I, Inc., dated November 15, 1995.

253: "Disney Hall is not about steel and concrete": *Los Angeles Times*, February 1, 1995. For a similar plea, see Michael Webb, *Los Angeles Times*, April 16, 1995.

253: Frequently drew parallels to the Disney opera house: For a defense that discusses the Sydney Opera House, see Richard Weinstein, "Great Cities, Great Public Works," *Los Angeles Times*, August 30, 1994. For an alternative view of the Disney Hall project in the context of the Sydney Opera House, see Stephen Games, "Another Bunker on the Hill," *Los Angeles Times*, September 11, 1994.

Chapter 10: Welcome to Sales Tax Canyon

Much of my knowledge of the Sales Tax Canyon story comes from the fact that I have lived in the Ventura/Oxnard area since 1987. Not only have I witnessed its construction on an almost daily basis, but I have also attended a dozen or more public meetings and public hearings on various aspects of Sales Tax Canyon.

My research was greatly assisted by two court files: the file from Ventura's lawsuit against Oxnard over Oxnard Town Center (*City of San Buenaventura v. City of Oxnard,* Ventura County Superior Court No. 89647, filed October 15, 1986) and the file from Stephen Maulhardt's lawsuit against Camarillo over Camarillo Factory Stores (*Stephen J. Maulhardt and Richard L. Lundberg v. City of Camarillo,* Ventura County Superior Court No. 124843 consolidated with No. 124855, filed February 3, 1993.). There were actually several Maulhardt lawsuits, but this was the file I used.

I also relied heavily other official documents, especially environmental impact reports and the state controller's annual report on the financial transactions of cities, which was the source of the sales and property tax revenue data. In addition, I compiled a time line for the Sales Tax Canyon story based on news accounts in the *Ventura County Star* (formerly *Star-Free Press*) and the *Los Angeles Times* over a 15-year period. This time line contains more than 300 news stories between 1981 and 1996.

Significant interviews: Matthew Winegar, Linda Windsor, Steve Chase, Donna Landeros, Tony Boden, Steve Kinney, Dorothy Maron, John Sullard.

256: Oxnard Factory Outlet traffic counts: Traffic Count, Highway 101 at

Rose Avenue, contained in Caltrans' "1994 Traffic Volumes on California State Highways."

258: Ventura County history: Judy Triem, *Ventura County: Land of Good Fortune.*

258–259: Ventura County population growth: Actual U.S. Census count: 1940, 69,685; 1950, 114,647 (+64.2%); 1960, 199,138 (+73.7%); 1970, 374,520 (+88.1%); 1980, 532,300 (+42.1%)

260: History of Proposition 13: The best source for a comprehensive political history of Proposition 13 is Clarence Y.H. Lo, *Small Property Versus Big Government: Social Origins of the Property Tax Revolt.*

261: "I'd be out getting every Buick dealership": Peter Detwiler, quoted in *The Wall Street Journal,* June 14, 1991.

262: Details of Gruen plan for Oxnard: Winegar interview.

264: "We certainly don't need the extra tax dollars": Ventura City Councilman John Chaudier, quoted in the *Star-Free Press,* June 4, 1985.

264: Number of retail establishments in Ventura and Oxnard: Mountain West Research, "Oxnard Economic Development Strategy, Final Working Papers #1–8," August 22, 1989. See especially "Working Paper No. 5: Regional Retail Market Enhancement Study."

265: Oxnard-Price Club deal: Winegar interview.

265: Oxnard Auto Center deal: Kinney interview. Also "Public Financial Participation in Land Use Development Projects," report from The Natelson Co. to the City of Ventura, February 8, 1996.

266: "great milestone": *Star-Free Press,* April 25, 1987.

266–267: Oxnard Town Center details: Michael Brandman Associates, Oxnard Town Center Environmental Impact Report, May 1985.

267: Emerald City: Winegar interview.

267–268: Ventura criticism of Oxnard Town Center: Letter from Mayor Dennis Orrock to Oxnard Planning Commission, June 5, 1995; testimony

of Shelley Jones to Oxnard City Council, September 12, 1985; Orrock letter to Oxnard City Council, August 29, 1985; Orrock testimony to Oxnard city Council, August 27, 1985.

268: Michael Mackin quote: *Star-Free Press,* June 8, 1985.

269: $25 million cost estimate for bridge: Ken Steele, Caltrans district director, to Ginger Gherardi, Ventura County Transportation Commission, July 25, 1995.

269: Terms of Oxnard Town Center settlement: Settlement Agreement, March 1986.

269: "Oxnard Town Center...has ceased to function": *Star-Free Press,* January 8, 1992.

270: "I buy just about everything from outlets": "The Wholesale Success of Factory Outlet Malls," *Business Week,* February 3, 1986.

270: Wal-Mart project announcement: *Star-Free Press,* December 14, 1991.

271: "We need revenue": *L.A. Times,* July 29, 1992.

271: Details of Shopping at The Rose deal: Kinney interview; Natelson report.

272: "causes an economic disadvantage": Camarillo response in Maulhardt suit, May 17, 1993.

272–273: Larry Davis quote: *Los Angeles Times,* October 10, 1992.

273: "Horse race": *Los Angeles Times,* October 15, 1992.

273: "Not more than $1 million": Kinney to Oxnard City Council, March 3, 1993. Details of deal: Kinney interview, Natelson report.

274: "benefit to the developer": Judge Melinda Johnson ruling, July 14, 1993.

274: "Revlon nail polish": *Los Angeles Times,* May 28, 1994.

275: Ventura economic analysis of Buenaventura Mall: Summarized in 1992 environmental impact report for Buenaventura Mall expansion prepared by Fugro-McClelland.

276–277: Details of Buenaventura

Mall deal: "Buenaventura Mall Memorandum of Understanding Announced," City of Ventura news release, May 24, 1995; accompanying package included text of MOU.

278: Council goes on three-city tour: *Ventura County Star,* December 6, 1995.

278: Oxnard Town Center deal revived: Kinney interview; *Ventura County Star,* December 8, 1995.

278: Tax-sharing proposal: *Los Angeles Times,* December 9, 1995.

279: "This is not about creating new business": Comments of Tom Holden on Carl Haeberle Show, KVEN, January 12, 1996.

279: "Sellscape": Richard Moe, quoted in "Alternatives to Sprawl," 1995 report issued by Lincoln Institute of Land Policy and National Trust for Historic Preservation.

280: "Have you looked for one?": Comments of citizen Bill Locey at public meeting on Buenaventura Mall, January 3, 1996.

Chapter 11: Whose Riot Was This, Anyway?

Like most typical Southern Californians, I did not have much personal acquaintanceship with South Central prior to the 1992 riots. Since then, however, I have done research for several magazine and newspaper articles in the area, toured the area several times, and interviewed many people.

There is a rich literature about Los Angeles's black community, but I am particularly indebted to two books. The first is Rafael Sonenshein's *Politics in Black and White,* an outstanding scholarly analysis of the history and current forces shaping black political power in Los Angeles. The second is *No Crystal Stair* by Lynelle George. Though I have not drawn on this book directly in this chapter, it is the best contemporary journalistic account of African-American life in L.A. Simply put, it is great journalism.

I am especially indebted to my colleague Morris Newman, who lives in the West Adams district, for his many insights on this topic over the years. Some of the themes in this chapter are drawn from our article, "Whose Riot Is It, Anyway?" (*California Republic,* June 1992) I am also indebted to UCLA geographer Jim Johnson, who has done considerable work on the "black flight" phenomenon. Though he surely does not recall this, he provided my introduction into the issue of "race and space" in a geography class I took from him in the summer of 1982. His insights have remained with me since.

Significant interviews: Denise Fairchild, Lois Medlock, Julia Simmons, Maxine Waters, David Cobb, Mark Ridley-Thomas, Anthony Scott, Eugene Grigsby, Richard MacNish, Al Jenkins, Roy Willis, Ed Avila, Con Howe, Davis Rogers, Tom Hawkins, Gary Squier, Michael Woo, Roberto Levato, Jane Blumenfeld, Sterling Barnes, John Gray, Rodney Shepard, James H. Johnson, Jr.

286: "voracious flames left only charred storefronts": *Los Angeles Times,* March 26, 1995.

288–289: History of L.A.'s historically black neighborhoods: Lawrence DeGraaf, "The City of Black Angels: Emergence of the Los Angeles Ghetto, 1890–1930," *Pacific Historical Review* 39 (1970), and Lonnie G. Bunch, "A Past Not Necessarily Prologue: The Afro-American in Los Angeles," in Klein and Schiesl, editors; *Twentieth Century Los Angeles.*

290: "We could walk to the show": Medlock interview.

291: "Blacks are no longer choosing": James H. Johnson, Jr., "A Note on Recent Black Migration Trends in the U.S.," unpublished paper dated February 25, 1990.

291: "Competition for race and space": Comments of Eugene Grigsby at UCLA Graduate School of Architecture and Urban Planning Dean's Council Forum, October 27, 1992.

291: Jews in the Bronx: Sonenshein, *Politics in Black and White*, pp. 172–173.

292: Damage was estimated at $450 million: "Rebuilding L.A.'s Neglected Communities," RLA, May 1996.

293: Background on RLA board composition: See, for example, *Los Angeles Times*, June 27, 1992, which describes "vast expansion" of RLA board.

293: "The whole idea of rebuilding L.A. is a joke": Scott interview.

296: Background on Local Initiative Support Corporation: See, for example, Local Initiative Support Corporation 1991 Annual Report.

296: Dunbar background: Scott, Fairchild interviews.

296: "The myth of community development": Nicholas Lemann, "The Myth of Community Development," *The New York Times Magazine*, January 9, 1994, pp. 27+.

297: "These people are all land-grabbers": Medlock interview.

297: "It must be because somebody else wants it": Jenkins interview.

298: Fate of Tucker's redevelopment bill: *California Planning and Development Report*, August 1992.

299: 14,000 new affordable units per year: City of Los Angeles Comprehensive Housing Assessment Survey (CHAS).

300: ULI panel findings: "Vermont Avenue Corridor, Los Angeles, California: Recommendations for Revitalization of the Vermont Avenue Corridor in South Central Los Angeles," Urban Land Institute Advisory Services Panel Report, November 13, 1992.

300–301: Background on First Interstate competition: Gray interview.

301: "We want to show": "First Interstate Creates Statewide Design/Build Competition for Affordable Housing in South Central Los Angeles," First Interstate Bank press release, January 10, 1994.

303: "This is not a poor neighborhood": Simmons interview. An account of the freeway chase from Fontana was carried in the *Los Angeles Times* on October 28, 1995. I recall other details because I happened to see this chase on television on October 27.

304: "Righteous anger is a constant companion": Mills, Kay, "Maxine Waters: The Sassy Legislator Who Knows There's More Than One Way to Make a Political Statement," *Governing*, March 1988.

304: "If I could live ...": Waters interview.

304: "Garantuan ego": Ridley-Thomas interview.

306: "I've got low-income housing to the south of me": *Los Angeles Times*, February 28, 1994.

306: "This is not a 'not-in-my-backyard' kind of attitude": *Los Angeles Times*, March 16, 1994.

306: "Go to hell, Ron": *Los Angeles Times*, March 4, 1994.

306: Sentinel plea to work together: *Los Angeles Sentinel*, April 14, 1994.

306: Picketing of First Interstate Bank building: *Sentinel*, May 26, 1994.

306–307: Specifics of winning development proposal: First Interstate Bank competition binder.

307: Solomon admitted that the neighbors had been agitated: *Los Angeles Times*, December 27, 1994.

307: Specifics on subsidy: Report from the Chief Administrative Officer to the Mayor re council File No. 95-1950, dated October 27, 1995.

307–308: Account of City Council hearing: Los Angeles City Council videotape, Item 95-1950, November 3, 1995.

308: Riordan's attitude toward finances of: Cobb interview; Mayor's Veto Message, Council File No. 95-1950, November 16, 1995.

308: Specifics of Riordan veto-signing ceremony: *Los Angeles Times*, November 20, 1995.

308: "Interestingly, this community": Mayor's Veto Message, Council File No. 95-1950, November 16, 1995.

309: "Dick Riordan just because he has a hatred": *Los Angeles Times*, November 20, 1995.

309: Ridley-Thomas quickly recovered: *Los Angeles Times*, November 30, 1995.

309: Veto override: *Los Angeles Times*, December 7, 1995.

309: "A community came to me": Riordan comments on "Bob Navarro's Journal," KCBS Channel 2, December 17, 1995.

Chapter 12: Cloning Los Angeles

This chapter was based on several personal visits to Las Vegas in 1995, interviews, and gathering of background documents.

Significant interviews: David Gay, Karen Marshall, Jerry Sanstrom, Gary Arnt, Morris Newman, Donald Staley, Eugene Moehring, Patricia Mulroy, Wayne Laska, Melissa Warren.

313: Pereira and Irvine: Frantz, *From the Ground Up*; Schiesl, "Designing the Model Community" in Kling et al., eds, *Postsuburban California*.

314–316: Description of Clark County Planning Commission meeting: Based on author's eyewitness account at meeting of July 31, 1995.

317: "From Vice to Nice": Trip Gabriel, "From Vice to Nice," *The New York Times Magazine*, December 1, 1991.

317: *Learning from Las Vegas:* Robert Venturi et al., *Learning from Las Vegas: The Forgotten Symbolism of Architectural Form*.

317: "a New Florence": Carl Abbott, *The Metropolitan Frontier: Cities in the Modern American West*, p. 128.

317: "Las Vegas and Disneyland": Alan Hess, *Viva Las Vegas: After-Hours Architecture*, p. 8.

318: As Denver author Ed Quillen has written: Ed Quillen, "Now That Denver Has Abdicated . . . Who Will Coordinate and Inspire the West?," *High Country News*, May 3, 1993.

318–319: Las Vegas development in the 1930s: Eugene P. Moehring, *Resort City in the Sunbelt: Las Vegas, 1930–1970*, especially chapter 1, "The Federal Trigger."

319: The Strip drew its name from the Sunset Strip: Hess, *Viva Las Vegas*, p. 46.

319–320: Tom Hull and the McAllisters: Moehring, *Resort City in the Sunbelt*, chapter 2, "A City Takes Shape"; Hess, pp. 28–29; Moehring interview.

320: School of Los Angeles modernism: Hess, p. 41.

320: "It is a western phenomenon": Hess, p. 40.

320–321: The city's history contrasts dramatically with Phoenix: Moehring, *Resort City in the Sunbelt*, chapter 7, "The Struggle for Industry."

321: Description of Potlatch plant: Arnt interview; Potlatch Corporation Annual Report 1994.

323: History of Don Staley and Basic Food Flavors: Staley interview; "Driven Out," *Forbes*, October 29, 1990.

323: Lewis Homes data: Laska interview.

325: Background on Las Vegas Valley Water District: Mulroy interview.

326: Population growth: Chart provided by Nevada Development Authority.

326: Increase in water use: Charts contained in presentation of Richard Holmes, Clark County Planning Director, to the American Planning Association national conference, May 3, 1993.

326: "In '89 we were": Mulroy interview.

326: "You try telling people": *San Diego Union Tribune*, July 31, 1995.

327: Dates of conservation ordinances: Holmes material.

328: "The Southwest is an urban economy": Mulroy interview.

329: "This is something": *Las Vegas Review-Journal*, December 5, 1995.

329–330: Political opposition to MWD-Las Vegas deal: *Sacramento Bee*, January 21, 1996; *Political Pulse* (California newsletter), February 9, 1996; *Las Vegas Review-Journal*, February 3, 1996.

330: "Is the Met selling water to Las Vegas? The short answer is NO.": MWD press release, March 19, 1996.

330: "If California and Nevada can agree": *Las Vegas Review-Journal,* December 9, 1995.

Chapter 13: Cocoon Citizenship and Toon Town Urbanism

This chapters owes many debts to my colleague and erstwhile writing partner Morris Newman, who lives in a different part of the reluctant metropolis and has provided me with many valuable perspectives. Among other things, he and I have, over the years, chewed over the Pacific Pipeline, the *Los Angeles Times,* CityWalk, and urbanism and citizenship in general. I also drew upon my own speech, entitled "Toon Town Urbanism," delivered to the West Hollywood Urban Design Symposium, Pacific Design Center, March 21, 1994.

334: Details of Pacific Pipeline hearing in Los Angeles, June 14, 1993: Eyewitness account of Morris Newman.

334–336: *Los Angeles Times* coverage: *Los Angeles Times,* June 13, 1993; June 18, 1993; June 20, 1993.

338: Suburbs as partial cities: Lewis Mumford, *The City in History: Its Origins, Its Transformations, and Its Prospects,* p. 492.

338: "the temptation to retreat": Mumford, p. 494.

338: Edge cities: Joel Garreau, *Edge City: Life on the New Frontier.*

338: "economically inert bedroom communities": Hise, "The Roots of the Postwar Urban Region," pp. 265–267.

339: As Alan Ehrenhalt pointed out: Alan Ehrenhalt, *The Lost City: Discovering the Forgotten Virtues of Community in the Chicago of the 1950s,* Part IV, "Suburb."

339: the cocoon is literal: Edward Blakely, and Mary Gail Snyder, "Fortress America: Gated and Walled Communities in the United States," Working Paper, Lincoln Institute of Land Policy, 1995.

340: Calabasas and Agoura Hills: Attitudes of these residents were gleaned from interviews I conducted in researching the policy paper *The 101 Corridor: Land Use Planning and Intergovernmental Relations* (UCLA Extension, 1993).

340: One tract in Santa Clarita: "Device Impales Unwelcome Autos," *San Jose Mercury News,* February 7, 1993.

340: "There isn't a week that goes by...": Interview with Bill Torrence, board member, Camarillo Springs Master Common Area Association.

340: "It's not that I have anything against": *Los Angeles Times,* August 4, 1993.

343: As Boston architect Steven Cecil once pointed out: Remarks of Steven Cecil, West Hollywood Urban Design Symposium, March 21, 1994.

343: Central Park in the 1860s: For an excellent discussion of the uses of Central Park as a public space, Roy Rosenzweig and Elizabeth Blackmar, *The Park and the People: A History of Central Park.*

344: A century ago, the historian Frederick Jackson Turner: There is far, far more to the debate among historians about Frederick Jackson Turner's work than I have included here. A good overview of the debate is Richard Hofstadter and Seymour Martin Lipset, editors, *Turner and the Sociology of the American Frontier.*

344: Many of Europe's now-venerated older cities: Mumford, *The City in History,* p. 256.

344: As Daniel Boorstin has so eloquently explained: Daniel J. Boorstin's monumental three-volume series, *The Americans* provides a useful synthesis of the development of the American Midwest and West. Especially useful is "Book One: Everywhere Communities," in volume 2 of *The Americans: The Democratic Experience.*

Bibliography

Abbott, Carl. *The Metropolitan Frontier: Cities in the Modern American West.* Tucson: University of Arizona Press, 1993.

Acuña, Rodolfo F. *Anything But Mexican: Chicanos in Contemporary Los Angeles.* London: Verso, 1996.

American Planning Association. *The Best of Planning.* Chicago: American Planning Association, 1989.

Bail, Eli. *From Railway to Freeway: Pacific Electric and the Motor Coach.* Glendale, California: Interurban Press, 1984.

Banham, Reyner. *Los Angeles: The Architecture of Four Ecologies.* New York: Harper and Row, 1971.

Basten, Fred E. Santa Monica: *The First Hundred Years.* Los Angeles: Crest Publications, 1982.

Bicentennial Heritage Committee. South Gate: 1776–1976. South Gate, California: South Gate Press, 1976.

Boorstin, Daniel. *The Americans: The Democratic Experience.* New York: Vintage Books, 1974.

Bottles, Scott M. *Los Angeles and the Automobile: The Making of the Modern City.* Berkeley: University of California Press, 1987.

Brodsly, David. *L.A. Freeway: An Appreciative Essay.* Berkeley: University of California Press, 1981.

Carnoy, Martin and Derek Shearer. *Economic Democracy: The Challenge of the 1980s.* Armonk, New York: M.E. Sharpe Inc., 1980.

Chandler, Raymond. *Farewell, My Lovely.* Vintage Crime/Black Lizard Edition, 1992 (originally published in 1940).

Conot, Robert. *Rivers of Blood, Years of Darkness: The Unforgettable Classic Account of the Watts Riots.* New York: William Morrow and Company, 1968.

Cooper, Irwin. *Aqueduct Empire: A Guide to California in California, Its Turbulent History, Its Management Today.* Glendale, California: The Arthur H. Clarke Company, 1968.

Crump, Spencer. *Ride the Big Red Cars: How Trolleys Helped Build Southern California*. Costa Mesa, California: Trans-Anglo Books, 1970 (3d Edition).

Davis, Mike. *City of Quartz: Excavating the Future in Los Angeles*. London: Verso, 1990.

Didion, Joan. *The White Album*. New York: Simon and Schuster, 1979.

Downs, Anthony. *New Visions for Metropolitan America*. Washington, D.C.: The Brookings Institution, 1994.

Ehrenhalt, Alan. *The Lost City: Discovering the Forgotten Virtues of Community in the Chicago of the 1950s*. New York: Basic Books, 1995.

Elliott, Charles. *City of Commerce: An Enterprising Heritage*. Los Angeles: Hacienda Gateway Press, 1991.

Fante, John. *Ask the Dusk*. Santa Barbara: Black Sparrow Press, 1982 [originally published in 1939].

Fogelson, Robert M. *The Fragmented Metropolis: Los Angeles, 1850–1930*. Cambridge, Massachusetts: Harvard University Press, 1967.

Frantz, Douglas. *From the Ground Up: The Business of Building in the Age of Money*. New York: Henry Holt and Company, 1991.

Friedrichs, William B. *Henry E. Huntington and the Creation of Southern California*. Columbia, Ohio: Ohio State University Press, 1992.

Garreau, Joel. *Edge City: Life on the New Frontier*. New York: Doubleday, 1991.

Gebhard, David and Robert Winter. *Los Angeles: An Architectural Guide*. Salt Lake City: Gibbs Smith, 1994.

George, Lynelle. *No Crystal Stair: African-Americans in the City of Angels*. London: Verso, 1992.

Glickfeld, Madelyn and Ned Levine. *Regional Growth...Local Reaction: The Enactment and Effects of Local Growth Control and Management Measures*. Cambridge, Massachusetts: Lincoln Institute of Land Policy, 1992.

Gottlieb, Robert. *A Life of Its Own: The Politics and Power of Water*. San Diego: Harcourt Brace Jovanovich, 1988.

Gottlieb, Robert and Irene Wolt. *Thinking Big: The Story of the Los Angeles Times, Its Publisher, and Their Influence on Southern California*. New York: G.P. Putnam's Sons, 1977.

Gottlieb, Robert and Margaret FitzSimons. *Thirst for Growth: Water Agencies as Hidden Government in California*. Tucson: University of Arizona Press, 1991.

Halberstam, David. *The Reckoning*. New York: William Morrow and Company, 1986.

Hart, John, editor. *The New Book of California Tomorrow: Reflections and Projections from the Golden State*. Los Altos, California: William Kaufmann Inc., 1984.

Hayden, Tom. Reunion: A Memoir. New York: Random House, 1988.

Heskin, Allan David. *Tenants and the American Dream: Ideology and the Tenant Movement*. New York: Praeger Publishers, 1983.

Hess, Alan. *Viva Las Vegas: After-Hours Architecture*. San Francisco: Chronicle Books, 1993.

Hofstadter, Richard and Seymour Martin Lipset, editors. *Turner and the Sociology of the American Frontier*. New York: Basic Books, 1968.

Hubbard, Carson B., editor-in-chief. *History of Huntington Park*. Huntington Park, California: A.H. Cawston Co., 1935.

Hundley, Jr., Norris. *The Great Thirst: Californians and Water, 1770s–1990s*. Berkeley: University of California Press, 1992.

Kahrl, William L. *Water and Power: The Conflict over Los Angeles' Water Supply in the Owens Valley*. Berkeley: University of California Press, 1982.

Kann, Mark. *Middle-Class Radicalism in Santa Monica*. Philadelphia: Temple University Press, 1986.

Kilty, James. *Leonis of Vernon*. New York: Carlton Press, 1963.

Klein, Norman M. and Martin J. Schiesl, editors. *Twentieth Century Los Angeles: Power, Promotion, and Social Conflict*. Claremont, California: Regina Books (1991).

Kling, Rob, Spencer Olin, and Mark Poster, editors. *Postsuburban California: The Transformation of Orange County Since World War II*. Berkeley: University of California Press, 1991.

Lo, Clarence Y.H. *Small Property Versus Big Government: Social Origins of the Property Tax Revolt*. Berkeley: University of California Press, 1990.

Logan, John R. and Harvey Molotch. *Urban Fortunes: The Political Economy of Place*. Berkeley: University of California Press, 1987.

Lotchin, Roger W. *Fortress California, 1910–1961: From Warfare to Welfare*. New York: Oxford University Press, 1992.

Lunsford, James. *Looking at Santa Monica*. Self-published, 1983.

Massey, Douglas and Rafael Alarcon, Jorge Durand, and Humberto Gonzalez. *Return to Aztlan: The Social Process of International Migration from Western Mexico*. Berkeley: University of California Press, 1987.

Mayo, Morrow. *Los Angeles*. New York: Knopf, 1933.

McPhee, John. *The Control of Nature*. New York: Farrar, Strauss and Giroux, 1989.

McWilliams, Carey. *Southern California: An Island on the Land*. Santa Barbara, California: Peregrine Smith, Inc., 1973 (update of 1946 edition).

Miller, Gary L. *Cities by Contract: The Politics of Municipal Incorporation*. Cambridge, Massachusetts: MIT Press, 1981.

Moehring, Eugene P. *Resort City in the Sunbelt: Las Vegas, 1930–1970*. Reno: University of Nevada Press, 1989.

Moran, Tom and Tom Sewell. *Fantasy-by-the-Sea*. Culver City, California: Peace Press, 1979.

Mumford, Lewis. *The City in History: Its Origins, Its Transformations, and Its Prospects*. New York: Harcourt Brace, 1961.

Reisner, Marc. *Cadillac Desert: The American West and Its Disappearing Water*. New York: Viking Penguin Inc., 1986.

Robinson, W.W. *Santa Monica: A Calendar of Events in the Making of a City*. Los Angeles: Title Insurance and Trust Company, 1959.

Roe, David. *Dynamos and Virgins*. New York: Random House, 1984.

Rosenzweig, Roy and Elizabeth Blackmar. *The Park and the People: A History of Central Park*. New York: Henry Holt and Company, 1992.

Schickel, Richard. *The Disney Version: The Life, Times, Art, and Commerce of Walt Disney*. New York: Simon and Schuster, 1988.

Schwarz, Joel. *A Water Odyssey: The Story of the Metropolitan Water District of Southern California*. Los Angeles: Metropolitan Water District, 1991.

Scott, Mel. *Metropolitan Los Angeles: One Community*. Los Angeles: The Haynes Foundation, 1949.

Shanks, Thomas H. *From Horse Car to Red Car to Mass Transit: A Century of Progress*. Virginia Beach, Virginia: Donning Company/Publishers, 1991.

Simon, Ted. *The River Stops Here*. New York: Random House, 1994.

Smith, Adam. *Paper Money*. New York: Dell Publishing, 1981.

Sonenshein, Rafael J. *Politics in Black and White: Race and Power in Los Angeles*. Princeton, New Jersey: Princeton University Press, 1993.

Starr, Kevin. *Material Dreams: Southern California through the 1920s*. New York: Oxford University Press, 1990.

Taylor, John. *Storming the Magic Kingdom: Wall Street, the Raiders, and the Battle for Disney*. New York: Knopf, 1987.

Triem, Judy. *Ventura County: Land of Good Fortune*. Woodland Hills, California: Windsor Publications, 1985.

Tygiel, Jules. *The Great Los Angeles Swindle: Oil, Stocks, and Scandal During the Roaring Twenties*. New York: Oxford University Press, 1994.

Venturi, Robert, Denise Scott-Brown, and Steven Izenour. *Learning from Las Vegas: The Forgotten Symbolism of Architectural Form*. Cambridge, Massachusetts: MIT Press, 1972.

Warner, Sam B. Jr. *Streetcar Suburbs: The Process of Growth in Boston, 1870–1900*. Cambridge, Massachusetts: Harvard University Press and MIT Press, 1962.

Warner, Sam Bass Jr. *The Urban Wilderness: A History of the American City*. New York: Harper and Row, 1972.

Weiss, Mark. *The Rise of the Community Builders: The American Real Estate Industry and Urban Land Planning*. New York: Columbia University Press, 1987.

Index

A

aerospace industry, 10, 24, 72, 144, 169, 289, 319, 320
affordable housing, 35, 66, 206
  in black neighborhoods, 295-301, 304-309
  in Santa Monica, 28-29, 37-38, 57, 195
  See also apartments; housing
Aggregate Recycling Systems Inc., 90
Agoura Hills/Old Agoura, 178, 184, 187, 189, 341
Agran, Larry, 61
agricultural land conversion, 9, 15, 256-258, 317-318
  See also real estate development
agriculture, 16, 82
  hobby farms, 8, 13, 14, 18, 73
  water supply affecting, 106-107, 110-113, 118-120
Ahmanson, Howard, 9, 237, 239
Ahmanson Ranch, 180, 192-199
air pollution, 155, 157, 165, 191, 196, 323
  La Montaña, 67-71, 90-97
  smog, 6, 10-11, 22
Alameda Street, 67, 70, 74, 76, 91, 149, 289, 322
Alarcon, Richard, 336
Albright, Stanley, 186
All-American Canal, 329
American Savings and Loan, 237
anti-urbanism, 11-15, 17-18, 29, 154
  of *Los Angeles Times*, 336
  suburban, 338-347
  See also suburbs
Antonovich, Michael, 233-234
Apartment Owners of Los Angeles, 260

apartments, 13, 30-31, 35, 55, 193
  Hub Cities, 77, 82-84
  Santa Monica, 24-26, 28, 36, 39, 40, 56
  See also housing
Arizona water claims, 114, 326-329
Asian immigrants, 5, 10, 82, 258, 288, 291, 293, 345
assessment districts, 226-227, 260, 265-266, 271, 340-341
  See also taxes
Atlantic Monthly, 43
Atwood, Jonathan, 208, 211
auto dealerships, 75, 77-78, 265-266
  See also retail development
automobile
  carpooling requirements, 135, 158, 160, 169
  role in decentralization, 7, 9, 72, 104, 126-136, 290, 313, 317, 320
  See also freeways; transportation
Automobile Club of Southern California, 133

B

Babbitt, Bruce, 201-203, 216-218, 221-223, 330
Backyard Politics, 22
Baggerly, Russ, 194
Banham, Reyner, 10, 17, 125-126
Bank of America, 286
bankers
  role in growth machine, 7, 15, 21, 25, 33, 41, 128, 229, 318
  See also savings-and-loan institutions
Basic Food Flavors, 323

water supply *(continued)*
   relation to growth, 13, 44, 104-105
   See also City of Los Angeles
   See also Metropolitan Water District
water transfers, 118-124
Watt, James, 182
Wieder, Harriett, 161
Weisbrock, Mary, 180, 187-188,
   195-197, 199
Welk, Lawrence, 25, 29
Welton Becket Associates, 36-41, 57, 238
West, Mae, 23
Western Center for Law
   and Poverty, 211
Westside, 30, 34-35, 49, 291-292
   Latino immigration, 83
   political activism, 26, 52-53, 55-58, 63
   See also Yaroslavsky, Zev
Westside Pavilion, 54, 64, 65
Wheeler, Douglas, 212-213, 222
White, Franklin E., 146-147, 149-150
white flight, 76, 82, 148, 283, 288-290,
   311, 344-345
Whiteson, Leon, 245
Who Framed Roger Rabbit?, 342
Williams, Willie, 308
Wilshire Boulevard, 49, 131-132, 136
Wilshire District, 5, 285, 291-292
Wilson, Pete, 16, 90, 119, 165-167,
   191-192, 201, 202, 212-213,
   218, 329
Witte, Bill, 306-307
Wodraska, John, 123, 329-330
Woo, Michael, 305

working class
   alliance with homeowner
      associations, 57, 65
   Latino, 70-71, 82
   mobilization of in Santa Monica,
      24, 31, 35, 39, 41
working-class neighborhoods, 67, 69
   Hub Cities, 70-71, 75
   response of to growth machine,
      17-18, 338
   Riverside County, 61-62
   Santa Monica, 24
   See also black neighborhoods;
      Latino neighborhoods
World Wildlife Fund, 221

Y

Yannatta, Ruth, 30, 32, 38
   See also Goldway, Ruth
Yaroslavsky, Zev, 46, 51-56, 58, 59,
   60, 63-66, 143-144, 148-149
Yoo, Wan, 116
Young, Bruce, 141-142

Z

Zane, Dennis, 33, 38-39, 40
Zanuck, Darryl F., 23
zoning
   affected by politics, 22, 49
   affecting black neighborhoods, 62-63
   court-ordered rezoning, 48-51, 65
zoning changes, 40, 43

PHOTOGRAPHY CREDITS

About the Author

William Fulton is a journalist and urban planner who has lived and worked in Southern California since 1981. A former chairman of the West Hollywood Planning Commission, Mr. Fulton is editor of *California Planning and Development Report* and the author of *Guide to California Planning,* the standard textbook on urban planning in California. He lives in Ventura, California with his wife, Victoria Torf Fulton, an artist, and their daughter, Sara.

**Of Related Interest from
Solano Press Books**

Code Enforcement

*Curtin's California Land Use
and Planning Law*

Guide to California Planning

*Lusk Review for
Real Estate Development
and Urban Transformation*

*Public Needs and Private Dollars:
A Guide to Dedications
and Development Fees*

Redevelopment in California

Transfer of Development Rights

*Understanding Development
Regulations*

Cover illustration and design
by Victoria Torf Fulton

Book design by Solano Press Books

Maps by CartoGraphics

Printed by by Braun-Brumfield, Inc.

Index by Paul Kish